HISTORY AND MEMORY IN MODERN IRELAND

EDITED BY

IAN McBRIDE

PUBLISHED BY THE PRESS SYNDICATE OF THE UNIVERSITY OF CAMBRIDGE
The Pitt Building, Trumpington Street, Cambridge, United Kingdom

CAMBRIDGE UNIVERSITY PRESS
The Edinburgh Building, Cambridge CB2 2RU, UK
40 West 20th Street, New York, NY 10011-4211, USA
10 Stamford Road, Oakleigh, VIC 3166, Australia
Ruiz de Alarcón 13, 28014 Madrid, Spain
Dock House, The Waterfront, Cape Town 8001, South Africa

http://www.cambridge.org

First published 2001

Printed in the United Kingdom at the University Press, Cambridge

Typeface Baskerville Monotype 11/12.5 pt. *System* LaTeX 2ε [TB]

A catalogue record for this book is available from the British Library.

Library of Congress cataloguing in publication data
History and memory in modern Ireland / edited by Ian McBride.
p. cm.
Several of the chapters in this volume originated as papers presented at the Eleventh Conference of Irish Historians in Britain, which met in Durham in April 1998.
Includes bibliographical references and index.
ISBN 0 521 79017 4 – ISBN 0 521 79366 1 (pbk.)
1. Ireland – Historiography. 2. Historiography – Ireland – History – 20th century.
I. McBride, Ian.
DA908 .H57 2001
941.5′007′2 – dc21 2001025827

ISBN 0 521 79017 4 hardback
ISBN 0 521 79366 1 paperback

HISTORY AND MEMORY IN MODERN IRELAND

This book is about the relationship between the past and the present in Irish society, and the ways in which Irish identities have been shaped by oral tradition, icons and images, rituals and re-enactments. It examines pivotal moments in Irish history, such as the 1798 rebellion, the Famine, the Great War and the Northern Ireland troubles, investigating the ways in which they have been recalled, commemorated and mythologised.

Beginning with the conviction that commemoration has its own history, the essays address questions concerning the workings of communal memory. How have particular political and social groups interpreted, appropriated and distorted the past for their own purposes? How are collective memories transmitted from one generation to the next? Why does collective amnesia work in some situations and not in others? What is the relationship between academic history and popular memory?

Such questions are central to the study of nationalism and national identity, the 'invention of tradition', post-colonial studies and the development of the heritage industry, as well as ongoing debates on Irish historiography and current cultural politics on both sides of the border. The range of contributors is interdisciplinary and international, and includes many of Ireland's leading historians and literary critics.

IAN McBRIDE is Lecturer at King's College London. His publications include *The Siege of Derry in Ulster Protestant Mythology* (1997), *Scripture Politics: Ulster Presbyterians and Irish Radicalism in the Late Eighteenth Century* (1998) – which was shortlisted for the Ewart-Biggs memorial prize – and, co-edited with Tony Claydon, *Protestantism and National Identity: Britain and Ireland, c. 1650–c. 1850* (1998).

Contents

Illustrations

Contributors

D. GEORGE BOYCE is Professor in the Department of Politics, Universitiy of Wales, Swansea. His *Nationalism in Ireland* (1982) is now in its 3rd edition, and he has edited *Political Thought in Ireland since the Seventeenth Century* (1993), with Robert Eccleshall and Vincent Geoghegan. He is currently working on the religious and political ideas of William King.

DAVID FITZPATRICK is Associate Professor of Modern History at Trinity College, Dublin. His books include *Politics and Irish Life, 1913–1921* (1977, 1998); *Oceans of Consolation* (1995); and *The Two Irelands, 1912–1939* (1998).

ALAN FORD is professor in the Department of Theology, University of Nottingham. He is the author of *The Protestant Reformation in Ireland, 1590–1641* (1987, 2nd edn 1997) and co-editor, with James McGuire and Kenneth Milne, of *As by Law Established: The Church of Ireland since the Reformation* (1995).

ROY FOSTER is Carroll Professor of Irish History at the University of Oxford. His books include *Modern Ireland, 1600–1972* (1988); *Paddy and Mr Punch: Connections in Irish and English History* (1993) and *W. B. Yeats: A Life I: The Apprentice Mage 1865–1914* (1997).

LUKE GIBBONS is Professor of English, and Film, Theatre and Television, at the University of Notre Dame, Indiana, and formerly taught at Dublin City University. He has written extensively on Irish literature, the visual arts and popular culture, and is the author of *Transformations in Irish Culture* (1996), co-author of *Cinema and Ireland* (1988), and was a contributing editor for *The Field Day Anthology of Irish Writing* (1991). His next book, *Edmund Burke and Ireland: Aesthetics, Politics and the Colonial Sublime, 1750–1850* (Cambridge University Press), is due for publication in 2001.

JOEP LEERSSEN is Professor of Modern European Literature at the University of Amsterdam, and director of the Huizinga-Instituut (Dutch national research institute for cultural history). He has published on Irish cultural and literary history; on the theory of national and cultural stereotyping; and on the history of European borders and border regions. His most recent book is *Remembrance and Imagination: Patterns in the Historical and Literary Representation of Ireland in the Nineteenth Century* (1996).

EDNA LONGLEY is a Professor of English at Queen's University, Belfast. She is the author of *The Living Stream: Literature and Revisionism in Ireland* (1994) and *Poetry and Posterity* (2000). She co-edits the interdisciplinary journal *The Irish Review*.

IAN McBRIDE is a Lecturer in the Department of History, King's College London. He is the author of *The Siege of Derry in Ulster Protestant Mythology* (1997) and *Scripture Politics: Ulster Presbyterians and Irish Radicalism in the Late Eighteenth Century* (1998); and co-editor, with Tony Claydon, of *Protestantism and National Identity: Britain and Ireland, c. 1650–c. 1850* (1998).

NIALL Ó CIOSÁIN is a Lecturer in the Department of History, National University of Ireland, Galway. He studied at Trinity College, Dublin and the European University Institute, Florence, and is the author of *Print and Popular Culture in Ireland, 1750–1850* (1997).

KEVIN O'NEILL is Associate Professor of History at Boston College and co-director of the Irish Studies Program. He is author of *Family and Farm in Pre-Famine Ireland: The Parish of Killeshandra* (1984), and is completing a major study of Mary Leadbetter.

DAVID OFFICER is Education, Training and Development Officer in Democracy and Citizenship at the Ulster People's College, Belfast. He has published articles on the Ulster Division, the architecture of Stormont Buildings and the Ulster question in Scottish politics, and he is preparing his doctoral thesis, on Ulster Protestant ethnic identity, for publication.

Acknowledgements

Several of the chapters in this volume originated as papers at the Eleventh Conference of Irish Historians in Britain, which met in Durham in April 1998. The Irish have long been great observers of anniversaries, but that year, the bicentenary of the 1798 rebellion, witnessed a commemorative fever of unprecedented proportions. It seemed fitting then, that 'Memory and Commemoration' had been chosen as the conference's theme. I am grateful to the organisers, Marianne Elliott and Roy Foster, for maintaining the intellectual and convivial traditions of these biennial gatherings. In the course of assembling this collection, I have contracted a number of considerable debts to many other Irish scholars: Guy Beiner, Ray Gillespie, Jane Leonard, Tadhg O'Sullivan, Senia Pašeta and Chris Woods all helped in different ways. In particular, I am deeply grateful to George Boyce, who has given valuable advice and assistance throughout the editorial process. For permission to reproduce illustrations, I should like to thank the Cultural Relations Council of Northern Ireland, Keith Haines of the East Belfast Historical Society, Judith Hill, Neil Jarman, Senia Pašeta once again, Bill Rolston, the Ulster Museum and the trustees of the National Museums and Galleries of Northern Ireland. Finally, I owe a great debt of gratitude to William Davies at Cambridge University Press for his patience and support during the last two years.

IAN MCBRIDE

CHAPTER 1

Memory and national identity in modern Ireland

Ian McBride

For national communities, as for individuals, there can be no sense of identity without remembering. In his pioneering essay, 'What is a nation?' (1882), Ernest Renan suggested that the principle of nationality is founded upon the desire to live together or, in his famous phrase, 'a daily plebiscite'. Yet this was only one of two essential constituents, for the existence of a nation also required 'the possession in common of a rich legacy of memories'.[1] None of the familiar objective criteria – racial origins, language, religious affiliation, natural frontiers – adequately explained the division of western Europe into nation-states. More fundamental, he reasoned, was the cult of ancestors, a shared heritage of glorious triumphs and common suffering. Forgetting, or 'historical error', was equally vital to the maintenance of communal solidarity; it was for this reason, Renan remarked, that the advance of historical studies posed a threat to the principle of nationality. French citizens were therefore obliged to erase from their minds such divisive episodes as the massacre of St Bartholomew or the brutal unification of northern France with the Midi in the thirteenth century.[2]

In Ireland, as is well known, the interpretation of the past has always been at the heart of national conflict. Indeed the time-warped character of Irish mindsets has become a cliché of scholarly and unscholarly writing. After the eruption of the Northern Irish Troubles, when the recrudescence of ancestral hatreds perplexed outside observers, there was renewed academic interest in the communal psychology of the protagonists. 'Ireland', one political scientist discovered, 'is almost a land without history, because the troubles of the past are relived as contemporary

I am greatly indebted to Tadhg O'Sullivan, Senia Pašeta and Oliver Zimmer for stimulating comments on earlier versions of this chapter.

[1] Ernest Renan, 'What is a nation?', trans. Martin Thom, in Homi K. Bhabha (ed.), *Nation and Narration* (London, 1990), p. 19. The lecture was delivered at the Sorbonne, 11 March 1882.

[2] Ibid., p. 11.

events.' The Ulster historian A. T. Q. Stewart agreed, suggesting that the recurrence of older patterns of conflict could only be explained by some 'mysterious form of transmission from generation to generation'.[3] Thus loyalism had been constructed upon a grid of talismanic dates – 1641, 1690, 1912 – all underlining the durability of ethnic antagonism in Ireland, the unchanging threat posed by Roman Catholicism and the ultimate assurance of providential deliverance. For nationalists, on the other hand, the myth of a pre-Norman golden age, the recollection of conquest and persecution, and the pantheon of republican martyrs which stretched from Wolfe Tone to Patrick Pearse have all performed corresponding ideological functions.

What is so striking about the Irish case is not simply the tendency for present conflicts to express themselves through the personalities of the past, but the way in which commemorative rituals have become historical forces in their own right. An obvious example is the 1898 centenary of the United Irish rebellion, which not only established Wolfe Tone as the unrivalled icon of resistance to British rule, but accelerated the radicalisation of Irish nationalism at the turn of the century. Arthur Griffith later claimed, that 1898, was 'the beginning of all modern efforts towards a return to the ideals of independence'.[4] The self-sustaining character of the republican cult of violence was neatly captured by Seósamh Ó Cuinneagáin, an internee during the 'border war' of 1956–62, who argued that the only appropriate way to commemorate Wolfe Tone's death was to avenge it.[5] When the 'armed struggle' was renewed in the 1970s, the Provisional IRA mounted attacks to coincide with key dates in the republican calendar such as Easter or the anniversary of internment. At the same time, sites of remembrance also became targets for political violence: an Irish custom of blowing up monuments and statues was revived with the detonation of Nelson's Pillar (Dublin, 1966), the Walker Testimonial (Derry, 1973) and a statue of the evangelical street-preacher 'Roaring' Hugh Hanna (Belfast, 1970).[6] One such attack, the horrific

[3] Richard Rose, *Governing without Consensus: An Irish Perspective* (London, 1971), p. 70; A. T. Q. Stewart, *The Narrow Ground: Aspects of Ulster* (Belfast, 1977), p. 16.

[4] Senia Pašeta, '1798 in 1898: the politics of commemoration', *Irish Review*, 22 (Summer 1998), 50.

[5] Seósamh Ó Cuinneagáin, *Lecture on the Tones in a Decade of Irish History: Delivered at the Curragh Concentration Camp on Sunday, 27th April, and Sunday, 4th May, 1958* (Enniscorthy, 1970), p. 36. The author was echoing Tone's own comment on the death of Lord Edward Fitzgerald.

[6] These acts continued a well-established tradition of explosive de-commemoration. An earlier phase had seen the eradication of British symbols from the Free State, including Grinling Gibbons' equestrian statue of William III, blown up in 1929, and John Van Nost's statue of George II at St Stephen's Green, destroyed in 1937.

Enniskillen bombing of 1987, claimed eleven lives. During the Troubles worshippers have been killed in church, and mourners have been attacked at funeral processions, but no other act caused such profound revulsion throughout the island as the desecration of a Remembrance Day service.

For unionists, too, political life has revolved around the calendar of commemoration. The right to march on Orange anniversaries has been a source of inter-communal conflict for 200 years. As a number of observers have recognised, the ritualised parades of the marching season constitute an attempt to overcome the ideological contradictions of an embattled 'Ulster': with flags and banners, bands, bonfires and arches, Protestants have symbolically asserted their territorial presence in the absence of a stable national identity.[7] Narratives of the modern Troubles often take as their starting point the Twelfth of August 1969, when the Apprentice Boys of Derry, despite government requests to cancel their celebration of the seventeenth-century siege, commenced their annual circuit of the city walls. But historians have paid insufficient attention to the communal celebrations of the previous years, which saw both unionism and republicanism revitalised by the fiftieth anniversary of the Home Rule crisis. Rival claimants to the heritage of Carson and Craig clashed over the half-centenaries of the Solemn League and Covenant (1912) and the Larne gun-running (1914). Meanwhile the 200th anniversary of Wolfe Tone's birth (1763), and the centenary of the Fenian Rising (1867), brought nationalists onto the streets, challenging the unionist monopoly of the public sphere guaranteed by the Flags and Emblems Act. Above all, the fiftieth anniversary of the Easter Rising, which laid to rest the spirit of 1916 in Dublin, spawned a new generation of republicans in Belfast, rekindling the fears of loyalist extremists who took for themselves another commemorative name, the Ulster Volunteer Force.[8]

In Ireland, perhaps more than in other cultures, collective groups have thus expressed their values and assumptions through their representations of the past. There is no evidence, moreover, that this preoccupation is abating; if anything, questions of collective memory and commemoration have assumed a new prominence in recent years. One novel source of disquiet is the exponential growth of the heritage

[7] See e. g. Desmond Bell, *Acts of Union: Youth Culture and Sectarianism in Northern Ireland* (Basingstoke, 1990).

[8] Bob Purdie, *Politics in the Streets: The Origins of the Civil Rights Movement in Northern Ireland* (Belfast, 1990), p. 31.

industry, which threatens to reduce the historical landscape to a series of free-floating tourist attractions.[9] Seamus Deane has decried the repackaging of Ireland as a supermarket for overseas visitors, where neolithic burial chambers, Joyce's *Ulysses* and Kilmainham prison are presented as 'the exotic debris thrown up by the convulsions of a history from which we have now escaped into a genial depthlessness'.[10] At the same time, recent anniversaries of such pivotal events as the Easter Rising or the 1798 insurrection have prompted bouts of self-examination in the Dublin media. The Great Famine which devastated Ireland 150 years ago has re-entered Anglo-Irish relations, prompting an apology from Tony Blair. Meanwhile the construction of a Peace Tower at Messines, in honour of the Irish soldiers who fought for Britain in the First World War, has been hailed as a symbol of reconciliation between the two countries. Not content merely to remind us of ancient quarrels, then, Irish anniversaries have an uncanny way of making history themselves.

This book is about the relationship between the past and the present in Irish society, and the ways in which historical consciousness has been shaped and structured by oral tradition, icons and monuments, ritual ceremonies and re-enactments. Our understanding of such key moments as the 1798 rebellion, the Famine and the Great War is not static, but has been shaped by a complex interaction of individual actors, cultural patterns, social forces and technological developments. Beginning with the assumption that memory is itself historically constructed, the following chapters address questions concerning the workings of collective recall. How are particular political and social orders maintained or undermined by the use of historical ideas and representations? Why does collective amnesia work in some situations and not in others? What is the relationship between academic historians and popular memory? It should also be borne in mind, as Edna Longley has remarked, that 'one man's iconography, commemoration or ritual is another's coat-trailing'.[11] Whenever the Irish past is invoked we must therefore ask ourselves not only by which groups, and to what end, but also against whom?

The study of collective memory is a sub-field of the study of identity, that most ubiquitous of topics, and the literature on the subject is vast

[9] Fintan O'Toole, 'Tourists in our own land', in his *Black Hole, Green Card: The Disappearance of Ireland* (Dublin, 1994), pp. 33–50.

[10] Seamus Deane, 'Wherever green is red', in Máirín Ní Dhonnchadha and Theo Dorgan (eds.), *Revising the Rising* (Derry, 1991), p. 98.

[11] Edna Longley, 'What do Protestants want?', *Irish Review*, 20 (Winter/Spring 1997), 109.

and bewildering. 'Remembering' is defined here in the broadest sense, encompassing not only events recalled from personal experience but also those inherited recollections that prompt feelings of collective shame, pride or resentment on behalf of our real or metaphorical ancestors. As we shall see, this 'social memory' also shades off into the areas of oral history, folklore, myth and tradition. The best documented, and consequently the most thoroughly researched aspects are the ceremonies and monuments of the nation-state, examples of which are discussed in this volume by David Fitzpatrick, Roy Foster and David Officer. Several of the essays below, however, notably those by Joep Leerssen and Niall Ó Ciosáin, show that we must balance institutionalised memories with oral or folk traditions if we are to understand the ways in which past events have been creatively reworked by different social groups. By way of introduction, this chapter will attempt to survey the literature on social memory, to sketch a brief history of commemorative occasions in Ireland, and to address the role of academic historians in the interpretation and representation of the past.

MEMORY AND SOCIETY

That the remembrance of injustice and persecution, endurance and deliverance, has been fundamental to the shaping of modern Ireland is indisputable, but how should we characterise the relationship between past experience and present antagonisms? According to one view, reactivated by the conflict in the north, the Irish are prisoners of their past, impelled towards violent confrontation by their atavistic passions. The notion that the (northern) Irish are essentially tribal, driven to blood-sacrifice in order to appease the dark gods of their ancestors, has often coloured British journalism. Its implication – that Northern Ireland is an intractable, timeless problem, impervious to the solutions proposed by liberal policy-makers – lends it an unmistakable ring of self-exoneration. A similar tendency towards determinism, however, can sometimes be detected in the 'clash of cultures' interpretation of Irish history pioneered by F. S. L. Lyons, who examined the explosive juxtaposition of 'seemingly irreconcilable cultures, unable to live together or to live apart, caught inextricably in the web of their tragic history'.[12] What I would like to explore here is the possibility that present actions are not determined

[12] F. S. L. Lyons, *Culture and Anarchy in Ireland 1890–1939* (Oxford, 1979), p. 177.

by the past, but rather the reverse: that what we choose to remember is dictated by our contemporary concerns.

For a theoretical formulation of this view, we might turn to the French sociologist Maurice Halbwachs, who first drew attention to what he called 'the social frameworks of memory' in the 1920s.[13] Where Freud believed that an archive of memories was housed within the unconscious of the individual psyche, Halbwachs proposed that recollections cannot endure outside social networks of communication. In isolation, our individual images of the past are fragmented and transitory; to be properly stabilised they require repeated confirmation by other members of our community. When we recall the past, then, we do so as members of groups – a family, a local community, a workforce, a political movement, a church or a trade union. What we remember or forget therefore has as much to do with external constraints, imposed by our social and cultural surroundings, as with what happens in the frontal lobes of our brains.[14] And as those external forces evolve over time, so too our memories must evolve with them, reflecting the shifting power relations that have taken place within our communities. This is true not only of autobiographical recollections, but also of historical memories – those transmitted to us from previous generations by oral tradition, literature or anniversary rituals. Approached in this way, it becomes easier to explain why pivotal events and personalities which possess self-evident and spontaneous meanings for us have been understood in very different ways by previous generations. Memory, in other words, has a history of its own, and like the best forms of history it teaches us to think again about what we have taken for granted.

There are some similarities between this approach and the work of the Cambridge psychologist, Frederick Bartlett, who explored the contextual structures that order individual recollections in the 1930s. Shortly after, the anthropologist Evans-Pritchard developed the concept of 'structural

[13] See Maurice Halbwachs, *On Collective Memory*, ed. and trans. Lewis A. Coser (Chicago, IL, 1992); Mary Douglas, 'Maurice Halbwachs, 1877–1945', in Maurice Halbwachs, *The Collective Memory*, trans. Francis J. Ditter and Vida Yazdi Ditter (New York, 1980), pp. 1–21, reprinted in Mary Douglas, *In the Active Voice* (London, 1982), pp. 255–71; Patrick H. Hutton, *History as an Art of Memory* (London, 1993), ch. 4. The best survey of the literature is Jeffrey K. Olick and Joyce Robbins, 'Social memory studies: from "collective memory" to the historical sociology of mnemonic practices', *American Review of Sociology*, 24 (1998), 105–40. Other introductions to the subject include Peter Burke, 'History as social memory', in Thomas Butler (ed.), *Memory: History, Culture and the Mind* (Oxford, 1989), pp. 97–113; John R. Gillis, 'Memory and identity: the history of a relationship', in John R. Gillis (ed.), *Commemorations: The Politics of National Identity* (Princeton, 1994), pp. 3–24.

[14] For the psychology of memory and its epistemological background see James Fentress and Chris Wickham, *Social Memory* (Oxford, 1992), ch. 1.

amnesia' in his classic study of the Nuer people of the Sudan.[15] Yet it is only in the last twenty years that sociologists such as Barry Schwartz and Yael Zerubavel, psychologists such as David Middleton and Derek Edwards and historians such as Pierre Nora and Raphael Samuel have put social memory at the top of an interdisciplinary agenda.[16] One common link is a growing interest in the social and political dimensions of remembrance, prompted partly by the rise of multiculturalism, with its political vocabulary of victimhood, restitution and, in the Irish context, 'parity of esteem'.[17] The creation of ethnic minorities in western Europe and the United States as a result of immigration, the fragmentation of the Soviet bloc along ethnic lines, and the demands of 'aboriginal' populations for territorial entitlements in Canada, Australia and New Zealand – all have encouraged greater sensitivity among scholars to the ways in which the past has been used to underpin social privilege and political power. A corresponding shift has taken place within the social sciences, away from the social dynamics of nationalism towards a focus on language and symbolism as the keys to understanding how collective identities are forged. Scholarly inquiry now focuses on the means by which communities have been 'imagined' or 'narrated' with the aid of newspapers, novels and other texts during the modern era.[18]

The rediscovery of Halbwachs, whilst long overdue, has not been uncritical. Most contemporary readers would agree that Halbwachs, as a pupil of Emile Durkheim, placed excessive emphasis on the collective nature of social consciousness, to the extent that the individual was reduced to the sum total of his or her collective parts. For this reason, James Fentress and Chris Wickham prefer to speak of 'social memory', a term which avoids the organic and consensual connotations attached to notions of collective identity.[19] Subsequent scholars have distinguished

[15] Olick and Robbins, 'Social memory studies', 106.

[16] Yael Zerubavel, *Recovered Roots: Collective Memory and the Making of Israeli National Tradition* (Chicago, IL, 1995); David Middleton and Derek Edwards (eds.), *Collective Remembering* (London, 1990); Barry Schwartz, 'The reconstruction of Abraham Lincoln', in ibid., pp. 81–107; Barry Schwartz, Yael Zerubavel and Bernice M. Barnett, 'The recovery of Masada: a study in collective memory', *Sociological Quarterly*, 27/2 (1986), 147–64; Raphael Samuel, *Theatres of Memory* (London, 1994); Nora's work is discussed below.

[17] For Northern Ireland see Tom Hennessy and Robin Wilson, *With all Due Respect: Pluralism and Parity of Esteem* (Belfast, 1997); Neil Jarman and Dominic Bryan, *Parade and Protest: A Discussion of Parading Disputes in Northern Ireland* (Coleraine, 1996); more widely, see Charles Taylor *et al.*, *Multiculturalism: Examining the Politics of Recognition* (Princeton, NJ, 1994).

[18] For the 'cultural turn' in studies of nationalism see Geoff Eley and Ronald Grigor Suny, 'Introduction: from the moment of social history to the work of cultural representation', in Eley and Suny (eds.), *Becoming National: A Reader* (Oxford, 1996), pp. 3–37.

[19] Fentress and Wickham, *Social Memory*, p. ix.

between varieties of memory – official/vernacular, public/private, elite/popular – reminding us that behind the blotting out of painful episodes, the sudden recollection of long-forgotten events, or the preparation of commemorative rituals, there are often fierce clashes between rival versions of a common past. Others have highlighted the dangers of the 'presentist' tendency shared by many followers of Halbwachs. As Barry Schwartz has warned, an undue emphasis on the malleability of the past destroys any sense of historical continuity, leaving us unable to account for the extraordinary durability and recurrence of some historical images and myths over time.[20] It can be argued, indeed, that the arrangement of experience through narrative frames is such a basic part of cognition that events are encoded with meaning as they actually occur.[21] Some of these difficulties can be elucidated further by briefly examining two of the most prominent models adopted by historians of collective memory, the 'invention of tradition' and the '*lieux de mémoire*'.

Among British historians the dominant paradigm for the study of commemorative rituals and symbols was established by Eric Hobsbawm and Terence Ranger's *Invention of Tradition* (1983). Although Hobsbawm, the guiding spirit behind the collection, deconstructed a diverse range of traditions, from the royal Christmas broadcast to the Wimbledon tennis tournament, his chief preoccupation was with the emergence of the western nation-state during the years between 1870 and 1914. This period saw the introduction of national systems of education, the institution of public ceremonies such as Bastille Day (1880), and the mass production of commemorative statues and monuments. The sudden proliferation of national celebrations was a response, so the Hobsbawm thesis ran, to a crisis of legitimacy experienced by established ruling élites. Just as social patterns were disrupted by accelerated industrialisation and the extension of the franchise to the working classes, western states were forced to mobilise their populations on an unprecedented scale as economic and military competition between the European powers intensified. 'Invented traditions' therefore encompassed the whole panoply of national festivals, symbols and rituals employed to assert a 'largely factitious' continuity with the past.[22]

Following Hobsbawm's lead, many historians have taken delight in exposing the recentness of traditions which lay claim to an ancient pedigree.

[20] See note 16 above.

[21] David Carr, 'Narrative and the real world: an argument for continuity', *History and Theory*, 25 (1986), 117–31.

[22] Eric Hobsbawm, 'Introduction: inventing traditions', in Eric Hobsbawm and Terence Ranger (eds.), *The Invention of Tradition* (Cambridge, 1983), p. 2.

In practice, however, the distinction between pre-industrial 'custom' and the artificial ceremonies of the nation-state is difficult to maintain. In Ireland, as elsewhere, the years between 1870 and 1914 were central to the formation of national identities. Many 'traditions' were consolidated, as incipient party organisations utilised commemorative occasions as a means of accessing a mass constituency. The marching season, with its distinctive parades, bands and regalia, was co-opted by Conservative leaders following the legalisation of 'party processions' in 1872. With the production of standardised banners and street-arches, the Twelfth of July assumed something like its modern form, and the practice was established of using 'the Field' as a political platform for party politicians.[23] At the same time, the Irish Parliamentary Party harnessed an elaborate historical symbolism, incorporating Grattan's Parliament, the United Irishmen, Daniel O'Connell, the Young Irelanders and the early Fenian movement, to secure the loyalties of a mass following.[24] These rival iconographies and rituals are sometimes regarded as inventions designed to serve the interests of political élites who forged electoral blocs out of communities split by social differences. Yet the reality is much more complicated. The extension of parading represented the formalisation of festive practices which had been maintained by the rural lower classes since the 1790s, while nationalist iconography can be dated back to the same period.

Repeated reference to the 'manufactured' or 'artificial' aspects of nineteenth-century remembrance results in a restricted view of the role played by commemorative practices in shaping group identities. As a historian trained in a broadly Marxist tradition, Hobsbawm emphasised the manipulation of symbols and memories by official élites which sought to indoctrinate the masses with accepted values and behaviour through the repetition of collective rituals. Such an approach fails to explain why some versions of the past carried a popular resonance that others lacked. An antidote can be found in Anthony Smith's work on ethnic groups, which highlights the constraints imposed on nationalist intellectuals by the customs and institutions of the communities to which they belong. While nationalist mobilisation sometimes involves outright fabrication, it more often requires the imaginative reworking of pre-existing materials.[25] In a study of the Gaelic revival, John Hutchinson has applied Smith's approach to Irish nationalism, arguing that the success of Gaelic

[23] Neil Jarman, *Material Conflicts: Parades and Visual Displays in Northern Ireland* (Oxford, 1997), p. 62.

[24] Peter Alter, 'Symbols of Irish nationalism', *Studia Hibernica*, 14 (1974), 104–23.

[25] See the essays reprinted in Anthony D. Smith, *Myths and Memories of the Nation* (Oxford, 1999).

revivalists depended on their 'ability to evoke and appropriate genuine communal memories linked to specific homelands, cultural practices and forms of socio-political organisation'.[26]

Although it bears some similarities to Hobsbawm and Ranger's collection, Pierre Nora's *Les lieux de mémoire* (1992) differs in scope, method and ambition. This multi-volume work brought together 120 contributors from a variety of disciplines – literary criticism, political science, and sociology as well as history.[27] Most French traditions, as Nora observed, were either created or refashioned during the nineteenth century. Consequently much space is devoted to the monuments, symbols and anniversaries established during the nation-building ventures of the Third Republic – the same timespan which had interested Hobsbawm. Yet the definition of a *lieu de mémoire* extends far beyond the invented traditions of Bastille Day and the Tour de France to include 'any significant entity, whether material or non-material in nature, which by dint of human will or the work of time has become a symbolic element of the memorial heritage of any community'.[28] In addition to physical sites (the prehistoric caves of Lascaux), rituals (the ceremonial annointment of kings at Rheims), historical figures (Joan of Arc) and institutions (the role of the *Acadamie Française* as guardian of the French language), Nora explored the fundamental spatial and temporal categories which have structured representations of the French past, such as right/left, *ancien régime*/revolution, and Paris/provinces.

A full understanding of Nora's objectives must begin with his analysis of the shattered relationship between history, memory and national identity in France. Nora traced the development of historiography through four stages, each characterised by the exploration of new sources and methods, but ultimately propelled by upheavals in the wider social world. The first phase, the romantic, achieved its apotheosis with Michelet's poetic understanding of the French Revolution as a triumphal manifestation of the national soul. The second dates from the Franco-Prussian war when, in an apparent effort to emulate German efficiency, French scholars reconstructed their discipline around the scientific exploration of archival sources. Beginning with the manifesto of the *Revue historique* (1876), this positivist historiography culminated in Ernest Lavisse's twenty-seven volume, *Histoire de France*, a historiographical counterpart

[26] John Hutchinson, *The Dynamics of Cultural Nationalism: The Gaelic Revival and the Creation of the Irish Nation State* (London, 1987), p. 20.

[27] Pierre Nora, *Realms of Memory*, English language edn, ed. with a foreword by Lawrence D. Kritzman (3 vols., New York, 1996). This is a revised and abridged translation of the original work in French.

[28] Nora, 'From *Lieux de mémoire* to *Realms of Memory*', in *Realms of Memory*, vol. i, p. xvii.

to the Third Republic's endeavours, via military service and a public education system, to turn 'peasants into Frenchmen'.[29] Following the First World War and the Crash of 1929, attention was redirected away from political, military and diplomatic concerns towards long-term economic trends and cycles with the creation of the *Annales* school; later their ambition to integrate history, geography and anthropology took an ethnological turn towards *mentalité*. Once more, academic trends were prefigured by social disruption – this time the shocks of decolonisation, which stimulated interest in marginal groups both inside and outside French society.

The fourth phase, naturally enough, is the age of Nora, a period scarred by political and cultural disorientation. As traditional ideas of Frenchness, centred on 1789, were challenged by international decline, European integration and immigration, so historians moved from celebrating the national past to the analysis of national celebrations. With a characteristically postmodern twist, Nora proclaimed that the relentless packaging of history in fact serves as an index of our memory loss. Thus the proliferation of archives, the heritage craze, the popularity of genealogical research and the obsession with anniversaries are all ways of compensating for the loss of an organic relationship with the past:

> Memory is life, always embodied in living societies and as such in permanent evolution, subject to the dialectic of remembering and forgetting, unconscious of the distortions to which it is subject, vulnerable in various ways to appropriation and manipulation, and capable of lying dormant for long periods only to be suddenly reawakened. History, on the other hand, is the reconstruction, always problematic and incomplete, of what is no longer.[30]

Disconnected from their origins by globalisation and the advance of mass culture, contemporary societies can only simulate a past which premodern communities had experienced as spontaneous, collective and ritualistic. Our *lieux de mémoire*, those images, places and relics inscribed by residues of the past, are sanctified by an impoverished culture which has abandoned its *milieux de mémoire*, the 'settings in which memory is a real part of everyday experience'.[31]

Where *The Invention of Tradition* contrasted the artificial ceremonies of the nation-state with the organic customs which had often nurtured oppositional politics in pre-modern societies, Nora's portrait of contemporary alienation represents an even more radical, pessimistic reading of modern historical consciousness. Once again, a simplistic contrast is

[29] Eugen Weber, *Peasants into Frenchmen: The Modernisation of Rural France* (London, 1979).
[30] Nora, 'General introduction: between memory and history', in *Realms of Memory*, vol. i, p. 3.
[31] Ibid., p. 1.

made between *popular* culture, viewed as vibrant and participatory, and the passive rituals of a *mass* culture. His grandiose project was conceived as an alternative method of compiling a national history of France, one that would serve the needs of its current inhabitants by abandoning conventional thematic or chronological arrangement in favour of a typology of French symbolism. *Les lieux de mémoire* remains undecided between subversion and retrieval: the urge to dismantle and analyse the constituent blocs of the national imagination is offset by a desire to disclose 'the unbroken path, the permanence of an identity even now in the throes of a fundamental change'.[32] Although Nora's portrait of alienated postmoderns may be contested,[33] and his nostalgia has attracted criticism,[34] his monumental project offers an imaginative genealogy of the symbolic sites which have formed French historical consciousness.

As this brief survey suggests, there is no straightforward or predictable relationship between past and present – no clear-cut distinction between genuine and artificial traditions. On the one hand, there is a basic consensus running through the sociological literature that the recollection of the past is not simply a matter of filing away and retrieving information, but an active, continuing process. The past has to be reconstructed over and over again, with all the attendant transferences, short-circuits and distortions which that process involves. Sometimes these activities may require social engineering of the kind envisaged by Hobsbawm; at others they appear to be part of the unconscious methods which social groups use to reproduce themselves. Either way, remembering and forgetting are social activities, and our images of the past are therefore reliant upon particular vocabularies, values, ideas and representations shared with other members of the present group. Whilst journalists may resort to the metaphors of tribalism, historians can and should analyse the structures which enable recollections to be preserved and transmitted – the roles played by parents, schoolteachers, by church and state, and by organisations such as the Orange Order, the Ancient Order of Hibernians or the National Graves Association.

It quickly becomes obvious, however, that a 'presentist' position of this kind runs the risk of circularity. The selection of past experiences, according to Halbwachs, is determined by the groups to which we

[32] Nora, 'Conflicts and divisions', in *Realms of Memory*, vol. i, p. 23.

[33] More satisfying are those analyses which characterise our contemporary condition as a kind of accelerated modernity. For a number of very different approaches see Frederic Jameson, *The Cultural Turn: Selected Writings on the Postmodern 1983–1998* (London, 1998); Anthony Giddens, *The Consequences of Modernity* (Stanford, CA, 1990); David Brett, *The Construction of Heritage* (Cork, 1996), esp. ch. 2.

[34] Steven Englund, 'The ghost of nations past', *Journal of Modern History*, 64 (1992), 299–320.

'Blessed are those who hunger for justice': dying hunger striker and the Blessed Virgin Mary depicted in a mural, Rockmount Street, Belfast, 1981. Photo: © Bill Rolston

belong – groups whose needs are continually changing. Yet it is equally true that our 'social frameworks' – the family, the community, the nation – are themselves constituted by memories, for how can we locate ourselves in relation to others without a sense of continuity based on common experiences? The relationship between memory and identity is always a two-way one, with ideas of the communal past setting limits to the perceptions and aspirations of the current generation. Part of the difficulty here is that the tension between our contemporary needs and our cultural resources is inseparable from wider debates over agency and structure, or between 'primordialist' and 'instrumentalist' perspectives on ethnicity.[35] If it is to be useful, the duality of 'past' and 'present' needs to be disaggregated. When we speak of the 'present' we are dealing with the conflicting demands of intellectuals, political activists, state institutions and different social groups; the 'past' comprises not only written and oral records, but also archaeological discovery and scholarly interpretation. Although remembrance is always selective, the selections depend upon a complex interaction between the materials available and the dominant modes of political and social organisation.

[35] For a helpful summary of some of these debates see Thomas Hylland Eriksen, *Ethnicity and Nationalism: Anthropological Perspectives* (London, 1993).

It may be worth reiterating this point by raising perhaps the hardest case of all, the 1981 Hunger Strikes. The slow deterioration and eventual death of ten republican prisoners inside the H-Blocks, and the widespread sympathy they attracted in Ireland and in the United States, focused the attention of academics on the cult of sacrificial martyrdom that stretched back through Terence MacSwiney and Thomas Ashe to the Fenian martyrs and beyond. The criticism was frequently voiced that republicans had made armed struggle an end in itself, that blood-sacrifice was primarily a matter of fidelity to previous generations rather than a means of furthering a practical goal. The rise of Sinn Féin, culminating in the election of Gerry Adams to Westminster in 1983, was attributed by Richard Kearney to the fact that the H-Block campaign had 'articulated a tribal voice of martyrdom, deeply embedded in the Catholic tradition'.[36] Where collective memories have become basic constituents of ethnic identities, there obviously arises the danger that they may become dysfunctional. For many commentators the key to the hunger-strikers' deaths lay in a pathological fixation with sacrifice and death which characterised republicanism, a view put forward in Padraig O'Malley's influential study, *Biting the Grave* (1990):

> Their actions, ultimately, were not the actions of autonomous individuals but rather a reflexive embrace of the way in which political prisoners throughout Irish history were presumed to have behaved. Their self-images, reinforced by the chronicles of oppression on which they had been raised and the experiences of their young lives, impaired their ability to act independently and diminished their capacity to act in their own behalf. In the end, they were the victims of our myths.[37]

And yet the death of ten republican prisoners must also be seen against the background of an escalating protest against the withdrawal of 'special category status' in 1976, involving the refusal to wear prison clothes, to wash and to slop out. Several years of 'dirty protest' had been followed by an earlier hunger strike, called off in December 1980 in the false belief that the British government had agreed to concessions. Accordingly, John McGarry and Brendan O'Leary have rejected 'culturalist' interpretations, preferring to describe the campaign as a miscalculation on the part of 'rational agents pursuing strategic objectives,

[36] Richard Kearney, 'Myths of motherland', in his *Postnationalist Ireland: Politics, Culture, Philosophy* (London, 1997), p. 113. This article was originally published in 1984.

[37] Padraig O'Malley, *Biting the Grave: The Irish Hunger Strikes and the Politics of Despair* (Boston, MA, 1990), p. 117.

namely a united Ireland'.[38] The actions of Bobby Sands and his colleagues, they contend, cannot be explained by the romantic mythology of nationalism, but rather by 'oppression at the hands of Protestants or the state authorities'.[39] This is a welcome corrective to the tendency to account for communal violence by falling back on the peculiarities of the Irish psyche. And yet, to expect a *causal* connection between the actions of the hunger strikers and the cult of martyrdom is unnecessarily crude. It is obvious that Gaelic, Catholic nationalism does not 'explain' their decisions, in the sense of providing a motivation for them. The more interesting question concerns the choice they made in legitimating their behaviour, both to themselves and to the public: the rhetoric of blood-sacrifice on the part of a 'risen people'.[40] The task for scholars, as the Swiss historian Oliver Zimmer has phrased it, is to 'avoid the trap of political functionalism without resorting to naively culturalist account'.[41]

MODES OF MEMORY

While nationalists and unionists have both acquired the 'Irish habit of historical thought', they have not only recalled different events but have evolved different ways of recalling them. The nationalist past, as Oliver MacDonagh has observed, turns on 'subjection and struggle', takes 'heroic defeat' as its recurring motif; and prizes 'the bearing of witness as against success'. The *locus classicus*, of course, is the cult of violent resistance focused on Patrick Pearse and the martyrs of 1916 – though republican precursors such as Wolfe Tone and Robert Emmet have been retrospectively conscripted into a single canon. The Protestant self-image, on the other hand, envisages 'an endless repetition of repelled assaults, without hope of absolute finality or of fundamental change'.[42] In this section I intend to explore the origins and development of these two mnemonic frameworks. Since, as Edna Longley observes, they have

[38] John McGarry and Brendan O'Leary, *Explaining Northern Ireland: Broken Images* (Oxford, 1995), p. 245.

[39] Ibid., p. 246.

[40] In his diary Sands maintained that he was dying 'not just to attempt to end the barbarity of H-block or to gain the right recognition of a political prisoner but primarily because what is lost in here is lost for the Republic and those wretched oppressed whom I am deeply proud to know as the "risen people"': O'Malley, *Biting the Grave*, p. 57.

[41] Oliver Zimmer, 'Competing visions of the nation: liberal historians and the reconstruction of the Swiss past, 1870–1900', *Past & Present*, 168 (2000), 199.

[42] Oliver MacDonagh, *States of Mind: A Study of Anglo-Irish Conflict, 1780–1980* (London, 1983), pp. 1, 13–14.

been shaped by the different denominational cultures of Protestant and Catholic,[43] they may be characterised as 'providential' and 'redemptive'. These frameworks draw upon different repertoires of images and narrative forms; they are also shaped by their historically uneven relationship with the British state.

The first state-sponsored anniversary in Ireland, the thanksgiving day of 23 October, was established in 1661 following the restoration of both the Stuart monarchy and the Anglican Church. In addition to a series of dynastic commemorations observed across the three kingdoms, Protestant Ireland was to have its own distinctive holy day, recalling the discovery of the plot to seize Dublin Castle in 1641. Though Dublin had been spared from the Catholic rebels, the Ulster plantation had not. An act of parliament, annually recited by clergymen before their congregations, described how the massacre of many thousands of English and Scots settlers had been orchestrated by 'malignant and rebellious papists and Jesuits, fryers, seminary priests and other superstitious orders of the popish clergy'.[44] This conspiracy theory was elaborated in grisly detail in Sir John Temple's often-reprinted *History of the Irish Rebellion* (1646), and tirelessly rehearsed in annual commemoration sermons, many of them published. Temple's version of events endured, providing both a ready explanation for the disloyalty and savagery of Catholic Ireland, and a convincing rationale for the eighteenth-century penal code. In parts of Ulster, the official version may also have interacted with oral tradition, which seems to have preserved memories of the confessional and ethnic violence of the 1640s.[45]

Although a specifically Irish occasion, 23 October was rooted in a broader Protestant culture of commemoration which originated with the English Reformation.[46] In the early modern period the relationship between western societies and historical time had been very different from that experienced by the inhabitants of twentieth-century nation-states. Agrarian, pagan and biblical occasions were blended in an annual cycle of birth, death and re-birth in the calendar of traditional societies. In addition to the Christian festivals, the year was punctuated by a

[43] For what follows I am indebted to Edna Longley, 'The Rising, the Somme and Irish memory', in Ní Dhonnchadha and Dorgan, *Revising the Rising*, pp. 29–49.

[44] James Kelly, '"The glorious and immortal memory": commemoration and Protestant identity in Ireland 1660–1800', *Proceedings of the Royal Irish Academy*, 94/C/2 (1994), 27.

[45] Toby Barnard, '1641: a bibliographical essay', in Brian Mac Cuarta (ed.), *Ulster 1641: Aspects of the Rising* (Belfast, 1993), p. 182.

[46] For what follows see David Cressy, *Bonfires and Bells: National Memory and the Protestant Calendar in Elizabethan and Stuart England* (London, 1989).

profusion of holy days – some dedicated to the early founders of the church venerated throughout Christendom, others instituted by the medieval church in honour of national or local saints. In the towns, a further layer of local festivities comprised civic rituals in honour of the dynasty, the nobility, professional élites or various corporate bodies. What was absent, however, was the celebration of the ethnic past, so central to modern societies. It was not until the last quarter of the sixteenth century that religious reform intersected with the dynastic ambitions of the Tudors to produce a new *national* calendar centred on the anniversaries of the Protestant monarchy.

The background to these developments was the Reformation assault on the liturgical calendar of the Roman Catholic Church. Although some puritans went so far as to reject the observance of Christmas and Easter as unscriptural, it was the saints' days, associated with both idolatry and idleness, which constituted the principal target. As a rival focus for popular loyalties, a new set of anniversaries was instituted, celebrating Protestant England's break with Rome. During the reign of Henry VIII, Sir Richard Moryson had called for the adoption of 'an annual triumph, with bonfires, feasts and prayers, to act as a perpetual memorial to the good fortune of the English people in their deliverance from the bondage of the Papacy'. It was not until the 1580s, however, that 17 November, the anniversary of the Elizabeth's accession, provided a nationwide celebration, described by one contemporary as 'a holiday which passed all the pope's holidays'.[47] More enduring was Gunpowder Treason day, marking the miraculous preservation of monarch and parliament, whose place in the prayer book was spectacularly confirmed in 1688 when William III landed at Torbay on the sacred date of 5 November. 'Well doctor', William is supposed to have said to Gilbert Burnet as they arrived on English soil on Guy Fawkes night, 'what do you think of predestination now?'[48]

This annual cycle of Protestant deliverances was observed in a variety of ways, both official and popular. Proclamations and sermons linked the state-building ambitions of the Crown to local communities throughout England and Ireland. In addition to special church services, national anniversaries were marked by the ringing of church bells, civic processions, banquets and, in the evening, bonfires, fireworks displays and the lavish dispensation of alcohol. In Dublin, a typical 23 October

[47] Ibid., pp. 67, 56.
[48] Quoted in J. G. A. Pocock, 'The significance of 1688', in Robert Beddard (ed.), *The Revolutions of 1688* (London, 1991), p. 271.

commemoration began with the lord lieutenant and members of the nobility processing to Christ Church cathedral, where an admonitory sermon was preached by a distinguished clergyman. At noon the canon at Dublin Castle were discharged, and the day ended with the ringing of bells, bonfires and illuminations.[49] The Williamite celebrations followed a similar pattern, with a vice-regal levée held at the Castle, followed by a procession of notables to the equestrian statue of William III at College Green. These proceedings, accompanied by flags and music, were imitated in provincial towns, where local customs developed involving pageants, bonfires or ritual doles to the poor. In Cork, for example, the corporation inaugurated an annual commemoration for the liberation of the city on 29 September 1690, while veterans of the Siege of Derry quickly established the shutting of the gates and the relief of the city as annual commemorations.[50]

Like other official occasions, such as the monarch's birthday, the elaborate public rituals surrounding these anniversaries were designed to renew the bonds of paternalism and deference by enacting in dramatic form an idealised model of the social hierarchy. Alongside these state-sponsored festivities, however, a parallel tradition of plebeian festivity was tolerated, focusing on the anniversaries of the battles of the Boyne (1 July O.S.) and Aughrim (12 July O.S.). The First of July, marked with bonfires, fireworks, the wearing of Orange cockades and ritual toasts to King William's memory, remained the highpoint of the commemorative year for the broader Protestant public. By the 1740s, groups like the Boyne Club and the Protestant Society, whose members embraced 'gentlemen, shopkeepers, dealers and tradesmen', were organising marches through the main thoroughfares of Dublin, accompanied by drums and trumpets, cheers and pistol shots. In retrospect, these more populist processions can be seen as the forerunners of the Orange lodges which took root in rural Ulster at the end of the century. In the shorter term, however, the appearance of a more assertive, middle-class opinion gave expression to oppositional and even radical currents within the Protestant population. With the rise of the Volunteers in 1778 the Williamite anniversaries became displays of patriotic sentiment, with William revered as parliamentary monarch rather than Protestant champion. For a brief moment the First of July even shed its sectarian character as Catholics, now admitted to some Volunteer corps, joined with their

[49] Kelly, 'Commemoration and Protestant identity', 30.
[50] For Derry see Ian McBride, *The Siege of Derry in Ulster Protestant Mythology* (Dublin, 1997).

Protestant compatriots in praising the Williamite Revolution as the keystone of civil liberty and religious toleration.[51]

Within this shared set of commemorative customs it is possible to isolate a number of themes which would acquire new meanings as they entered the Irish context. The first concerns the idea of Protestant England as an elect nation, the heir to the children of Israel, existing under the special protection of God and defined through its struggles with the Church of Rome. The accession of Elizabeth, the discovery of the Gunpowder Plot and the arrival of William III were not merely royal occasions: each represented an important turning-point in religious and constitutional history, when the Reformation had been preserved from its enemies by the continuance of a Protestant succession to the throne. Troubled by the spectre of invasion from Spain and later France, or by suspicions of crypto-Catholicism at Court, the English instinctively drew parallels between their beleaguered position in a predominantly popish Europe and the trials and tribulations of the Hebrews, surrounded by hostile unbelievers. Each escape from the international conspiracy that radiated outwards from Rome was taken as a renewal of God's covenant to deliver his chosen people from their enemies. And like the people of Israel, Anglicans felt that it was their duty to commemorate such instances of God's favour. Thus the Rev. Joseph Stearne, in a sermon preached on the ninth anniversary of the Boyne, called for an act of parliament to establish an annual service for William's victory, just as the Jews had set apart the days of Purim to commemorate their deliverance from Haman's conspiracy.[52]

Protestant triumphalism, however, was tempered by a note of anxiety which echoed the jeremiad tradition of Old Testament prophecy. Heavily formulaic in design, the commemorative sermons of the seventeenth and eighteenth centuries usually fell into three parts. Following a preliminary discussion of a biblical text, God's mercy to the Protestant English was compared to his earlier protection of the Jews, and the providential direction of worldly affairs was explained. Vivid examples then followed of the atrocities committed by papists in their attempts to establish earthly dominion, often echoing the folk-images of the Marian burnings popularised by Foxe's *Book of Martyrs*. Finally, preachers considered the appropriate means of giving thanks to God for his mercy.

[51] Patrick Rogers, *The Irish Volunteers and Catholic Emancipation (1778–1793)* (London, 1934).

[52] Joseph Stearne, *A Sermon to Bring to Remembrance GOD's Wonderful Mercies at the Boyn[e]; Preach'd on the Second Day of July, 1699* (Dublin, 1699), p. 2.

Occasionally, direct calls were made for a fresh offensive against Catholicism, either by coercion or conversion; more often, however, preachers reflected on the need for further reformation and greater solidarity *within* the Protestant community. Self-congratulation, at this point, usually gave way to self-flagellation. Were the English really worthy of God's continuing protection? Might they, like Israel of old, lose his favour? Stearne, mentioned above, feared that forgetfulness of God's mercies would expose an apostate people to divine retribution once again, this time with fatal results:

> Shou'd We or Our Posterity ever suffer God's Great and Compendious Mercy at *the Boyn* to grow into neglect, the Astonish'd World may justly tell us (in the Psalmist's Words) that *We have sinn'd with our Fathers, who regarded not God's Wonders in Egypt, neither kept his great Goodness in Remembrance, but were disobedient at the Sea, even at the Red Sea.*[53]

Secondly, it is important to realise that national anniversaries offered a licence for the criticism of authorities who failed to live up to their godly predecessors. Though designed to promote social cohesion, there was the constant danger of a gulf emerging between the polite observances of the Court and the popular festivities of the streets. During the Restoration, Protestant anniversaries were used to attack the Declaration of Indulgence (1672) which suspended penal laws against Catholics and Dissenters, and to express anxieties about the threat posed by the Catholic James, duke of York and successor to the throne. Inflamed by anti-Catholic preachers and encouraged by Whig politicians, London artisans and apprentices participated in elaborate theatrical pageants designed to dramatise the threat posed by popish despotism. It was at this juncture, when the English élite was divided along political and religious lines, that the burning of effigies – devils, whores of Babylon and popes – was added to the repertoire of anti-Catholic demonstrations. At the same time in Ireland, when the ministers of Charles II attempted to find a modus vivendi with sections of the Catholic élite, they were embarrassed by the strident anti-popery perpetuated by the 23 October service and by Temple's *Irish Rebellion*.[54]

A similar disjunction occurred in the decades following the Union, as the Williamite festivals became occasions for regular sectarian clashes.[55]

[53] Ibid., p. 3.

[54] Barnard, '1641: a bibliographical essay', p. 178.

[55] Jacqueline R. Hill, 'National festivals, the state and "Protestant Ascendancy" in Ireland, 1790–1829', *Irish Historical Studies*, 24/93 (May 1984), 30–51.

During the later 1790s a combination of insurgency at home and the threat of French invasion produced a relapse to sectarian casts of mind and the Williamite monument at College Green became the centrepiece of anti-Catholic displays once again. As the British government moved towards neutrality on the Catholic question, however, the vice-regal court withdrew from participation in the Orange anniversaries associated with the Protestant Ascendancy. In July 1823 squadrons of troops lined the streets around College Green to prevent the decoration of the equestrian statue, effectively marking the end of Orange public celebrations in Dublin; the Castle henceforth promoted St Patrick's day as a means of expressing a separate Irish identity within the Union. Consequently, the guardianship of the Williamite anniversaries now passed to the more demotic Orange Order and the Protestant lower classes. Founded in Armagh in 1795, the Order drew its symbolic forms and organisational structures from a variety of traditions: the Protestant paramilitarism of the Volunteers, Freemasonry, the rituals of communal solidarity associated with the oathbound secret society, as well as the iconography and pageantry of state ceremonial.[56]

Commonly dismissed as assertions of Protestant triumphalism, the confrontations of the marching season continue to echo the providential memory of Ulster loyalists as a persecuted people. In remembering 1690, loyalists implicitly recall the lessons of 1641: the need for eternal vigilance, the dangers of backsliding, and the implacability of Roman Catholic vengeance. The Old Testament paradigm of nationhood was made explicit by one loyalist clergyman in 1866:

> Can we forget our history? Were the Israelites to forget theirs? To please the Philistines and the Amalekites, were the monuments erected to commemorate their battles and deliverances to be overthrown? Was the land of their possession to be given back to them or divided between them, because they were the original possessors? . . . Were the banners of the tribes not to be carried in procession – no horns blown by the priests and Levites, because the Philistines might take offence at it? The Israel of God thought not thus.[57]

The same Old Testament stories, depicting a godly people exiled in a heathen land, are represented in the regalia of the Loyal Institutions.[58] Even the Orange parades of contemporary Northern Ireland, as Joep

[56] Jarman, *Material Conflicts*, ch. 3.

[57] Frank Wright, *Two Lands on One Soil: Ulster Politics before Home Rule* (Dublin, 1996), p. 341.

[58] A. D. Buckley, 'The chosen few: Biblical texts in the symbolism of an Ulster secret society', *Irish Review*, 1 (1986), 31–40.

12 July procession, Belfast, 1913. East Belfast Historical Society, courtesy of Keith Haines

Colonel Robert Wallace, Lord Londonderry and Sir Edward Carson at the 12 July procession, 1913. East Belfast Historical Society, courtesy of Keith Haines

Orange arch. *c.* 1900, Nelson Street, Belfast. Reproduced by kind permission of the Trustees of the National Museums and Galleries of Northern Ireland

Commemoration of the 1798 rebellion in Belfast, 1898. Reproduced by kind permission of the Trustees of the National Museums and Galleries of Northern Ireland

Leerssen writes below, are not confident declarations of ascendancy, but acts of defensiveness and defiance.

While anniversary rituals are designed to provide the impression of continuity and sameness, their annual repetition paradoxically allows the original events to become overlaid with contemporary preoccupations. Loyalist commemoration has evolved in both form and content since the eighteenth century, assimilating new confrontations – such as the sectarian affray at Dolly's Brae (1849) or the recent clashes at Drumcree – to the template outlined above. Although the most common historical image on Orange banners is still William III, the nineteenth century saw the incorporation of local figures such as the Orange populist William Johnston, the clerical demagogue Thomas Drew and the parliamentarian Edward Saunderson.[59] As the Protestant population was mobilised against Home Rule in the years before the First World War, the mass demonstrations organised by James Craig provided a second creation myth for Ulster Unionism: the cult of Carson, the ceremonial signing of the Solemn League and Covenant on 'Ulster Day' and the Larne gunrunning would become shibboleths of political orthodoxy for subsequent Unionist leaders.[60] Yet it is striking that Ulster Day (28 September) – surely more relevant to the Stormont regime than a seventeenth-century battle fought south of the border – never displaced the Williamite anniversaries. Ulster Protestants continue to recall the Battle of the Boyne or the Siege of Derry because, like the Serbs and the Battle of Kosovo (1389) or Israelis and the suicide at Masada (73 CE), they continue to find it expressive of their current predicament.

By contrast, the episodic history of republicanism, focused on successive waves of insurgency, has generated a more innovative pattern of commemoration as each generation of icons has subsumed its predecessors. The tensions between varieties of nationalism – clerical and secular, constitutional and physical force – have also been more clearly articulated and more publicly aired. Nevertheless, the core narrative in modern nationalist memory is that expressed here in Eamonn McCann's classic account of the Civil Rights Movement, *War and an Irish Town*:

> One learned, quite literally at one's mother's knee, that Christ had died for the human race and Patrick Pearse for the Irish section of it. . . . Pearse ranked high in the teeming pantheon of Irish martyrdom. There were others. They had all died in the fight to free Ireland from British rule, a fight which had paused in partial victory in 1922 when twenty-six of our thirty-two counties won their

[59] Jarman, *Material Conflicts*, p. 68.

[60] See Alvin Jackson, 'Unionist myths 1912–1985', *Past & Present*, 136 (1992), 164–85.

independence. It was our task to finish the job, to cleanse the remaining traces of foreign rule from the face of Ireland.[61]

In contrast to the providential framework which shaped loyalist memory, the historical vision of republicans may be described as redemptive, concerned with the promissory words and deeds of individual martyrs rather than the collective sacrifices associated with Portadown bridge, Derry's Walls, or the Somme. Republicans, too, follow a calendar of parades, but the paradigm here is less the battle march or the border patrol than the funeral procession. Although there are areas of overlap, a comparison of loyalist and republican commemorations reveals not merely rival accounts of the same events, but alternative cultural codes which give rise to different ways of structuring historical experience.

While the 'official' memory of Protestant Ireland received the sanction of church and state after 1660, the nationalist representation of the past as a succession of triumphant failures was a later nineteenth-century creation. This is not, however, to deny the existence of older counter-memories concentrated around the conquests and expropriations that had taken place under the Tudors and Stuarts. Among historians of early modern Ireland, accustomed to working with official sources and printed material, Catholic *mentalités* have not received the attention they deserve; it seems likely that the customary emphasis on the primitive and localised character of Catholic loyalties will not survive for much longer.[62] Nevertheless, before Catholic Emancipation (1829) no public bodies existed to give institutional expression to Catholic images of the past. As Joep Leerssen observes below, it was an effusion of monuments dedicated to the Liberator himself that announced the advance of the Catholic middle classes into streets and public squares of the Irish towns. Only the 'patriot parliament' summoned in 1689 by James II had previously disrupted the Protestant monopoly of the public sphere, and while the Jacobites quickly abolished the 23 October commemoration they did not survive to establish rival anniversaries of their own.

In order to track the development of a proto-nationalist memory, we are therefore forced onto the more difficult terrain of popular culture, oral tradition and ballads. The classic treatment of the subject is Daniel Corkery's *Hidden Ireland* (1924) which contended that a powerful folk-memory of dispossession was formulated first at élite level, and by the

61 Eamonn McCann, *War and an Irish Town* (3rd edn, London, 1993), p. 65.

62 See, for example, Marc Caball, *Poets and Politics: Reaction and Continuity in Irish Poetry, 1558–1625* (Cork, 1998); Vincent Morley, 'The American Revolution and opinion in Ireland, 1760–83', Ph.D. thesis, University of Liverpool, 1999.

early nineteenth century had been diffused among the rural Catholic population. The notion of two antagonistic Irelands – the world of the Gaelic underclass, the cottier's cabin and the hedge school abruptly juxtaposed against that of the Big House – is a misleading one; rural Ireland possessed an increasingly complex social hierarchy of large and small tenant farmers, dairymen, artisans, cottiers and labourers.[63] Yet the trend of recent work has been towards a qualified rehabilitation of the 'hidden Ireland' thesis. Particular attention has focused on the displaced Catholic gentry, still regarded as the legitimate owners of the forfeited estates by their former tenants; as Kevin Whelan has shown, their presence provided 'a matrix of memory which encoded an attainable future enabled by the available past'.[64] Both the sense of a past marked by collective loss and the often apocalyptic expectation of future deliverance were most clearly voiced in Jacobite poetry, which continued to denounce the Hanoverian monarchs as usurpers, the followers of Luther and Calvin as heretics and the Protestant élite as foreign upstarts.[65]

At a popular level, meanwhile, the Williamite processions of the eighteenth century found their counterpart in Jacobite demonstrations, which continued to flourish into the 1710s and 1720s. On the birthday of the Pretender, Catholic crowds gathered, white roses were worn in honour of the Stuart dynasty, and bonfires were lit.[66] A tradition of anti-commemoration also testified to the continuing rejection of Ascendancy rule. In 1740, for example, a Quaker meeting-house in Co. Kildare was set on fire, when it was reported that the Quakers had burned an effigy of the Virgin Mary as part of their 5 November celebrations.[67] This violent opposition conflicted with the assimilationist tactics of the Catholic gentry and the merchant classes, who hoped that their professions of loyalty would be rewarded with some amelioration of their position. As early as the 1720s the Catholic priest Cornelius Nary praised William 'of happy memory' for his role in negotiating the Treaty of Limerick.[68] With little prospect of military or diplomatic aid, the public

[63] L. M. Cullen, *The Hidden Ireland: Re-Assessment of a Concept* (Mullingar, 1988).

[64] Kevin Whelan, 'An underground gentry? Catholic middlemen in eighteenth-century Ireland', in his *The Tree of Liberty: Radicalism, Catholicism and the Construction of an Irish Identity 1760–1830* (Cork, 1996), p. 3.

[65] Breandán Ó Buachalla, 'James our true king: the ideology of Irish royalism in the seventeenth century', in D. G. Boyce, Robert Eccleshall and Vincent Geoghegan (eds.), *Political Thought in Ireland since the Seventeenth Century* (London, 1993), pp. 7–35.

[66] Kelly, 'Commemoration and Protestant identity', p. 33.

[67] S. J. Connolly, *Religion, Law, and Power: The Making of Protestant Ireland 1660–1760* (Oxford, 1992), p. 126.

[68] Kelly, 'Commemoration and Protestant identity', p. 35.

utterances of Catholics were naturally shaped by the constraints ir by Protestant dominance; it was not until the 1790s that Catholi phleteers such as Theobald McKenna cast off 'the obsequious jargon which many Catholics think themselves bound to use'.[69]

As we are now beginning to appreciate, native traditions of resistance interacted with the republican ideologies imported from America and France by the United Irishmen during the 1790s. Where the ruptures of seventeenth-century settlement continued to shape demographic patterns, as in Armagh or Wexford, hereditary antagonisms remained close to the surface of local society. The Wexford insurgent Miles Byrne recalled that his father had often shown him 'the lands that belonged to our ancestors now in the hands of the sanguinary followers of Cromwell', while the radical priest James Coigley rejoiced in the part played by his ancestors at Derry, the Boyne and Aughrim.[70] As visitors to Ireland often noted, this dispossession mentality remained strong among the lower orders. In the aftermath of the '98 rebellion one commentator discovered that the Irish peasantry had been taught that 'the lands had once belonged to their ancestors, who had been driven out of them by powerful invaders; and they never lost sight of the prospect of being one day reinstated in them'.[71] During this transitional period, as Ireland moved from a predominantly oral and Irish-speaking culture to a predominantly literate and English-speaking one, the republican propaganda of the United Irishmen, who had set out to 'abolish the memory of past dissensions', was reworked in creative, and sometimes contradictory, ways.[72]

After the Union, Catholic opposition to the Williamite commemorations, increasingly viewed by London as partisan rather than 'national' occasions, was steadily intensified. The equestrian statue of William III at College Green, defaced, damaged and once even decapitated during the eighteenth century, was the prime target. In April 1836, following three unsuccessful attempts, it was blown up.[73] As the Catholic middle classes made their presence felt in central and local government, however, it

[69] Thomas McKenna, *Some Thoughts on the Present Politics of Ireland* (Cork, 1792), pp. 12–13.

[70] Whelan, 'Underground gentry', p. 10; Dáire Keogh, *A Patriot Priest: The Life of Father James Coigley, 1761–1798* (Cork, 1998), pp. 29–30.

[71] Robert Bell, *A Description of the Condition and Manners as well as of the Moral and Political Character, Education, &c. of the Peasantry of Ireland* (London, 1804), p. 27.

[72] See generally Niall Ó Ciosáin, *Print and Popular Culture in Ireland, 1750–1850* (Basingstoke, 1997). For the combination of Jacobin and Jacobite in Irish-language texts see Tom Dunne, 'Subaltern voices? Poetry in Irish, popular insurgency and the 1798 rebellion', *Eighteenth-Century Life*, 22 (November 1998), 31–44.

[73] The statue was restored but destroyed again in 1929; it is said that the head remains hidden in a secret location: Maurice Craig, *Dublin 1660–1860* (revised edn, London, 1992), p. 77.

was natural that they should seek their place in the streets and squares of Ireland's towns and cities. From the 1840s nationalist spokesmen, often with newspaper editors to the fore, contrasted the embarrassing scarcity of memorials to Irish heroes with the monuments to British military and naval figures dotted around the country. At times the competition with unionist remembrance was explicit, as when the Albert memorial committee, formed after the death of the prince consort in 1861, applied to the corporation for a site in College Green. A. M. Sullivan, proprietor and editor of *The Nation*, countered with a rival campaign to save the site of the old Irish parliament for a Grattan monument, arguing that nationalists should 'kiss the stones of that place and declare them holy, for the national memories they consecrated'.[74] Similarly, the 1898 United Irish centenary, examined by Roy Foster below, was devised as a riposte to Diamond Jubilee celebrations for Queen Victoria held during the previous year.

The most notable commemorative project of this period was the O'Connell monument by John Henry Foley and Thomas Brock, situated at the bottom of what was then Sackville Street, completed in 1882. The foundation stone had been laid in August 1864, at a time when O'Connell was remembered primarily as the successful Liberator of Catholic Ireland rather than the failed Repealer.[75] For several decades the cult of O'Connell dominated the memory of Catholic Ireland, before the writings of the Young Ireland veterans John Mitchell and Charles Gavan Duffy effectively demolished his reputation. By the last quarter of the century, however, when the Irish Parliamentary Party harnessed public festivals and national emblems to the cause of Home Rule, other figures had been added to the central streets and squares of Dublin, Cork and Limerick.[76] They included the Young Ireland leader William Smith O'Brien, whose statue, erected in Dublin in 1870, was the first monument raised to an advocate of armed resistance to British rule. By the outbreak of the First World War, nationalists had erected some forty monuments in honour of United Irishmen, Young Irelanders and Fenians, all of whom, like O'Brien, and in stark contrast to O'Connell, had practised or preached armed resistance against British rule in Ireland.

[74] Judith Hill, 'Ideology and cultural production: nationalism and the public monument in mid nineteenth-century Ireland', in Tadhg Foley and Séan Ryder (eds.), *Ideology and Ireland in the Nineteenth Century* (Dublin, 1998), p. 59.

[75] Donal McCartney, 'The changing image of O'Connell', in Kevin B. Nowlan and Maurice R. O'Connell (eds.), *Daniel O'Connell: Portrait of a Radical* (Belfast, 1984), pp. 19–31.

[76] Hill, 'Ideology and cultural production', pp. 55–68.

It was claimed that the unveiling of the O'Connell monument brought together half a million people, probably the largest crowd to assemble in Dublin during the nineteenth century. Other significant mass gatherings, sometimes compared to the 'monster meetings' of the 1840s, were occasioned by the series of public funerals – for O'Connell himself, the Fenian Terence Bellew MacManus (1861), Charles Stewart Parnell (1891) and Jeremiah O'Donovan Rossa (1915) – which established Glasnevin cemetery as a site of nationalist pilgrimage. None of these four, who included constitutional politicians as well as separatists, had been executed by Crown forces; in fact all had died outside Ireland. Yet their burials, often marked by tussles between parliamentarians, revolutionaries and the Catholic church, established the rhetorical and ritual framework for the messianic style of nationalist remembrance. The MacManus funeral procession set the precedent by taking a long circuitous route through Dublin, halting at a number of symbolic spots – on Thomas Street where Robert Emmet was hanged in 1803 and where Lord Edward Fitzgerald was shot in '98. Although he had died peacefully in San Francisco, MacManus was retrospectively claimed as a republican martyr. The messianic note underlying these demonstrations achieved its classic articulation with Patrick Pearse's famous graveside oration for O'Donovan Rossa: 'Life springs from death; and from the graves of patriot men and women spring living nations . . . the fools, the fools, the fools ! – they have left us our Fenian dead and while Ireland holds these graves, Ireland unfree shall never be at peace.'[77]

The climax to the commemorative craze of the pre-war period was the spectacular centenary of the 1798 rebellion, described by Gary Owens as a 'year-long indulgence in patriotism and anglophobia'.[78] Some thirty memorials were erected in towns and villages across the country, as hundreds of thousands of Irish men and women participated in commemorative occasions. In Dublin the centrepiece was to be the erection of a large monument to the United Irish leader Wolfe Tone; and on 15 August, the capital officially closed down for the laying of a foundation stone at the top of Grafton Street. As Owens noted, the enormous

[77] Pauric Travers, 'Our Fenian dead: Glasnevin Cemetery and the genesis of the republican funeral', in James Kelly and U. MacGearailt (eds.), *Dublin and Dubliners* (Dublin, 1990), pp. 66–7. See also Gary Owens, 'Constructing the martyrs: the Manchester executions and the nationalist imagination', in Lawrence W. McBride (ed.), *Images, Icons and the Irish Nationalist Imagination* (Dublin, 1999), pp. 18–36.

[78] Gary Owens, 'National monuments in Ireland, *c.* 1870–1914: symbolism and ritual', in Brian P. Kennedy and Raymond Gillespie (eds.), *Ireland: Art into History* (Dublin, 1994), p. 106. See also Nualla C. Johnson, 'Sculpting heroic pictures: celebrating the centenary of the 1798 rebellion in Ireland', *Transactions of the Institute of British Geographers*, 19/1 (1994), 78–93.

procession, attracting 100,000 people, re-enacted the rituals of the Fenian funeral procession: 'How else can we interpret the veneration that the stone engendered, its public lying in state, its place at the head of a solemn procession that slowly wound its way along a circuitous route to the final resting place?'[79] It is surely no coincidence that the rhetoric and rituals of nationalist remembrance were popularised at the highpoint of the 'devotional revolution' which reshaped the doctrines and practices of Catholic Ireland: this was the same period which saw the popularisation of the benediction, stations of the cross, novenas, processions and retreats. Ironically, the United Irish mission to replace confessional allegiances with 'the common name of Irishman' would spawn a specifically Catholic style of remembrance.

The development of nationalist remembrance during the age of invented traditions presents us with a series of contradictions. From the 1880s the parliamentarians of the Home Rule movement closed their meetings with 'God Save Ireland', an anthem celebrating the revolutionary separatism of the Fenians. At a time when the tiny Irish Republican Brotherhood maintained only a shadowy existence, the most popular commemorative occasion, surpassing even St Patrick's day, was the memorial day for the Manchester Martyrs, three Fenians executed in 1867 for the killing of a policeman. In 1870, the year in which Cardinal Cullen denounced the Fenians as 'men without principle or religion', Father Patrick Kavanagh published his best-selling history, *The Wexford Rebellion*, which established the popular image of 1798 as a patriotic rising of priesthood and peasantry. A few decades later, the clergy who had denounced the Fenian societies in the 1860s would be participating in graveyard vigils held in memory of executed Fenians.[80] The climax of the 1898 centenary, the dedication of the foundation stone for the Wolfe Tone memorial, would see the parliamentary leaders Dillon and Redmond share a platform with the veteran rebel John O'Leary. Maud Gonne's bitter complaint that the parliamentarians both 'eulogis[ed] Wolfe Tone and tr[ied] to keep the people from following his teaching'[81] reflected both the political dominance of constitutional nationalism and the fact that – in symbolic terms at least – the physical-force men had won the battle for the Irish past.

[79] Owens, 'National monuments in Ireland', p. 114.

[80] Brendán Mac Giolla Choille, 'Mourning the martyrs: a study of a demonstration in Limerick City, 8 December 1867', *North Munster Antiquarian Journal*, 10/2 (1967), 173–205.

[81] Pašeta, '1798 in 1898', p. 49.

As Oliver MacDonagh has argued, this ambiguous relationship between rhetorical violence and political pragmatism was related to Ireland's anomalous status as a metropolitan colony.[82] The chronic conflict between constitutionalism and physical force, that is, cannot be separated from the contradictory character of the union itself, presented both as a framework for the assimilation of Ireland to British norms, and a device for containing its intractably Catholic majority. Those who found themselves mediating between state authority and popular nationalism – the parliamentary party and the Catholic clergy – adopted a number of tactics to hold the line between the two. One tactic was what MacDonagh describes as 'recessional' separatism: as particular episodes of revolutionary violence receded in time so they might be the more safely pressed into service in contemporary campaigns. Thus the Wexford rebels of 1798, condemned by the Catholic hierarchy in their own day, were later held up as noble idealists in contrast to the sordid conspiracies of the Fenians. As the *Dublin Review* observed of the mock funerals held for the Manchester Martyrs in 1869, the sympathy of the clergy was 'a kind of posthumous sympathy, limited to such objects as the saying of Masses for the souls of executed Fenians, or the collections of funds for the relief of the families of incarcerated Fenians'.[83]

The final, and most difficult question to be considered here concerns the role of Patrick Pearse in the evolution of a republican reading of Irish history. As the reaction against 'revisionism' has gathered pace, a number of critics and historians have recently sought to circumvent the discredited Catholic militarism associated with Pearse in order to reconstruct a more variegated and a more sympathetic picture of Irish nationalism. It has been pointed out that Pearse's politics of redemption resembled the 'old chivalric claptrap that it was a sweet and noble thing to die for your country', then popular all across Europe.[84] Less convincingly, it has been claimed that Catholic militarism was a retrospective imposition of the Free State, designed to boost conservative nationalism at the expense of the more radical strains of the republican heritage, such as the socialism of James Connolly.[85] And, most ambitiously,

[82] Oliver MacDonagh, 'Ambiguity in nationalism: the case of Ireland' (1981), reprinted in Ciaran Brady (ed.), *Interpreting Irish History: The Debate on Historical Revisionism 1938–1994* (Dublin, 1994), pp. 105–21.

[83] Ibid., p. 117.

[84] Declan Kiberd, 'The elephant of revolutionary forgetfulness', in Ní Dhonnchadha and Dorgan, *Revising the Rising*, p. 12.

[85] Ibid., p. 5.

post-colonial theorists have sought to distinguish between official versions of nationalism, which simply produced a mirror-image of the sectarian and militaristic ideology of British imperialism, and the subaltern nationalism of the Gaelic underclass, as manifested in nineteenth-century street ballads and agrarian insurgency. All of these arguments tend towards the same point: that Pearse's fusion of Catholic mysticism and militarism is essentially foreign or incidental to the republican tradition.[86]

A study of nationalist memory offers some qualified support for this view. To begin with, it must be acknowledged that the idea of blood sacrifice was not exclusively Catholic, nor was it an invention of the *fin de siècle*. The motifs of patriotic martyrdom were prominent in the United Irish propaganda of the 1790s, not least in the elegies produced by the *Presbyterian* poets William Drennan and William Hamilton Drummond following the trial and execution of the Antrim farmer William Orr in October 1797.[87] We should be wary, moreover, of easy generalisations about nineteenth-century Irishmen fearing to speak of '98. Recent research has begun to piece together the connections between United Irish iconography and the literary nationalism of Thomas Davis and Young Ireland. Some of the most interesting links can be found in the writings of Thomas Moore, author of the best-selling *Memoirs of Captain Rock* (1824), verses on Robert Emmet and a biography of Lord Edward Fitzgerald (1831).[88] Although it was only in the 1890s that Wolfe Tone's grave at Bodenstown was established by the Irish Republican Brotherhood as a major annual commemoration, it had been a local site of pilgrimage long before it was 'discovered' by Richard Madden and Thomas Davis in the 1840s.[89] And underpinning memories of '98 there was the dispossession mentality: the popular appeal of Jacobite verse endured right through the nineteenth century, as demonstrated in the massive sales of Edward Walsh's *Reliques of Irish Jacobite Poetry*, first published in penny-weekly numbers in 1844. Introducing the composite 1866 edition, John O'Daly commented that their popularity among the Irish lower classes derived

[86] Catholic symbolism, of course, was blended with the image of Mother Ireland calling her sons to shed their blood in the cause of national liberation. See S. W. Gilley, 'Pearse's sacrifice: Christ and Cuchulain crucified and risen in the Easter Rising, 1916', in S. W. Sykes (ed.), *Sacrifice and Redemption: Durham Essays in Theology* (Cambridge, 1991), 218–34.

[87] Mary Helen Thuente, *The Harp Re-Strung: The United Irishmen and the Rise of Irish Literary Nationalism* (New York, 1994).

[88] Tadhg O'Sullivan, ' "The violence of a servile war": three narratives of Irish rural insurgency post 1798', in Laurence M. Geary (ed.), *Rebellion and Remembrance in Modern Ireland* (Dublin, 2000), pp. 73–92.

[89] C. J. Woods, 'Tone's grave at Bodenstown: memorials and commemorations, 1798–1913', in Dorothea Siegmund-Schultze (ed.), *Irland: Gesellschaft und Kultur* VI (Halle, 1989), pp. 138–48.

not from their specific ideological content but from 'the vague sentiment of having been wronged and the far hope of sometime retrieving their position'.[90]

And yet Pearse's hold over nationalist remembrance is inescapable. It was 1916 that facilitated the retrospective ordering of earlier rebellions into a cumulative sequence of inspirational defeats; and it was Pearse who defined the ideal of sacrificial martyrdom for future generations. Moreover, as Gary Owens has demonstrated, redemptive memory had roots in the rituals of the Fenian funeral procession and in the patriotic educational enterprise of the 1898 centenary. The spread of nationalist symbols and rituals during that year, the erection of monuments, and the circulation of print media all make it difficult to disentangle folk memory from official commemoration.[91] Indeed, as Niall Ó Ciosáin demonstrates below, the relationship between text and oral tradition was a dynamic one, with the written history of the Famine feeding back into folklore. The idea of the crucified nation is difficult to disconnect from the decisive shift towards the new nationalism that took place at the end of the nineteenth century. It is an idea, too, which is profoundly alien to Protestants, for reasons that lie ultimately in Reformed theology. *Pace* Declan Kiberd, it is unlikely that 'many Protestant sects would have perfectly understood Pearse's equation of "the people labouring, scourged, crowned with thorns, agonising and dying, to rise again immortal and impassable" with the mystical body of Christ'.[92] Nor is there a loyalist equivalent of the prison poems and memoirs of Bobby Sands; the closest candidate, Ian Paisley's *Messages from the Prison Cell* (1969) draws its imagery from the Old Testament, and in particular 'the slave days of Israel in Egypt'.[93]

If we return to the 'tribalism' of Northern Ireland, we can now begin to construct a more complex understanding of the relationship between collective memory and communal violence. For both loyalists and republicans, as we have seen, it has been argued that history works not by linear progression but a process of accretion, where one violent outbreak is laid on top of another. Yet cultural traditions cannot be understood apart from experiences rooted in social and structural relationships, that is, the group's position in the economy, its demographic strength, and

[90] Dunne, 'Subaltern voices?', p. 35.

[91] Research currently being undertaken by Guy Beiner will illuminate this subject.

[92] Declan Kiberd, *Inventing Ireland: The Literature of the Modern Nation* (London, 1995), p. 211.

[93] Quoted in Patrick Grant, *Breaking Enmities: Religion, Literature and Culture in Northern Ireland, 1967–97* (Basingstoke, 1999), p. 159.

its access to political decision-making.[94] One telling similarity between loyalist and republican myths is the feeling of powerlessness and dependence evinced by the two groups: both represent themselves in ways that are designed not only for internal consumption, but for British public opinion. 'The Northern Irish', as McGarry and O'Leary have written, 'are only exceptional in that their debates, conflicts and wars have not been resolved, an irresolution which owes little to local atavism.'[95] In the south, meanwhile, the ideal of blood-sacrifice has lost much of its political relevance. In David Fitzpatrick's study of commemoration in the Free State, below, he shows how rival claims to the patriot graves at Glasnevin and Bodenstown prevented both Cosgrave and de Valera from appropriating nationalist remembrance for themselves. '[N]either Fianna Fáil nor any other party had yet managed to secure sole custody of the Easter legacy when, recently and quite suddenly, it became worthless.'[96]

The remembrance of missed opportunities, evident in nationalist readings of 1798, permits the imagination of an alternative history. On the one hand, 'posthumous sympathy' for republican martyrs may serve as a pressure-valve, compensating nationalists for the realities of British rule by fostering a sense of self-regard rooted in the noble words and actions of their insurgent ancestors. On the other hand, of course, the unfinished business of Irish rebellion functions as a reminder of the injustices of the existing order and an inspiration for future generations. Denied equal access to political processes and economic resources, it is not surprising that Catholics have recalled ancestral rebellions to offset feelings of powerlessness. Nor is it strange that Ulster Protestants, confronted with attempts to make them a permanent minority in a hostile state, have invoked the seventeenth-century Siege of Derry. The potency of these collective memories does not derive from their accuracy or comprehensiveness but, on the contrary, from their ability to reduce complex historical processes to basic images and narrative types that answer specific ideological needs. For both Protestants and Catholics, however, memories take root most successfully when they are patterned in accordance with the culture's accepted customs of telling stories about itself.

[94] Joseph Ruane and Jennifer Todd, ' "Why can't you get along with each other?": culture, structure and the Northern Ireland conflict', in Eamonn Hughes (ed.), *Culture and Politics in Northern Ireland 1960–1990* (Milton Keynes, 1991), pp. 27–43.

[95] McGarry and O'Leary, *Explaining Northern Ireland*, p. 244.

[96] See below, p. 198.

HISTORY AND MEMORY

Renan's provocative aside that 'historical error' is an essential part of nation-building coincides with the received notion that historians and remembrancers make uneasy companions, if not outright enemies. We commonly speak of memories as vague and unreliable, while historical scholarship purports to be dependent upon chronological precision, the critical investigation of primary sources, and 'scientific' processes of verification. In contrast to oral tradition, which appears to flow spontaneously across the generations, history – in the sense of historiography – is manufactured by professional academics, based on written documents, and remains fixed in textbooks, monographs and journals. During the twentieth century, academic historians sought to justify their professional existence by distinguishing between the living past and scholarly history. While the former was used to sanctify political institutions, social hierarchies or religious beliefs, the progress of the latter, it was suggested, would purge the human story of such 'deceiving visions'.[97] For some recent commentators, like Nora, this demystification of the past is construed in terms of loss rather than gain – the impoverishment of the contemporary imagination rather than the triumph of truth over error. On all sides, however, it is usually claimed that the historians are winning, as they steadily encroach on the territory once occupied by myth, custom and tradition.

At a general level, the evolution of historical scholarship in Ireland conforms to this trajectory. Since the crystallisation of Irish history as an academic discipline in the 1930s, its practitioners have distanced their investigations from the nationalism disseminated by memorialists and hagiographers and embodied in de Valera's constitution. It was not until the late 1970s, however, following a decade of upheaval in Northern Ireland, that the antithesis between history and memory became a common topic. In an address to the Trinity College History Society in 1977, T. W. Moody contrasted mythology – the consciousness of the past derived 'from popular traditions, transmitted orally, in writing, and through institutions' – with the knowledge acquired by the historian through 'the application of scientific methods to his evidence'.[98] A year later, F. S. L. Lyons spoke of the need to divorce 'the realities of what has happened

[97] J. H. Plumb, *The Death of the Past* (Basingstoke, 1969), p. 17.

[98] T. W. Moody, 'Irish history and Irish mythology' (1978), reprinted in Brady, *Interpreting Irish History*, p. 71.

on this island' from 'the myths we have chosen to weave around certain symbolic events'.[99] The historian's duty to address the causes of communal division in Ireland was a common theme: both men associated historical revisionism – the re-evaluation of received opinions in the light of new evidence – with the demythologising of the past. The embarrassment surrounding the seventy-fifth anniversary of the Easter Rising in 1991 suggested that the historiographical revolution of the previous forty years was beginning to percolate into the public mind.

There was nothing peculiarly Irish about the detached tone of historical writing adopted in the middle decades of the twentieth century; nor was there anything unusual about the more iconoclastic position of those younger historians who challenged national teleologies from the 1960s onwards. In England, whig historiography suffered its own revisionist incursions, as Conrad Russell and others overturned conventional assumptions concerning the evolution of constitutional government under the Tudors and Stuarts. By the 1980s David Cannadine was questioning the cult of professionalism in the British universities whose triumph, he argued, had robbed British history of its core themes, structural coherence and vigour.[100] On the tercentenary of the Glorious Revolution in 1988, attempts to celebrate the constitutional foundations of parliamentary government were swamped by objections that the deposition of the last Stuart king had led to religious intolerance, the oppression of the Irish and the consolidation of a narrow propertied élite.[101] A year later, the pyrotechnic bicentennial of the French Revolution, the largest historical commemoration ever undertaken, was marked by best-selling books which focused public attention less on the Declaration of the Rights of Man and the Citizen than the victims of the Terror.[102]

In important respects, however, Ireland was not like England or France. The latter have often been taken as paradigms of the western nation-state, their underlying stability guaranteed by a fortuitous coincidence of ethnic identity and territorial boundaries. By contrast, the two polities on the island of Ireland have their origins in the relatively recent convulsions of 1912–22; on both sides of the border the victors rapidly institutionalised the historical ideology of the majority population. Prosecuting the unfinished business of the nationalist revolution

[99] F. S. L. Lyons, 'The burden of our history' (1979), reprinted in Brady, *Interpreting Irish History*, p. 88.

[100] David Cannadine, 'British history: past, present – and future?', *Past & Present*, 116 (1987), 169–91.

[101] Lois G. Schwoerer, 'Celebrating the Glorious Revolution, 1689–1989', *Albion*, 22 (1990), 1–20.

[102] S. L. Kaplan, *Farewell, Revolution: Disputed Legacies, France, 1789/1989* (Ithaca, NY, 1995).

remained the theoretical objective of the southern state, and later the practical aim of republican paramilitaries in the north. Like Moody and Lyons, those who joined the academic expansion of the 1970s were disturbed by the prominence of the gun in Irish politics. Had historians, in their preoccupation with the seventeenth-century wars of religion or the romantic nationalism of Patrick Pearse, helped to shape modern attitudes? Had they incurred a responsibility for communal strife? As Moody reminded his audience, the eight-centuries-of-British-oppression version of Irish history which sustained the Provisional IRA had long been part of the political culture of the Republic.[103] While British and French historians responded to the painful readjustments brought about by imperial decline, decolonisation and postwar immigration, neither was confronted so directly with the violent expression of historically based ideologies.

It was the remarkable, and seldom acknowledged achievement of Moody and his generation to maintain a shared sense of enterprise across two mutually antagonistic jurisdictions; in an era of cultural retrenchment and introspection the imagined community of the historians extended to the island as a whole. Arguably, however, the price of this latitude was the estrangement of the academic élite from the nationalist and unionist mentalities which still dominated lay understandings of the past. By the late 1980s a backlash was underway, as Brendan Bradshaw launched a critique of mainstream Irish historiography, asking 'whether the received version of Irish history may not, after all, constitute a beneficent legacy – its wrongness notwithstanding'? Historical revisionism, he regretted, had cleansed the Irish past of heroic figures, rejected the concept of an aboriginal Gaelic race, and replaced the central dynamic of nationhood with an emphasis on complexity, ambiguity and contingency. Above all, the scientific research techniques developed by professional historians had inhibited their understanding of the 'catastrophic' episodes in Irish history – conquest and colonisation, the brutal suppression of insurrections and the Famine. Blinded by their commitment to objectivity, historians had disconnected themselves from a 'communal memory' still traumatised by ancestral suffering.[104]

A further, more radical, challenge to conventional scholarship has emerged in association with post-structuralist approaches to historical

[103] Moody, 'Irish history and Irish mythology', p. 85.

[104] See Brendan Bradshaw, 'Nationalism and historical scholarship in modern Ireland', *Irish Historical Studies*, 26 (1989), reprinted in Brady, *Interpreting Irish History*, quotations on pp. 205 and 212.

writing. Conventionally, as we have seen, history and memory have been viewed as alternative routes to the past. Yet, as Hayden White has been arguing for some thirty years now, historical narratives are not innate within past events, waiting to be found or discovered, but must be constructed by the historian. A greater appreciation of the role of metaphor and narrative in the writing of historical texts has made it increasingly difficult to maintain the epistemological superiority of history over memory, myth and tradition.[105] A growing number of Irish literary critics, inspired by theories of post-colonialism and subalternity, have contended that the distinction between professional and lay versions of the past is founded on disciplinary power rather than epistemological soundness: history, in other words, is merely officially sanctioned memory. The argument finds its extreme form in the essays of David Lloyd, for whom historians are irretrievably implicated in the 'coercive project' of the European state.[106] On such a view, historical discourse is encoded with an unexamined contrast between civility and violence that legitimates capitalist notions of 'modernity' while consigning alternative conceptions of culture to the realms of folklore or mythology.

On one level, of course, it is undeniable that historians themselves construct the meaning of their objects of study. The 'devotional revolution' which transformed popular Catholicism after the Famine is just one example of the imposition upon the past of retrospective frameworks. Few historians these days, moreover, pretend to be immune from the pressures of their intellectual and social milieu. Yet the analysis of historical texts in terms of the rules of literary genre and style offers a very limited account of what historians actually do. The inventiveness of historical scholars is usually constrained by the documentary record itself, that is, by the accumulation of a recognised corpus of primary sources, and by the established procedures and conventions of the discipline. The reconstruction of historical contexts and processes certainly involves narration and therefore contains a 'fictive' element, but narration is no longer the dominant form of historical writing. Even the basic

[105] Elizabeth Tonkin questions the distinction between history and myth from the point of view of an anthropologist in 'History and the myth of realism', in Raphael Samuel and Paul Thompson (eds.), *The Myths We Live By* (London and New York, 1990), pp. 25–35.

[106] David Lloyd, *Ireland after History* (Cork, 1999). Needless to say, most historians would reject his argument that the historical profession is the mouthpiece of the establishment; for an informed discussion of the relationship between historians and the state see Stefan Berger, Mark Donovan and Kevin Passmore (eds.), *Writing National Histories: Western Europe since 1800* (London, 1999).

task of mapping a chain of events raises questions about background conditions, relationships of cause and effect, and social context which are not reducible to the choice of plot structures or discursive tropes.[107]

Certainly Moody's positivistic faith in scientific method, like his 'mental war of liberation from servitude to the myth', sounds naïve to a generation of historians which has absorbed many of the insights of postmodernism. As we have already seen, 'myth' can be used in another sense, to signify stories told about the past which serve to legitimate or undermine contemporary practices. The real question then, as Raphael Samuel and Paul Thompson have suggested, is not how myths relate to 'reality', but how they relate to other myths and to 'the imaginative complexes which sustain them'.[108] As historians we need to scrutinise collective myths and memories, not just for evidence of their historical accuracy, but as objects of study in their own right. This necessarily brings us into contact with the practitioners of other disciplines where narrative is a key issue, whether cultural anthropology, psychoanalysis or literary criticism. Irish historians, who once lamented the laity's tendency to cling to error, have thus moved on to ask why it should be that images and interpretations which seem self-evidently 'mythical' to us have exercised such a tenacious hold on the historical consciousness of different audiences.

Such an approach, exemplified in the essays in this volume, contrasts with Moody's conception of the historian as crusader against error. It is equally distant, however, from Bradshaw's bardic notion of the historian as custodian of tradition. Both views fail to see that historiography and commemoration, whilst shaped by shared cultural patterns, have divergent objectives. The direction of history is always towards the specificity and particularity of events: it is an essentially contextualising discipline. Memory, on the other hand, succeeds best when it travels in the other direction, when the details that supply the social and cultural context are stripped away to reveal the moral of the tale. By combining sensitivity with a critical standpoint, this volume aspires to the kind of history which is, as Pierre Nora puts it,

> less interested in events themselves than in the construction of events over time, in the disappearance and re-emergence of their significations; less interested in 'what actually happened' than in its perpetual reuse and misuse, its influence

[107] Noël Carroll, 'Interpretation, history, and narrative', in Brian Fay, Philip Pomper and Richard T. Vann (eds.), *History and Theory: Contemporary Readings* (1998), pp. 34–56.

[108] Samuel and Thompson, 'Introduction', *Myths We Live By*, p. 12.

on successive presents; less interested in traditions than in the way in which traditions are constituted and passed on.[109]

Rather than speaking of a 'communal memory' linking the Irish across the centuries, a social and cultural history of remembering would unravel the various strands of commemorative tradition which have formed our consciousness of the past. In attempting this task, the essays in this volume help us to understand some of the ways in which different people at different times have claimed to be, or refused to become, 'Irish'.

[109] Nora, 'From *Lieux de mémoire* to *Realms of Memory*', p. xxiv.

CHAPTER 2

Martyrdom, history and memory in early modern Ireland

Alan Ford

Twere happy for our holy faith to bleed:
The blood of martyrs is the churches feed.[1]

No one can deny the power of political martyrdom in modern Irish history. The blood of those who died for the nationalist faith has repeatedly been invoked to inspire and stiffen the sinews of their successors fighting to free Ireland from foreign rule. The consequent creation of an apostolic succession of heroic suffering, from Wolfe Tone to Bobby Sands, along with their cults and shrines, from Bodenstown to the gable ends of houses on the Falls Road, has provided a fascinating challenge for later interpreters. Historians, with their instinctively reductionist focus upon 'what really happened', have often found it difficult to come to terms with the protean power of martyrdom, where the stark and depressing facts of abject failure and death can be mysteriously transfigured into triumph by the powerful but perplexing interplay between history and memory, belief and imagination.[2]

But behind this much-studied political tradition there lies, of course, a religious one, which has received rather less attention from modern Irish historians.[3] In mainland Europe this tradition dated back to the invention of the very concept of martyrdom in the early church, when brave men

[1] James Shirley, *St Patrick for Ireland. A Tragi-comedy. First Acted by His Majesty's Company of Comedians in the year 1639* (Dublin, 1750), p. 73.

[2] S. L. Williams, 'Another martyr for old Ireland', Ph.D. thesis, University of Massachusetts (1996); Marianne Elliott, *Wolfe Tone: Prophet of Irish Independance* (New Haven, CT, 1989); Padraig O'Malley, *Biting at the Grave: The Irish Hunger Strikes and the Politics of Despair* (Belfast, 1990); S. W. Gilley, 'Pearse's sacrifice: Christ and Cuchulain crucified and risen in the easter Rising, 1916', in S. W. Sykes (ed.), *Sacrifice and Redemption: Durham Essays in Theology* (Cambridge, 1991); W. I. Thompson, *The Imagination of an Insurrection: Dublin, Easter 1916: A Study of an Ideological Movement* (New York, 1967); S. F. Moran, 'Patrick Pearse and patriotic soteriology: the Irish republican tradition and the sanctification of political self-immolation', in Yonah Alexander and Alan O'Day (eds.), *The Irish Terrorism Experience* (Aldershot, 1991); S. F. Moran, *Patrick Pearse and the Politics of Redemption: The Mind of the Easter Rising, 1916* (Washington, DC, 1994) and other references there cited.

[3] A considerable amount of hagiographical research has been conducted on the cause of the Irish martyrs, producing an impressive corpus of factual information: M. W. P. O'Reilly, *Lives of the Irish*

and women, following Christ, went joyfully to their deaths and helped forge the Christian sense of community and identity. The memory of martyrdom was reinforced by ritual, as popular cults grew up around the dead and tombs became places of pilgrimage; and was preserved (and even on occasions invented) by oral tradition and the new genre of martyrology. In Ireland, however, the early and mediaeval churches were notable for their distinct lack of martyrs.[4] Indeed, early Irish Christians had to invent new forms of non-lethal martyrdom to compensate for the embarrassing shortage of deaths due to religious persecution.[5] As a result, the roots of modern Irish martyrdom are to be found much later, in the sixteenth-century Reformation and Counter-Reformation, the second great period of martyrdom in European history.

The Reformation, in this as in so many other matters, added new layers of complexity to a previously simple story. Across Europe, martyrdom was brought back to the centre of the stage, but it was now a contested martyrdom, not a battle between Christianity and paganism, but fought over *within* the Christian community. 'Truth', as the theologian Thomas Stapleton put it, 'purchaseth hatred.'[6] The mutually conflicting truths of the Reformation and the Counter-Reformation doubled the hatred. Though each side sought to preserve appearances by insisting that

Martyrs and Confessors (New York, 1881); Denis Murphy, 'Our martyrs' in *Irish Ecclesiastical Record,* (3rd ser.) xiii (1892), pp. 42–7, 124–30, 350–5, 720–9; Denis Murphy, *Our martyrs, a record of those who suffered for the Catholic faith under the penal laws in Ireland* (Dublin, 1896); J. Brady, 'Canonisation of the Irish martyrs: the apostolic process', in *Irish Ecclesiastical Record* (5th ser.), xi (1918), 311–21; Ciaran Brady, 'The beatified martyrs of Ireland (4): Margaret Ball (née Birmingham)', *Irish Theological Quarterly,* 64 (1999), 379–84; James Coombes, 'The beatified martyrs of Ireland (5): Maurice MacKenraghty', *Irish Theological Quarterly,* 65 (2000), 57–64; P. J. Corish, 'The beatified martyrs of Ireland (2): Matthew Lambert, Robert Meyler, Edward Cheevers, Patrick Cavanagh, and companions', *Irish Theological Quarterly,* 64 (1999), 179–87; Francis Finnegan, 'The beatified martyrs of Ireland (6): Dominic Collins, S. J.', *Irish Theological Quarterly,* 64 (2000), 157–68; J. J. Meagher, 'The beatified martyrs of Ireland (3): Dermot O'Hurley, Archbishop of Cashel', *Irish Theological Quarterly,* 64 (1999), 285–98; Benignus Millett, 'The beatified martyrs of Ireland (1): Patrick O'Healy, OFM, Conn O'Rourke, OFM', *Irish Theological Quarterly,* 64 (1999), 67–78. However, much less attention has been paid to the broader historical interpretation of early modern Irish martyrdom. A notable and impressive exception is Clodagh Tait, 'Harnessing corpses: death, burial, disinterment and commemoration in Ireland, *c.*1550–1655', National University of Ireland, Cork, Ph.D. thesis (1999), pp. 320–54.

4 Dáibhí Ó Cróinín, *Early Medieval Ireland, 400–1200* (London, 1995), p. 37; *cf.* Giraldus's taunt, and the response of the Archbishop of Cashel: Gerald of Wales, *The History and Topography of Ireland,* ed. J. J. O'Meara (Harmondsworth, 1982), pp. 113, 115f.

5 Clare Stancliffe, 'Red, white and blue martyrdom', in Dorothy Whitelock, Rosamond McKitterick and David Dumville (ed.), *Ireland in Early Mediaeval Europe: Essays in Memory of Kathleen Hughes* (Cambridge, 1982), pp. 21–46.

6 Thomas Stapleton, *The History of the Church of England Compiled by the Venerable Bede* (Antwerp, 1565), Epistle, cited in Patrick Collinson, 'Truth, lies, and fiction in sixteenth-century Protestant historiography', D. R. Kelley and D. H. Sacks (eds.), *The Historical Imagination in Early Modern Britain: History, Rhetoric, and Fiction, 1500–1800* (Cambridge, 1997), p. 46.

those they were executing were not martyrs, but heretics, blasphemers or traitors, the horrifying reality was that Christians were once more being put to death for religion, just as in the days of the early church, but this time not by pagan monsters such as Nero, but at the hands of emperors, princes and states who claimed to be Christian.

As a result, early modern martyrdom flourished most on the frontiers (both internal and external) of Christianity – at doctrinal, missionary or political boundaries, where the intensity and ferocity of the conflict with the enemy made extreme demands upon the combatants.[7] Such conflict occurred most notably when the new post-Reformation religious boundaries crossed and conflicted with civil ones. Here, confessional and secular insecurities intersected, as rulers, instinctively attached to the principle of uniformity, saw religious division as a direct threat to the unity of their state. The resultant tensions in countries such as the Netherlands, France, England and, of course, Ireland, marked the beginning of this new era of Christian martyrdom, distinguished by bitter sectarian rivalry, hostility and violence. With terrifying logic, each side of the confessional divide claimed exclusive ownership of the title martyr. Catholic martyrs, as a result, now vied with their Protestant rivals to prove by their zeal and bravery the rectitude of their particular cause.

The result of this fatal competition was renewed interest in the history of martyrdom, with the emergence of parallel and competing literary and propagandist genres – Protestant and Catholic martyrology.[8] Historians began to compile new and strictly confessional lists, using the power of print to ensure that, through text and woodcuts, the bravery and steadfastness of the martyrs' witness was recorded so as to preserve their memory and strengthen the faith of ordinary Christians. Reflecting the early modern conviction that 'what was ancientest was best', they went further and linked their modern martyrs with those of the early church, creating a kind of apostolic succession of suffering for the truth, which served at one and the same time to legitimise their own side of the confessional divide, whilst implicitly denigrating their persecutors as barbaric, the direct descendants of the pagan emperors. Sectarian martyrology was born: the Catholics had Baronius; the Lutherans Rabanus, the Huguenots Crespin, the English Protestants Foxe and the English

[7] J. T. Rhodes, 'English books of martyrs and saints in the late sixteenth and early seventeenth centuries', *Recusant History*, 22 (1994), 7–25. I am grateful to Dr Rhodes for her stimulating conversation on the subject of martyrs.

[8] B. S. Gregory, *Salvation at Stake: Christian Martyrdom in Early Modern Europe* (Cambridge, MA, 1999).

Catholics Sanders, while the poor Anabaptists, slaughtered impartially by Catholic and Protestant alike, preserved their woes in powerful oral traditions of song and story.[9]

It was towards the end of the sixteenth century, in the wake of Protestant persecution, that pious historians began to collect the names of those who had suffered for the faith in Ireland and compose the first native martyrologies. The purpose of this investigation is to look at that initial process of memorialising in order, first, to establish some essential facts – when the deaths started to be recorded, who it was that recorded them, and in what form; second, to look at whose deaths were recorded and why; third, to use this information to examine the wider contemporary importance of these martyrs and the martyrologies, looking in particular at the way in which the latter helped to reshape the way in which Irish Catholics viewed their recent history; and, finally, to gain some insight into the complex and sometimes delicate triangular relationship between truth, memory and history which is exposed in the stories of those unjustly killed.

I

It is possible to divide the development of early modern Irish martyrology into four stages, the first two of which are of primary interest to us here. Initially, in the 1580s and 1590s, the challenge was taken up by Catholics outside Ireland, who added a small number of Irishmen to their general Counter-Reformation memorials of those who had suffered for the faith. In 1582 an English friar, Thomas Bourchier, included in his lengthy history of the sufferings of his fellow Franciscans the story of two Irish martyrs, Patrick Hely, bishop of Mayo, and his companion, Con O'Rourke, killed in 1578.[10] Bourchier's account both conformed to the general pattern of Counter-Reformation martyr stories, and provided a model for subsequent Irish martyrologists. Caught on their return to Ireland from the continent, betrayed to the English authorities by the countess of Desmond, Hely and O'Rourke were first

[9] Cesare Baronius, *Martyrologium Romanum* (Venice, 1584); Ludwig Rabanus, *Historien der Martyrer* (2 vols., Strasbourg, 1571–2); Jean Crespin, *Histoire des martyrs*, ed. Daniel Benoit (3 vols., Toulouse, 1885); John Foxe, *Acts and monuments of these latter and perilous days, touching matters of the church* (London, 1563); Nicholas Sanders, *De visibili monarchia ecclesiae* (Wurzberg, 1592); T. J. van Braght, *The Bloody Theatre or Martyrs Mirror of the Defenceless Christians* (Scottdale, 1990).

[10] Thomas Bourchier, *Historia Ecclesiastica de martyrio Fratrum Ordinis Divi Francisci* (1st edn, Paris, 1582; 2nd edn, Ingolstadt, 1583). There was also one Italian and two German abridgements: A. F. Allison and D. M. Rogers, *The contemporary printed literature of the English Counter-Reformation between 1558 and 1640 : an annotated catalogue* (2 vols., Aldershot, 1989–94), i, p. 20.

imprisoned for several months, then taken before Sir William Drury, president of Munster, 'a savage persecutor of Catholics'. Under examination they both acknowledged that they were Franciscan priests, sent to minister unto the Catholic people of Ireland, and when pressed to acknowledge the royal supremacy they rejected the Reformation legislation. Offered riches and honours if they conformed, threatened with torture and death if they did not, they remained resolute. Infuriated, Drury ordered that they be tortured and hanged by martial law, without even a trial. They were beaten with sticks, racked, their fingernails prised up with sharp objects, their fingers cut off, their limbs broken with hammers, yet they remained firm and determined. After further offers of reward if they conformed, the Franciscans were hanged by their own girdles on 22 August. The bodies were left exposed for fourteen days, so the wild animals could eat them but, miraculously, they remained untouched. Instead, their features remained smiling and unchanged, and far from decomposing, they exuded a pleasant smell. The local people flocked to see them, taking away parts of their clothing as relics.[11] In a final confirmation of the rectitude of the Catholic cause, just fourteen days later Drury collapsed and died from a mysterious illness.[12]

In 1587 the Dutch–English Catholic historian, Richard Verstegan, published the one truly international, and highly popular, contemporary Catholic account of Protestant persecution, *Theatrum crudelitatum haereticorum*, with twenty-nine vivid, not to mention gruesome, woodcuts.[13] He gave an account of the deaths of Hely and O'Rourke, and added a more recent, and horrific, case, that of the archbishop of Cashel, Dermot Hurley. Captured by the Dublin government in 1583, Hurley was first tortured in April 1584 by having his legs boiled in oil, then allowed to recover for two months before being condemned to death under martial law and hung by an improvised noose of rough twigs (see illustration).[14] Contemporary English Catholic writers, including the Catholic apologist

[11] Bourchier, *Historia Ecclesiastica* (Paris, 1582), fols. 162r–165v.

[12] Christopher Holywood, *Supplicia magna*, in P. F. Moran (ed.), *Spicilegium Ossoriense: being a collection of original letters and papers illustrative of the history of the Irish church from the Reformation to the year 1800* (3 vols., Dublin, 1874–84), iii, 27.

[13] Richard Verstegan, *Theatrum crudelitatum haereticorum* (Antwerp, 1587); Gregory, *Salvation at Stake*, 290.

[14] Verstegan, *Theatrum crudelitatum haereticorum* (2nd edn, Antwerp, 1588). pp. 80f.; Peter Milward, *Religious Controversies of the Elizabethan age: A Survey of Printed Sources* (London, 1978), p. 73; Allison and Rogers, *Printed Literature*, i, 171; J. H. Pollen, 'Verstegan, Richard', in *The Catholic Encyclopedia* (1913); A. C. Petti, 'Richard Verstegan and the Catholic martyrologies in the later Elizabethan period', *Recusant History*, 5 (1959–60), 64–90.

Engraving showing Protestant cruelties towards Catholic clergy in Ireland, 'Persecutiones adversus Catholicos a Protestantibus Calvinistis excitae in Hibernia', from Richard Verstegan, *Theatrum Crudelitaum Haereticorum Nostri Temporis*, Antwerp, 1588

Nicholas Sanders, who himself died in Ireland, also included Irishmen amongst their lists of martyrs.[15]

These works by foreign writers, however, only recorded the fate of the more notable Irish martyrs and confessors.[16] Far greater depth and detail was provided by our second strand of martyrology, the Irish writers who began the task of collecting and preserving the stories of persecuted Irish Catholics from the late sixteenth century, initially in manuscript, subsequently in printed works. The first was John Howlin, a Jesuit from Wexford who was one of the founders of the Irish College at Salamanca in 1592.[17] Well placed in exile in Spain and Portugal where he had regular contact with Irish travellers and students, but

[15] Nicholas Sanders, *De visibili monarchia ecclesiae* (1st edn, s.l., 1571; 2nd edn, Wurzberg, 1592), pp. 664, 672, 674, 676; John Fen and John Gibbon, *Concertatio ecclesiae Catholicae in Anglia adversus Calvino-Papistas et Puritanos sub Elizabetha regina* (Trier, 1588), Appendix.

[16] Confessors were those who suffered severely, but did not die directly for their religion.

[17] Edmund Hogan, *Distinguished Irishmen of the Sixteenth Century* (London, 1894), pp. 29–47; T. J. Walsh, *The Irish Continental College Movement: the Colleges at Bordeaux, Toulouse, and Lille* (Cork, 1973), pp. 50–5.

also with recent experience of the Irish mission, he compiled *c.* 1590 the *Perbreve Compendium*, a list of forty-six Irish people who had suffered for religion.[18]

Howlin considerably expanded upon the few clergy who had been included in the foreign compilations, but also used his local knowledge to record the fates of less prominent sufferers, ordinary Catholics who had been tragically caught up in the troubles – men such as Robert Meiler, Patrick Canavan and Edward Cheevers, sailors who had helped Robert Rochford the Jesuit and other priests and nobles to flee to France and were, as Howlin recounted, hanged, cut down whilst half alive, castrated, disembowelled, beheaded and then quartered.[19]

Howlin was followed by Conor O'Devany, bishop of Down and Dromore, who was himself martyred in 1612. Before his death he compiled a manuscript 'Martyrs' Index' listing those bishops and priests who had died since 1585, which was passed on to David Rothe, who was provided to the see of Ossory in 1618 and became the leading resident Catholic bishop in Ireland.[20] Rothe oversaw the crucial transition from manuscript to print. Combining O'Devany's list with Howlin's and Sanders', and adding evidence from his own sources, in 1619 he published the most comprehensive catalogue yet, of eighty-seven martyrs and confessors.[21] This appeared as part of his *Analecta*, dedicated to the Catholic princes of Europe, which aimed to provide a comprehensive account of the persecution of the Irish at the hands of the English Protestant sectaries. Rothe's work was quickly followed by three further books. In 1620 an Irish priest trained on the continent, John Copinger, published in France *The theatre of Catholique and Protestant religion divided into twelve bookes*, which listed seventy-three martyrs and confessors. The following year two more martyrologies came out: Henry Fitzsimon, an Irish Jesuit, included fourteen modern martyrs in his list of Irish saints, while Philip O'Sullivan Beare recorded forty-six martyrs in his two accounts of Irish history, the first published in 1621, the second in 1629.[22] Also in 1629, an Irish professor at the Sorbonne, John Mullan, completed the

18 Moran (ed.), *Spicilegium Ossoriense*, i, pp. 82–109.

19 Ibid., i, p. 103.

20 P. F. Moran (ed.), *The Analecta of David Rothe, Bishop of Ossory* (Dublin, 1884) [hereafter, Rothe, *Analecta*], pp. civ, 386.

21 [David Rothe], *De processv martyriali quonrandam fidei pugilum in Hibernia, pro complemento sacrorum analectorvm. Collectore et relatore T. N. Philadelpho* (Cologne, 1619), part III of the *Analecta*, printed in Rothe, *Analecta*, pp. 357–589; Rothe, *Analecta*, p. 386 (Sanders), pp. 390f. (Howlin), p. 489 (Howlin).

22 Veridicus Hibernus, *Hiberniae sive antiquioris Scotiae vindiciae adversus immodestam parecbasim Thomae Dempsteri moderni Scoti nuper editam Catalogus praecipuorum sanctorum Hiberniae recognitus et auctus per R.P.*

first generation of native Irish martyrologists with his detailed account of the suffering of one particularly heroic Dubliner, Francis Taylor, and his comprehensive listing of Irish martyrs published in Paris.[23]

The third stage in the development of Irish martyrology saw these fuller listings being taken up in the first half of the seventeenth century and after by other Catholic historians and martyrologists in Europe, most especially those dedicated to the sufferings of members of particular religious orders, and included in their broader accounts and calendars.[24] The final stage, in the second half of the seventeenth century, involved the compilation of further histories of the persecution of Irish Catholics by Irish Catholic writers based abroad, who, stimulated by the recrudescence of persecution under Cromwell in the 1650s recorded the new martyrdoms together with the earlier accounts.[25]

II

Who was included in these early martyrs' lists? In all, for the 100 years from 1529 to 1629 there are 162 named people – 19 confessors and 143 martyrs. Of these 162, 46 were lay people (2 of whom were women), 116 were clergy, of whom 49 were secular and 67 regular.[26] Geographically, though the clergy ranged across the country, they, and more especially the lay sufferers, tended to be concentrated in the south, especially the province of Munster. Amongst the religious orders, the Franciscans were

Henr. Fitz-Simon (Antwerp, 1621); Paul Grosjean, 'Édition du Catalogus praecipuorum Sanctorum Hiberniae de Henri Fitzsimon', in John Ryan (ed.), *Féilscríbhinn Eoin Mhic Néill* (Dublin, 1995), pp 335–93; Richard Sharpe, 'The origin and elaboration of the Catalogus Praecipuorum Sanctorum Hiberniae attributed to Fr Henry Fitzsimon, S. J.', *Bodleian Library Record*, 13 (1989), 202–30; William O'Sullivan, 'A Waterford origin for the Codex Salmanticensis', *Decies*, 54 (1998), p. 23 draws attention to the exisentence of a part of the first (1611) edition of Fitzsimon's *Catalogus,* though this does not contain any later martyrs; Philip O'Sullivan-Beare, *Historiae Catholicae Iberniae compendium* (Lisbon, 1621); Matthew Kelly, ed. (Dublin 1850); Philip O'Sullivan Beare, *Patritiana decas sive libri decem quibus de divi Patricii vita Archicormiger mastix sive Usheri haeresiarchae confutatio descriptioque accesit* (Madrid, 1629).

23 John Mullan, *Epitome tripartita martyrum fere omnium qui in Britannicis insulis nostra patrumque memoria de haeresi gloriose triumpharunt* (Paris, 1629); John Mullan, *Idea togata constantiae* (Paris, 1629).

24 The early work of Bourchier on the Franciscans was followed by similar compilations for the Cistercians (1630), Dominicans (1635), Jesuits (1640) and finally the massive work on the history of the Franciscans by an Irishman, Luke Wadding, his *Annales Minorum*, published between 1625 and 1654: for a fuller listing of martyrologies see Murphy, *Our martyrs*, pp. xxiii–xxviii.

25 Peter Redan, *Commentaria in libros Machabaeorum canonicos* (Lugduni, 1651); Maurice Conry, *Threnodia Hiberno-Catholica sive planctus universalis totius cleri et populi regni Hiberniae* (Innsbruck, 1659); Anthony Bruodin, *Propugnaculum catholicae veritatis* (Prague, 1669); Franciscus Porter, *Compendium annalium ecclesiasticorum Regni Hiberniae* (Romae, 1690); and cf. Murphy, *Our martyrs*, pp. xxiii–xxviii.

26 Compilation of these statistics is fraught with difficulty: in the case of the best-known martyrs, identification is straightforward, but for some of those where only the name and a few details are known, establishing their race and origin involves a certain amount of guesswork.

dominant, with forty-eight out of the sixty-eight regular clergy, reflecting their place in the vanguard of Irish resistance to the Reformation (and the assiduousness of their martyrologists). Nearly all the Franciscans had native Irish names, hardly surprising given their strength in the Gaelic areas of the country. As a result, amongst the regular clergy it was those with Irish names who dominated; amongst the laity, however, English and Anglo-Irish names outnumbered native Irish almost 3 to 1. Amongst the secular clergy the racial division was roughly even.

Why were these particular people included in the lists? It might be imagined that the relationship of the martyrs to the martyrologies would be fairly straightforward. Martyrs die for the faith; martyrologists record their death. But the process of creating martyrs had always been a complex one in western Christendom, as much a matter for informal negotiation and local initiative as official ecclesiastical decision. Initially, it was entirely a matter for particular churches and bishops, and, indeed, for those who wrote and circulated the accounts of the martyrs' sufferings and deaths – exaggeration and even invention were, accordingly, not unknown. Only gradually did the papacy centralise the procedure for canonisation and assert its right to conduct the increasingly elaborate judicial inquiry, or 'process' into the cause of the martyr or saint. And even after Urban VIII had formalised procedures in 1625 and 1634, martyrdom remained a special case. For saints it was necessary to inquire whether the candidate had led a life of heroic virtue. But martyrdom was by its very nature more dramatic and less complicated: all was focused upon the heroic death. However, the very ease with which it could be recognised created certain tensions between centre and periphery, as unofficial, local martyrs frequently gained wide followings without ever receiving, or even seeking, official sanction.[27]

The martyrologies of Howlin, Rothe and the others were clearly inspired by a desire to secure the canonisation of their fellow-Irishmen. To judge from the initial phrase – *De processu martyriali* – in the title of the section of the *Analecta* dealing with the martyrs and confessors, Rothe saw himself as providing material for a formal process. But the cause never got under way – indeed, for all the religious bitterness and bloodshed in the early modern period across Europe, remarkably few martyrs were even considered for formal canonisation until centuries later.[28] The reasons for this are unclear – the tightening up of the procedures

[27] Gregory, *Salvation at stake*, p. 252.

[28] Peter Burke, 'How to be a Counter-Reformation saint', in Kaspar von Greyerz (ed.), *Religion and Society in Early Modern Europe, 1500–1800* (London, 1984), p. 51. It was not in fact until 1892 that a formal canonical process was begun by the Irish hierarchy, but the early efforts to collect

by Urban VIII may have been responsible, or, more likely, papal reluctance to antagonise Protestant states and risk further persecution of Catholic minorities.[29] This absence of any central response, however, merely focuses our attention upon the local and unofficial cults which were inspired by the deaths of the Irish martyrs, and, more significantly, upon the criteria used by the martyrologists themselves. For, in default of higher authority, it was partly their decisions, partly the response of the Catholic faithful, that decided whether or not one was considered to be a martyr for the faith in early modern Ireland.

As the first native martyrologist, Howlin is the obvious starting point: he not only had the privilege of deciding on his criteria for inclusion without having to pay any attention to those of his predecessors; nearly all those he did include were also recorded by his successors. The most striking feature of his list is its remarkably narrow chronological and geographical focus. His seven confessors and thirty-nine martyrs all suffered between 1578 and 1588. They came overwhelmingly from southern Leinster or Munster, reflecting his close ties with Wexford; thirty were Anglo-Irish, fifteen native Irish, one English; just over half (twenty-four) were lay people (including one woman), and of these all but two were of Anglo-Irish origin. The reason for these biases become apparent when examining the individual histories.

Amongst those included were the earl of Desmond's chaplain, Maurice Mc Enright, portrayed as inspiring the Catholic troops, administering the sacraments and enduring many calamities in the war against the heretics, before being captured, imprisoned and eventually executed as a traitor in Clonmel in 1585.[30] He also included Nicholas Sanders, the English priest and Counter-Reformation leader, a staunch advocate of military resistance who came over to Ireland under the papal flag with James Fitzmaurice in 1579.[31] Another similar case was that of Edmund McDonnell, one of the early Jesuit missionaries, arrested and

evidence to secure the canonisation of 258 martyrs proved over-ambitious. A more selective approach led to the beatification of seventeen Irish martyrs in 1992. Murphy, 'Our martyrs', pp. 42–7, 124–30, 350–5, 720–9; Michael O'Riordan, 'Sanctification and canonisation of the Irish martyrs: the articles of the apostolic process', *Irish Ecclesiastical Record*, 5th ser., 7 (1916), 287–413; P. J. Corish, *The Irish Martyrs* (Dublin, 1989); P. J. Corish, 'The Irish martyrs and Irish history', *Archivium Hibernicum*, 47 (1993), 89–93; *The 17 Irish Martyrs* (Dublin, 1992); Desmond Forristal, *Dominic Collins: Irish Martyr, Jesuit brother, 1566–1602* (Dublin, 1992); Thomas Morrissey, 'An Irish Jesuit martyr: Dominic Collins', *Studies*, 81 (1992), 313–25; Augustine Valkenburg, *Two Dominican Martyrs of Ireland* (Dublin, 1992).

[29] See the fate of the effort to canonise the English martyrs in the 1640s: Archdiocese of Westminster, *Cause of the canonisation of blessed martyrs . . . put to death in England in defence of the Catholic faith (1535–1582)* (Vatican, 1968), pp. vi–vii.

[30] Moran (ed.), *Spicilegium Ossoriense*, i, pp. 89–91.

[31] Ibid., pp. 98f.

put to death for treason on the charge of carrying letters from the pope to James Fitzmaurice. But the most significant inclusions were those laymen who had fought against the Dublin government. 'Nor should we forget the many noted and noble laymen who for the sake of the faith, at the insistence of the supreme pontiff, Gregory XIII, fought in Ireland between 1576 and 1588.'[32] Howlin stressed the religious nature of the struggle, specifically mentioning the deaths of Walter and Thomas Eustace, brothers of James Viscount Baltinglass, and the earl of Desmond and his brothers John and James, together with many others who were judged to be 'glorious martyrs'.[33] In sum, what Howlin was doing was recording those who had died for the faith in the 1570s and 1580s, a period of martial law and savage fighting in Munster and Leinster during the Desmond, Baltinglass and Nugent risings. Hence the dates and the narrow time frame, hence the bias towards the Anglo-Irish.

O'Devany's list has not survived, but it is possible to reconstruct its contents. It was narrower and less potentially controversial than Howlin's, omitting laymen who had died in the recent risings, confining itself instead to clergy who had been killed in Ireland since 1585, and was again a product of the compiler's personal knowledge, being dominated by native Irish clergy from O'Devany's own province of Armagh.[34] Rothe, on the other hand, was more comprehensive in his approach, using O'Devany's list, including a number from Sanders and other English sources, and all but three from Howlin, whilst adding a further twenty himself, to produce a total of eighty-seven.[35] Of those twenty original to Rothe, all bar one were subsequent to Howlin, fifteen of them from the early seventeenth century; nearly all were from Leinster or Munster; five were laymen, fifteen priests; thirteen were probably of Anglo-Irish origin, seven native Irish. Rothe, in other words, brought the list up to date by adding those more recent martyrs of whom he had personal knowledge – two of his additions came from his native city of Kilkenny.[36] He also exercised his judgement by omitting some of those included by earlier compilers.[37]

[32] Ibid., p. 105.

[33] Ibid.

[34] See the reconstruction of this list by John MacErlean, Irish Jesuit Archives, Dublin, MS MACE/MTYR, 'The Index martyrialis of Conor O Devany, Bishop of Down and Connor'. I would add to MacErlean's proposed twelve, one further martyr: Daniel O'Harran.

[35] John Travers was taken from Nicholas Harpsfield, *Dialogi sex* (Antwerp, 1566), and William Tynsby from Maurice Chauncy, *Historia martyrum, Angliae* (1573).

[36] Walter Archer and George Power: Rothe, *Analecta,* p. 392; Murphy, *Our martyrs,* p. 209.

[37] From Howlin he left out Sanders and two of those executed after the Baltinglass rising, Christopher and Thomas Eustace. From Sanders he omitted Thomas Fleming, baron of Slane, whom Rothe saw not as an heroic, but a lukewarm Catholic: Rothe, *Analecta*, p. 429.

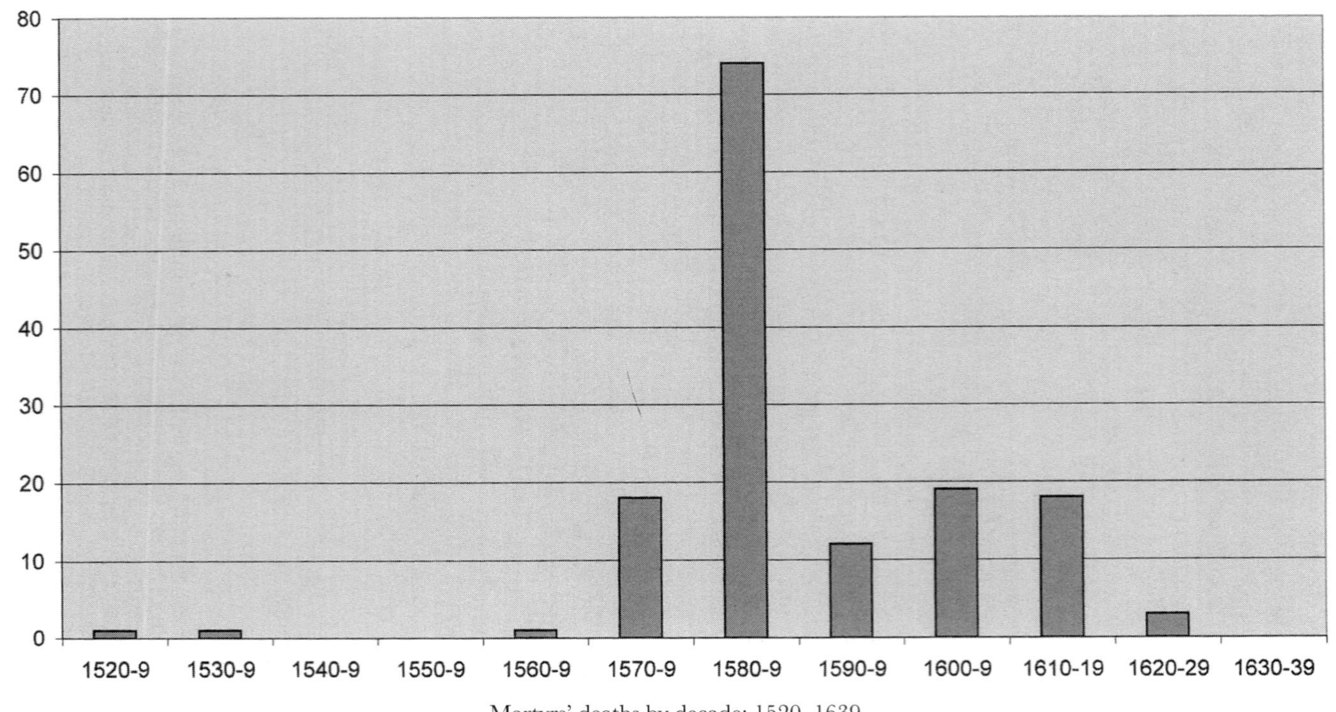

Martyrs' deaths by decade: 1520–1639

Coppinger's list of seventy-three martyrs and confessors was more selective and original. It seems unlikely that he had access to Howlin and Rothe, since he includes only thirty of Howlin's total of forty-six, and only forty-six from Rothe's eighty-seven. He does, however, supply us with an additional twenty-five, most of them from the 1580s. Like his predecessors, Philip O'Sullivan Beare's criteria for inclusion reflected his origins: but since he, unlike them, was native Irish, a layman and a soldier who had fought against the English forces in the Nine Years War, his list was very different. It contained no confessors: for him, death was the crucial qualification. It was also overwhelmingly native Irish – there were only seven Anglo-Irish names out of forty-five martyrs; and clerical – there were just eight laymen. Again it reflected his personal knowledge: his martyrs came predominantly from his native Munster. Most significantly, for O'Sullivan the crusade had not ended with the end of the Nine Years War. He, unlike Rothe, Copinger or Mullen, included as martyrs four of the leaders of the O'Doherty rising of 1615.[38] Finally, Mullan's martyrology was largely derivative – eighty-one of his eighty-five martyrs and confessors also appeared in Rothe.

III

Though the original inspiration of Howlin, Rothe, Fitzsimon, Coppinger, O'Sullivan and Mullan was simply to record the suffering of their fellow Irishmen and to provide evidence for canonisation, their work had a significance well beyond the field of martyrology. In that typically reflexive way of all martyrologists, they both contributed to and responded to a significant shift in the way that Irish Catholics viewed their faith, as part of that transition from traditionally minded to Counter-Reformation Catholicism, from a secular to a religious view of recent Irish history. In short, Irish martyrology in its early decades was linked to the forging of a new Irish Catholic identity. Though proof of this contention can at best be indirect, since it is difficult to trace the response of Catholic readers in Ireland and abroad to the martyrologies, it is possible to demonstrate the marked shift in the interpretation of the deaths of Irish Catholics during the 1580s, and assess the ideological use to which martyrdom was put.

The simplest way to approach this issue is by looking at the distribution by decade of the deaths of named martyrs (see table, p. 54). Clearly,

[38] O'Sullivan-Beare, *Historiae Catholicae*, pp. 73–9; Raymond Gillespie, *Conspiracy: Ulster Plots and Plotters in 1615* (Belfast, 1987), pp. 54–5.

something dramatic happened in the 1580s. But what? The obvious response is simply to point to the Desmond, Baltinglass and Nugent risings, and the associated death toll. After all, the last quarter of the sixteenth century saw the climax of the bloody struggle for control of Ireland between English, Anglo-Irish and native Irish. But violent death, opposition to the Dublin government, and even open revolt by disgruntled feudal magnates, were by no means unusual in earlier decades. What made the deaths of the 1570s and 1580s different from those who had died in earlier risings? The answer is threefold: the change in the risings' context, severity and interpretation, each of which gave a new prominence to religious motivations.

The shift in context can be precisely dated. The excommunication of Elizabeth in 1570 led, albeit slowly but nevertheless inexorably, to a hardening of positions on either side of the religious divide. Since Elizabeth was a heretic, Catholics were released from their duty to obey her. Since the pope was Antichrist, Protestants had an apocalyptic duty to fight the forces of Catholic darkness. The interchange between William Cecil, representing the views of the English government, and William Allen, the leader of the exiled English Catholics, in 1583–4 established the starkly opposed views of the implications of the excommunication.[39] For Cecil, the Catholics, following *Regnans in excelsis*, had a religious duty to overthrow the English government. Repeated plots involving Catholic priests proved that they were potential, and indeed on occasions actual, traitors, trying to replace the established government and its ruler. Catholics, on the other hand, soon worked out that it was impractical, not to mention dangerous, to follow the Bull and refuse to obey the queen. Instead they stressed their secular loyalty, while insisting on their right to retain their allegiance to the Catholic religion.[40] Persecution, therefore, had to be on account of their religion. As Allen's book explained in his title page:

> Wherein is declared, how unjustly the Protestants do charge Catholics with treason: how untruly they deny their persecution for religion; and how deceitfully they seek to abuse strangers about the cause, greatness and manner of their sufferings . . .

One practical result of this increasing religious tension was vastly to increase the stakes in the periodic risings and rebellions that had always

[39] R. M. Kingdon (ed.), *The Execution of Justice by William Cecil and A True, Sincere and Modest Defence of English Catholics by William Allen* (New York, 1965).

[40] Elliot Rose, *Cases of Conscience: Alternatives Open to Recusants and Puritans under Elizabeth I and James I* (Cambridge, 1975); Patrick McGrath, *Papists and Puritans under Elizabeth I* (London, 1967).

been such a feature of Irish history. No longer was it just a matter of a local magnate, dissatisfied with his treatment, seeking to make a political and military point in order to emphasise his importance. The moment James Fitzmaurice Fitzgerald unfurled his papal banner in Ireland in 1579 marked a highly significant change in context – the integration of Ireland into the wider diplomatic and military Counter-Reformation struggle in Europe between the Protestant and the Catholic powers. Like Fitzmaurice, many of the conspirators in the Baltinglass and Nugent risings of 1580 and 1581 were also inspired by the ideal of an anti-Protestant crusade. The resultant fear, indeed paranoia, on the part of the Dublin authorities, when faced with this new combination of revolt and crusade, fuelled their savage response to these risings. Catholic bishops and priests such as O'Hely and O'Rourke were not seen as harmless missionaries, but as agents of enemy powers, even supporters of Antichrist, dedicated to the overthrow of the Protestant church and state.

Legal niceties and normal military conduct were thrown aside as the government resorted to martial law, torture, and even massacre in an effort to keep its grip on Ireland.[41] Martial law was used extensively and pre-emptively, reaching its peak in the early 1580s under the rule of Lord Deputy Grey, who boasted that he had used it to execute 1,500 of the chief men and gentlemen, 'not accounting those of meaner sort . . . and killing of churls, which were innumerable'.[42] The willingness to use torture, previously shunned by English governments and judges, points most clearly to the exceptional nature of the official perception of the Catholic threat. The treatment of Hurley in 1584 thus marked a new departure for the Irish authorities, the beginning of a period of two decades in English and Irish history when torture was regularly used in order to gather evidence of treason.[43]

Even those on the official side recognised the consequences of the escalation in the use of state violence. In 1582 William Lyon, a Protestant Englishman newly appointed to the See of Ross in Munster, warned about the 'disorder of the soldiers among the people, which breedeth

41 David Edwards, 'Ideology and experience: Spenser's *View* and martial law in Ireland', in Hiram Morgan (ed.), *Political Ideology in Ireland, 1541–1641* (Dublin, 1999), pp. 127–57.

42 Cited by David Edwards, 'Beyond reform: martial law and the Tudor reconquest of Ireland', *History Ireland*, 5 (1997), p. 20.

43 S. P. 63/106/7, transcribed in Rothe, *Analecta*, pp. xxxiv–xxxv. On the use of torture generally, see John Langbein, *Torture and the Law of Proof* (Chicago, IL, 1976); James Heath, *Torture and English Law* (Westport, 1983); Elizabeth Hanson, 'Torture and truth in renaissance England', *Representations*, 34 (1991), 53–84; Elizabeth Hanson, *Discovering the Subject in Renaissance England* (Cambridge, 1998), ch. 2.

great hatred to our nation, and not without cause'.[44] By 1590, Robert Gardiner, chief justice of the Queen's Bench, was deeply concerned about the free rein given to 'inferior governors' over the past decades: 'our poor subjects have been frequently shamefully deprived of life, liberty and goods, and no decorum has been observed either in prosecution or execution, but a butcherlike spoiling of Christian blood'.[45]

And, of course, for those on the Catholic side such treatment provided the raw material for martyrdom and martyrology. The savage punishments inflicted on the Counter-Reformation martyrs were already being recorded in horrified detail by Catholic authors across Europe as final proof of the rectitude of their cause.[46] 'Go on you good magistrates, rack us, torture us, condemn us, yea grind us: your iniquity is proof of our faith.'[47] Now the risings of the 1570s and 1580s, replete with Counter-Reformation rhetoric and savage Protestant persecution, enabled Catholic writers on the continent to include Ireland in their modern martyrologies, and provided Irish Catholic historians with the opportunity to identify the modern Irish with the ancient Christian martyrs.

Shifting religious and political contexts, together with the increasing severity of the conflict in Ireland, go part of the way, then, towards explaining the sudden interest in martyrdom towards the end of the sixteenth century. Yet there is one final piece of this explanatory jigsaw that remains to be explored – the way in which the interpretation and, indeed, even the self-interpretation of these deaths, not only reflected the changing context, but also decisively altered that context, by reshaping Catholic memories of the risings and those who died in them. Sainthood, it has been observed, 'depends upon a community's recollection of a dead person's past existence'.[48] In the case of martyrdom, the martyrs themselves, by their conduct at their execution, and the martyrologists, by the way in which they record the life and death of their subjects, had a decisive role in influencing the formation of community memory.

Even the public execution of ordinary criminals offered a theatrical stage on which was played out many of the tensions and conflicts of early

[44] PRO (London), SP 63/96/10.II.

[45] PRO (London), SP 63/90/4. Responding to such complaints, Elizabeth suspended the use of martial law in 1591: Edwards, 'Ideology and experience', p. 142.

[46] Gregory, *Salvation at stake*, pp. 287–97.

[47] Robert Southwell, *An Epistle of Comfort to the Reverend Priests* (St Omer, 1616), 387, quoted by Hanson, *Discovering the Subject*, p. 33.

[48] Pierre Delooz, 'Towards a sociological study of canonized sainthood in the Catholic church', in Stephen Wilson (ed.), *Saints and their Cults: Studies in Religious Sociology, Folklore and History* (Cambridge, 1983), p. 194.

modern society. In the case of martyrs, though, the conflicting claims to truth and rectitude, and the contested legitimacy of the judicial process, together with the presence of committed members of the public as audience, offered an even more highly charged atmosphere in which the various participants could seek to shape the meaning of the drama.[49] The execution of four of those involved in the Nugent rising provides the clearest evidence of such refashioning. Thomas Jones, the strongly Protestant, English-born bishop of Meath, who escorted George Netterville, John and Robert Scurlock and Christopher Eustace to their deaths on 18 November 1581, left a detailed account of the drama of their last hours. His task was to make the prisoners openly acknowledge their treason and renounce their Catholicism, to ensure that they died a 'good death', serving as a warning to the assembled crowds. The condemned men, however, rejected his attempts contemptuously, determined to use the occasion to bear public witness to their faith.

> Netterville and Robert Scurlock joining together at the Castle gate began with the Lady's psalter, and said it verse by verse one answering another in the streets of Dublin. When they came to their Sancta Maria, mater Dei, ora pro nobis, etc. I interrupted their prayers and exhorted them to pray only unto God . . . but Mr Netterville answered me saying: 'You lose your labour Mr Parson, for it is not possible to bring us from our religion'. When yet I urged them, Netterville gnashing his teeth against me, and punching me with his elbows said '*Vade Satana, vade Satana, vade post me Satana*'.[50]

Further efforts to harangue them were rebuffed by their reciting Psalms in Latin. When they reached the place of execution they were urged to pray in English, but Netterville refused and tried to snatch the Book of Common Prayer from Jones's hand. When told to ask for the queen's forgiveness 'they spat for anger'. Their last words as they ascended the ladder were 'Now all good Catholics pray for us.' Christopher Eustace was similarly determined and religiously aware, shouting over to Netterville and Scurlock when Jones was haranguing them 'answer him nothing, take heed, *non licet disputare cum heretico*'. When asked to pray for the queen just before his execution, 'I will', said he, and therewith he said, 'God amend her.'[51]

49 Peter Lake and Michael Questier, 'Agency, appropriation and rhetoric under the gallows: puritans, Romanists and the state in early modern England', *Past & Present*, 153 (1996), 64–107; David Nicholls, 'The theatre of martyrdom in the French Reformation', *Past & Present*, 121 (1988), 49–73.

50 PRO, London, SP 63/86/69; cf. Matthew 16.23: 'Get thee behind me, Satan.'

51 SP 63/86/69.

Howlin repackages the death of Scurlock as a family drama. He stresses the victim's noble birth, the son of a judge, his youthful beauty and goodness, and his commitment to the Catholic faith. He was even, Howlin claims, imprisoned for several years before his death, and was eventually brought to court, where he was confronted by his father, sitting as a judge. His aged father begged him to accept the royal supremacy and avoid an ignominious death, only to be firmly rejected by his son in a lengthy and moving speech in which he affirmed that even if he had a hundred lives he would happily expend all of them in defence of the Catholic faith. He could not, he explained, obey an heretical queen, excommunicated by the pope, and condemned by the whole Catholic church. Rather he begged his aged father to reconsider his position and the danger in which it placed his soul. Condemned to death, he bravely journeyed to the gibbet, setting an example to the crowds by exhorting them to remain faithful to the Catholic religion, before dying a martyr.[52]

The first test of the commitment of the Irish Catholics to their new-found martyrs' heritage came in the early seventeenth century, when, after the end of the Nine Years War in 1603, the Dublin government was finally in a position to enforce conformity. In a bitter campaign between 1605 and 1607, the Protestant church and state in Ireland sought to use the full power of the law – and more – to force Catholics to come to church. Against the ordinary people the authorities used the 12d fine of the Act of Uniformity. But the richer urban recusants were singled out, and were issued with mandates requiring them to conform, and then subjected to massive fines and lengthy imprisonment if they refused. The results were instructive. Some of the ordinary people went to church, but there was a resolute refusal of the leading Catholics to make the slightest compromise.[53] The reports of the Irish Jesuits convey an atmosphere of defiant courage and solidarity in the face of terrifying persecution.[54]

Last week a proclamation was posted in the public places condemning all priests who are caught to be hanged from the nearest tree or gallows. Blessed be the name of the Lord Jesus, of whose divine love these are most evident

[52] Moran (ed.), *Spicilegium Ossoriense*, pp. 97–9.

[53] Alan Ford, *The Protestant Reformation in Ireland* (2nd edn, Dublin, 1997), ch. 3; H. S. Pawlisch, *Sir John Davies and the Conquest of Ireland: A Study in Legal Imperialism* (Cambridge, 1985), ch. 6; John McCavitt, *Sir Arthur Chichester, Lord Deputy of Ireland 1605–1616* (Belfast, 1998), ch. 7; John McCavitt, 'Lord Deputy Chichester and the English government's "mandates policy" in Ireland, 1605–7', *Recusant History*, 20 (1991), 320–35.

[54] Edmund Hogan (ed.), *Ibernia Ignatiana seu Ibernorum Societas Jesu patrum monumenta* (Dublin, 1880); Henry Fitzsimon, *Words of Comfort . . . letters from a cell . . . and diary of the Bohemian war of 1620*, ed. Edmund Hogan (Dublin, 1881).

marks and tokens, since his members are treated with the same ignominy with which he . . . was treated by the Jews! Arms and ropes have now been distributed to a brutal and treacherous soldiery, in order that they may slay or hang the priests of Christ. Three Catholics, one of whom was a priest, being taken prisoners, and suspected of being priests, were immediately hanged. May this island be now fruitful in martyrs as it once was of confessors and virgins! . . . The bearing of the Catholic laity has been glorious up to this, and they cheerfully suffered the miseries of prison life and the loss of their goods and fortunes.[55]

The image of a united Catholic nation opposed to the cruel oppression of their heretical rulers was partly, of course, propaganda, designed to convince the papacy and the continental powers to put pressure on the English government to lighten the burden on Irish Catholics. But it also helped to reflect and confirm what was also a growing reality, which even the Irish Protestant authorities had reluctantly to acknowledge – that the Irish people were indeed being drawn together in their commitment to Counter-Reformation Catholicism.

This was confirmed by the last great public martyrdom of the first half of the seventeenth century, the execution of Conor O'Devany and Patrick O'Loughran in 1612. O'Devany, an aged Franciscan from Donegal, had made the familiar trip to Rome, where in 1582 he was ordained bishop of Down and Connor. Though associated with the promulgation of Tridentine decrees in Ireland, and the signatory of a letter appealing to Philip II of Spain to intervene in Ireland, O'Deveny was not in the forefront of the fight for faith and fatherland. Hence when he was captured by the Dublin authorities in 1588, he was released after two years' imprisonment. O'Loughran, it has been plausibly argued, was a chaplain to the earl of Tyrone, and had accompanied him into exile, but later returned to Ireland. Their misfortune was to be seized by the Dublin authorities at a time when the firmly anti-Catholic lord deputy, Sir Arthur Chichester, had finally been allowed by the normally cautious English authorities to vent the full force of his hostility on the Catholic clergy. Hoping to make an example of them and perhaps cow the Catholic opposition in the forthcoming parliament, Chichester put O'Deveny and O'Loughran on trial for treason, making much of their connections with the earl of Tyrone.[56]

[55] Fitzsimon, *Words of Comfort*, p. 134.

[56] J. J. Silke, 'Bishop Conor O Devanney, OFM *c.* 1553–1612', *Seanchas Ardmhacha*, 13 (1988–9), 9–32; Kieran Devlin (ed.), 'The capture of Conor O'Devany, martyr', *Clogher Record*, 14/3 (1993), pp. 125–8; Ciarán Ó Doiblin, 'Giolla Phádraig Ó Luchráin *c.* 1577–1612', *Seanchas ArdMhacha*, 15 (1992), 50–96.

Their inevitable conviction was followed by a public execution. Accounts of their deaths, both Catholic and, significantly, Protestant, confirm that the considerable crowds – 'such a multitude as the like was never seen before at any execution about Dublin' – who flocked to their hanging, drawing and quartering were by now fully attuned to both the drama and the religious significance of martyrdom.[57] As O'Deveny and O'Loughran were led through the city, people went down on their knees, braving the blows of the guards to seek the priests' blessing.[58] Even the deeply hostile Protestant polemicist, Barnaby Rich, tells of the broad range of spectators from all sections of Catholic society, and recounts the dramatic scenes after the executions, as the crowds sought to secure relics from the holy martyrs:

The execution had no sooner taken off the bishop's head but the townsmen of Dublin began to flock about him . . . some cut away all the hair from the head, which they preserved for a relic; some others gave practice to steal the head away . . . Now when he began to quarter the body, the women thronged about him, and happy was she that could get but her handkerchief dipped in the blood of the traitor; and the body being dissevered into four quarters, they neither left finger or toe, but they cut them off and carried them away . . . and some others who could get no holy monuments that appertained to his person, with their knives they shaved off chips from the hallowed gallows; neither could they omit the halter with which he was hanged, but it was rescued for holy uses.[59]

In short, by the second decade of the seventeenth century the cult of martyrdom was fully established in Dublin. The execution of two Gaelic priests was able to attract a huge and sympathetic crowd of people in the very centre of the English presence in Ireland, who were prepared to cast personal safety aside in their desire to secure relics from the persecuted saints. Despite Chichester's efforts, this marked the end of official efforts to put Catholic priests to death as traitors. The response of the populace, and the publicity accorded to the deaths in Europe, forced even the Dublin government to accept that it had signally failed to win the argument over the status of Catholic martyrs.[60] The battle to define their historical memory had been decisively lost. It was not till

[57] C. L. Falkiner (ed.), 'William Farmer's Chronicles of Ireland', *English Historical Review*, 22 (1907), 544.

[58] Moran (ed.), *Spicilegium Ossoriense*, i, p. 124.

[59] Barnaby Rich, *A Catholic Conference* (London, 1612), pp. 5f.

[60] P. J. Corish (ed.), 'A contemporary account of the martyrdom of Conor O'Devany, O. F. M., Bishop of Down and Connor, and Patrick O'Loughran', *Collectanea Hibernica*, 26 (1984), 13–19; Benignus Millett, 'Who wrote the *Martyrium . . . Cornelii Dovenii*, Cologne, 1614?', *Recusant History*, 17 (1984–5), 358–61.

Cromwell's arrival in Ireland that the cycle of religious persecution and martyrdom resumed.

IV

The execution of O'Deveny has been identified as a decisive moment in the history of the Counter-Reformation in Ireland.[61] In fact, it may well have been merely a symbolic public confirmation of something which had already taken place well before – the forging of a separate and distinct sense of Catholic identity in which common religious belief and suffering transcended previously insurmountable barriers of race and national identity to create an ideology of Catholic faith and fatherland which could be shared by Irish and Anglo-Irish alike.[62] Underpinning this sense of religious solidarity was the discourse of martyrdom, with its capacity to take the raw material of popular experience and memories and structure them as narratives of official savagery and Catholic heroism. Such, indeed, was the power of this new form of discourse, that it reshaped the way in which Catholics viewed their recent history. This can be observed in the way it transformed past deaths and often rather complex historical events into much more simple and starkly dualist struggles between Protestant persecution and Catholic sanctity. It can even be seen in the capacity of some exiled martyrologists to transcend fact altogether and ascend into the realms of invention.

Take the case of the earl of Desmond. While it can be granted that James Fitzmaurice Fitzgerald, and many of those involved in the Baltinglass and Nugent risings, were consciously committed to the cause of the Counter-Reformation, it is much more difficult to paint the earl of Desmond as a religious crusader. The most acute modern analysis of the reasons why he joined the 1579 rising paints a convincing portrait of an unstable feudal magnate trapped by economic, political and ultimately military pressures beyond his control, but scarcely mentions religion as a motivating force.[63] Yet, when one reads Howlin's and even Rothe's account, the earl is improbably included amongst the leading participants in the Desmond, Nugent and Baltinglass risings as one of

[61] T. W. Moody, F. X. Martin and F. J. Byrne, *A New History of Ireland* (Oxford, 1976), iii, p. 209.

[62] Hiram Morgan, 'Faith and fatherland in sixteenth-century Ireland', *History Ireland*, 3 (1995), 13–20; Glyn Redworth, 'Beyond faith and fatherland: the appeal of the Catholics of Ireland, *c.* 1623', *Archivium Hibernicum*, 52 (1998), 3–23.

[63] Ciaran Brady, 'Faction and the origins of the Desmond rebellion in 1579', *Irish Historical Studies*, 22/88 (1981), 289–312.

those glorious martyrs inspired by the desire to 'restore the Catholic religion'.[64]

A similar attempt to rewrite history can be seen in the case of O'Sullivan Beare's inclusion of those executed for their part in the O'Doherty rising of 1615. The Rising was a complicated affair, with, it is true, some clerical participation, but the primary motivating forces do not seem to have been religious, and the leaders were neither as socially important or as principled as O'Sullivan claimed. Though the most recent characterisation of the Rising as a botched conspiracy hatched by a one-eared man, a social undesirable, a highway robber and a dwarf may be somewhat reductionist, the fact remains that O'Sullivan's claims stretched the definition of martyrdom to its limits, and demonstrated not merely the significant gap which could arise between ecclesiastical and popular evaluations, but also the distorting effect of long exile.[65]

Portraying the history of the 1570s and 1580s as a story of oppression and martyrdom was neither difficult nor inaccurate. But some martyrologists, unhappy at the long gap between the beginning of the Reformation and the later martyrdoms, wanted to go back to the 1530s. If the Reformation in Ireland had begun in the reign of Henry VIII, then, surely, so too had Catholic opposition. In fact, the early decades of the Reformation in Ireland, apart from Silken Thomas's rising and the deaths of Travers and Tynsby in England, were largely free from the religious savagery of the 1580s and 1590s: it was difficult to find Irish equivalents to Thomas More and John Fisher.[66] But that did not stop the more inventive of the Irish martyrologists from trying. Anthony Bruodin, the most comprehensive of the late seventeenth-century chroniclers, solved the problem by elevating the earl of Kildare and his five sons to the status of having died 'for the defence of the Catholic truth', just about arguable in the case of Silken Thomas, rather less convincing in the case of his siblings and father.[67] Most inventive of all was the Irish exile monk, Thomas Gold. A member of a thoroughly respectable Munster family, Gold was a Trinitarian, an order with a very limited presence in Ireland. He provided O'Sullivan Beare with accounts of horrendous

64 Rothe, *Analecta*, p. 390. Normally, none of those who died fighting would be considered for martyrdom by the church. But in unofficial lists like these, such caveats could be ignored. See the later efforts of the Irish Jesuit, Peter Redan, to make the case that those who had fought in the Irish wars of religion were worthy of the martyr's crown: Redan, *Commentaria*.

65 Gillespie, *Conspiracy*, pp. 54–5.

66 Indeed, even in England, martyrological interest in the early Reformation did not develop until the latter part of the sixteenth century: Gregory, *Salvation at stake*, pp. 254f.

67 Bruodin, *Propugnaculum*, p. 427.

massacres of members of his order, dating from the early decades of the Reformation, which suggested that nearly all the members of Chapter of the Trinitarians, when meeting in their Dublin convent in 1539 to oppose the royal supremacy, had been arrested, tortured and executed.[68]

Though full of circumstantial detail, Gold's accounts are undermined by their utter lack of contemporary evidence. It is difficult to prove the existence of either the personnel or even, in some cases, the Trinitarian houses, nor does anything appear of the events in official state sources. It is faintly possible that these stories have some basis in fact. But the balance of probabilities is that they are simply invention, inspired by a twofold desire: to glorify the history of his own order; and to fill in that surprising gap between the 1530s and the 1570s.[69] Anthony Bruodin was perhaps a more subtle exponent of the invention of memory. He recorded the fate of eighty-five martyrs, giving precise dates for all their deaths. In many cases surviving sources allowed such precision; in a small minority Bruodin may have had access to additional information from his own family or acquaintances which enabled him to improve on the imprecision of earlier memorialists; but in a significant number of cases we simply do not have a definite date for martyrdom, and here Bruodin, presumably anxious to ensure that the Irish victims could be included in the calendars of Catholic martyrs, seems simply to have resorted to invention.[70]

V

The power of the concept of martyrdom in early modern Ireland was such that it could forge a new understanding of historical events, even, as we have seen, lead to the invention of such events. The linkage between divine providence and human suffering which martydrom offered provided Irish Catholics with a powerful and reassuring overarching framework within which they could evaluate their experience at the hand of the Protestant authorities and define themselves as Catholics. Indeed, it

[68] O'Sullivan, *Patritiana decas*, fols 161v–164r; cf. Domingo Lopez, *Noticias historicas de las tres florentissimas provincias del celeste orden de la santissima Trinidad* (Madrid, 1714), i, p. 450.

[69] Aubrey Gwynn and R. N. Hadcock, *Medieval Religious Houses Ireland* (London, 1970), p. 217; Earl of Dunraven and Countess of Dunraven, *Memorials of Adare Manor with Historical Notices of Adare* (Oxford, 1865), pp. 36–44; Irish Jesuit Archives, MACE/MTYR, Letter to MacErlean from Father M. H. McInerny, 25 March 1920: 'Who was the Irish joker who foisted that pile of audacious fables on O'Sullivan . . . in regard to the Irish Trinitarians? I am afraid it was Richard Gould . . .'

[70] For examples of his personal knowledge, see his accounts of Phelim O'Hara, Donough O'Mullony, *Propugnaculum*, pp. 444, 467.

is no coincidence that the period of greatest persecution was precisely when two separate and mutually hostile confessional identities began to emerge in Ireland. What Howlin and the martyrologists on the one side, and Jones and the Protestant church-state on the other side both helped to create were two starkly different and mutually uncomprehending discourses which explained the deaths of Catholics in such as way as to validate two conflicting views of history. What was to Protestants the disposal of arrant traitors, the apposite civil punishment of those who refused to recognise the Protestant church-state, discussed in the appropriately judicial and unemotional language of the state papers, was to the Catholics a religious drama, replete with divine intervention and miracles and marked by the Christ-like heroism and suffering of the unjustly killed at the hands of their ruthless persecutors. The power of these two discourses is evident both in their ability utterly to ignore the other – to create, as it were, parallel but separate universes – and also in the way in which they reshaped the people's perceptions and interpretation of history.[71]

What early modern martyrdom presented, in its most irreducible form, was the claim to absolute truth, and the willingness of men, both ordinary and extraordinary, to die for that claim. The force of that fact, both brutal and transformative, decisively altered the way in which contempories viewed the world, and also posed a twin and continuing challenge to later historians. First, how to do justice to the power of early modern martyrdom with its complex relationship between history and memory, fact and imagination; and second, how to unpick the continuities and discontinuities between the willingness to die for Christ and the tradition of dying for Ireland. The former demands a sensitive treatment of the martyr stories and a detailed analysis of the context of martyrdom; the latter requires closer investigation of the extent to which the often parallel streams of religious hagiography and political martyrdom actually met and influenced each other, whether in Dublin in 1916, or in the H-blocks in 1981.

[71] See the way in which the Reformation and Counter-Reformation in Ireland produced two parallel but utterly different schools of historiography: Alan Ford, '"Standing one's ground": religion, polemic and Irish history since the Reformation', in Alan Ford, James McGuire and Kenneth Milne (ed.), *As By Law Established: The Church of Ireland since the Reformation* (Dublin, 1995), pp. 1–14.

CHAPTER 3

Remembering 1798

Roy Foster

I

In 1972, as a postgraduate student working on Charles Stewart Parnell and Wicklow, I went to visit Mr Robert Barton of Glendalough House. He was then over ninety, and his father had been an exact contemporary and close friend of his neighbour Parnell, though politics sundered them. Among much else, Robert Barton told me that the two friends, both owners of well-timbered demesnes, cooperated in the 1870s on building sawmills; and his father decided that one particularly large and aged beech should be scheduled for the mills, as its impressive circumference would test the new machinery. But none of the men on the place would agree to cut it down, without saying why, except that it was 'unlucky'. Barton's father brought in workers from somewhere else, who began to saw it down. The blade of their saw was unable to get through the trunk without grinding to a halt, because the wood was densely peppered with lead. The tree stood for more than bad luck. In the 1798 Rising, particularly bloody in Co. Wicklow, local rebels had been tied to it and shot. The memory persisted, and the taboo; the actual association was suppressed, whether for reasons of tactfulness or trauma. Or both.

The folk memory of 1798, like that of the Famine, the next traumatic caesura in Irish history, tends to be repressed: it often takes the form of re-remembering in the following generation. The most famous commemorative ballad was published anonymously in the *Nation* on 1 April 1843 (and reprinted in *The Spirit of the Nation* anthology later that year). It was called 'The Memory of the Dead', but is inevitably known by its first line 'Who Fears to Speak of '98'. It was written, ironically, by an idealistic twenty-year-old who subsequently became a notably conservative vice-provost of Trinity College, Dublin.[1] 'Fearing to speak' or not, it is

[1] The claim that he tried to disown it is often made but, according to the author himself, is without foundation: see J. Kells Ingram, *Sonnets and Other Poems* (London, 1900), p. 6

a truism that historical understanding and suppressed or re-edited memory are closely interwoven: a recent study on the subject refers sweepingly to 'History as an Art of Memory'.[2] Commemoration of 1798, 200 years later, has shaken off any fear; it has, indeed, run like a riptide. There have been dozens of books, yards of newsprint, countless conferences, even – in the most harmless possible way – attempted re-enactments of key junctures.[3]

But this is not new; 1798 has, in fact, a history of commemoration, as well as a history of itself. The impetus behind this is obvious: an astonishing historical crisis, a moment when the Irish – and possibly European – future could have been decisively changed, demands attention; and there is also the wished-for association with the evident heroism of the United Irishmen and their admirable, and still relevant, principles. Wolfe Tone's charismatic insouciance ('the *beau-ideal* of Irish rebels' as Sean O'Faolain put it[4]), Lord Edward Fitzgerald's self-sacrifice, Bartholomew Teeling's address at the foot of the gallows: all these demand a certain empathy as well as respect.

> If to have been active in endeavouring to put a stop to the blood-thirsty policy of an oppressive government has been treason, [said Teeling], I am guilty. If to have endeavoured to give my native country a place among the nations of the earth was treason, then am I guilty indeed. If to have been active in endeavouring to remove the fangs of oppression from off the heads of the devoted Irish peasant was treason I am guilty. Finally if [to] have strove to make my fellow men love each other was guilt, then I am guilty.[5]

Two hundred years later, these sentiments make him seem more innocent than his prosecutors; and the United Irishmen remain, in Ian McBride's word, spellbinding.[6]

But commemoration is, of course, always present-minded; and future historians will be interested in how we remembered to remember 1798, and what was forgotten in the process. It is tempting to quote a memorable open letter sent by George Bernard Shaw, in response to an invitation to join the commemorationists in 1898. 'It was proposed to me that I should help to uplift my downtrodden country by assembling

[2] Patrick H. Hutton, *History as an Art of Memory* (Hanover, NH, 1993).

[3] The best summation of the commemorative literature is Ian McBride, 'Reclaiming the rebellion: 1798 in 1998', *Irish Historical Studies*, 31/123 (May 1999), 395–410.

[4] Sean O'Faolain, *The Irish* (Harmondsworth, 1947), p. 99.

[5] PRO HO 100/82/160, quoted as Appendix D to Liam Kelly, *A Flame Now Quenched: Rebels and Frenchmen in Leitrim 1793–1798* (Dublin, 1998), p. 141. It seems likely that this influenced Robert Emmet's much more celebrated speech from the dock four years later.

[6] I. R. McBride, *Scripture Politics: Ulster Presbyterians and Irish Radicalism in the Late Eighteenth Century* (Oxford, 1988), p. 231.

with other Irishmen to romance about 1798. I do not take the slightest interest in 1798. Until Irishmen apply themselves seriously to what the condition of Ireland is to be in 1998 they will get very little patriotism out of yours truly GBS.'[7]

What happened in 1798? The year comes as the climax of a decade of radical activity – which changed ideological direction, and political strategy, after Britain went to war with France in 1793, and government policy towards British and Irish radicals became accordingly severe and eventually violently oppressive. Behind the savage episodes of 1798 lay a complex recent history of parliamentary reform, short-circuited from the early 1790s, agitation for the lifting of all disabilities against Catholics, mounting tension in the countryside, and most significantly of all the foundation and transformation of the Society of United Irishmen: French-inspired radicals, embracing modern, egalitarian, secular ideals. A founder member, the cautious Ulsterman William Drennan, had called for 'the establishment of societies of liberal and ingenious men, uniting their labours, without regard to nation, sect or party, in one grand pursuit, alike interesting to all, by which mental prejudice may be worn off, a humane and truly philosophic spirit may be cherished in the heart as well as the head, in practice as well as theory'. The 'general end', he said, was 'real Independence to Ireland' and republicanism 'the general purpose'.[8]

Drennan rather withdrew later, and he was a less fashionable icon in 1998 than Teeling.[9] But this quotation, as inspiring in its way as Teeling's, serves as a reminder that the United Irishmen represented the Dissenter (mostly Presbyterian) merchant classes of Belfast as well as the middle classes of Dublin and some liberal-minded gentry; with the change in government policy, they too radicalised. Their exclusion by the Anglican establishment gave them a certain sense of fellow-grievance with Catholics, though their ideology remained resolutely anti-papal. Their links with France, brilliantly investigated by Marianne Elliott,[10] were

[7] George Bernard Shaw to T. P. O'Connor's journal *MAP*, 17 Sept. 1898, reprinted in *Sixteen Self-Sketches* (London, 1949), p. 47.

[8] McBride, *Scripture Politics*, p. 168.

[9] See Louis Cullen's hostile remarks in 'The internal politics of the United Irishmen', in David Dickson, Dáire Keogh and Kevin Whelan (eds.), *The United Irishmen: Republicanism, Radicalism and Rebellion* (Dublin, 1993), pp. 176–96; but see also Ian McBride's essay 'William Drennan and the Dissenting Tradition', in ibid., pp. 49–61, and the same author's extended consideration of Drennan's views in *Scripture Politics*. Perhaps a further shift in Drennan's favour may be seen in A. T. Q. Stewart, *A Deeper Silence: The Hidden Origins of the United Irishmen* (London, 1993) and Adrian Rice, 'No lithe interloper', *Causeway*, 1/1 (Sept. 1993).

[10] Marianne Elliott, *Partners in Revolution: The United Irishmen and France* (London, 1982); *Wolfe Tone: Prophet of Irish Independence* (London, 1989).

strengthened as they went underground. By 1796, French invasion forces were planned, and in December there was the cliff-hanging episode of a huge French fleet in Bantry Bay, with Wolfe Tone on board. At the same time, the United Irishmen were moving towards rapprochement with a more shadowy strand of the Irish subversive tradition – the Defenders, a rurally based secret society with roots in the radical-agrarian tradition, who had been involved in confrontational activity since the early 1790s.[11]

By late 1797, revolutionary plans were so clearly afoot that the government commenced a deliberate policy of aggression, through newly raised forces of yeomanry and militia. And they also used the growing network of the Orange Order, formed after the 1795 Battle of the Diamond, to drive home the identification of loyalism and Protestantism. While the United Irishmen conspired with their French allies, a stream of information came to the government from a wide range of informers. Ulster was ruthlessly 'pacified', with martial law and sweeping arrests, from the spring of 1797. Nonetheless, in February 1798 there were still about 500,000 sworn United Irishmen, with perhaps 280,000 in possession of arms. A month later, Ireland was proclaimed as in a state of rebellion, and draconian measures were inflicted far and wide. The insurrection of that summer happened as a series of disparate episodes, beginning in Leinster on 23 May. Until the Battle of Vinegar Hill outside Enniscorthy, Co. Wexford on 21 June, Wexford and Wicklow were ablaze, despite severe checks such as the Battle of Ross on 5 June. In early June a belated insurrection broke out in Ulster, but lasted only a week. The percussion of incidents ended with (at last) a French landing in Mayo, too little and too late, in August. By then, the only rebels holding out from the first wave were some bands of skirmishers in the Wicklow mountains. In all these linked outbreaks, perhaps 30,000 died (3,000 alone at the battle of Ross on 5 June). Numbers remain conjectural, but the rebellion stands as the most concentrated outbreak of violence in recorded Irish history.

That staggered nature of the outbreak was one reason for the revolutionaries' failure; another was the incoherence of the cause for which so many fought so bravely, at least when compared to the firm revolutionary theory of the United Irishmen before its outbreak. Yet another was the unexpected geographical dispersal of the activity: hearing of the Wexford conflagration, Wolfe Tone (in Paris) was astounded, and

[11] Thomas Bartlett, 'Select Documents XXXVIII: Defenders and Defenderism in 1795', *Irish Historical Studies*, 24 (May 1985), 373–94.

wondered at once what had happened to the North, where it had been expected: rather than in the south-east where – as records subsequently seemed to show – the United Irishmen network was tenuous in the extreme. All these imbalances have been interrogated anew over the past few years, but a certain sense of disparateness remains (especially as so many of the studies are, by intention and definition, local).

There is another imbalance too, which concerns the amount of material surviving: records are vastly disproportionate on each side, the governmental archive hugely outweighing that reflecting the rebels. Thomas Pakenham, writing in *The Year of Liberty* thirty years ago, pointed out that there were 10,000-odd documents in the Rebellion papers then at Dublin Castle, of which all but around a hundred originated from the government side; they are now in the new National Archives, and have been added to, but a recent analysis by Deirdre Lindsay comes to much the same conclusion.[12] Only a few first-hand records from the rebel side are more or less contemporary, notably those of Thomas Cloney and Joseph Holt, and even these did not see the light of day until 1832 and 1838 respectively. Other materials were gathered in R. R. Madden's great seven-volume collection about the United Irishmen, published from 1842 to 1846, which fixed the men of '98 in the mould of heroic nationalism, nineteenth-century style. Perhaps the most useful first-hand account of all, the remarkable three-volume reminiscences of Miles Byrne, were not published until 1863. Byrne, a United Irishman in his teens in 1798, subsequently became an experienced soldier in France, and Parisian correspondent for the *Nation*; his account, dictated to his wife, denied any sectarian input in Wexford and stressed the coherence of United Irish organisation there. Both these issues were already the subjects of hot debate, and remained so.

Madden's first volume had stated a case generally followed until very recently, regarding the relationship between the Wexford Rising and the rest of the island. It was 'sufficiently established by the universal acknowledgement of all the inhabitants of the county of Wexford', he wrote, 'officers and men, who bore a part in this insurrection, that there was no concert between this rising and the plan of a general insurrection in and about Dublin, and that it was no more than a tumultuary and

[12] Pakenham defined what he found as a complete run of Irish newspapers, the confidential letters of protagonists such as Pitt, Camden, George III, Dundas and Wycombe, and the copious reports of Edward Cooke, whereas for the rebel side he had to rely on spy reports, early nineteenth-century biographies, folksongs and local tradition. For an up-to-date analysis see Deirdre Lindsay, 'The Rebellion papers', *History Ireland*, 6/2 (Summer 1998), 18–22.

momentary exertion of popular resistance to a state of things found or considered insupportable, the sole object of which was an attempt to get rid of oppression, and to retaliate with equal violence what they had been for some time experiencing'; this was not, in other words, an ideologically inspired United Irishman revolution, and there was in fact only a sketchy United Irish organisation in the county.[13]

At any rate, the Rising went wrong; few would disagree about that. In the image of a later radical, Fintan Lalor, the metaphorical wolfdog lying chained in every Irish peasant's cabin did not slip his leash: or at least, too few of them did, and at different times. Notable dogs that did not bark, or were quickly muzzled, included the Dublin dog, that resilient urban mongrel; the city did not act as the nerve centre of revolt. The local United Irishmen were thrown off course by the early arrest of Lord Edward Fitzgerald and others, by insufficient arms, and by a fatally effective ring of informers. The plan had been for Dublin to give the signal, when United Irish organisation in the city was ready – which it never was. Though planned for 23 May, the outbreak was rapidly suppressed by the Yeomanry, and liaison with groups outside the capital was never effectively established.[14]

The western dog was equally quiet – or at least only woke up when the French finally arrived, apart from some unrest around Leitrim in 1795 which was apparently agrarian and Defenderist in inspiration.[15] And a dog that barked early but then fell notably silent was the noble, secular-minded dog of French revolutionary idealism, as mediated through the merchants and intellectuals of Belfast. There, in a sense, the inspiration had all begun; there, it faded most quickly into oblivion, as early-nineteenth-century Ulster solidified into confessional mode and sectarian patterns were etched yet further into economic, social and political life.

The subsequent historiography reflected these silences and embodied fixed positions of partisanship. The historical treatments of the Rising set hard into orthodoxy during the nineteenth century. From the loyalist

[13] Quoted and discussed in Anna Kinsella, 'The nineteenth-century interpretation of 1798', M. Litt. thesis, University of Dublin (1992), p. 5. Madden was taken to task by the local historian Luke Cullen, who contradicted these statements, but they generally held the field – repeated, with careful argument, by Charles Dickson in *The Wexford Rising in 1798: Its Causes and its Course* (Tralee, [1953]).

[14] See Thomas Graham, 'Dublin in 1798: the key to the planned insurrection', in Dáire Keogh and Nicholas Furlong (eds.), *The Mighty Wave: The 1798 Rebellion in Wexford* (Dublin, 1996), pp. 65–78. The case there presented for the existence of a logical plan is more convincing than the assertion that the outcome was anything but a fiasco.

[15] See Kelly, *Flame now Quenched*, ch. 2.

side (emblematised by the enormous collections of material published by the rabidly partisan Richard Musgrave), it was a bloodthirsty religious war for the expropriation of Protestants, led by priests and fuelled by the memories of the seventeenth century. On the other hand, writers like Tom Moore had early on established the nobility of the enterprise; so did the cult of Robert Emmet. Much as the resistance struggle waged by Hugh O'Neill and Red Hugh O'Donnell against the Elizabethan Conquest was praised by Irish Tory romantics like Samuel Ferguson and Standish O'Grady, the glamour of Lord Edward Fitzgerald and Emmet (young, handsome, articulate, liberal, Protestant) was covertly celebrated by some unlikely protagonists from the mid-nineteenth century. For the radical nationalist tradition (at least from the growth of the Young Ireland movement in the late 1830s, and further bolstered by the Fenian journalism of the 1860s[16]), 1798 was a heroic rising against oppression, after a series of reverses for the cause of Catholic equality, precipitated by government *agents provocateurs*.

Both sides rather played down the French input, and the pre-existing tensions in the countryside at large; both put the events of 1798 firmly into a continuum of linked struggles for 'freedom', an interpretation greatly boosted by the 'faith and fatherland' version popularised from the 1870s by the Wexford Franciscan Patrick Kavanagh and the nationalist journalist A. M. Sullivan, and apostrophised in a more mystical way by Patrick Pearse when he hailed Tone as the greatest apostle of Irish nationalism because 'he died for us'.[17] The original ideas of the United Irishmen were rather downgraded in the process, and for Wexford, the 'faith and fatherland' interpretation seemed logical enough: there was Father Murphy, the priest who led the rebels, and there were not, apparently, many United men; moreover, that pleasant south-eastern corner was a prosperous and largely English-speaking area, with a long history of colonisation. From the late 1970s, however, the distinguished social historian Louis Cullen (himself a Wexfordman) began analysing this interpretation, from two angles. In a series of pioneering articles, he established a prehistory of social and agrarian conflict in the county, breaking along lines of land settlement and helping explain

[16] See Kinsella, 'Nineteenth-century interpretation of 1798', pp. 9ff., for the profuse references to '98 in the *Irish People* during the early 1860s. John O'Leary (the editor) later said that the inspiration of Wolfe Tone, relayed through Thomas Davis, did more to inspire the Fenian movement than 'famine or failure': O'Leary, *Recollections of Fenians and Fenianism* (2 vols., London, 1896), p. 78.

[17] Patrick Kavanagh, *A Popular History of the Insurrection of 1798* (1870); A. M. Sullivan, *The Story of Ireland* (1867 and countless reprints); Patrick Pearse, 'Ghosts', in *Political Speeches and Writings* (Dublin, 1922), pp. 223–55.

the savagery of intercommunal violence there; from another angle, he examined the state of United Irish organisation in Wexford, and radically revised the picture which up to then had been readily accepted from fortuitously assembled government records.[18] More recently, others have shown how far these rely upon chance survivals: Kevin Whelan, for instance, repeating Miles Byrne, has laid great emphasis on the fact that a United Irishman delegate from Wexford, through dallying with a girl in a pub, failed to turn up at the meeting subsequently raided in Dublin – so a list of the Wexford membership of the organisation did not fall into the hands of Dublin Castle, and subsequently of no less rapacious historians. It should be said, however, that cold water was poured on this attractive idea by Charles Dickson over forty years ago.[19]

Still, with the gathering momentum through the 1990s, towards the long-awaited bicentenary, other lacunae were addressed. Most of all, and sparked perhaps by the bicentenary of 1789 a decade ago, the French were welcomed back into the picture. Their inspirational, secularist ideal has been re-established, displacing the interpretation of a brave, tragic but essentially reactive and atavistic jacquerie asserted by Charles Dickson in the 1950s and Thomas Pakenham in the 1960s.[20] In the process, what the French could have done for the Irish future has been framed as one of the most tragic might-have-beens of Irish history – a hypothesis, it might be added, first advanced some time ago, and with considerably more irony, by that good friend to Ireland, John Stuart Mill. It should be said that another strain of heavyweight historical research from the 1980s on, notably from Marianne Elliott, preserved more of the older interpretation – notably regarding the sectarian input of the Defenders; and in 1994 Nancy Curtin published a study of the United Irishmen which is a classic of its kind and which echoes Elliott more closely than the commemorationists.[21] Tom Dunne also produced an interpretative short study of Wolfe Tone as a 'colonial outsider' which

[18] See L. M. Cullen, *The Emergence of Modern Ireland 1600–1900* (London, 1981), pp. 210–33; 'The 1798 rebellion in its eighteenth-century context', in Patrick J. Corish (ed.), *Radicals, Rebels and Establishments* (Belfast, 1985), pp. 91–113; Corish, 'The 1798 rebellion in Wexford', in Kevin Whelan and William Nolan (eds.), *Wexford: History and Society* (Dublin, 1987), pp. 248–95. Also see Kevin Whelan, 'Politicisation in County Wexford and the origins of the 1798 rebellion', in Hugh Gough and David Dickson (eds.), *Ireland and the French Revolution* (Dublin, 1990), pp. 156–78.

[19] Kevin Whelan, *The Tree of Liberty: Radicalism, Catholicism and the Construction of Irish Identity 1760–1830* (Cork, 1996), p. 159. But see Dickson, *Wexford Rising*, pp. 22, 180–1.

[20] For how the Pakenham interpretation was received in Wexford, see Colm Toíbín, 'New ways of killing your father', *London Review of Books*, 18 Nov. 1993.

[21] Nancy Curtin, *The United Irishmen: Popular Politics in Ulster and Dublin 1791–1798* (Oxford, 1994).

sits rather athwart the general drift.[22] But it is fair to say that the new wave of 1798 historians are all United Irishmen now. The appeal of their bracing Northern vision of egalitarianism has been re-established; the notion of 'the Republic in the Irish Village', paraphrasing Maurice Agulhon, has been put at the very centre of their enterprise. A recent article on 1798 even took this very title in homage, though the actual content contained nothing at all to bear the parallel out.[23] More convincingly, James Livesey's thought-provoking edition of the United Irishman Arthur O'Connor's 1798 pamphlet, *The State of Ireland*, shows how significantly 'French Ideas' were grafted on to the rather antiquated forms of Irish oppositionism.[24] To be French is to be radically fashionable, historiographically speaking; it is also to be European, and Modern, and non-Anglocentric.

Thus the Wexford Rising has been reinterpreted as forward-looking rather than atavistic. The fact that it broke out in an Anglophone area makes sense, if it is seen as epitomising the avant-garde secularist ideals of the United Irishmen. The relation of this elite group to 'popular culture' has been the subject of cheery if inconsistent generalisation.[25] For a current generation of historians, lively, *engagé* and above all imaginative, 1798 represents the moment when the North came South, and opened up a 'space' for an 'inclusive, democratic, non-sectarian' united Ireland. We are told briskly by more than one historian that 'Understanding the reason for its momentous defeat in the 1790s can help us to ensure that history does not tragically repeat itself in the 1990s.'[26] To scent a whiff of dangerous anachronism about this can only mark one down as a spoilsport.

II

Still, if this is where we stand now, it may be interesting to look back a hundred years to the first centenary of the Rising: because commemoration

[22] Tom Dunne, *Theobald Wolfe Tone, Colonial Outsider: An Analysis of his Political Philosophy* (Cork, 1982).

[23] Kevin Whelan, 'The republic in the village: the United Irishmen, the Enlightenment and popular culture', in *Tree of Liberty*, pp. 59–98.

[24] Arthur O'Connor, *The State of Ireland*, ed. James Livesey (Dublin, 1998).

[25] Thus Whelan, *Tree of Liberty*, p. 95 stresses the distance of this group from popular culture; elsewhere he identifies the spread of the movement as intimately linked to pastimes such as hurling, *meitheal* and Maying. For a more detailed consideration of Whelan and 'popular culture' see T. C. Barnard, 'Gentrification of eighteenth-century Ireland', *Eighteenth-Century Ireland*, 12 (1997), 142–3.

[26] Kevin Whelan, 'Reinterpreting the 1798 rebellion in county Wexford', in Keogh and Furlong, *Mighty Wave*, p. 10.

1798 memorial by Oliver Sheppard, 1908. Enniscorthy, Co. Wexford.
Photo: © Judith Hill

for the purposes of present politics is nothing new. In September 1898 the Irish Quaker, Alfred Webb, nationalist, printer, ex-secretary of the Land League and treasurer of the Evicted Tenants' Fund, wrote to a colleague: 'The country appears *memorial mad*'; he complained about 'no less than 4' monuments to the United Irishmen in County Wexford, and remarked caustically that this expenditure was 'absorbing the funds that should go to supporting a Home Rule fight and towards relieving the evicted ... What is going on is *talk* about the past, and inaction regarding the present.'[27] Certainly the period from 1880 to 1914 was a great age of jubilees and commemoration, and squarely in the middle came the centenary of 1798; by now firmly established as an episode in the continuing struggle for faith and fatherland against the Saxon. Father Kavanagh was the accepted historian of the Rising, rather than O'Kelly or others more or less forgotten now: much less the partisan Musgrave, who was after all seen as a crank even in his own day – as latter-day commentators tend to forget. Jonah Barrington's 'character' of him bears repeating: 'a man who (except on the abstract topics of politics, religion, martial law, his wife, the pope, the Pretender, the Jesuits, Napper Tandy, and the whipping post) was generally in his senses'.[28] Certainly by the late 1890s Father Kavanagh held the field. Laying the Foundation Stone of the Wexford '98 Monument, he announced that it was 'proof to future generations that we were imbued with the spirit of the men of '98 ... The men whose memory we honour today, died for a persecuted creed as well as an oppressed country ... Their blood was not poured forth in vain. It made the earth which drank it ever sacred to freedom; with their expiring breath they kindled the embers of a fire which burnt still.'[29] The creed mentioned was clearly not that of the French Revolution; a fellow historian who worked with Kavanagh on the commemorations rather nervously described him as a fanatic in matters of religion, who wanted to impose a boycott on Protestant businesses in Wexford town, which would certainly have been one method of commemoration.[30] By now 1798 had been firmly annexed, and would be celebrated accordingly.

The centennial movement had probably begun in 1879, when a group of Wexford men in Dublin formed the '98 Club, with a view to commemorating the Rising; two years before, there had been significant

[27] A. Webb to J. F. X. O'Brien, 21 Sept. 1898 and 21 July 1898, NLI MS 13, 431(5).

[28] Quoted in Dickson, *Wexford Rising*, pp. 215–16.

[29] Quoted in J. Turpin, '1798, 1898 and the political implications of Sheppard's monuments', *History Ireland*, 6/2 (Summer 1998), 45.

[30] Sir James O'Connor, *A History of Ireland 1798–1924* (London, 1925), i, p. 3, quoted in Kinsella, 'Nineteenth-century interpretation of 1798', p. 132.

commemorative meetings in Wexford. The 1898 initiative should probably be seen as part of the enterprise which produced the Young Ireland Clubs a few years later, in the mid-1880s. Both represent the colonisation by Fenian elements of aspects of cultural politics, at a time when the IRB was prospecting other strategies than the traditional one. (This is a process that coincides with the apparent success of the constitutional movement, rather than succeeding it after the fall of Parnell, as so influentially claimed by Yeats.) It was therefore highly politicised, as people expected it to be – on the Unionist side as well. Inspired by the early-warning commemorationists, the sardonic Unionist, Alexander Donovan, published in 1893 an only-just-futuristic pamphlet, a sort of Irish *Battle of Dorking*, called *The Irish Rebellion of 1898*. Set in post-Home Rule anarchy five years on, this cod-historical squib grafted memories of massacres in Wexford a century before onto the idea of an insurrection helped by Britain's enemies during a future war, quelled only by loyal Ulster.[31]

What began in the literary societies soon spread to the politicians – inside and outside the system. On the one hand, the movement for commemoration was seized by old Fenians like John O'Leary and his younger acolytes, including William Rooney, Maud Gonne and W. B. Yeats; on the other hand, the separated wings of the Irish parliamentary party, floundering in the wilderness after the shattering fall and death of Parnell, decided to climb on the bandwagon too. John Redmond, after all, was a Wexfordman *pur sang*, whose ancestors had been much involved; in 1886 he had published a pamphlet, *The Truth About '98*, and lectured prolifically on the subject on both sides of the Atlantic, usually with the aim of demonstrating the illegitimacy of the Union, as well as invoking neo-Fenian rhetoric for fundraising purposes. However, for several months the organising committee remained firmly in the hands of 'advanced nationalists', who managed to exclude both the Redmondite and Dillonite wings of the parliamentary party from any part in their deliberations.

[31] Rev. Alexander Donovan, *The Irish Rebellion of 1898: A Chapter in Future History, from the Supplement to the Imperial History of England, AD 1900* (Dublin, 1893). Though Britain's continental opponents are Russia and France, the conditions anticipated strangely predict Easter 1916. Irish MPs set up a provisional assembly and government, civil war breaks out with 'loyal Volunteers' in Ulster, parts of Dublin are burned by the rebels. However, after General Wolseley brings pacification the insurrectionary leaders are exiled, while incendiary newspaper editors are hanged. 'McC-, who had been chosen President of the Irish republic because he had some shred of character, and was almost an imbecile, was placed in a lunatic asylum, where he amuses himself by writing novels.'

Thus 1898 became the high point of Irish 'demo' politics, coming between the anti-Jubilee of 1897 and the agitation against the Boer War.[32] In the end, the enterprise of commemorating 1798 a hundred years later helped bring about the reunion of the constitutional nationalists; but it also helped spark the revival of the IRB, usually placed some years later, after the anti-war elements had regrouped as Sinn Féin in the early 1900s.

In many underground ways 1898 was important; it also intersected decisively with the projects of the young W. B. Yeats, public and private. He was one of the founder members in 1891 of the Young Ireland League, a Fenian cultural society which took a leading part in the 1898 organisations. It came at a time when, after a brief estrangement, he was once more determined to win the beautiful revolutionary Maud Gonne; but also when he was moving into the orbit of Augusta Gregory and planning the Irish Literary Theatre. It also coincided with a high point of mystical involvements and astrological frenzy, for Yeats and his circle of occultist would-be adepts, and their schemes to commemorate 1798 are inextricably mixed with plans for the creation of a Celtic Mystical Order, based in a Castle of Heroes on a lake isle in Connacht (Richard Wagner meets Standish O'Grady); if, Yeats cautioned, it could be done for 30 shillings a week. He was determined to seize control of this and other enterprises, and actually became president of the '98 Centennial Committee for Great Britain and France, while Gonne set herself to collecting money in the United States for a Wolfe Tone memorial, and bringing in revolutionaries as diverse as the Garibaldi veteran Cipriani, and sundry English hangers-on like the deranged vicar of Plumstead. She was better at it than Yeats, whose determined adherence to the cause was at least partly inspired by astrological calculations which promised that 1898 was a year of historic conjunctions, in his personal as well as his public life.[33] But neither of them, in the end, was a match for the hard-headed politicos, from the extreme and the constitutional wings of the nationalist movement, who eventually took over proceedings. Either way, the project seems to have had less and less connection with anything that 1798 had actually been about.

[32] Senia Pašeta, '1798 in 1898: the politics of commemoration', *Irish Review*, 22 (Summer 1998), 46–53; T. J. O'Keefe, 'The 1898 efforts to celebrate the United Irishmen: the '98 centennial, *Eire-Ireland*, 23 (1988), 51–73, and " 'Who fears to speak of '98?": the rhetoric and rituals of the United Irishmen centennial, 1898', ibid., 28 (1992), 67–91; Kinsella, 'The nineteenth-century interpretation of 1798', passim; L. Ó Broin, *Revolutionary Underground: The Story of the IRB 1858–1924* (Dublin, 1976); W. Gould, J. Kelly and D. Toomey (eds.), *The Collected Letters of W. B. Yeats, vol. II, 1896–1900* (Oxford, 1997), pp. 695–707.

[33] See R. F. Foster, *W. B. Yeats, A Life: I, The Apprentice Mage, 1865–1914* (Oxford, 1997), pp. 179–97.

Yeats and Gonne were not the only ones. From Ulster, commemorative plans were launched by the influential nationalist Alice Milligan, not without opposition; convivial visits to the graves of dead rebels were organised, and societies founded in their honour. Here too the constitutional nationalists (organised by the young Joseph Devlin) tried to outflank the Fenians, and effectively took over, while the centenary parade sparked off riots in the Shankill.[34] Those who recalled the Presbyterian radical tradition did so by emphasising how different it appeared to the sectarian republicanism which they now perceived in the south. Moreover, the Union had – it was claimed – given the Northern heirs of the United Irish tradition exactly the freedoms their ancestors had fought for a hundred years before.

Still, an interestingly ambivalent note sounded through the *Belfast Newsletter*, which opposed a Wolfe Tone memorial, but cautiously admitted there was a case for commemorating William Drennan. In fact, ambiguity dogged the 1898 activities: even that quintessential Fenian John O'Leary can be found reading a message from it all that faces both ways. Before the stone-laying ceremony he told the Lord Mayor's Banquet that 'he infinitely preferred that Ireland should be under her own laws and not under English laws, and he did not mind whether it was a republic, an absolute monarchy or a limited monarchy; however, he was not an impractical, and he could conceive Ireland accepting something short of that'.[35]

As O'Leary's speech hints, politics were breaking in all round. Yeats and Maud Gonne had ended up in the camp of the Irish National Alliance, a breakaway Fenian group, and were accordingly distanced from their patron O'Leary. They found themselves the targets of an ex-comrade, the unbalanced firebrand Frank Hugh O'Donnell, whose pamphlets denouncing their revolutionary agitprop and commemorative activities still burn off the page – as where he accused 'the Daughter of Erin from Essex' of aligning Ireland's holy cause with a secret plan to destroy the Vatican, funded by Parisian stock-jobbers.[36] Yeats's own ambivalence came through more and more clearly, as Maud Gonne dragged him round committee rooms from Limerick to Liverpool. 'We tare each

[34] Ian McBride, 'Memory and forgetting: Ulster Presbyterians and 1798', in Thomas Bartlett, Dáire Keogh and Kevin Whelan (eds.), *The 1798 Rebellion* (Four Courts Press, forthcoming), and O'Keefe, 'Rhetoric and rituals', 84 ff.

[35] News-cutting in O'Leary Coll., UCD/SA. 'The remainder of the remarks did not reach the reporters', which was a pity. He was speaking in response to Lord Mayor Tallon, a Parnellite who had surprisingly declared that Irishmen were best governed under English laws.

[36] TS of 'Fuath na Gall' handout to members of the Paris Young Ireland Society, O'Leary Coll., UCD/SA.

others character in peices [*sic*] for things that don't matter to anybody', he lamented to Lady Gregory, who riposted with a firm public statement that anyone who wanted to commemorate the men of 1798 should simply plant a tree, and then get on with their lives.[37] Maud Gonne's money-raising efforts also caused bitter antipathy among the revolutionaries, and by the high point of the celebrations in August 1898 there was a campaign to squeeze her out of the picture. Meanwhile, the rival parliamentary leaders Redmond and Dillon managed, from their different sides, to get the constitutional nationalists in on the act (rather as Redmond, an underrated political operator, would later effect a takeover of the Irish Volunteers in 1913). This required aligning themselves with Fenian rhetoric, and other complicated manoeuvres; their rival commemorative organisations only just came uncomfortably together in time for the great day, 15 August 1898.[38]

The commemorations attracted great publicity, and were closely watched by the authorities; but they were effectively colonised by mainstream Irish nationalism and the clerical establishment. Detectives noted that Gonne was excluded from the platforms, and the socialist James Connolly mordantly attacked the conventional direction things had taken, denying 'that the United Irishmen had anything to do with a union of classes', and attacking the commemoration committees for choosing Lady Day, a festival of the Catholic church 'and therefore, if not absolutely prohibitive to, at least bound to raise grave suspicion in the minds of our non-Catholic fellow-countrymen'.[39] Nevertheless, he sold the first copies of his new Marxist-nationalist magazine, the *Workers' Republic*, to the crowds assembling for the celebrations on 15 August.

The commemorations had made their mark. During the confused period of Yeats's life when he found his way back to advanced nationalism, after the Easter Rising of 1916, his correspondence shows that he was preoccupied by his memories of 1898 and what had happened then, when the millennium was deferred. The whole episode was a prophetic demonstration of the potent fission when politics meet history in Ireland. It also proved the inherent tourist appeal of such conjunctions. The 'diaspora' (or, as we were then called, the 'Irish race worldwide') were warmly encouraged to participate, and much was hoped for from this injection

[37] Yeats to Gregory, 3 Oct. 1897, *Collected Letters II*, p. 135; *Tuam Herald*, 12 Mar. 1898.

[38] Fully described in *Irish Daily Independent*, 15 Aug. 1898, and *Daily Express* (Dublin), 16 Aug. 1898.

[39] Cutting from *Workers' Republic* in O'Leary Coll., UCD/SA. He also claimed Mitchel and Tone were both direct ancestors of his own Irish Republican Socialist party, rather than any of the organisations represented on the platforms.

of 'wealth and influence'.[40] The '98 Centennial Association of America offered a 'Grand Pilgrimage' tour to Ireland, France and England – which included, as an unexpected highlight for the Republican pilgrims, a visit to Shakespeare's home at Stratford.[41] However, Dr Whelan's claim that the 1898 commemorations 'knitted together' strands of Irish nationalism[42] is hard to sustain; all the evidence seems to be – as Timothy O'Keefe has made clear – that it did the opposite.[43] While the two wings of the post-Parnellite parliamentary party came together two years later, this was in response to the challenge posed by William O'Brien's United Irish League rather than the uneasy co-operation on commemorative platforms; and O'Brien, in fact, had sharply disapproved of the political narrowness of the '98 organisations.[44]

As for the Fenian element, it was further distanced than ever. Superficially, the movement for commemoration had been 'parliamentarised' by the constitutionalists. The site at the top of Grafton Street in Dublin where the foundation stone had been laid for a monument to Wolfe Tone remained unoccupied. There was an embarrassing amount of trouble about the money,[45] and it was finally used for an arch to commemorate the Dublin Fusiliers at the end of the Boer War.

Down in Wexford, it was different. When Oliver Sheppard's impressive statue to the United Wexford men of '98 was finally unveiled in 1905, the language used was significant: 'it was the duty of everyone claiming to be an Irishman', said the mayor, 'not to waver until the aspirations of those brave men had been fulfilled'.[46] This could be read as a safe call for Home Rule, and the proceedings were described as 'a model of constitutional propriety'. But 1898 had all the same reintroduced a certain tone. Perhaps the most potent results of the 1898 project lay in the experience gained by William Rooney (a prominent organiser) and Arthur Griffith, later channelled into the movement against the Boer War, the significantly named newspaper *United Irishman*, and the creation of Sinn Féin. Even more prophetic was the creation of the 'Dungannon Clubs', whereby the IRB was reconstructed from the inside. All this took its rise

[40] O'Keefe, 'Rhetoric and rituals', 75. However, the intervention of the Spanish–American War short-circuited much planned transatlantic activity.
[41] This detour was $75 extra. Booklet in O'Leary Coll., UCD/SA.
[42] Whelan, *Tree of Liberty*, p. 172.
[43] See O'Keefe, '1898 efforts', pp. 68ff.
[44] Letter of 22 Sept. 1897 to M. J. Quinn, O'Leary Coll., UCD/SA.
[45] By the end of 1898 only £561 of the projected £14,000 had been found, most of it by Maud Gonne: see Ó Broin, *Revolutionary Underground*, p. 91.
[46] Turpin, 'Sheppard's monuments', 46.

from the 1898 activities. Timothy O'Keefe has engrossingly analysed the quasi-religious and hagiographical format of organisations named for United Irishmen, like the Oliver Bond Club,[47] and the secretary of that club, the Sinn Féiner George Lyons, would long afterwards trace the pedigree of the 1916 Rising back, not (as Yeats did) to Parnell's death in 1891, but to the 1898 commemorations, which began 'all our modern efforts towards an ideal of independence'.[48] And though the subsequent years saw a considerable stir of polemical and political activity in Irish nationalist circles, Fenians and constitutionalists were not particularly 'knitted together' by the memory of the dead United Irishmen. The most influential nationalist ideologue of the early twentieth century, D. P. Moran, liked to deny that Wolfe Tone was Irish at all, since he was born of English parents, became a Frenchman, and was an atheist to boot.

III

With the slightly divisive example of 1898 in mind, it is time to turn to the present day and consider how the 1798 Rising was remembered 200 years later. This was not left to chance. The Irish government appointed a 1798 Commemoration Committee, based at the Office of the minister of state at the Department of the Taoiseach,[49] and on 10 April 1997 this issued a six-point 'Mission Statement on 1798' to relevant civil servants and diplomats:

(i) To commemorate the ideals of the United Irishmen and the 'Fellowship of Freedom' that inspired them in 1798.
(ii) The recognition of the 1798 rebellion as a forward looking, popular movement aspiring to unity; acknowledging that what happened in Dublin and Wexford was part of what happened in Antrim and Down.
(iii) Attention should shift from the military aspects of 1798 and be directed towards the principles of democracy and pluralism which the United Irishmen advocated.
(iv) A focus on the international perspective of the United Irishmen and the enduring links which 1798 forged with America, France and Australia.

47 O'Keefe, 'Rhetoric and rituals', pp. 73ff.
48 G. A. Lyons, *Some Recollections of Griffith and his Times* (Dublin, 1923).
49 Since 1995 the annual estimates of the taoiseach's department have included a budget for commemorative programmes. My thanks to Mary Daly for this and other points.

Centenary of Ireland's Gallant Struggle for Freedom

1798

"They rose in dark and evil days to right their native land."

"They kindled here a living blaze that nothing shall withstand."

1898

To the Memory of the United Irishmen

This is to Certify that

M..........

of..........

was admitted a Member of the '98 Centenary Committee.......... Branch

.... 189 John O'Leary President.

Counter-signed by

.... Branch Sec.

M. J. Quinn Hon Sec. for self and Committee

"It is new strung and shall be heard"

"Nil desperandum"

Dollard, Printinghouse, Dublin

1798–1898 Centenary Committee membership card, by courtesy of Dr Senia Pašeta

(v) To acknowledge the Ulster dimension and particularly the contribution of the Presbyterian tradition, with its emphasis on justice, equality and civil liberty.
(vi) To focus attention on the ideals of the leaders of 1798 which still live in Irish history.

It is tempting to add a seventh: 'Don't talk about the war.' Certainly, the historians retained by the government for the purposes of commemoration, and sent forth on the mission, acted up to the mark. There was a good deal of rather self-congratulatory commentary, to the effect that we have learned from the mistakes of our great-grandparents. Instead of stridently remembering '98 as a festival of faith and fatherland (*one* faith, *one* fatherland), the Irish were enjoined to embrace '98 as a confluence of traditions in a pluralist, secular 'space'. Certainly there was a profuse outpouring of research and commentary, much of it highly suggestive. The canonical accounts were interrogated, and pursued back to their sources – leading to the re-establishment of General Holt's memoirs before Croker bowdlerised them, and the reassessment of Miles Byrne's evocative account.[50] The disingenuous reasons behind, for instance, Edward Hay's contemporary claims that the Wexford Rising had no plan or structure behind it have been clarified, and the collections of local historians like Luke Cullen given their full due. The European dynamic has been re-established at this juncture of Irish history, as at others; the local texture of events, people, alliances, kinships has, following the pioneering work of Louis Cullen, been built upon by several scholars. The intended connections between what happened in the North and the South have been reasserted, and the structure of the United Irishmen and their intentions more clearly delineated than ever before. All this is extremely interesting and self-evidently worthwhile.

At the same time, 1798 has been repackaged, and the intentions of the principal actors prioritised above the actual outcome of events. The language used is significant. 'The United Irishmen', according to one historian, 'were trying to negotiate a political structure here and with Britain, capable of representing Irish people in all their inherited complexities and allegiances; the peace process today is trying to do the same thing.'[51]

[50] Peter O'Shaugnessy (ed.), *Rebellion in Wicklow: General Joseph Holt's Personal Account of 1798* (Dublin, 1998); Thomas Bartlett, 'Miles Byrne: United Irishman, Irish exile and *beau sabreur*', in Keogh and Furlong, *Mighty Wave*, pp. 118–38. James Livesey's edition of Arthur O'Connor, mentioned above, might also be instanced, and Tom Bartlett's collection of Wolfe Tone's autobiographical writings.

[51] Kevin Whelan in the *Irish Times*, 24 Mar. 1998.

A pluralist, Europeanised, dynamic Ireland was proleptically asserted for the 1790s, as for the 1990s: today's 'Republic', declared in 1948, was described as a lineal descendant of what is called, in rather gingerly fashion, the 'embryonic Republic of Wexford'.[52] Others, less evasive, proclaimed the actual Republic as established in Wexford, and even the ecumenical 'Senate' which allegedly ran that Republic during its existence.[53] This rather ignored the debate over whether the term 'Republic' was ever used for Wexford, except by one antagonistic commentator determined to raise the spectre of French revolutionism: Daniel Gahan, author of the most recent history of the Rising in that county, specifically denied that the rebels declared a 'Republic of Wexford', and Tom Dunne sharply dismissed the actuality of either Republic or Senate, in terms which were not effectively rebuffed.[54] Nonetheless, as commercialised theme-park history took over, that 'Senate' was re-established in the town as a sort of fancy-dress exhibit for 1998, manned by local – and other – worthies prepared to pay £2,000 for the privilege. 'It was like what John Hume calls "an agreed Ireland" today', explained one over-excited local historian.[55] Senate membership, like entry to the Rose of Tralee competition, was open to anyone of 'Irish extraction', so the diaspora were welcomed in too.

The senatorial fees, where they were forthcoming, went to fund the Enniscorthy 1798 memorial centre, built at a cost of £2.3m, where visitors walked over a Bridge of Democracy, past plaques commemorating the great Republics from Athens onwards, when History could – it is implied – have changed for the better. (These sportingly include the English republic of 1649, thus providing Ireland's only monument celebrating Oliver Cromwell.) There was a lot of dressing up and posing with pikes. There were exhibitions all over – some, like the one in the Ulster Museum, utterly admirable, others, like the ongoing 'Puppet Show of '98' in Fingal, less intellectually demanding. In the old Wicklow jail, reopened by President MacAleese as the 'National Centre for Convict Transportation to Australia', tape-recordings were played of suggestive jail rape scenes, and actors dressed as jailors threatened tourists with hanging; visitors

52 Ibid.

53 See Brian Cleary, 'The battle of Oulart Hill: context and strategy', in *Mighty Wave*, p. 79: 'The nation's first republic was established . . . governed by a Committee or Directory of four Catholics and four Protestants.'

54 Daniel Gahan, *The People's Rising: Wexford 1798* (Dublin, 1995), p. 88; Tom Dunne, '1798: memory, history, commemoration', *Journal of the Wexford Historical Society*, 16 (1996–7), 115–16.

55 Brian Cleary in *Irish Times*, 28 Jan. 1998.

were promised the further frisson of 'meeting some of the Wicklow men of '98' (on the Other Side, presumably – an aspect which Yeats and his friends would have thoroughly approved). Re-enactment took ever more surreal forms, with the 're-creation' of the battles of Ballinamuck and Carrignagat – complete with muskets.[56] Best of all, in 1998 the French returned in force – though in the form of squadrons of Lycra-clad bicyclists taking part in the first leg of the Tour de France, which took place, by a happy chance, in Ireland that summer.

Historical memory was bewilderingly recycled into spectator sport and tourist attraction. This had been, as is so often the case, already forecast in satirical form. About twenty-five years ago, Hugh Leonard's play *The Patrick Pearse Motel* opened in Dublin, a mordant farce set in an Irish hotel where the rooms were named after events in Irish history: the illicit lovers were apprehended in the Parnell Suite, while the restaurant was called 'The Famine Room'. How we laughed, in 1973. At least one great Irishman, Oscar Wilde, would have appreciated the way that reality has slavishly imitated art.

It may not seem to matter; tourism is one thing, the demands of current politics another, and the practice of history yet another.[57] But what gives one pause for thought is the extent to which professional historians were involved in the repackaging and alterations of emphasis. There seemed, in some quarters at least, to be an agreed agenda, which owed more to perceived late-twentieth-century needs than to a close reading of events and attitudes 200 years ago. Firstly, sectarianism in Wexford in 1798 was to be skimmed over – or, even more damagingly, attributed to one side only. It may have been self-evidently in operation in Armagh and Down during the disturbances of 1796–7, but – for these purposes – North and South are to be kept firmly apart. The leadership of the Wexford and Wicklow rebels was retrospectively removed from Father John Murphy, and handed back to supposedly liberal Protestants like Bagenal Harvey or General Holt. Historians whose work a decade ago dealt with the sectarian aspects of local society in the county revised themselves with surprising completeness.[58] Most strikingly of all, the burning alive of about a hundred Protestant civilians locked into a barn by rebel forces at Scullabogue, which passed into history as one of

[56] *Irish Times*, 24 Mar. 1998.

[57] Emblematised by the handout in Wicklow Jail claiming that 6 million died in the Famine: a significant confusion with the statistics of the Holocaust.

[58] See, for instance, Kevin Whelan's views in Patrick O'Flanagan, Paul Ferguson and Kevin Whelan (eds.), *Rural Ireland 1600–1900: Modernisation and Change* (Cork, 1987), pp. 62–85.

the worst atrocities on either side, was repainted. There were Catholics there too (if only eight, who were there as servants of the imprisoned Protestants); moreover, it was claimed, the government forces had already burnt down a rebel hospital, so Scullabogue was the understandable if regrettable riposte. Tom Dunne, again, working closely from local sources, has shown that this 'hospital' is an invention, and the story represents a confusion with a similar atrocity which happened a fortnight *after* Scullabogue, in Enniscorthy:[59] separate incidents were elided, and chronology reversed, in order to provide some sort of rationalisation for what otherwise seems a clearly sectarian outrage. Dr Dunne was not thanked for his pains, but accused of engaging in 'scullaboguery': a new coinage, which appears to mean asserting that sectarian atrocities and communal antipathies are a deep-laid and unavoidable theme in Irish history. To 'scullabogue' could also, at the moment, be taken to mean drawing attention to the fact that a new-look Emperor has no clothes on.[60]

Here, again, the politicians had their say: whatever party they belonged to, they read from the same script. Thus the Fine Gael minister, Avril Doyle, on 24 November 1995 announcing future plans for commemoration:

> Firstly we must discard the now discredited sectarian version of '98, which was merely a polemical post-rebellion falsification. Secondly, we must stress the modernity of the United Irish project, its forward-looking, democratic dimension, and abandon the outdated agrarian or peasant interpretation. Thirdly, we must emphasise the essential unity of the 1798 insurrection: what happened in Wexford was of a piece with what happened in Antrim and Down.

Two and a half years later a politician from the opposing Fianna Fáil party, Síle de Valera, delivered herself of the following remarks: 'Firstly, we must continue never to entertain a sectarian version of '98. Secondly, we must stress the modernity of the United Irish project, its forward looking, democratic dimension. Thirdly, we must emphasise the essential unity of the 1798 insurrection: what happened in Wexford was of a piece with what happened in Antrim and Down.'[61] Actually, each of these three cardinal points is, in historical terms, vigorously disputed: but the Mission

59 Tom Dunne, 'The politics of atrocity: Scullabogue, representation and reality', forthcoming; also article in *Irish Times*, 6 Jan. 1998, and letters in *Irish Times*, 1 Apr., 15 Apr., 20 Apr., 24 Apr., 4 May 1998.

60 For 'Scullaboguery' see Brian Cleary in *Irish Times*, 23 Mar. 1998.

61 Speech by Síle de Valera at the opening of the 1798 Exhibition in the National Museum, Collins Barracks, 25 May 1998. My thanks to Mary Daly for these references.

Statement continued to provide the government songsheet, whoever was singing.

Thus the idea that sectarianism was an artificial invention of the government moved back into fashion.[62] Sectarianism was certainly encouraged by the authorities in some areas, especially through the Orange Order; invented, it was not. In much of the current historiography, 'atavistic visceral appeal'[63] is, correctly, attributed to popular Protestantism – but not to popular Catholicism. By the same token, the revolutionaries are allowed their Jacobinism, but not their Jacobitism: the ancient memory of dispossession, and the ancient belief in driving out the heretic invader, with foreign aid. In fact, much of this is evident in the contemporary literature of poem and ballad associated with the Rising; colonial confiscations are a raw wound, and the enemy are described as 'Luther's clan' rather than Pitt's creatures.[64] But commemorationist history glided over these motivations, preferring to stress that the Catholic hierarchy were pro-government, and that Catholic loyalism had been critically underestimated – which is true; and going on to imply that active rebels were all French-minded secularists – which seems dubious. Similarly, much was made of the fact that the Rising happened in the modernised, English-speaking areas of the east, and therefore supposedly looked forward – to French ideas – rather than backwards, to Stuart or Gaelic inspirations. The reminder that the rebels who fought at Ross were Irish-speaking (which came, again, from the splendidly tactless Dr Dunne) was – to say the least – unwelcome.[65] The most that commemorationist historians like Brian Cleary would allow was that this demonstrated 'the complex political, cultural and social effects of imperialism',[66] which does not get us very far. Too often, an easy accommodation was made between 1790s 'republicanism' and an implicit 'nationalism' – forgetting, as James Livesey has put it, that Arthur O'Connor, for instance, was an Irish republican but not an Irish nationalist.[67]

This is a pity, because this trend goes against much of what has been most stimulating in eighteenth-century studies over the last ten years or so: the study of the rise of Catholic consciousness from about 1770, the

[62] See *Tree of Liberty*, pp. 134ff.; P. Collins in *Irish Times*, 24 Feb. 1998; and Kevin Whelan, 'The origins of the Orange Order', *Bullán*, 2/2 (Winter/Spring 1996), 19–37.

[63] Whelan, 'Republic in the village', p. 96.

[64] Tom Dunne, 'Subaltern voices? Poetry in Irish, popular insurgency and the 1798 Rebellion', *Eighteenth-Century Life*, 22 (Nov. 1998), 31–44.

[65] Tom Dunne, 'Wexford's *Comoradh '98*: politics, heritage and history', *History Ireland*, 6/2 (Summer 1998), 53.

[66] Cleary, 'Oulart Hill', p. 96.

[67] O'Connor, *State of Ireland*, p. 21.

importance (and complexity) of confessional identification, the nature and development of the Defender network, the revival of Whiteboyism in the early 1790s, the establishment by Louis Cullen of what he discerned as sectarian 'frontiers' in the social geography of the south-east well before the outbreak of the Rising. Similarly, the desire to elide the Rising in Ulster into that in Wexford (in obedience to the guidelines from the taoiseach's office) meant ignoring the drift of Northern opinion against the French Republic by the later 1790s, and basic structural differences too. The first-hand description by David Bailie Warden of the state Northern United Irishmen had been thrown into after the brutal government 'pacification' of 1797 is worth remembering, though not much quoted by commemorationists: 'instead of the forces meeting at any point in collected and organised bodies, they met rather by accident than by design; and they were in no better order than *a mere country mob*'.[68] The mobilisation of 1798 in Ulster, in Ian McBride's authoritative treatment, was keyed closely to 'the basic categories of ethnic and denominational identity . . . [and] shaped by the magnetic pull of the settlement-patterns created by seventeenth-century colonisation'. The tensions that came to the fore were those between Protestant, Catholic and Dissenter. Nancy Curtin's work confirms this. Musgrave's picture of Presbyterian United Irishmen (still often called 'the Scotch' by contemporaries) never quite coalescing with Catholic Defenders is borne out by many contemporary reports.[69] And after their failed rising, there is a significantly different record of victimisation and violence compared to the south-east: there were proportionately ten times as many claims for compensation in Wexford and Wicklow than in Antrim and Down, and Presbyterians were in no way harassed like Catholics. The elision of what was happening in Ulster and Wexford in the summer of 1798 required cutting a good many corners.

It is true that too much has been made of the Presbyterian United Irishman James Dickey's supposed statement on the scaffold, that the 'eyes of the Presbyterians had been opened too late' to the sectarian nature of the Wexford Rising; like other such statements, it may have been orchestrated by the authorities.[70] But the speed with which Presbyterian radicals shifted their ground from 1798 still tells its own story. They

[68] Quoted in McBride, 'Memory and forgetting'.

[69] McBride, *Scripture Politics*, pp. 186–94; Curtin, *United Irishmen*, passim. Also see Allan T. Blackstock, '"A dangerous species of ally": Orangeism and the Irish yeomanry', *Irish Historical Studies*, 30/119 (May 1997), 393–405.

[70] Frank Wright, *Two Lands on One Soil: Ulster Politics before Home Rule* (Dublin, 1996), p. 42.

were heavily influenced by negotiations with the government over their *regium donum* grant, and by the attractions of a Union which did away with a parliament in which they had not been represented. First survivalism, and then respectability, enforced a deliberate distancing from the Protestant United Irishman tradition. The reaction to O'Connellism, and the rise of the Presbyterian leader, Henry Cooke, would solidify the process.[71] But there is also the fact that for the Presbyterian radicals the new French dawn had seemed to promise the twilight of Roman Catholic 'superstition': their own millennial surge had therefore very different roots from the Jacobite tradition clearly discernible in the polemic of the Southern rebels, and their civic republicanism was far from being proto-nationalism. Certainly when the old Presbyterian reformer Henry Joy, in his *Historical Collections* of 1817, advanced the case that Wexford had shown 'all the bigotry and intolerance of the middle ages', he was not saying so on government orders. Nor was the heroic United Irishman, Samuel Neilson, when in 1802 he wrote that Christ's true morality would win through 'in spite of superstition and priestcraft'. Here, he was simply following William Steel Dickson's three sermons on 'scripture politics' in 1793, which claimed the Bible as 'almost entirely political', being devoted to 'denouncing the tyranny of kings, the corruption of governments, and the unprincipled connivance and rapacity of priests and prophets'.[72] As James Livesey put it, for thinkers like these, 'Catholics might be given political rights because history had transformed them into Protestants.'[73] Early on, the movement was set in process whereby – as Ian McBride has neatly put it – left-wing intellectuals in modern Ulster 'would value Presbyterian radicalism not so much as a bridge to mainstream republicanism as a non-sectarian alternative to it'.[74]

Above all, commemorationist history tended to avoid the implications of the uncomfortable fact that so much of the evidence from this tragic era comes from informers: indeed, the nature of the evidence in court martials indicates much about the intimate resentments of local relations.[75] The idea, firmly held in the North, that the Rising in

[71] See McBride, 'Memory and forgetting', for how 'New Light' rebels were identified with the '98 tradition as aberrations in the true Presbyterian tradition.

[72] Neilson quote in Whelan, *Tree of Liberty*, p. 163; Dickson in epigraph to McBride, *Scripture Politics*.

[73] O'Connor, *State of Ireland*, p. 6.

[74] McBride, 'Memory and forgetting'.

[75] For attempts to play down informers, see Tom Bartlett, 'Informers, informants and information: the secret history of the 1790s', *History Ireland*, 6/2 (Summer 1998), 23–6, which does not really address the significance of their prevalence. Oliver Knox, *Rebels and Informers: Stirrings of Irish Independence* (London, 1997), though racy and written for a popular audience, contains much of insight.

Wexford had taken a sectarian turn is not just an invention of Musgrave and other polemicists.[76] Wexford may have sustained religiously 'mixed' communities in the eighteenth century, and been notably prosperous; but this is, tragically, no reason why, under circumstances of crisis and oppression, sectarian passions cannot spiral into a whirlwind of paranoia and brutality – as Mostar and Sarajevo have demonstrated all too recently.

It is worth looking at the tone employed by commemorationist historians to address these worrying issues. Ruan O'Donnell, for instance, describes the Wicklow rebels under Holt 'venting their frustration' by 'burning over twenty loyalist homes in the Roundwood area which were singled out from the general citizenry with great discipline and discrimination'.[77] Leaving aside the question as to how this discipline and discrimination must have appeared to those thus singled out, the implication that the 'loyalists' were not part of the general citizenry is ominous. Stressing that 'on the issue of rape the rebels occupied the moral high ground' and respected women and children, Kevin Whelan provides the consoling rationalisation that the women and children nonetheless burned at Scullabogue were – after all – attached to members of the North Cork Militia. Recollections that fit into the commemorationist agenda are prioritised, like Miles Byrne's memoirs; the fact that these were dictated half a century later is taken as specific evidence of 'detachment'.[78] This approach is exemplified by the Introduction to Kevin Whelan's interesting collection of reprinted essays, *The Tree of Liberty*: which makes a present-minded agenda triumphantly clear, boasts 'a non-talmudic irreverence to textual authority', trumpets the credentials of 'radical history' and claims for the author the description 'croppy' – the appellation given to the rebels of '98 by their adversaries. This kind of feel-good identification, while no doubt uplifting for the writer in question, suggests a certain limitation of approach. It is also significant that the same author moves smoothly to attacking Daniel O'Connell, traditionally seen by a certain tradition in Irish historiography (beginning with John Mitchel and climaxing with Patrick Pearse) as a worse enemy to Irish nationalism than even perfidious Albion: partly because he accepted confessional realities, and partly because he operated within a pacifist framework. In this as in some other ways, the redefinition of

[76] Henry Joy, quoted in McBride, 'Memory and forgetting'.

[77] Ruan O'Donnell, 'Keeping up the flame: General Joseph Holt', *History Ireland*, 6/2 (Summer 1998), 41.

[78] Whelan, *Tree of Liberty*, p. 168.

1798 seems to have brought us back to a familiar resting-place. What Hubert Butler wrote of Irish history sometimes seems true of Irish historiography as well: it is all like a journey on 'a scenic railway in a funfair: we pass through towering cardboard mountains and over raging torrents and come to rest in the same well-trodden field from which we got on board'.[79]

The point is, of course, that what happened in Ireland in 1798 was not a cardboard simulacrum, and the raging torrents were both real and bloody. It has now become part of historical memory, and has been fictionalised and poeticised: retrospectively inspired creations like Seamus Heaney's moving 'Lament for the Croppies', or the elegiac memory of marching to '98 in Brian Friel's play *Translations*, become treated as sources which somehow stand in for the painful reassembling of material about that blood-soaked summer, while modern Wexford treats commemoration as idealised re-enactment. Memory, as the mother of the Muses, is creatively selective.

And I come back to my visit to Robert Barton, the story of that bullet-riddled tree, and why no-one wanted to remember why it was 'unlucky'. Mr Barton, as it happens, knew about remembering and forgetting. When I went to talk to him about Parnell and Wicklow, I was less focused on the fact that he had been a revolutionary guerrilla in 1919–21 (despite an Ascendancy family and a British Army background), had gone to London to negotiate the Anglo-Irish Treaty, had signed but later reneged on it, fought in the brutal Civil War on the side of the anti-Treaty Republicans – probably influenced by his cousin, Erskine Childers, who was subsequently executed without mercy by the Free State. After our Parnell conversation, I longed to go back and ask him about his own life: but I was courteously told that he never discussed the Civil War. He was probably right: it was a terrible time, his own position must have been agonised, and he retired to private life at the cessation of hostilities. For politicians, scrupulous silence about the past is sometimes the right course. Historians *have* to remember, even – or especially – the most unwelcome aspects. But as Bernard Shaw and Alfred Webb suggested in 1898, others would do better to look to the future than to a past which has been romanticised and sanitised for present purposes.

It is in this sense that the literary critic Edna Longley suggested, during the commemorative year of 1998, that the Irish raise a monument to

[79] Hubert Butler, *Escape from the Anthill* (Mullingar, 1985), p. 7.

Amnesia and forget where they put it.[80] Less brutally, it might be salutary to remember G. M. Young's dictum that the historian must 'read until you hear the people talking'. True, and admirable: but the trouble with commemorative history is that, if those distant people were saying unwelcome things, it is all too tempting to put words in their mouths.

80 *Belfast Telegraph*, 17 Feb. 1998.

CHAPTER 4

Famine memory and the popular representation of scarcity

Niall Ó Ciosáin

The term 'memory' has become ubiquitous in recent historical writing. It is used to refer variously to historiography, to the subject matter of that historiography, and to an entire range of commemorative practices, both public and private, which constitute historical consciousness. This versatility and fluidity results in a degree of uncertainty of definition, however, and before embarking on a study of the 'memory' of the Great Famine, it is worth outlining two contrasting conceptions of memory which may be germane to such an inquiry.

The first and more familiar is the psychological one, the recollection of an individual, usually of events through which that person has lived. In historical writing, it is most often associated with oral history, whose practitioners have recorded the experiences, memories and life stories of individuals. A focus on individuals brings with it the problem of all microhistories, that of typicality. Oral historians have generally tackled this difficulty by taking testimony from a number of informants. Some have interviewed whole groups, such as villages, neighbourhoods or the workers of a particular industry, while others have selected large numbers of scattered informants as representative of an overall population. Whatever the size of the group, however, the technique remains that of the interview aimed at recording the reminiscences of an individual.[1]

If this first usage of memory emphasises personal recollection, the second usage, which has become general only in recent decades, emphasises memory as social representation. It studies the frameworks in which collectivities construct, embody and renew their shared sense of the past. These collectivities can range from small communities, whether urban or rural, through occupational groups, to nations or states. The most prominent studies of such memory deal with nations and states, and

[1] Yves Lequin and Jean Métral, 'A la recherche d'une mémoire collective; les métallurgistes retraités de Givors', *Annales ESC*, 35 (1980), 149–65; Luisa Passerini, *Torino Operaia e Fascismo* (Bari, 1984); Paul Thompson, *The Edwardians: The Remaking of British Society* (London, 1985).

reflect a growing awareness of the public and political uses of history in the creation or evolution of nation-states, national communities and national identities. The shared memory which underlies or is created by nations is manifested in public commemoration and monuments, in state institutions such as national museums, and in official histories.

The drawback of these studies is that they have a tendency to emphasise the public or political aspects of memory, and consequently to treat memory as an extension or reflection of politics or ideology, equivalent to 'political rhetoric about the past'. Their focus on public and official memory often leaves little room for informal or private opposition or appropriation, for the possibility that readers of historical texts or participants in public rituals may have had quite different ideas about their meaning and significance.[2]

I

It has become increasingly common in the historiography of the Great Famine to claim that there is little memory of the Famine. Such claims usually refer to the second of these two types of memory, the social and official. Until recently, it is maintained, there were few public commemorations or institutional expressions such as museums; the centenary passed largely unremarked; and academic historiography, the ultimate arbiter of official national memory, is held to have ignored the Famine. Whether these assertions are justified or not, and it is by no means clear that they are, they tend to share the shortcomings of the approaches to institutional memory outlined above, in particular a concentration on public memory, and a neglect of popular, oral or folk memory.[3]

The principal documentation of such a popular memory of the Famine was itself the product of an act of national institutional commemoration of the centenary of the Famine. This was a survey and collection of folklore relating to the Famine which was undertaken by the Irish Folklore Commission in 1945. It circulated a short questionnaire to its full-time and part-time collectors, and accumulated about 3,500 pages of testimony in both English and Irish. There is also a wealth of other Famine material in the archives of the Commission, much of it collected in the 1930s and early 1940s, again in both languages.

[2] Alon Confino, 'Collective memory and cultural history: problems of method', *American Historical Review*, 102/5 (1997), 1386–403.

[3] The arguments are summarised in Niall Ó Ciosáin, 'Was there silence about the Great Famine?', *Irish Studies Review*, 13 (1995–6), 7–10.

As memory, this material can be approached in both of the ways discussed. On the one hand, the Folklore Commission and its archive was established precisely as a repository of national memory, manifest in the oral tradition, and can itself be considered a form of institutionalised public memory. On the other hand, the work of the Commission in practice conceived of memory as personal recollection. Most of its material, even in the national surveys, was collected from individuals in ways which most resemble the methods of oral historians, making field recordings, for example, and concentrating on older informants rather than on the population at large.

Although the Famine material was conceived by the Commission as personal recollection, however, it is not entirely satisfactory to approach it using the methods of oral history. None of the informants had lived through the Famine, and moreover were not solely reliant on oral tradition for their knowledge of it. There are, of course, studies by oral historians of local memories of a distant past, notably Philippe Joutard's study of traditions among the Protestant communities of the Cevennes concerning the revolt of the Camisards, a religious rebellion which took place in the region in the early eighteenth century. Joutard notes the strong influence of written sources on such memories, as well as a tendency to assimilate later historical events to the rebellion, a process he refers to as the 'Camisardisation' of local memory.[4] Joutard's conclusions are illuminating, but his method is not directly transferable to the Famine folklore, principally because it is based on his own fieldwork, which permitted repeated visits to informants and a continuous dialogue with them. The Famine folklore, on the other hand, is a written archive, and does not permit interrogation, in the literal sense, of informants. Given, therefore, the distance of the informants from the Famine, the fixed nature of the testimony and its origins in a project of national memory, it is more appropriate to approach it as a type of representation of one aspect of the national past.

The influence of the Commission's conception of folklore as national memory is very clear in the material collected during the 1945 survey, which, by organising narratives around the event, itself shaped or constructed Famine memory. This process operated in a number of ways. To begin with, the circulation of an identical set of questions to all localities tended to produce a certain uniformity of response, with similar

[4] Philippe Joutard, *La légende des Camisards: une sensibilité au passé* (Paris, 1977), esp. part 3, 'Une autre histoire'.

phenomena being described in areas which may well have had different experiences. In the second place, the specific questions, grouped in six sections, tended to prejudge the way in which the Famine was experienced in any particular area.[5] (These are standard criticisms of the questionnaire method – in the expression of one French folklorist, 'If you ask questions, all you get are answers.'[6]) One section of the questionnaire, that on soup-kitchens, for example, inquired about 'conditions (if any) attached to the receipt of food at some of these centres. Souperism and proselytism in your district during the Famine (it is necessary to distinguish between centres at which proselytism was carried on and those at which it was not).' Proselytism, in other words, was to be enquired into whether it happened or not, and there is a wealth of material on it as a result, with some informants discussing cases which happened well outside their own localities.

If the inclusion of questions can distort the responses, the absence of others can have a similar effect. It is striking that the questionnaire shows little interest in supernatural or magical explanations or presentations of the Famine. In practice, many collectors came across narratives of this kind, and two of these are in fact quite frequent in the material. These are, first, the attribution of the Famine to divine displeasure at some aspect of Irish society or government, and second, stories concerning the various types of miraculous deliverance from hunger, particularly of those who had shown faith or charity. This neglect of the supernatural is largely the result of the survey's conception of folklore as recollection, in that the questionnaire envisages the material as memories of 'what really happened'. This positivism is reflected in the structure and content of the questions, which are derived from a conception of the Famine which is heavily influenced by written, documentary histories.[7]

II

Most subsequent discussions of the Famine folklore have also tended to start from the assumption that it consists primarily of recollection. The

[5] The English-language version of the questionnaire is reproduced in Cathal Póirtéir (ed.), *Famine Echoes* (Dublin, 1995), p. 283.

[6] Michel Balint, quoted in Max Caisson, 'Réflections méthodologiques sur des situations d'enquête utilisant la "tradition orale"', *Le Monde Alpin et Rhodanien*, I – II (1976), 103–6. For more favourable views of the questionnaire method, see the discussion in *Oral History*, 4 (1972), 126ff.

[7] The questionnaire was in fact compiled by an academic historian of the Famine, T. P. O'Neill: see Cormac Ó Gráda, 'Making history in Ireland in the 1940s and 1950s: the saga of *The Great Famine*', in Ciaran Brady (ed.), *Interpreting Irish History: The Debate on Historical Revisionism* (Dublin, 1994), pp. 269–87, 272.

earliest appeared in 1956, in an essay contributed by Roger McHugh to the collection *The Great Famine*. McHugh in fact characterised his work as a 'survey of traditional recollections of the Famine'. A similar approach is found in two recent anthologies of selections from the folklore edited by Póirtéir.[8] One aspect of the presentation of material in these anthologies subtly underlines the emphasis on direct recollection. In the original collectors' manuscripts, the age of the informant is given. Póirtéir gives instead their date of birth, so that, for example, instead of 'Séamus Reardon, age 72', as it appears in the manuscript, we read 'Séamus Reardon, born 1873'. The rhetorical effect is to place the source of information in the late nineteenth instead of the twentieth century, proposing a far more immediate link with the Famine.

McHugh and Póirtéir also reflect the questionnaire's positivism, using material which is drawn from the questionnaire and following its historical categories. Póirtéir in fact relegates a selection of supernatural legends to the end of both anthologies, as a type of appendix to more 'historical' material. The result in both cases is that an approach which promises an alternative perspective to documentary sources and official histories to a large extent reproduces the viewpoint of those histories, and makes the folklore an addendum to them rather than something qualitatively different.

In a series of articles and books, Cormac Ó Gráda has been more sceptical of the factual accuracy of the folklore, and has shown that some of the most frequently occurring assertions are not borne out by documentary evidence. These include statements that the speaker's area escaped lightly, and the linked tendency to declare that those who died were outsiders passing through, beliefs which are attributed to shame. Ó Gráda's analysis is instead more psychological, concentrating on what folklore reveals about people's attitudes and feelings, an approach which is also adopted by Carmel Quinlan. Ó Gráda focuses on 'a few interesting and recurrent themes that bear, directly or indirectly, on people's feelings about the Famine', while Quinlan concentrates on 'themes… which seem to reveal its psychological legacy'.[9] This approach, while moving away from straightforward recollection,

[8] Roger McHugh, 'The Famine in folklore', in R. Dudley Edwards and T. D. Williams (eds.), *The Great Famine: Studies in Irish History* (Dublin, 1956), pp. 391–406, quotation on p. 435; Cathal Póirtéir (ed.), *Famine Echoes* and *Glórtha ón nGorta* (Dublin, 1995).

[9] Cormac Ó Gráda, *An Drochshaol: Béaloideas agus Amhráin* (Dublin, 1994) and *Black '47 and Beyond: The Great Irish Famine in History, Economy and Memory* (Princeton, NJ, 1999), ch. 6, 'Famine memory', quotation on p. 203; Carmel Quinlan, 'A punishment from God: the Famine in the centenary folklore questionnaire', *Irish Review*, 19 (1996), 68–86, quotation on 84.

nevertheless remains predominantly positivist in that it invokes attitudes and emotions largely to explain inaccuracy of recollection, narratives which contradict what is known to have 'really happened'. As Quinlan, quoting Paul Thompson, writes, 'the importance of oral testimony "often lies not in its adherence to facts, but rather its divergence from them, where imagination, symbolism, desire break in"'.[10]

Moreover, an approach which insists on separating truth and fiction often risks losing sight of the coherence of popular representation. Ó Gráda, for example, finds much of the material 'flawed and confused' and 'usually innumerate (or anumerate)'. The case used to illustrate this is that of wages on the public relief works. A substantial majority of witnesses quote fourpence as the daily wage, a sum far below the average of what was actually paid.[11] If, however, this testimony was indeed the result of confusion and innumeracy, there should be a far more random selection of answers. The striking unanimity of so many informants suggests that a different logic was at work rather than no logic at all, though its precise nature remains to be elucidated.

The writer who moves farthest towards examining the folklore as representation is Patricia Lysaght, who emphasises the prominence of historical legends and international oral tale types which would have predated the Famine. She points out that 'groups of popular legends have developed around certain themes'. Thus 'the image of the starving mother and child is used to represent the Famine's worst consequences, though this is often tempered by the parallel image of the generous woman who comes to their assistance'. These legends also include the stories of charity rewarded and supernatural deliverance referred to above. However, Lysaght's ultimate aim, as her title indicates, is the same as that of the writers discussed previously, that is, an understanding of conditions during the late 1840s.[12] To carry further the study of the folklore as representation would require a slightly different starting point. It would not approach and classify the material according to the historical subject matter, that is, according to nineteenth-century historical events or phenomena, but would begin with the different types of knowledge which constitute the twentieth-century folklore itself.

[10] Quinlan, 'A punishment from God', p. 69.

[11] Ó Gráda, *Black '47*, p. 195.

[12] Patricia Lysaght, 'Perspectives on women during the Great Irish Famine', *Béaloideas*, 64–5 (1996–7), 63–130, quotations on 76, 128–9.

III

The types of knowledge (or representations) within the folklore correspond to the different ways in which that knowledge was formed, and I would like to propose a model of analysis consisting of three structural types or levels. Given that there is little agreed terminology in this field, I will also propose labels for them, calling them local memory, popular memory and abstract or global memory.

Global memory consists of a level of information which is abstract and usually national, and which probably derives from written, even academic, accounts. By 1945 Ireland had had near-universal primary education and literacy for over half a century, as well as a substantial number of newspapers both local and national. It would be surprising if these had had no impact on perceptions of local or national history. None of the studies mentioned above explores in any detail the possible influence of written sources, such as history books or newspaper articles, on the material. Quinlan notes the existence of a phrase deriving from A. M. Sullivan's *Story of Ireland* in one account, but concludes that, since 'references to England's Famine role are rare', the influence of written accounts of the Famine on the folklore is limited.[13] I would suggest, however, that the influence of written accounts is felt in the mode of presentation as much as in the specific content of the testimony. One example, with a wide geographical scope and the concept of a mathematical average, comes from Michael Gorman, a 77-year-old man in Mayo: 'Subscriptions were made up all over England and Scotland and in other countries and it was estimated that the amount collected would give £5 to every family in Ireland.'[14]

At the other extreme is local memory, which corresponds roughly to the conception of folklore as recollection. It consists of strictly local knowledge, rarely following an extended or elaborated narrative, and very often featuring named individuals. Informants often differentiate between good and bad local landlords, those who employed their tenants and those who evicted them, or name those who were in charge of local relief efforts or workhouses. Although this knowledge is often atomised and fragmentary, it is not necessarily a pure unmediated recollection. There is usually a form of mnemonic involved, such as situating that knowledge in space, in the local landscape, in a way which is familiar from oral history collected particularly in rural areas. Some informants,

[13] Quinlan, 'A punishment from God', pp. 73–4.
[14] Póirtéir, *Echoes*, p. 157.

for example, begin their accounts by noting depopulation and naming the families who had occupied those houses that are now in ruins.

The remaining type, popular memory, can be characterised as a popular representation of scarcity and famine within a predominantly oral culture. Informants draw on a repertoire of images, motifs and short narratives, many of which predate the Famine and which were part of a wider international narrative repertoire. These might be classified as representational, explanatory and exhortatory. The representational motifs illustrate the extent to which normal behaviour was abandoned and taboos broken. Perhaps the most familiar type describe dead bodies being found with mouths coloured green from eating grass, entire families dying and leaving no-one to bury them, burials in mass graves, sometimes with reusable coffins, and human corpses being eaten by animals. The most common explanatory form attributes the crop failure to divine displeasure. Finally, stories of charity or faith miraculously rewarded constitute in this context a recommendation that normal social responsibilities and beliefs should not be abandoned.

As in much oral narrative, individual motifs are available to be combined into a larger framework. Take the following example, told in 1938 by Diarmuid Ó hÚrdail, a farmer and fisherman in Eyeries, Co. Cork:

> *Bhí fear ar an mbaile . . .*
> There was a man in this town, during the famine times, and his wife died, a young woman, and they had a single child. He had to bury her on the hill, outside the wall. He couldn't bring her to the cemetery, he was too weak, and the neighbours were too weak, and the pigs dug her body up later, and he went wandering, himself and the child. He left the child in Kenmare workhouse, and when he returned after having walked all over Co. Kerry he couldn't recognise the child and he had to leave him behind.[15]

Here people are buried in unconsecrated ground and disinterred by animals, and every family bond is broken. Moreover, it is not simply the Famine whose brutalising effects are being illustrated, but also the state system of relief.

To point up the contrast of a classification based on types of knowledge and one based on historical phenomena, this example of popular memory can be compared with examples of the other two levels, the local and the global, concerning the same historical domain, the Poor

[15] Póirtéir, *Glórtha*, p. 147. To indicate a source in the Irish language, I have followed the style used in Ó Gráda, *Black '47*.

Law and the workhouse. As an example of the local, we can take a short description by Padraig Ó Sé, 68, a farmer from Caherdaniel:

Beait Rua a bhí san áit . . .
Beait Rua used to live in the farm my uncle had. The poor man had an old horse, and when he was able, those people who were going to the workhouse, it was Beait's horse that would bring them, and when one died, it was Beait's horse that would bring them to Derrynane.[16]

This is a local detail, remembered presumably because the narrator's uncle now occupies Beait's land. It does not form part of the popular memory because it does not signal any departure from normality.

Tomás Aichir, a farmer in his eighties from Kilmaley, Co. Clare, gives an example of the abstract from a written source:

By 1852 however, matters had much improved and the Poor Law commissioners could report that the rate of mortality in the Co. Clare was less than the average for Ireland and the workhouse accommodation in the county exceeded the actual number of inmates by 2,000.[17]

The categorisation of the material into three levels is not intended as a hard and fast taxonomy, applicable in every instance. The testimony of individual narrators can contain elements of all three, and those elements are not always neatly distinguishable. It is clearly possible for the different levels to interact. There is a double process here. On the one hand, popular memory can 'migrate' to the local or national level. Legends can attach themselves to named historic individuals, and appear to belong to the concrete local level; equally, writers of abstract accounts could incorporate legends into document-based narratives. On the other hand, the corpus of legend can provide the context within which local or national events are dramatised or highlighted, and it appears that these events are influential or remarkable to the extent that they conform to popular memory. The crucial level, therefore, is that of 'popular memory', and we need to look at this level in some more detail.

This popular memory can be broadly characterised as a popular culture of scarcity or catastrophe. The corpus of legend within the Famine folklore is part of a more general system of representation which was contained in behaviour, in action and ritual as well as in narrative form. This system is perhaps best characterised by looking in turn at popular representations of famine in early modern and modern Europe, distinguishing between those narratives and rituals which deal with production

[16] Póirtéir, *Glórtha*, p. 150.
[17] Póirtéir, *Echoes*, pp. 125, 127–8.

and those which deal with distribution (or, more precisely, the failure of production and distribution). The former were found in both subsistence and market economies, the latter in market economies.

In societies which practised subsistence – usually low-technology – agriculture, crop failures, animal diseases, and consequently food shortages, were frequent, and substitute foods and other survival strategies were well known. Failure was usually interpreted in the context of the supernatural. If the crop of an individual failed, or if his animals died, this was possibly the result of aggressive magic by an enemy. If the same happened to an entire community or locality, where interpersonal tensions could not be the cause, it was taken to be the result of divine displeasure, as a punishment from God. Such a view did not, of course, preclude a concrete understanding of disease or crop failure. It was clear, for example, that a storm could level a field of wheat, or that drought killed crops and animals. Storms and drought, however, were simply the instrument of punishment. Scarcity, in other words, was a metaphysical as well as a physical phenomenon.[18]

This type of explanation is dominant in folk tradition on the Famine, and also in contemporary reaction in the 1840s. It is expressed in a classic way as a waste of plenty:

> So plentiful were potatoes before the famine that it often happened that farmers filled them into sacks, took them to market in Moate, Athlone or Ballymahon, offered them for sale but nobody could be found to buy, so that on the return journey the farmers often emptied them into the ditch on the roadside for they weren't worth the sacks they were in. Afterwards it was said that the famine was a just retribution from God for the great waste of food.[19]

Other versions were more historically specific, looking for possible causes in the decade or so before 1845. Some focused on the pledges which had been taken during the Temperance crusade of the late 1830s and which subsequently had been broken. To renege on such a solemn promise would certainly be offensive to the divinity.

The corollary of adducing a supernatural cause for scarcity or calamity is that rescue was also supernatural. An individual or community which suffered a calamity might practise penance and appeal to God or saints in

[18] William Christian, *Local Religion in Sixteenth-Century Spain* (Princeton, NJ, 1981), ch. 2; for examples, see Abel Poitrineau, 'Le paysan et l'adversité: des calamités, des mentalités, des comportements', in *Le Paysan: Actes du 2e Colloque d'Aurillac* (Paris, 1989), pp. 109–34, 127, and David Gentilcore, *From Bishop to Witch: The System of the Sacred in Early Modern Terra d'Otranto* (Manchester, 1992), p. 183; Max Gluckman, 'The logic in witchcraft', in his *Custom and Conflict in Africa* (Oxford, 1955), pp. 81–108.

[19] Póirtéir, *Echoes*, p. 38.

other ways. In the 1940s folklore, the most common form of supernatural deliverance was individual, in the form of legends about those whose charity was rewarded. Those who continued to share their food, even if in danger of shortage themselves, found food miraculously appearing in their kitchens.[20]

To this supernatural framework, the development of a market in food and of associated systems of distribution added the concept of shortage being due to human agency. Among early modern urban dwellers, and particularly among wage earners, food shortage and high prices were often attributed to the machinations of food merchants who were guilty of hoarding and forestalling. This popular conception of the food market, the 'moral economy' and the forms of collective action or violence which accompanied it, are familiar from the work of Thompson and others on seventeenth- and eighteenth-century England, and were typical of western Europe in the period. Their existence in Ireland has been partly obscured by the fact that the most characteristic forms of collective action or violence in Ireland, and certainly those most investigated by historians, were directed at land rather than food prices or wages. However, between 1845 and 1847, and in previous periods of shortage, price and wage riots were typical reactions, as Eiríksson and McCabe have shown.[21]

This 'early market' perception of shortage or famine is more visible in action and ritual than in narratives or legends. Broadly speaking, these actions were of two kinds, urban and rural. Urban action concerned the supply and price of food. A large crowd would target merchants, retailers and sometimes bakers, accusing them of hoarding or selling short weight, and forced them (or made the authorities force them) to bring food to sale, to lower prices and increase size. Food riots were very frequent in the early years of the Great Famine, and were reported from most towns and cities. The forms of action were carried over into state relief schemes, which saw frequent riots against the level of wages and demanding increased employment.[22]

[20] Christian, *Local Religion*; Póirtéir, *Echoes*, ch. 17; Póirtéir, *Glórtha*, pp. 260–84.

[21] E. P. Thompson, 'The moral economy of the English crowd in the eighteenth century', *Past & Present*, 50 (1971) 76–136; Louise Tilly, 'Food entitlement, famine and conflict', *Journal of Interdisciplinary History*, 14 (1983), 333–49; Andrés Eiríksson, 'Food supply and food riots', in Cormac Ó Gráda (ed.), *Famine 150* (Dublin, 1997), pp. 67–94; Des McCabe, 'Social order and the ghost of moral economy in pre-Famine Mayo', in Raymond Gillespie and Gerard Moran (eds.), *A Various Country: Essays in Mayo History* (Westport, 1987) pp. 91–112.

[22] Eiríksson 'Food supply and food riots'; William Fraher, 'The Dungarvan disturbances of 1846 and sequels', in Des Cowman and Donald Brady (eds.), *Teacht na bPrátaí Dubha: The Famine in Waterford 1845–50* (Dublin, 1995), pp. 137–52.

In rural areas, the most visible form of collective action was the attack on transport to prevent the export of food from an area, often accompanied by insistence that food be sold to local people at a reasonable price. This action was grounded in the idea that in a time of shortage, the area which produced food had prior claim on its consumption. McCabe cites an instance in Ballina in 1817, described by Henry King, a local magistrate:

A mob consisting of no less than 500 persons came to my house carrying with them several carts, laden with meal, intended to be sent by land carriage to the town of Sligo, which they admitted they had seized upon and declaring in the most violent and outrageous manner their determination of not allowing provisions of any sort to be conveyed out of the country.

As McCabe comments, the fact that they went to a magistrate to explain the event shows how convinced they were of the justice of their case.[23]

IV

These were, in broad outline, some of the features of the popular culture of scarcity, the 'popular memory' of the folklore. Not all of it has survived in the twentieth-century oral narrative. There is little talk of food or wage riots, probably because the informants of the 1930s and 1940s were not drawn from urban areas. The ideology or morality of the rural action survives, however, in the many accounts of theft of food, many of which stress that such theft was moral in times of shortage.[24] This popular memory forms the basic framework through which the story of the Famine was constituted, and has a major influence on the ways that the other memories, the local and the national, were constructed. As regards local memory, narratives and images from popular memory are usually told as if they were local events. This is the case, for example, of the stories of supernatural aid. In Co. Laois,

I heard my father say that there was a poor widow with five children living outside the town. She and her family were on the verge of starvation and she had no means of securing food. She prayed fervently to almighty God and

[23] Tilly 'Food entitlement, famine and conflict'; McCabe 'Social order and the ghost of moral economy', p. 99. There were similar attacks on food transports on both the Royal and the Grand canals in the early nineteenth century: W. A. Maguire, *The Downshire Estates in Ireland 1801–1845* (Oxford, 1972), pp. 223–4, and Ruth Delany, *Ireland's Royal Canal 1789–1992* (Dublin, 1992), pp. 75, 100. For a continental example of a rural food seizure, see W. Gregory Monahan, *Year of Sorrows: The Great Famine of 1709 in Lyon* (Columbus, 1993), pp. 100–1.

[24] Póirtéir, *Echoes*, ch. 5; Póirtéir, *Glórtha*, pp. 88–109.

begged of Him not to let herself and her little ones die of hunger. On looking out one morning she was astonished to see a field at the back of the house white with mushrooms, though it was not the season of the year when mushrooms would be in the fields.[25]

Overall, those aspects of local experience which best conform to an existing repertoire of narrative, which are most tellable, are those which are highlighted in local memory.

The same argument can be made about global memory, although with some qualification, since the gap in perception between popular and local, which both tend towards the concrete, is less than that between popular and global. The global, in contrast, is frequently told in a more abstract historiographical mode, using numbers and a more complex notion of causality, and is also concerned with aspects of high politics which would be far removed from the popular experience. The influence of the global is felt more strongly in the English-language folklore, with some informants clearly comfortable with precise numbers and dates. Estimating the influence of written accounts of the Famine on the folklore of the 1930s and 1940s is difficult, since the number of possible routes of such influence is so large. At the same time, however, those written accounts would tend to be interpreted in the light of the popular representation outlined above.

One instance of this is in the presence of elements of the most influential nationalist treatment of the Famine, that of John Mitchel. Mitchel's presentation, published in *Jail Journal* (1854) and *The Last Conquest of Ireland (perhaps)* (1860) contains two fundamental arguments which had a major influence on subsequent writing about the Famine. First, 'during each of those five years of famine, from '46 to '51, that famine-struck land produced more than double the needful sustenance for all her own people', but this food was exported. This was encapsulated by probably Mitchel's best-known image, that 'a government ship sailing into any harbour with Indian corn was sure to meet half a dozen sailing out with Irish wheat and cattle'. The second element was that this export was deliberately allowed by the government who had come to the conclusion a decade beforehand that Ireland was overpopulated, and saw the Famine as an opportunity to reduce population. The result was that 'a million and a half men, women and children were carefully, prudently and peacefully slain by the English government' – in other words, the Famine was a form of mass murder.[26]

[25] Poirtéir, *Echoes*, p. 269.

[26] John Mitchel, *The Last Conquest of Ireland (Perhaps)* (London, n.d.), pp. 112, 219.

As Ó Gráda and Quinlan have noted, the folklore does not tend to focus blame on the government, and there is no mention of deliberate extermination. The argument about export, however, is present among the more abstract folklore accounts, usually in the form of the image of the ships. According to Martin Manning, near Westport, Co. Mayo, 'In the year 1847 fourteen schooners of about 200 tons each left Westport quay laden with wheat and oats to feed the English people while the Irish people were starving. This happened one morning on one tide and was repeated several times during the famine.' Although Manning presents the schooners as bound for England, there is no extension of blame to the government. In fact, a Wexford informant makes the point about export in a purely Irish context: 'Although people died there was plenty of food in the country. Corn was stored in Wexford town at the time and in Briens of Coolmaine. The corn at Coolmaine was for Power's distillery, and the corn was drawn out to Dublin though there was famine.'[27] The immorality of food transports leaving an area was precisely what lay behind and justified rural collective action during scarcity. Its prominence as an image within the popular culture of scarcity probably accounts for its impact on the popular readership of Mitchel, whether they were encountering Mitchel's presentation directly or indirectly.

As noted earlier, we know about the popular culture of scarcity in a market economy principally through action and ritual, and the centrality of the image of boats leaving a port which was suffering shortage cannot be illustrated from any pre-Famine popular narrative. At the same time, an account of the famine of 1822 given before the Devon Commission in 1844 by Mathias McDonnel, a substantial merchant in Westport, Co. Mayo, is suggestive. In that famine, and presumably in others, the potatoes failed, oats were exported to pay rent, and then relief committees brought in cargoes of potatoes and meal for sale: 'In truth, the vessels had met each other going out and coming in. A man may have engaged his vessels for two months before and he must go on with his business, no matter what the consequences must be.'[28]

The nationalist narrative of the Famine, which probably had more currency among those younger than the informants of 1945, was not the only larger or more abstract conception available. There was also a Catholic narrative which emphasised the continuation during the Famine of the Protestant evangelical activity which had been substantial in pre-Famine

[27] Póirtéir, *Echoes*, p. 210.

[28] *Evidence Taken before the Commissioners Appointed to Inquire into the Occupation of Land in Ireland*, Part 2, pp. 1845, XX, p. 410.

decades. During the 1840s, this evangelism was said to have taken the form of food relief which was conditional on conversion, those who availed of it being known as 'Soupers'. In the denominational polemics of the later nineteenth century, Catholic writers frequently referred back to these events, and most of the 1945 informants would probably have been familiar with these issues from sermons and religious literature.[29]

The influence of a printed denominational literature is evident in the material collected from Tomás Aichir of Kilmaley, Co. Clare, quoted earlier. Aichir's account of the Famine is that of a well-read individual, and his discussion is less of Kilmaley than of Clare as whole, global rather than local memory. He also describes evangelical activity in Kilbaha and Carrigaholt, 30 miles away, rather than in Kilmaley. These events were notorious, and Aichir's account probably reflects a common regional knowledge.[30] Two of his sentences, however, come verbatim from a written source: 'Such was the state of things that faced Father Meehan at the commencement of his mission in Carrigaholt' and 'In this year [1849] the crowbar as well as the famine had done its fearful work.' Both of these occur in an article called 'Proselytism in West Clare: A Retrospect,' published in the *Irish Ecclesiastical Record* in 1887. The Catholic narrative, in the words of this article, is that the Famine, or more accurately proselytism during the Famine, was but an 'episode of... an unholy war against the faith of the Irish poor', but that the resistance of the poor and of the clergy strengthened the church, so that 'what seemed a curse proved a lasting blessing'.[31]

The influence of a clerical narrative is evident also in the presentation of the material collected by Ciarán Ó Síocháin in Cape Clear for the 1945 survey. He wrote to the Folklore Commission in August 1945 that

Ní bheadh puinn . . .
There would be nothing here. However, I happen to have received a copy of a manuscript which was printed in the 'Month and Catholic Review' Sept.–Dec. 1881 written by Father T. Davis about this island. That account is in English, and I don't think it could be bettered.[32]

[29] For the importance of sermons as a source for oral narrative, see Philippe Joutard, *Ces voix qui nous viennent du passé* (Paris, 1983), p. 224. Other possible sources of proselytism narratives include one of the earliest plays written in Irish, which was performed in branches of the Gaelic League at the beginning of the twentieth century. This was *Creideamh agus Gorta: Faith and Famine, a Tragic Drama relating to the Famine Period*, by the Rev. P. Dinneen, published in 1901. Its story was told to a collector in 1945 by Séamus Reardon, Eniskeane, Co. Cork (Póirtéir, *Echoes*, pp. 176–7).

[30] See the account in Ignatius Murphy, *The Diocese of Killaloe 1850–1914* (Dublin, 1995), pp. 38–44.

[31] P. White, 'Proselytism in West Clare: a retrospect', *Irish Ecclesiastical Record*, 3rd ser., 8 (1887), 411–21.

[32] Irish Folklore Commission (IFC) MS 1070, p. 157.

Davis's article, 'Cape Clear: a retrospect' is a description of Protestant missionary efforts on the island during the Famine, including the building of a church and a school. Again the Famine is presented as an episode in a longer history of inter-church conflict:

It was in this period of writhing national agony that the arch-enemy of our holy religion prompted his agents in Great Britain and Ireland to attempt the spiritual ruin of the faithful Irish people. What in the past could not be effected by the sword, by confiscation, by corruption, was to be accomplished by money and want . . . [33]

It appears from the folklore material collected by Ó Síocháin that this had become the accepted Famine narrative in the area. In a letter accompanying the material which was submitted in October 1945, he apologises for not having been able to fill the pages which he had been sent:

Ní chloisfeá puinn . . .
You would not hear anything about the Famine itself, it was said that the old people who witnessed it did not like to talk about it at all. There was nothing they would talk about more than faith and the minister during the Famine.

The material which follows is dominated by the story of proselytism, which amounts to almost half of the account (30 pages), with a description of pre-Famine life (22 pages) and other Famine material (17 pages) making up the rest.[34]

As with the nationalist narrative, the Catholic narrative was also filtered through and accommodated to popular memory, in this case the conception of Famine as a divine punishment. In Ó Síocháin's account:

Déarfadh cuid des na seandaoine . . .
Some of the old people would say that the Famine was a punishment sent by God to the Irish to see were they faithful to him and to their faith. God willing, such a scourge will not come again on the Irish, with their food being exported, the stores full of grain, that this would not happen unless they converted to Protestantism.

Ó Síocháin also presents part of the story of proselytism in the mnemonic idiom of local memory, attaching sections of his account to the ruins of the Protestant church and school buildings.

In the folklore concerning proselytism in general, however, the longer historical vision of the clerical writers is entirely lacking. What

[33] C. Davis, 'Cape Clear: a retrospect', *The Month and Catholic Review*, 24 (1881), 476–88.
[34] IFC MS 1070, pp. 168–223.

is repeatedly highlighted is the act of taking food in return for conversion, a narrative whose power derives from its exact inversion of one of the commonest motifs of supernatural deliverance, that of faith being rewarded by food. Here instead, the reward is for lack of faith, which clearly points up the immorality of those who took it, and many informants refer to the notoriety which attached itself to those who converted. The proselytism stories also occasionally mention, with less disapproval, the conditional or temporary nature of conversion, and the clever replies of those whose sincerity was questioned, usually by a Protestant minister. The narrative model here is the trickster who extracts himself from awkward situations through verbal facility.[35] As with the nationalist narrative, therefore, the aspects of the church's version which had most impact were those which corresponded to images and narratives within popular memory.

V

A discussion such as the above, which emphasises the power of a corpus of narratives/system of belief to constitute the perception of an event and the receptivity to alternative narratives, comes close to a type of narrative idealism. This would imply a view of culture as being slow to change or even resistant to change, and would have a double consequence for our view of the famine folklore.

In the first place, it implies that the experience of the Famine did not produce any radical or fundamental change in perceptions, in psychology or in culture. This probably seems counter-intuitive, and certainly runs counter to much writing on the Famine from different points of view. The attribution of cultural or psychological effects to the Famine goes back at least as far as K. H. Connell, writing in the 1950s and 1960s in a broadly Malthusian framework, who expressed his judgement on the economic and demographic impact in psychological terms. The Irish, according to Connell, 'were shocked by the Famine; they shook off some of the old, easy going ways and married with discretion'.[36] A more elaborate version was presented in the religious sphere by David Miller in the mid-1970s. According to Miller, since folk religious ritual was to a large extent directed at agricultural survival or prosperity, the unprecedented failure of the potato crop in successive years undermined faith in those rituals. This made people more receptive to orthodox Catholicism,

[35] For an example, see Póirtéir, *Echoes*, p. 167.
[36] K. H. Connell, *Irish Peasant Society* (Oxford, 1968), p. 118.

and was crucial in the 'devotional revolution' of the mid-nineteenth century.[37]

Most recently, a presentation of the effects of the famine has appeared which is expressed in the language of psychotherapy, specifically in terms of trauma and recovery.[38] It is found in the work of historians, but is more marked in that of non-historians, its most public exponent being John Waters, a columnist with the *Irish Times*. The model underlies most of the essays in *Irish Hunger*, a recent collection of essays by journalists, academics and writers from both sides of the Atlantic, which addresses the impact of the Famine on Irish culture. According to this model, traumatic events in the lives of individuals – and by extension, communities – are dealt with by an attempt to suppress them, to banish them from consciousness. This is never entirely successful, however, and the memories return in other forms, forms which are usually harmful to the mental well-being of the person. As David Lloyd puts it: 'The Famine recurs, as the repressed must, in indirect and equally deflected cultural form . . . ours is a culture constituted around and marked by an unworked-through loss.'[39] The symptoms of this loss – the psychological effects of the Famine – are said to be feelings of inferiority and shame, and linked social phenomena such as high rates of alcoholism and mental illness. Waters characterises these as 'Our congenital inability to realise our potential . . . the cravenness of our dependencies, our fear of self-belief, the culture of amnesia in which we live our lives, our willingness to imitate anything rather than think for ourselves.'[40]

This late-twentieth-century view of memory, which by projecting a model of individual psychodynamics onto a national population effectively defines Irishness as a syndrome, also envisages a cure for these symptoms. This is the recovery of the suppressed memory and its narration.

All the above presentations see the Famine as a turning point in perceptions. Although the terms of the debate about whether the Famine was a 'watershed' are imprecise, the drawbacks of such arguments are clear. There is, for example, an inverse relationship between the impact

[37] David Miller, 'Irish Catholicism and the Great Famine', *Journal of Social History*, 9 (1975), 81–98, esp. 91–2.

[38] The most frequently quoted text is Judith Herman, *Trauma and Recovery: From Domestic Abuse to Political Terror* (London, 1992).

[39] David Lloyd, 'The memory of hunger', in Tom Hayden (ed.), *Irish Hunger: Personal Reflections on the Legacy of the Famine* (Dublin, 1997), pp. 32–47, quotation on p. 45.

[40] John Waters, 'Confronting the ghosts of our past', in Hayden, *Irish Hunger*, pp. 27–31, quotation on pp. 28–9.

of the Famine and the extent of the supposed cultural or psychological effect. The Famine was most severe in western counties, and yet these were the areas in which older forms of demographic behaviour and religious practice continued after the Famine, along with other cultural forms such as the Irish language.[41] Moreover, even allowing for the concentration of folklore collectors on the west coast, it seems that these areas had the richest corpus of narrative forms for representing Famine, and consequently, one could argue, the least repressed memory of it. This is not to say that the Famine did not have a huge impact, and may well have been a turning point, in a structural sense. But for a language or a religion to decline because its practitioners died is not the same as decline due to a change of attitude among those practitioners.

If the Irish Famine did indeed bring about significant and permanent change in purely cultural and psychological ways, that would make it unusual and perhaps unique. Of course, it was an unusually severe famine in material terms by modern European standards, but it does not follow that it had exceptional cultural effects, and it is difficult to see how it could. The religious argument put forward by Miller, for example, suggests that when a particular religion fails to deal with catastrophe, it can be abandoned. But if that were the case, no religion, perhaps no system of belief which purported to explain the natural world, would have lasted until the middle of the nineteenth century. Indeed, it could be argued that providing a satisfactory explanation of catastrophe is in fact one of the strengths of a religious or magical view of the world as opposed to a scientific or material one.

Miller's argument, in which the explanatory power of popular religion is defeated by the magnitude of the Famine, finds echoes in the sphere of elite culture. David Brett argues that the visual modes available to artists and engravers, including those who worked for the newspapers of the time, were inadequate to convey or to represent the full extent of the Famine, while Chris Morash makes a similar argument with reference to poetry.[42] While these are powerful and necessary preliminaries to studying representations of the Famine, they have the same drawbacks as the accounts of the folklore discussed earlier, in that they depend on the invocation of some 'real' experience or understanding of the famine, which is external to the modes of perception and experience being

[41] Cormac Ó Gráda, 'Seasonal migration and post-famine adjustment in the west of Ireland', *Studia Hibernica*, 13 (1975), 48–76.

[42] David Brett, *The Construction of Heritage* (Cork, 1996), pp. 142–50; Chris Morash (ed.), *The Hungry Voice: The Poetry of the Irish Famine* (Dublin, 1989), intro.

studied. This runs the risk of privileging the perception of the analyst over that of the people being analysed.

This is in fact what happens when some of those who propose a psychological effect come to deal with the folklore material. According to two of the contributors to *Irish Hunger*, Luke Gibbons and David Lloyd, the perception that the Famine was divine punishment was a form of amnesia or complicity in catastrophe by its victims, deflecting attention from a presumably more 'real' explanation rooted in centuries of colonialism.[43] Such an explanation may be more real for a society which is post-religious and which has a more abstract and linear sense of time and causality, and the emphasis of these writers on apportioning blame for therapeutic purposes may be an accurate reflection of public memory in the late twentieth century, but it is not necessarily appropriate to an earlier period. If, as Gibbons writes, 'memory is not just a matter of retention or recollection but of finding the narrative forms that will do justice to this troubled inheritance without sanitising it, but also without succumbing to it', then the post-Famine generations certainly possessed those narrative forms, and they were part of a wider system of meaning which made sense of their world.[44]

A representation and understanding of the Famine built on these narrative forms is still evident in the folklore of the 1930s and 1940s, and this brings us to the other consequence of narrative idealism and its understanding of cultural change as slow. That is the implication that the stories and descriptions given by those folklore informants would correspond to a large extent with the perceptions of a century earlier. In other words, the reliability of the folklore is not in terms of empirical facts or events of the kind favoured by document-based historiography. Nor does it simply reflect 'attitudes', since attitudes are usually towards events or experiences. It is reliable in terms of perceptions and experiences, what people actually thought was happening, which consequently formed not just their attitudes but even the events and facts which they used to tell the story of the Famine.

VI

Many studies of collective memory have emphasised its layered nature. Lequin and Métral, in their discussion of the steelworkers of Givors, have distinguished between personal memory, organised around the principal

[43] Hayden, *Irish Hunger*, pp. 45, 262.

[44] Luke Gibbons, 'Doing justice to the past', in Hayden (ed.), *Irish Hunger*, pp. 258–70, quote on p. 269.

events of life, a communal memory in which shared experiences define the identity of the occupational group, and institutional or state memory, manifested in schooling and public commemoration. Elsewhere, studies of historical narrative have proposed a classification in terms of degrees of complexity and abstraction. In one such classification, Jerzy Topolski differentiates between annals, which record discrete events, chronicles, which introduce some idea of causality into the sequence of those events, and historiography, which deals with longer time scales and introduces a greater degree of interpretation.[45]

This chapter has proposed a certain correspondence between narrative types and forms of memory which brings together these two classifications, although its categories are not precisely the same as either. Local memory tends to consist of relatively atomised detail, rather like a set of annals. Popular memory draws on a particular vision of causality, both in the supernatural and the human realm. Finally, global memory takes a view which is more abstract and more long term. In the case of the Famine, this consists partly of attempts to situate it in a longer history, whether of Anglo-Irish relations or religious conflict.

It remains to be seen whether such an approach can be extended to other areas of memory. There are relatively few large collections of oral narrative similar to the archive of the Irish Folklore Commission (IFC). One such corpus is the Slave Narrative Collection of the Federal Writers' Project in the United States, which in the 1930s interviewed thousands of black men and women who had been slaves. This has many similarities with the IFC archive. It was collected on a large scale in most of the southern states and used standardised questionnaires. It also interviewed older people about events and conditions many decades before, although in the case of the slave narratives these were events which the informants themselves had lived through. Nevertheless, as some commentators have pointed out, many of the informants would have been too young in the 1860s to have experienced the full extent of a slave regime, but would have known of it through their parents and elders. Most historical analysis of these narratives, however, again like the case of the Famine folklore, has concentrated on its reliability as a source for empirical data and attitudes in the mid-nineteenth century rather than as a system of representation in the twentieth.[46]

[45] Lequin and Métral, 'A la recherche d'une mémoire collective'; Jerzy Topolski, 'Historical narrative: towards a coherent structure', *History and Theory*, 26 (1987), 73–86.

[46] See the essays collected in C. T. Davis and H. L. Gates (eds.), *The Slave's Narrative* (London, 1985); for the question of age, John. W. Blessingame, 'Using the testimony of ex-slaves: approaches and problems', ibid., pp. 78–89.

Another possibility would be to explore such typologies in the IFC archive on other historical subjects. The material collected in Ríonach Uí Ógáin's study of the folklore of Daniel O'Connell shows a similar pattern to the one suggested above.[47] There is local memory, although it is more geographically concentrated than that of the Famine, occurring particularly in Kerry, where O'Connell was a landlord. Then there is the assimilation of O'Connell to the forms of standard oral narrative, tales in which he appears as hero and trickster in particular. Finally, there is a version of O'Connell as political hero in a wider Irish or British context, deriving ultimately from newspapers, schoolbooks and the publicity material of O'Connell's political organisations.

Such typologies, however, need also to be set in the context of a wider reconstruction of popular memory as a whole, of a worldview which does not necessarily correspond to that of the historian. For Famine memory, such an investigation could be carried further in two directions. The first would be to try to take a broader view, and to see how a representation of scarcity was related to the overall corpus of oral narrative and the worldview reflected in it or constituted by it. A separate study of the Irish Folklore Commission collections other than the 1945 questionnaire would be illuminating in this respect. In what contexts, for example, were famine narratives told, were they concentrated among particular specialised narrators, and can all narratives which are set during the Famine be described as 'Famine narratives'?

The second direction would be towards an understanding of the popular sense of time and period. In looking at the oral narrative about the Famine, this chapter has attempted to move away from an approach whose aim is the illumination of the events of the 1840s and instead to reconstruct a wider popular representation of scarcity whose repertoire of images and narratives is used to discuss those events. It remains the case, however, that a study of 'the memory of the Famine' is still being guided, at least partly, by a category of academic historiography, taking more or less for granted that a corresponding category existed in popular consciousness, and that a relatively coherent and well-defined image or cluster of memories existed which referred to a particular national-historical event, the Great Famine.

This was not necessarily the case, as we can see if we consider the Irish-language version of the 1945 questionnaire, which is titled 'An Gorta Mór,

[47] Ríonach Uí Ógáin, *Immortal Dan: Daniel O'Connell in Irish Folk Tradition* (Dublin, 1995).

1846–52'.[48] The term 'Gorta Mór' was rarely used in the Irish-language folklore, and may well be a translation of the English 'Great Famine'. Irish speakers referred instead to 'An Drochshaol', 'The Bad Times', a concept which is broader and less chronologically precise. In Cape Clear, for example, the only account of emigration collected by Ó Síocháin was that some inhabitants were given paid passage to Newfoundland during the 'Drochshaol'. However, he could not ascertain precisely when the 'Drochshaol' was, and the story probably refers to an emigration scheme undertaken in the aftermath of a later potato failure in 1862.[49] In other ways, the sense of time in the folklore is quite precise, with individual years or seasons in the late 1840s being specifically remembered. In Kerry, the summer of 1846, with its freakish weather patterns, was remembered as 'Bliain na tuile' ['The year of the flood'], in Clare the winter of 1846 was 'Bliain an Board of Works', and in Donegal, 1848 was 'Bliain na Scidíní' ['The year of the small potatoes']. The single bounded entity, 'An Gorta Mór', lasting from 1845 to 1852, is by contrast less frequent, and narratives, memories and images were not grouped in the folklore in the chronologically tidy ways assumed by the questionnaire.[50]

Further investigation of a corpus of oral narrative of the Famine such as that collected by the Irish Folklore Commission, therefore, would take account not only of the forms of representation of scarcity, but also of the wider dynamics of oral narrative and the forms of a more general representation of time and of the past. Such investigation would reveal more fully the dynamics of popular memory and ultimately offer the outlines of the worldview and sense of identity of rural society in the early twentieth century.

48 Reproduced in Póirtéir, *Glórtha*, pp. 315–16.

49 IFC MS 1070, p. 207; Eamon Lankford, *Cape Clear Island: Its People and Landscape* (Cape Clear, Co. Cork, 1999), pp. 66–8.

50 Póirtéir, *Glórtha*, pp. 18–19 (Kerry); IFC MS 1071, p. 314 (Clare); Póirtéir, *Glórtha*, p. 25 (Donegal); in south Galway 1846 was remembered as 'Bliain na Spéire', 'The Year of the Sky': M. McNamara and M. Madden (eds.), *Beagh: A History and Heritage* (Beagh, Co. Galway, 1995), ch. 8.

CHAPTER 5

The star-spangled shamrock: meaning and memory in Irish America

Kevin O'Neill

In December 1996 my university, Boston College, hosted the official Irish government commemoration of the Famine. In the spring of 1998 we hosted the official Irish government bicentennial commemoration of the Rebellion of 1798. Both were very strong programmes with major scholars participating. The papers were of a very high order, they were well attended, and I am sure that a great deal was learned. But in North America the level of excitement for the bicentenary of 1798 was simply not comparable to that which surrounded the Famine commemoration.

Perhaps this needs little explanation. The Famine was an event of such horrifying tragedy that there is an obvious human logic for identifying it as the major event of the nineteenth century and perhaps of modern Irish history. And in Boston there is the added factor that in many real, and some mythical ways, the Famine provides Irish Americans with a 'charter myth' – a creation story that both explains our presence in the new land and connects us to the old via a powerful sense of grievance. But there are also reasons for expecting there to be more interest in the rebellion of 1798. After all, the United Irish effort was part of the same eighteenth-century revolutionary experience that created the United States of America. And the American and Irish revolutions of the eighteenth century shared not only a common republicanism but also a common foe in the Irish arch-enemy, England. In Concord, Massachusetts, a plaque adorns a stone fence. Every year hundreds of thousands of visitors come and stand on this spot where many feel our nation was born, and it is a place to which I drag visiting historians from Ireland and Britain – for the symbols deployed are provocative to those who focus upon issues of nationalism and violence. That stone stands where the British 'invaders' are buried. (I take the word from another monument at the site.) It reads:

'Grave of British Soldiers'
They came three thousand miles and Died
To Keep the Past upon its Throne
Unheard, Beyond the Ocean Tide
Their English Mother Made her Moan.

Just across the famous bridge that 'spans the rude flood' is the even more famous statue of the 'Minuteman' – perhaps the most powerful icon to emerge out of the American revolutionary struggle. It eloquently expresses homage to the bravery of citizen soldiers who left their ploughs to confront the crème de la crème of Europe's professional armies. Ironically, this monument to part-time soldiers has also been used in the twentieth century to stress the need for American military preparedness and hence support the establishment of the largest and best-endowed peacetime professional military establishment on the planet.

The iconography bears a striking resemblance to that produced by the rebellion of 1798. For instance, our heroic Concord farmer differs little from the figure to be found in the town centre of Dunlavin, Co. Wicklow. Of course one critical difference does separate the two, in image and reality: the victorious Concord rebel holds a most impressive musket in his hand. What might the rebellion of 1798 have been like had the United Irishmen been so armed? A good question for military historians, but surely there are even more interesting and important questions to be asked about the nature of the ideology and social structure in Concord and Dunlavin, in Boston and Belfast? Why have militant republicans and nationalists within the Irish-American community not invested more heavily in the possibilities inherent here?

One reason is that though there certainly were Irish heroes in the American Revolution, such as Commodore John Barry, 'founder' of the American Navy, the war was perceived as a 'Yankee' War. And this was not an accident: Anglo ethnocentric groups such as the 'Daughters of the American Revolution' imposed an ethnic litmus test upon access to the legacy of the Revolution that they still seek to protect. During the nineteenth century such ethnocentric behaviour was popular, public and state supported. But the undoubted role of elite efforts to keep Concord and the Minutemen free of any sort of multicultural interpretations was not the primary reason that immigrant Irish people did not look to eighteenth-century republicanism as a point of entry into American discourse and life. As this chapter will demonstrate, there existed a far more powerful and emotive place and time to find such an

'The Minuteman', Concord, Massachusetts. Photo by Kevin O'Neill

entrepôt, one that correlated much more closely to their own group experience.

Since the publication of Thomas Brown's pioneering work on Irish-American nationalism established the American nature of Irish-American politics it has been accepted by most that Irish-American nationalism has had more to do with American opportunities than Irish difficulties.[1] And, as Chris Wickham and James Fentress point out in *Social Memory*, all systems of memory are functional and suited to the present environments in which social groups find themselves.[2] For most groups this means that social memory changes along a fairly gentle gradient as both environment and group membership evolve in time. The evolutionary nature of this process means that for most social groups, at most moments, social memory, while in flux, seems to remain constant, allowing us to mistake it for 'tradition'. But for groups such as immigrant communities this process can be far more rapid, and produce a painful sense of dislocation in both temporal and social identity. This was especially true for immigrant groups who moved from rural and agricultural cultures in which place and landscape formed important structural elements of social memory to communities that were urban and industrial. Immigrant communities had other memory challenges. In most 'traditional' societies 'elders' played an important role as both repositories and interpreters of a community's past. They not only served as conduits for group experience, but they were frequently called upon to utilise their knowledge of the past to judge and validate responses to new phenomena. In this way the shock of the new was negotiated, while the past could be renegotiated. Immigrant communities, especially those composed of young unmarried migrants, often had a marked shortage of such memory negotiators.

All of the above was true for most Irish emigrants to the United States during most of the nineteenth century, but emigrants of the Famine era had additional traumas to contend with. They were distanced from their past and their place, not only by these 'normal' factors but also by the difficulty that accessing their memories of Ireland posed. They fled from Ireland with images of failure, devastation and pain etched deeply into their personal memories. Their arrival in a new social and political environment posed a serious challenge to the capacity of their social memory system to provide useful and coherent bridges to membership in the

[1] Thomas Brown, *Irish-American Nationalism, 1870–1890* (Philadelphia, PA, 1966).
[2] James Fentress and Chris Wickham, *Social Memory* (Cambridge, MA, 1992), esp. pp. ix–xii.

American community. From the emigrants' perspective this could often lead to the type of alienation and marginalisation that Kerby Miller describes in his *Emigrants and Exiles* (1985).[3] From the Yankee perspective this cultural dysphasia was yet another reason to categorise the arriving Irish as inferior to other European stock, and to question whether they might not need to create a new racial category to include this new pariah class.

Despite the very real nature of cultural despair that some immigrants no doubt suffered, and the well-documented anti-immigrant and Know Nothing racism of the mid-century, we know that most immigrants did not cease to function in the new world, and in a relatively short period of time they began to both form and project a new ethnic pride and identity. This was possible because social memory was not a fixed attribute acquired in Ireland and carried abroad; rather it was, and is, an active search for meaning that seeks to integrate the received knowledge of past times and spaces with the realities of contemporary place and necessity. The precise way in which this process took place in mid-nineteenth-century America would have enormous impact on Irish-American society, and upon Irish and American nationalisms.

My particular interest in this subject arose out of a casual conversation about the Famine that I had with a military historian. His remark was astonishing to me. 'Without the Irish Famine, the Union Army would have been defeated.' This simple, and debatable assertion of the connection between the most momentous mid-century events in these two very different countries, set me rethinking some earlier work I had done on Irish-American nationalism. Just how did the context of Civil War America shape the nature of immigrant perceptions? The diaries and letters of Irishmen serving in the Civil War reveal that the experience of this second great trial by ordeal had a very different effect and meaning to them from their first, the Great Hunger. And while it may seem odd to use the term 'positive' when commenting upon such a massive bloodletting, there is no question that for the Famine Irish of America the Civil War provided an opportunity to transform both their role in American society and their self-image in positive ways. This transformation was, without question, the single most formative fact in the reworking of Irish-American social memory, and Irish-American nationalism.

That the Irish community in America was in dire need of a transforming experience cannot be doubted. The woes of the Famine immigrants

[3] Kerby A. Miller, *Emigrants and Exiles: Ireland and the Irish Exodus to North America* (Oxford, 1985).

may be too well known to bear repeating. Stories of Famine experience in Ireland were followed by 'middle passage' stories complete with coffin ships and desperate immigrants washed up upon America's shore. These in turn were followed by stories of the new urban landscape; the 'No Irish need apply' signs, pogrom-type riots in Philadelphia and New York, convent burning in Charlestown and, most frightening of all, the emergence of the Know Nothing party in the 1850s. These events and images may have become too familiar, producing groans of recognition from most twentieth-century audiences, but in their own time these were very powerful memory narratives that tracked a crisis of survival as it became a crisis of assimilation.

Less visible, because it was primarily a psychological reality, was the doubt Irish people on the eve of the Civil War harboured about their place in America. Some of their apprehensions were simple and rational responses to the anti-Irish hysteria they experienced. But there were less rational responses as well, responses that were likely derived from Irish more than American experience. For example, when the *Boston Pilot* warned that abolitionists were 'bigoted and persecuting religionists . . . [desiring] the extermination of Catholics by fire and sword'[4] it was engaged with a semantics of Irish social memory as well as Boston reality. This connection with Irish historical memory could serve as a strong anti-assimilation force for Irish-born people who were suspicious of most forms of state power, and especially so of those which resonated with Anglo-Protestant cultural and moral values.

The abolitionist campaign of the 1850s brought this ethnic hostility out into the open: most Irish, following the lead of the Democratic party, and their own perceived economic interests, were hostile to abolition and certainly did not wish to engage in war in order to coerce the South. The political situation was further poisoned by the fact that Know Nothings and Republicans were often interchangeable in the New England and Mid-Atlantic states where most Irish lived. But when war came everything changed. Irishmen were ready to serve their new country in very large numbers.[5] Even the very anti-abolitionist *Boston Pilot* proclaimed in January 1861: 'Catholics have only one course to adopt, only

[4] Quoted in *Commanding Boston's Irish Ninth: The Civil War Letters of Colonel Patrick R. Guiney, Ninth Massachusetts Volunteer Infantry*, ed. Christian G. Samito (New York, 1998), p. xxii.

[5] While the Irish volunteered in very large numbers, they also resented and resisted conscription and the bounty system that allowed affluent men to escape military service. For a useful account of the most dramatic moment of resistance see: Iver Bernstein, *The New York City Draft Riots: Their Significance in American Society and Politics in the Age of the Civil War* (New York, 1990).

one line to follow. Stand by the Union; fight for the Union; die for the Union.'[6]

It is dangerous to generalise about the many reasons that led so many individual Irishmen to the armies of the Republic. This war, like most other long wars, would offer many different paths to service. Many Irish joined in a flush of enthusiasm for the Union which had offered them shelter from Famine; others enlisted for want of other employment; others to gain the bounty that was offered; and still others were drafted.[7] This chapter offers three very different cases of Irish Americans entering the fray. We can not even begin to imagine how 'typical' they were, but the point is not to attempt such a mapping of Irish motivations, but to present some preliminary observations upon the ways in which soldiers themselves began the process of interpreting their experience. The three primary examples I have chosen illustrate much variation, yet they also illustrate that different paths might lead to the same destination.

Peter Welsh of the 28th Massachusetts regiment may be the most 'typical'. The 32-year-old, newly married carpenter went on a wild drinking spree in Boston in September 1862. To avoid his wife's anger, he took the safer course and joined the most violent conflict ever experienced in the Americas. In a letter to her, written eleven days after his enlistment from the safety of a battlefield in Virginia, he explained,

> it grieves my heart to think that you are there so lonly . . . you know i never would have left you only i was crazy from that acursed missfortune i fell intoo however you need not be afraid of my drinking now for there is no licker allowed in the army nor no person is alowed to sell it to soldiers and that is much the best there is hundreds of men here who got in to it in the same way as i did but do not think that i am sorry for coming for it was my wish . . . the only thing i am sory for is leaving you allone and for the unfortuante spree drove me to it. [*sic*][8]

Of course not all joined in such cavalier fashion: another Irish American, Patrick O'Rorke, provides us with a very different perspective upon the Irish in the war, and in American society. Whereas Peter Welsh's experience seems to confirm the images of the reckless Boston Irish, O'Rorke's experience underscores the danger of stereotypes and the importance of social geography in understanding immigrant experience.

6 Guiney, *Civil War Letters*, p. xxiv.
7 See Miller, *Emigrants and Exiles*, pp. 359–61.
8 Peter Welsh, *Irish Green & Union Blue: The Civil War Letters of Peter Welsh*, ed. Lawrence Kohl with Margaret Cossé Richard (New York, 1986), p. 17.

O'Rorke's origins were as humble as any: he was born into a landless labouring family in Co. Cavan in 1836. He emigrated with his family to Montreal – the destination of the poorest of Irish people. The O'Rorkes followed a well-worn path crossing into upstate New York and eventually settled in Little Dublin, a neighbourhood of Rochester, New York. There Patrick O'Rorke senior worked as an unskilled labourer. In some ways this story parallels that of Peter Welsh, whose family history included a stay in Nova Scotia before arrival in Boston. But Rochester was a very different place than Boston; its rapidly expanding industrial economy created a very different social dynamic. The young O'Rorke did so well at the public elementary school that he was offered a scholarship to the new University of Rochester. But, in a reminder of the complex effects of sectarianism, his mother would not allow the young Patrick to enroll in the new Baptist University. Instead he went to work in the Hebard Steam Marble Works where he learned to be a marble cutter, a skilled labouring job that represented real social progress.

O'Rorke might have remained a marble cutter, but for the less ethnically and class-stratified nature of the rapidly growing industrial towns of New York. In 1857 Congressman John Williams, a native New Yorker, nominated O'Rorke for the US Military Academy, and the secretary of war, one Jefferson Davis, conferred an appointment upon O'Rorke. Upon his entry to West Point he became the only foreign-born member of his class and perhaps the first Irish Catholic to attend the academy. O'Rorke graduated on 24 June 1861, first in a class that was graduated early because of the war. On 3 July he met President Lincoln who came to greet the young officers on their way to the front. On 16 July he saw his first combat.

We can follow in detail the experience of a third Irish American presented in an unpublished war memoir written in the 1870s by William McCarter of Philadelphia. McCarter joined the 116th Pennsylvania Infantry, which was later combined with the 28th Massachusetts, the 69th New York, and the 140th New York to form the famous Irish Brigade. McCarter, who was born in Derry in 1840, emigrated with his parents to Philadelphia where he became a tanner. Unlike Peter Welsh, he enlisted with both a clear head and a coherent set of political reasons. As he explained it, he enlisted

> because of my love for my whole adopted country, not the North, nor the South, but the Union, one and inseparable, its form of government, its institutions, its Stars and Stripes, its noble, generous, brave and intelligent people ever ready

to welcome, and to extend the hand of friendship to the downtrodden and oppressed of every clime and people ... I owed my life to my whole adopted country.[9]

Such sentiments are to be found in many of the diaries and letters of Irishmen serving in the Union army. But even those who enlisted for less noble reasons felt the need to explain their situations in the context of Irish experience. And in fact one of the fullest discussions of the larger meaning of the war is to be found in a letter by our inebriated enlistee, Peter Welsh. In a letter to his father-in-law in Ireland, Welsh tried to explain why he was serving in the army, and why in particular he had accepted the honour and danger of carrying the regiment's battle flag.

First he had to contend with his father-in law's hostility to all military service, a hostility that Welsh located in an uncompromising Irish nationalism:

I know pretty well in what light people view soldiering in Irland Nor do i wonder that such a feeling exists For i consider an Irishman who volunterly enlists in the British service merits the utter contempt of his countrymen Seven centuries of persecution Chrurches Convents and Monesteries plundered and destroyed ... inocent women and children slaughtered in cold blood With inumberable other barbarities of the most fiendish description ... comited in unfortunate Irland by that prostitute of nations that amalgamation of hipocricy base treachry and debauchry called the British Government. [*sic*][10]

There is little to surprise here, but as Welsh moves to stress the differences which inform his life as an American we can see the process by which Civil War experience was both educating Irish Americans about their new nation and facilitating an emotional and psychological bond between soldiers and their adopted land:

In this country it is very different. Here we have a free goverment just laws and a Constitution which guarentees equal rights and privelages to all Here thousands of the sons and daughters of Ireland have come to seek a refuge from tyranny and persecution at home... Here they have an open field for industry. ... Here Irishmen and their decendents have a claim a stake in the nation and an interest in its prosperity Irishmen helped to free it from the yoke of Britain ... and have rushed by thousands to the call of their adopted country... Their blood stained every battlefield of this war... We who survive them have a double motive then to nerve us to action We have the same nationel political and social interests at stake not only for ourselves but for

[9] William McCarter, *My Life in the Irish Brigade: The Civil War Memoirs of Private William McCarter, 116th Pennsylvania Infantry*, ed. Kevin E. O'Brien (Campbell, CA, 1996), p. ix.

[10] Welsh, *Irish Green & Union Blue*, p. 100.

coming generations and the opressed of every nation for America was a comon asylum for all. [*sic*][11]

Welsh then returns to an overtly Irish nationalist argument, but with a special American spin:

America is Irland's refuge Irland's last hope destroy this republic and her hopes are blasted If Ireland is ever ever [to be] free the means to acomplish it must come from the shores of America.... When we are fighting for America we are fighting in the interest of Irland striking a double blow cutting with a two edged sword For while we strike in defence of the rights of Irishmen here we are striking a blow at Irlands enemy and opressor. [*sic*][12]

Welsh's linkage of Irish and American nationalism was common currency on both the real and virtual battlefields of the war. Even the *Boston Pilot,* which as we have seen opposed abolition and the coercion of the South before the war, could find its rationale for 'changing sides' in this sort of nationalism. The *Pilot* offered an amazingly simple view of the dynamic connecting the trans-Atlantic Irish community in hostility to Britain and the Confederacy:

When we Irish are side by side with England in any quarrel, we *must* be in the wrong. It is the natural instinct in our race to hate the English side, and take the other; and if the southern States of America have England for their backer, they must look on it as a thing of fate to have Ireland for their foe.[13]

The hardly educated Peter Welsh offered a more sophisticated perspective that fuses Irish nationalism with a very American positivism:

England hates this country because of its growing power and greatness She hates it for its republican liberty and she hates it because Irishmen have a home and a government here ... England hates this country because we have out riveled her as a naval power and are fast outriveling her as a commercial power There is but one step more which a few years of peacefull progress will acomplish that is to surpass her as a manufacturing nation and Englands star of asendency will have set to rise no more ... Such motives have influenced me with the desire that... i might one day have an oppertunity... to strike a blow for the rights and liberty of Irland. [*sic*][14]

Welsh ends his discussion of politics by shifting to the personal:

It is just nine months since i joined the service i am color sergeant of my regiment i carry the green flag of Erin all the Irish regiments cary the green flag as well

[11] Ibid., p. 101.
[12] Ibid., p. 102.
[13] Guiney, *Civil War Letters*, p. xxiv, note.
[14] Welsh, *Irish Green & Union Blue*, p. 103.

as the national flag I received the green flag on last St. Patricks day i feel proud to bear the emblem of Irelands pride and glory and it shall never kiss the dust while i have strenght to hold it. [*sic*][15]

Welsh's pride and nationalism provide an unusually full and eloquent example of the ways in which Irish and American nationalisms were engaging – and fusing. His ideas, expressed in correspondence, are especially useful to the historian. Unlike the memoirs and autobiographies composed after the war, Welsh's letters provide us with the immediate battlefield responses unmediated by either the knowledge of the war's resolution, or by the interpretations of other, more elite commentators. Of course, there are clear signs here of influence from the Nationalist press, and perhaps IRB education; and letters, especially to one's father-in-law, are subject to other forms of mediation. Still, their precise location in the moment of the event, rather than in memory, makes them invaluable – not only for what they clearly demonstrate about the currents of Irish and American nationalism at work in the 1860s, but also because they help us to evaluate the less precisely located sources such as memoirs and edited diaries.

What is most compelling about Welsh's letters was widely shared among men in Irish regiments. Though normally expressed with a less-developed analysis, nearly all those who have left records shared Welsh's pride in identity as a member of an Irish regiment and in the reputations that these regiments were earning for courage and spirit. In some ways the most interesting perspective on the identity question comes from William McCarter, for unlike the stereotype of Irish Brigade members, McCarter was not a Catholic.[16] One might expect an Ulster Protestant to be immune to, or at least somewhat insulated from, the appeal of Irish ethnic pride and nationalism. One might also suspect that membership in an overwhelmingly Catholic Brigade might have been the cause of some friction. But such presumptions seem an unwarranted imposition of latter-day sectarian realities into the Civil War era. Save for one overt comment, only a very careful reader of McCarter's memoir would discover his place in the sectarian geography of the Irish-American community. The primary clue is to be found in the delight that he took in the Protestant hymns that the regiment sang. In one poignant

[15] Ibid., pp. 103–4.

[16] McCarter does not reveal which church he belonged to, but makes clear his Protestant identity, and his ease and familiarity with Methodist services: see McCarter, *My Life in the Irish Brigade*, p. 49.

description he recounts the massed voices of the regiment singing the 'Old Hundredth':

> oh, what a thrill it sent through every heart. I never heard such strong music since then. Think of it 14 or 15 hundred men all in the uniform of United States soldiers, raising their voices in such a place and under such circumstances to the throne of God . . . But my powers to do justice in describing these meetings and their effects upon the troops come far short of what is necessary. I may, however, note that they were a source of much comfort and encouragement to myself and others.[17]

McCarter's disapproval of alcohol abuse is the only other apparent sign of his confessional distinction from the regimental fellows with whom he eagerly joined in manifestations of Irish pride and identity. He records with glee the importance of flags, Green and Star-spangled, as New York's 69th was given permission to lead the entry into a town from which the brigade had just driven the enemy: 'With banners gaily floating in the breeze – the glorious Stars and Stripes and the emblems of the little Emerald Isle over the sea, the Green Flag so feared, dreaded, and shunned by the Rebs.'[18] The iconography of these regimental flags varied, but certain elements were standard: the green background, the golden harp with sunburst, the wreath of shamrock, and the thirty-four Stars of the Union. The 28th Massachusetts stressed continuity with past Irish valour by adding the Irish rallying cry, 'Faugh a Ballagh' ['Clear the way'], while the 9th Massachusetts provided a fuller, more American commentary that announced to all that the Irish were part of the American family by both fact and choice: 'Thy Sons by Adoption, thy Firm Supporters and Defenders from Duty, Affection and Choice.' Elsewhere, William McCarter records with obvious pride a conversation with a rebel prisoner who had a different take on the shamrock flag. To the Rebel prisoner it was that 'damned infernal Green Flag'. The rebel continued: 'It gave us a sickening dose at Antietim . . . I tell you boys, we can lick you out of your Yankee shoes every day in the year with the musket or rifle. . . . But your "cold steel" and the way you wild Irishmen use it, we cannot stand.'[19]

Sadly, for the Irish Brigade, the rebel prisoner was wrong. The Irish charge could be withstood even when led by the Star-Spangled Shamrock flag. At Fredricksburg, the rebel forces demonstrated that the Irish could

[17] Ibid., pp. 49–50.
[18] Ibid. p. 33.
[19] McCarter, *My Life in the Irish Brigade*, p. 40.

not charge successfully uphill against well-prepared infantry defences supported by artillery. Of course, no sane commander would commit such a blunder. But that is what happened at the fierce battle of Fredricksburg where the Irish Brigade made their awful charge at Marye's Heights, and where they consolidated both their reputation and their self-image as the most determined Americans. After futilely trying to force Lee to engage on ground favourable to his army, General Burnside, commander of the Army of the Potomac decided to force the issue and try to achieve a breakthrough via a frontal assault on well-established Confederate positions overlooking the town of Fredricksburg, Virginia. On that fateful day, 13 December 1862, Burnside had already committed and lost an entire regiment in a hopeless charge up Marye's Heights. But he remained committed to the assault and the Irish Brigade was sent forward. They had to march past the demoralised survivors of the first charge, and then over their dead. The next few hours would end the war for many an Irishman, including Private McCarter who received multiple wounds in the desperate charge. He described the last moments before the charge:

> As Gen. Meagher was about to lead the Irish Brigade . . . where French's brigade had already been smashed . . . he appeared before his troops carrying green boxwood – ordering his officers to have each man place a sprig in his hat – so that the rebs would know who was coming.

The 28th Massachusetts was given centre place during the charge because the 69th New York, which would normally have held the centre of the line, had seen its battle flag destroyed in earlier action; Meagher insisted on the Green flag front and centre.

It is difficult to offer any useful observations about the actual charge at Fredricksburg. Militarily it was a blunder of immense proportions, a military insanity ominously prophetic of charges made by other Irishmen at the Somme a half century later. And ironically, the mayhem inflicted upon the Irish Brigade was partly the work of other Irishmen. The most serious damage inflicted upon Meagher's Irish Brigade came from the Georgia Brigade. Many of the Georgians were also recent Irish immigrants and recognised the Yankees advancing upon them as countrymen. They reportedly cried out: 'Oh, God, what a pity! Here comes Meagher's fellows!'[20] The deadly fire that the Georgia Irish then directed at their fellow Irish underscores the limits of ethnic solidarity, but it did not

[20] Ibid., p. vi.

prevent the formation of a narrative of this battle that identified, for well over a century, 'Irish', 'Union' and 'Heroism'.

The charge so caught the imagination of the Union that for over a century it would be recalled as one of the great tragic heroic moments of the war. And for each following generation of young Irish Americans it would be a powerful icon of Irish and American virtue that served to fix their identity as the core martial caste of America's citizen army – and separate it from the equally awful, but meaningless, suffering of the Famine. The recognition of the role of the Irish in the martial efforts of the Union was immediate. The importance of this battle in the narrative of Irish valour was recognised on the battlefield by friend and foe alike. Two of the most compelling descriptions of the charge came from those who watched the charge from behind the Confederate lines. The London *Times* correspondent connected it with past markers of Irish military valour in Europe:

> Never at Fontenoy, Aluera, or at Waterloo was more undaunted courage displayed by the sons of Erin. The bodies which lie in dense masses within 40 yards of Colonel Walton's guns are the best evidence what manner of men they were who pressed on to death with the dauntlessness of a race which has gained glory on a thousand battlefields, and never more richly deserved it than at the foot of Marye's Heights on the 13th day of December, 1862.[21]

The most telling, and eerie, account of this charge is that written by one of the Confederate generals who commanded against the Irish, General George E. Pickett. The Confederate positions were so secure on this December day that Pickett's regiment was not needed. He had the chance to watch the entire charge as it carried that Green Flag of the 28th to within 20 yards of the stone wall behind which Rebel infantry rained fire down upon the Irish. After the battle Pickett wrote to his fiancée:

> Your soldier's heart almost stood still as he watched those sons of Erin fearlessly rush to their death. The brilliant assault on Marye's Heights of their Irish Brigade was beyond description. Why, my darling, we forgot they were fighting us, and cheer after cheer at their fearlessness went up along our lines.[22]

Ironically, it was General Pickett who would lead just such a frantic charge at Gettysburg in a last-ditch effort to save the Confederate cause. And, with the grim irony of this most civil war, Irish survivors of

[21] Quoted ibid., p. viii.
[22] Ibid., p. vii.

Fredricksburg would be among those who repelled this equally famous display of hopeless bravery.

Of the 1,200 Irishmen of the Irish Brigade who charged Marye's Heights that day, 545 fell, including 3 of the 5 regimental commanders.[23] Only 250 men could answer muster the next day. After the battle, General Meagher travelled to Washington to plead personally with President Lincoln to remove the brigade from the front until it could be supplied with new recruits. Lincoln refused, it is said, because he believed that retiring the Green Flag at this dark time, even temporarily, would provide too great a victory for the Rebels.

So the Irish brigade soldiered on, filling in its voids with raw recruits, its survivors rapidly ascending in the ranks. Peter Welsh became a sergeant; Patrick O'Rorke rose to the command of the 140th New York. Both men were present at Gettysburg, the crisis battle of the war where Northern numbers finally broke Southern resolve. The two would play direct roles in the central dramatic pieces of the larger battle – O'Rorke at Little Round Top, and Welsh in the centre of the line. Welsh's role is obscured by the mayhem of that place and his relative anonymity amidst the thousands who fought there. However, Col. Patrick O'Rorke led his Irishmen in a furious action that saved the day on the Union flank, helped force Pickett's doomed charge, and created an important symbolic triumph for Irish America.

At the opening of this gigantic set piece of the Civil War, the Union army had managed to gain a rare tactical advantage of high ground, but with characteristic speed of analysis and deployment, Lee came close to turning the Union flank by taking a lightly defended outlying hill known as 'Little Round Top'. Col. O'Rorke, unaware of any crisis, was leading his regiment along a road on the uncontested and peaceful side of this hill. He had orders to bring his regiment into line in the centre of the Union lines some miles away. As he and the regiment marched along a rider suddenly galloped down the hill. The rider was Brigadier General Gouveneur K. Warren, chief engineer. While still 50 yards away from O'Rorke he began to shout orders. This presented O'Rorke with a dilemma: Warren outranked O'Rorke but, as an engineer, he had no authority to countermand orders of a field officer like O'Rorke. Warren excitedly explained that the Michigan regiment which was trying to hold the hill was evaporating under a massive and withering Rebel attack. Joseph Leeper, captain of Company E later reported the conversation

[23] Ibid., p. viii.

between the mounted officers:

GENERAL WARREN: Paddy, give me a regiment.
O'RORKE: We have been ordered to support 3rd Corps. Gen Weed . . . has gone to select a position.
WARREN: Is that the 140th? If so take your regiment up this hill . . . There is a gap there that must be filled without delay, or the position is gone.
O'RORKE: Head of the column to the left, forward.[24]

General Warren rode off to seek more assistance, while the 140th quick-marched up the steep, rocky and wooded slope. It was not until they were near the summit that they could hear gunfire, and even as they crested the top the heavily forested hillside did not give them any idea of what lay before them. The column had come up in its marching formation of a column of fours – not in position to execute a charge. They also carried unloaded muskets: in the scramble up the hill there had been no time to load their muskets or even fix bayonets.

O'Rorke dismounted his horse, for the descent was too steep, pulled his sabre, and was likely about to give orders to deploy his troops in a proper firing line when he realised that there were massed Rebel troops close and advancing unopposed upon his position. He immediately gave the most unprofessional order, 'Down this way, boys!' and led his men, without bullet or bayonet, forward in a desperate charge. The first two companies of the column followed him with a great cheer and as the forces joined the Rebels fired a murderous volley at point blank range. O'Rorke fell dead immediately but his troops rushed on over his body to engage the advancing rebels in hand-to-hand combat. Meanwhile his adjutant, Porter Farley, worked the remaining companies of the regiment off to the North to establish a firing line. Of the 400 men who climbed Little Round Top, 115 fell in this wild engagement. But they did hold, and the Union flank was protected, eventually forcing Pickett's desperate charge at the centre.[25]

As dramatic and heroic as the 140th's action was, it is the aftermath that fixed the meaning of this carnage. Col. O'Rorke's body was sent home to Rochester where he received a hero's funeral with a solemn funeral mass. After a moving eulogy by Father O'Brien in St Bridget's Church, he was buried in St Patrick's cemetery. The very Catholic and Irish nature of this event could not have been more obvious, but all was

[24] Brian A. Bennett, *The Beau Ideal of a Soldier and a Gentleman: The Life of Col. Patrick Henry O'Rorke from Ireland to Gettysburg* (Wheatland, NY, 1996), p. 117.
[25] Ibid., p. 123.

not Hibernian. The Rochester newspaper described the decoration of the church:

> The sacred edifice was hung in drapery . . . the national flag being everywhere conspicuous. The high altar was decorated with crape, white tassels and other ornaments appropriate to the occasion and produced an exquisite appearance to the eye of the spectators.[26]

These were very likely the first American flags to adorn St Bridget's. On the same day, in the field, his troops passed numerous resolutions in his honour, one ending with 'while the tree of freedom puts forth a single shoot, to his name a garland we shall weave, and keep green his memory in our hearts forever'.[27] Commentators in Rochester were keen to point out that Catholics, Protestants and Jews were present at O'Rorke's funeral, and Rochester's own historian of the nineteenth century noted that the funeral marked a turning point in ethnic and sectarian relations in the city:

> fights which had been quite numerous, with battles between groups of Irish and Germans and Irish and yankees and so forth, none of them appeared again. In other words he not only helped win [and] save the union, but he made a union of Rochester . . . [28]

Perhaps this is something of an exaggeration, but such comments can be found in various forms from every part of the victorious North. And O'Rorke and his grave would become important parts of Irish and American nationalist discourse and celebration for the next half century. The very first Memorial Day parade held in 1868 ended at his grave.

The sacrifices that other Irishmen made were memorialised in other ways. Patrick Guiney, colonel and hero of the Massachusetts 9th regiment who entered Massachusetts politics could find no better way to trace the great change that had taken place in the status of the Massachusetts Irish than to follow the course of the Irish battle flags. In an 1868 campaign speech he revealed both the bitterness of the pre-war era and the transformation that these few but intense years had created: 'Go up to the State House and you will find the torn and faded banners of the Ninth Regiment, and so long as they remain there no man will ever be heard to say that the Irish people living in Massachusetts are enemies of the

[26] Ibid., p. 134.
[27] Ibid., p. 137.
[28] Ibid., p. 140.

republic.'[29] It is impossible for us to understand the emotional charge that this statement carried for Guiney's fellow Irish Americans. But it is worth noting that these flags still hold the central place of honour in the rotunda of the State House in Boston.

Many Irishmen did not live to see that victory. Peter Welsh survived Gettysburg only to be wounded in the final days of the war. He died in hospital as his wife rushed in vain to see the young carpenter who had enlisted so casually two years before. These men paid an extraordinary price for the Union's victory. They also helped to win a great deal for the Irish in America.[30] Their sacrifice earned the larger community acceptance. But perhaps just as importantly it gave a generation that had begun life with the terror and humiliation of the Great Famine an opportunity to redefine themselves as a heroic group who were the authors, not the subjects, of one of the great defining moments of a nation.

Such notions of acceptance via war service are central to many ethnic and racial groups in the United States. But what is less clear, less explored, are the ways in which such a path to citizenship shapes the memory and identity of those who follow the war-time generation. What is the connection between the individual experience and interpretation of the war and the social memory and meaning of the Irish-American community in the post-war era?

In *Social Memory* Fentress and Wickham argue that 'If memory is to be preserved beyond the present continuum, it must be conceptualised and fitted into . . . context.'[31] In the 1860s the contexts in which Irish-American social memory was conceptualised were republicanism, war, blood sacrifice and a militant American nationalism. This was the transit point, the place not only where Irish people were accepted as Americans but, equally importantly, the place at which Irish Americans willingly accepted this new status. The actual experience of the war, and the commemoration and memory of it, also helped to fuse Irish and American nationalisms, and the solder that held them together was martial valour. In turn, these nationalisms, along with militant Catholicism, became the pillars of identity for the Irish in America. Irish Americans were very aware, as Patrick Guiney's reference to battle flags indicates, that their status in the United States was won by the military heroism

[29] Guiney, *Civil War Letters*, p. 252.

[30] See Thomas O'Connor, *Civil War Boston: Home Front and Battlefield* (Boston, MA, 1997) for an excellent discussion of the impact of the war on the urban landscape.

[31] Fentress and Wickham, *Social Memory*, p. 80.

and battlefield sacrifice of individuals such as Patrick O'Rorke and Peter Welsh. This in turn would doom many future Irish Americans to tests of courage that they could not win; but it also connected with a grim moral ethic that the Irish-American community learned during the war. Before the war the Irish had been opposed to efforts by the federal government to coerce the South, they had opposed the abolitionists as dangerous moral extremists and denounced them as fanatics who claimed a higher morality than that of the Constitution.

After the war, however, it was very hard for even the most racist Northern Americans to avoid the attraction of the argument that the war had been a great moral crusade to end slavery, a moral crusade in which the Irish had earned a great credit by dying, and by killing. For many Irish it was very hard to ignore the obvious question: 'Having fought and died to free the slaves, must not the children of Ireland wage a great struggle to free their own nation?' Indeed, having witnessed the ability of the Irish to command and follow during the war, many veterans chose to join the IRB and seek such an Irish republic through violence. Most Irish Americans chose instead to pursue their collective future in exclusively American political terms; but we should not lose sight of the parallel nature of these different paths. The moral and political acceptance of massive violence as a legitimate instrument of a just political cause; the belief that in the end only violence really produces results, and that individual self-sacrifices can redeem a people: these lessons were writ large in American – not Irish – copybooks. They were announced from the pulpit and discussed at the dinner table. And each new generation of Irish Americans had both to learn and rewrite these lessons.

As late as 1960, films such as 'Fighting Father Duffy' and 'The Fighting Sullivans' – wildly patriotic and emotional portraits of Irish-American life and military heroism – were shown in Catholic parochial schools as a way of preparing the next generation 'for your chance', as the nuns put it. Sadly, those nuns were neither alarmist nor romantics; they knew what they were about, and they had powerful allies. During the 1950s and early 1960s the cold warrior leadership of Irish Americans such as Joseph McCarthy, Bishop Fulton J. Sheen and William F. Buckley, each in their different ways, reminded Irish America of its role as the 'praetorian guard' of American democracy. Perhaps no one personified that time and moment better than the man who marked the next major transit point for Irish America in so many ways, John F. Kennedy. It is a cliché now to note that Kennedy's election marked the arrival of Irish Americans as members of the political and economic elite of the United

States. Cliché or not, it is still the essential fact of the public side of the Irish-American tale.

Yet, for the purposes of this chapter, there is another aspect of Kennedy's substance and symbol that is most striking. It was John F. Kennedy who gave the icon of the Irish-American military hero its final form, both by playing the part so well, and by helping to create the conditions that made such militant patriotism impossible to sustain. It would be impossible to imagine a better Irish-American hero than the skipper of PT109 – young, bold, heroic and loyal to his crew even after his ship was destroyed and he was seriously injured. But it is another part of the Kennedy legacy that marks him as the seminal figure in twentieth-century Irish America: Vietnam. It is perhaps appropriate to end this chapter by noting that just as Famine-era Irish people in America were militarised by American experience, their descendents in the late years of the twentieth century were demilitarised by American, not Irish, developments. The bitter legacy of Vietnam fatally injured the broad consensus that had held both left- and right-leaning Irish Americans together along a patriotic axis. Many of the right-leaning figures such as Bishop Sheen and William F. Buckley remained committed to a martial ideology, but nearly all left-leaning and most moderates could not reconcile the mayhem in Vietnam with the older perceived positive virtues of American patriotism.

Some believe that John F. Kennedy himself had come to this conclusion shortly before his murder. However real his reassessment of the morality of hot and cold wars, both of his brothers became vocal critics of the war, and a significant group of other Irish Americans helped to form the anti-war coalition that transformed American politics. Politicians such as Senator Eugene McCarthy and California Governor Jerry Brown and activist priests like the Berrrigan brothers played a critical role in the leadership of the anti-war movement. Most importantly, thousands of Irish-American young men, raised to follow in the footsteps of their fathers, found that military service was either immoral or inconvenient. And, during the course of this long war, the acceptance or rejection of one's military obligation was to matter much more than whether one was an Irish or an Italian American. Despite the divide created within the Irish-American community there was one element of continuity for all its young members: whether they served or resisted service, these young men encountered a radically different experience from the generations of Irish-American young men who had preceded them. Those who resisted the draft found support from dissident Catholic clergy such as the Berrigan brothers or from lay Catholic social radicals such as Michael Cullen of the Catholic Worker movement. The emergence of this Catholic pacifism deeply influenced by Irish Americans would have an important effect upon the Vietnam generation's attitudes towards both American and Northern Irish politics at a critical juncture.

As radical as this departure was, the situation for those who served was perhaps even more painfully different. While those who died in Vietnam did receive patriotic burials, with flags, eulogies and some civic ritual, there was nothing like the communal grieving experience of the Civil War or the world wars. And, for those who returned home alive there was little consolation for their troubles. The general public who did not wish to be reminded of the grim realities of the war often shunned the returning veterans, while those who opposed the war often greeted them with ridicule and open hostility. Yet for many who had marched off to war the most jarring aspect of the experience was the severe disjunction between the images and realities of a dirty colonial war. For such men, like Ron Kovic, author of *Born on the Fourth of July* (1976),[32] the patriotic celebrations that did welcome them home were often more than they could bear.

There were, of course, many other factors altering the nature of Irish-American identity in the post-Kennedy era. The decline in the Catholic church's role in everyday life, the very real improvement in the economic and social position of Irish Americans and their consequent movement from city to suburb, all seriously eroded the very concept of an 'Irish-American identity'.[33] Yet, while the core components of 'traditional' Irish-American identity – 'working class', 'Catholic', and 'urban' – may have eroded during this period, there has been no time in which more Irish Americans have played more important roles in forming US policy towards Irish nationalist issues. Political leaders, journalists, and even historians of this Vietnam generation have processed Northern Irish experiences through lenses tempered by very different martial experience. As we lose our memories of the nineteenth century, and struggle to recalibrate our personal calendars to think of the twentieth as 'the past century', could it be possible that Irish Americans in losing their martial identity have found a new one – that of peace-maker?

[32] Ron Kovac, *Born on the Fourth of July* (New York, 1976).

[33] See Lawrence J. McCaffrey, *Textures of Irish America* (Syracuse, NY, 1992).

CHAPTER 6

'Where Wolfe Tone's statue was not': Joyce, monuments and memory

Luke Gibbons

> Is it possible to wander around a town fraught with memories? . . . we might wonder if there is such a character as a flâneur in *Dubliners*, that is someone who would be immune to memory.
>
> Carle Bonafous-Murat

No self-image has been more reassuring to the modern historian of Ireland than that of debunking nostalgia for the past, of interring romantic Ireland, and all that 'delirium of the brave' as Yeats described it, firmly in its grave. Yet historical method has more in common with romantic nostalgia than it might care to admit, for both are, in fact, products of modernisation, and share a common assumption that the past is dead and gone. One may rejoice over this, while the other may regret it, but the conviction that we are dealing with a world that is lost is essentially the same. In its determination to convert memory into history, not the least of the concessions made by modern historical method to romantic nostalgia is to construe tradition itself as an undifferentiated, organic body of experience, all the more to contrast it to the critical intervention of history. 'A historically tutored memory', as Paul Connerton writes, 'is opposed to an unreflective traditional memory',[1] thereby giving romantic nostalgia precisely the image it craves of a holistic, prelapsarian past. Connerton, in his valuable book *How Societies Remember* (1989), has done much to renew intellectual interest in neglected (or discredited) modes of historical awareness, such as commemorative ceremonies, rituals and other 'performances' of the past bound up with a sense of place, which are often relegated by historians to mere mindless behaviour. As he expresses it:

> It is to our social spaces – those which we occupy, which we frequently retrace with our steps, where we always have access, which at each moment we are capable of mentally reconstructing – that we must turn our attention, if our

[1] Paul Connerton, *How Societies Remember* (Cambridge, 1989), p. 16.

memories are to reappear. Our memories are located within the mental and material spaces of the group.[2]

Yet the temptation remains, particularly where national memory is concerned, to depict any mode of negotiating the past, other than writing (preferably by a professional historian), to be, at best, deluded, or, at worst, a pathology to be purged from the civil sphere.[3]

The linear, cumulative logic of historical method has its equivalent in commemorative practices, however, in the stately, rigidly choreographed parade of the nation in official ceremonies, taking place in what Nietzsche referred to as a 'monumental' time. 'Tradition situates the daily life of the individual', writes Adam J. Lerner, 'in the nation's victory parade, which travels through the streets of the city and through time.'[4] But what of a 'tradition' under colonialism in which the nation is not a victor, and in which its members have, at most, walk-on rather than speaking parts in the official public sphere? Two ways of moving through the 'social spaces' of the modern city may be contrasted here: the orderly procession of state power through the main thoroughfares, with all its pomp and splendour, as against the movements of the 'flâneur', or city stroller, a key figure of modernity, who roams through the streets seemingly at random, but often in the shadow of a counter-public sphere. The latter, I will contend, corresponds to the condition of the inhabitants of Joyce's Dublin, who enjoy the same marginalised relation to the city as the modernist flâneur, at once part of, and yet detached from, official space. As Joyce depicts it, the impact of the massive mobilisation of national sentiment during the centenary of the 1798 rebellion testified not to the backward look of romanticism, but was more akin to the radical, unsettling strategies of the flâneur, with their gestures towards other futures, and alternative narratives of the nation. Instead of displaying the fixity of Nietzsche's 'monumental' time, these oppositional narratives could not even attain the condition of a monument, as is graphically demonstrated in *Ulysses* by the image of the 'five tallwhitehatted sandwich men' passing by the slab at the corner of St Stephen's Green 'where Wolfe Tone's statue was

[2] Ibid., p. 37.

[3] See, for example, the interdiction of popular memory and amateur history in T. W. Moody's 'Irish History and Irish Mythology', which contrasts 'the dead past that historians study' with the 'living present in which we all, historians included, are involved'. T. W. Moody, 'Irish history and Irish mythology', in Seamus Deane (ed.), *The Field Day Anthology of Irish Writing* (3 vols., Derry, 1991), iii, p. 576.

[4] Adam Lerner, 'The nineteenth-century monument and the embodiment of national time', in Marjorie Ringrose and Adam J. Lerner (eds.), *Reimagining the Nation* (London, 1995), p. 178.

not'.[5] It was as if certain forms of memory lodged in the body remained in perpetual motion, like the restlessness of the young Stephen Hero on his endless walks through the city. It is to the radical implications of this dislocated, somatic memory that I shall now turn.

THE SECRET TOUCH OF MEMORY

> Seems to a secret touch telling me memory. Touched his sense moistened remembered.
>
> *Ulysses*, pp. 175–6

In the 'Flâneur' section of his Arcades project, Walter Benjamin cites Ferdinand Leon's marvellous description of how the montage of time in the modern city infiltrates the mind of even the most casual passer-by:

> The most heterogeneous temporal elements thus coexist in the city. If we step from an eighteenth-century house into one from the sixteenth century, we tumble down the slope of time. Right next door stands a Gothic church, and we sink to the depths . . . Whoever sets foot in a city feels caught up as in a web of dreams, where the most remote past is linked to the events of today . . . Things which find no expression in political events, or find only minimal expression, unfold in the cities: they are a superfine instrument, responsive as an Aeolian harp – despite their specific gravity – to the living historic vibrations of the air.[6]

This could be a description of the tremulous cultural climate of Joyce's Dublin, in which various characters go about their business, seemingly oblivious to the forces that are orchestrating their lives. As if responding directly to these historical resonances, the young boy in Joyce's story 'Araby' mixes memory and desire as he carries parcels for his aunt through the busy streets of Dublin on Saturday evenings, the awakening of his ardour for Mangan's sister being interspersed with inchoate social and political experiences:

> Her image accompanied me even in places the most hostile to romance . . . amid the curses of labourers, the shrill litanies of shop boys who stood on guard by the barrels of pigs' cheeks, the nasal chanting of street-singers, who sang a *come-all-you* about O'Donovan Rossa, or a ballad about the troubles in our native land. These noises converged in a single sensation of life for me. . .

These sounds, mingled with his affections for her, take on the force of internal physical sensations, so that his 'body was like a harp and

[5] James Joyce, *Ulysses* (New York, 1961), p. 229.

[6] Walter Benjamin, 'The Flâneur', in *The Arcades Project*, trans. Howard Eiland and Kevin McLaughlin (Cambridge, MA, 1999), p. 435.

her words and gestures were like fingers running along the wires'.[7] In 'Two Gallants', the image of the harp invoked by Benjamin as a conduit between public and private, between culture and the body, acquires emblematic status. As the two emotional predators at the centre of the story, Corley and Lenehan, turn off Nassau Street and pass by the Kildare Street Club on their mission to exploit a vulnerable 'slavey' or servant girl, they encounter a forlorn harpist:

> Not far from the porch of the club a harpist stood in the roadway, playing to a little ring of listeners. He plucked at the wires heedlessly, glancing quickly from time to time at the face of each new-comer and from time to time, wearily also at the sky. His harp, too, heedless that her coverings had fallen about her knees, seemed weary alike of the eyes of strangers and of her master's hands. One hand played in the bass the melody of *Silent, O Moyle*, while the other careered in the treble after each group of notes.[8]

The sexually compromised condition of the harp, with 'her' body exposed pitilessly to the public gaze, links it to the poor servant girl, but also to the abject condition of Ireland, and its ignominious political servitude.[9] For the harp in question, with its allusion to a bare female torso, can only be the symbol of the most radical movement for Irish independence, the United Irishmen. Rather than raising itself to the level of consciousness, this association, with its 'mournful music', percolates physically through Lenehan's body, as is clear from his involuntary actions a short time later when Corley leaves him on his tryst with the servant girl. As Lenehan walks down one side of Merrion Square, his countenance changes:

> Now that he was alone his face looked older. His gaiety seemed to forsake him and as he came by the railings of the Duke's Lawn he allowed his hand to run along them. The air which the harpist had played began to control his movements. His softly padded feet played the melody while his fingers swept a scale of variations idly along the railings after each group of notes.[10]

The 'Duke's Lawn' is that of Leinster House, the family home of Lord Edward Fitzgerald, and this key site of memory in the popular imagination links the forlorn harp directly with the fate of the United Irishmen. It is as if, in keeping with Benjamin's image, Lenehan's comatose body has become an Aeolian harp, strummed not so much by his own fingers

7 James Joyce, 'Araby', in *Dubliners* (Harmondsworth, 1976), pp. 28–9.
8 'Two Gallants' in *Dubliners*, pp. 51–2.
9 For a discussion of the harp as the central image in the story, see Robert Boyle, '"Two Gallants" and "Ivy Day in the Committee Room"', *James Joyce Quarterly*, 1, 1 (Fall, 1963).
10 'Two Gallants', p. 54.

as by his historically charged physical surroundings in the gathering political ferment at the end of the nineteenth century. That Lenehan is no stranger to these memories of the dead is clear from his presence in the offices of *The Freeman's Journal* when the unresolved legacy of the 1798 rebellion, and the exploits of the notorious editor of the paper, the 'Sham Squire', who informed on Lord Edward Fitzgerald, introduce the theme of the Aeolian harp into the 'Aeolus' section of *Ulysses.*[11]

In 'Two Gallants', the reverberations of the past enter Lenehan's body at a somatic level, in keeping with the symptoms of hysterical paralysis which, according to Evelyn Ender,

> denies to its victims the ability to move from impressions and sensations into the realm of thought and language. The figures of hysteria acts as a vivid reminder of the fact that, for certain categories of subjects, consciousness remains secret, not because of a choice but as an imposed condition.

This condition, she continues, citing recent medical literature, surfaces 'among patients who have been cut away from their culturally distant home countries (such as exiles, refugees, and foreign emigrants) and who are deprived of a language in which to express their mental and emotional deprivation'.[12] In Ireland, however, these symptoms were also displayed by those who, like Corley or Lenehan, stayed at home, cut off from the culture which once sustained them, yet infused by its legacy in an almost intravenous fashion on their daily rounds of the city. As Joyce himself describes this pathology in *Ulysses*, in the ventriloquised voice of his favourite prose writer, Cardinal Newman:

> There are sins or (let us call them as the world calls them) evil memories which are hidden away by man in the darkest places of the heart but they abide there and wait. He may suffer their memory to grow dim, let them be as though they had not been and all but persuade himself that they were not or at least were otherwise. Yet a chance word will call them forth suddenly and they will rise up to confront him in the most various circumstances, a vision or a dream, or while timbrel and harp soothe his senses . . .[13]

This could be Lenehan, passing by the Kildare Street Club and the Duke's Lawn, the music of the harp disturbing rather than soothing the savage breast.

For many Dubliners at the turn of the nineteenth century, much of the discomfiture of the past can be seen as withdrawal symptoms from the

[11] *Ulysses*, pp. 125–7.
[12] Evelyn Ender, *Sexing the Mind: Nineteenth Century Fictions of Hysteria* (Ithaca, NY, 1995), p. 19.
[13] *Ulysses*, p. 421.

catastrophes of the 1798 rebellion and of the Great Famine fifty years later, the cultural debris of a fugitive and degraded popular memory. 'Famine, plague and slaughters', Stephen Dedalus ruminates, casting his mind (or body) over the centuries, 'Their blood is in me, their lusts my waves.'[14] In the *Portrait of the Artist as a Young Man*, even monuments seem to be in mourning as the abject condition of 'the droll statue of the national poet of Ireland' in College Green, who is not even named, moves Stephen in an unaccountable way, if only because 'it seemed humbly conscious of its indignity. It was a Firbolg in the borrowed cloak of a Milesian; and he thought of his friend Davin, the peasant student', who, though characterised by 'a quiet inbred courtesy of attention or by a quaint turn of old English speech', nevertheless could repel swiftly 'by a bluntness of feeling or by a dull stare of terror in the eyes, the terror of soul of a starving Irish village in which the curfew was still a nightly fear'.[15] That this residual terror has also coursed through Stephen's veins is clear from his confused response to the flower girl who accosts him outside Trinity College: 'he left her quickly, fearing that her intimacy might turn to gibing, and wishing to be out of the way before she offered her ware to another, a tourist from England or a student of Trinity'. The malaise here is not simply of a sexual or even a personal kind, but one that affects a whole culture in its attempt to come to terms with its shattered past, as is evident on his escape from the girl up Grafton Street:

> Grafton Street, along which he walked, prolonged that moment of discouraged poverty. In the roadway at the head of the street a slab was set to the memory of Wolfe Tone and he remembered having been present with his father at its laying. He remembered with bitterness that scene of tawdry tribute. There were four French delegates in a brake and one, a plump smiling young man, held, wedged on a stick, a card on which were printed the words: *Vive l'Irlande!*[16]

THE TRANSMIGRATION OF SOLES: WALKING AND MODERN MEMORY

> The great reminiscences, the historical shudder – these are a trumpery which he (the flâneur) leaves to tourists, who think thereby to gain access to the genius loci with a military password. Our friend may well keep silent. At the approach of his footsteps, the place has roused; speechlessly, mindlessly, its mere intimate nearness gives him hints and instructions. He stands before Notre Dame de

[14] Ibid., p. 45.
[15] James Joyce, *Portrait of the Artist as a Young Man* (London, 1992), p. 195.
[16] Ibid., p. 199.

Lorette, and his soles remember: here is the spot which in former times the *cheval de renfort* – the spare horse – was harnessed to the omnibus that climbed the Rue de Martyrs toward Montmarte.[17]

One of the highlights of the protracted ceremony on 15 August 1898, which laid 'the slab where Wolfe Tone's statue was not' at the corner of St Stephen's Green, was a stirring rendition of John Kells Ingram's famous poem, 'The Memory of the Dead', first published in *The Nation* newspaper in 1843. Ingram's ballad is striking, as it suggests that even half a century after the 1798 rebellion, a rush of blood to the face was still the most appropriate response of many to the full measure of the calamity: 'Who fears to speak of Ninety-Eight?/ Who blushes at the name?' The alarm displayed by the authorities in Dublin Castle at its publication in *The Nation* newspaper showed that there was good reason for fearing to speak of the memory of the dead.[18] The ballad formed a central part of the prosecution case against Daniel O'Connell, Charles Gavan Duffy (the editor of *The Nation*) and others for sedition in a state trial in 1844. At stake was what might be called the politics of embarrassment, but it is clear that at least where the sentiments of the poem were concerned, it was not the rebellion itself which occasioned shame but the ignominious disavowal by the subsequent generation of that heroic episode ('When cowards mock the patriot's fate,/ Who hangs his head for shame?). Ingram is perhaps playing here on what Christopher Ricks terms the 'ripples or chain reactions of embarrassment',[19] except in this case, the patriot's shame – itself a physical reaction ('Who hangs his head') – is meant to undo the original blushes of the coward, though it has not yet attained the ability to name itself. This inability – or reluctance – to name became part of the defence strategy in the trial, when the counsel for the defence, the colourful James Whiteside, questioned the alleged seditious content of the poem, and even its relation to the 1798 rebellion:

What '98 does it refer to? or how does he [i.e., the prosecution] connect it with the subject matter of this conspiracy? There is not a word of prefatory matter to explain what it refers to. I want to know by what right you are called to presume,

[17] Benjamin, 'The Flâneur'.

[18] As Kevin Whelan notes, the 1840s witnessed the first concerted attempts to reclaim the memory of 1798, with the publication of the first volumes of R. R. Madden's multivolume history of the rebellion; but the caution surrounding the discovery and rededication of Wolfe Tone's grave at Bodenstown, which 'was privately erected in 1844 to prevent embarrassment to O'Connell – indicat[ed] that in the 1840s it was still politically sensitive to engage in any open commemoration of the men of '98'. See Kevin Whelan, *The Tree of Liberty: Radicalism, Catholicism and the Construction of Irish Identity, 1760–1830* (Cork, 1996), p. 168.

[19] Christopher Ricks, *Keats and Embarrassment* (Oxford, 1974), pp. 51 2.

in a criminal case, that it refers to 1798 no more than to 1698, or 1598 or 1498. The expression 1798 does not occur in the song from the beginning to the end.[20]

This relationship between the body, memory and silence is picked up in the gallows humour of the 'Cyclops' section of *Ulysses* when the rush of blood involved in the male physical response to execution – on 'the poor bugger's tool that's being hanged'[21] – provides a cue for the citizen who 'was only waiting for the wink of a word and he starts gassing out of him about the invincibles and the old guard and the men of sixtyseven and who fears to speak of ninetyeight and Joe with him about all the fellows that were hanged, drawn and transported for the cause by drumhead courtmartial and a new Ireland and new this, that and the other'.[22] The citizen's 'gassing out of him' alludes to the earlier episode in 'Sirens' in which a line from Ingram's poem, 'True men like you men', prompts yet another physical response to the memory of the dead, this time in the form of a slow release of a fart by Bloom as he reads Robert Emmet's famous last words in a second-hand shop window along the quays. Emmet's words are rudely interrupted by Bloom's body noise and the sound of traffic which conveniently camouflages his indiscretion:

When my country takes her place among.
Prrprr.
Must be the bur.
Fff. Oo. Rrpr.
Nations of the Earth. No-one behind. She's passed. *Then and not till then.* Tram. Kran, kran, kran. Good oppor. Coming. Krandlkranskran. I'm sure it's the burgund. Yes. One, two. *Let my epitaph be.* Karaaaaaaa. *Written. I have.*
Pprrpffrrppff.
Done.[23]

It is commonplace in Joyce criticism to see this as ridiculing the pieties of nationalist sentiment, and as evidence of Bloom's/Joyce's cosmopolitan sophistication, but within the textual frame of Ingram's poem, it may be that Bloom represents precisely the type of coward who mocks the patriot's fate.[24] Some of the mockery and embarrassment, therefore, may

[20] Henry Shaw, *Authenticated Report of the Irish State Trials 1844* (Dublin, 1844), pp. 429–30.

[21] *Ulysses*, p. 304.

[22] Ibid., p. 305.

[23] Ibid., p. 291.

[24] The desecration of Emmet's speech, as Enda Duffy suggests, may be related to its relegation to a disused commodity in a second-hand shop – though, for Walter Benjamin, it may be precisely this release of commodities from fashion and the immediate pressures of the market which releases their potential utopian energy. See Enda Duffy, *The Subaltern Ulysses* (Minneapolis, MN, 1994), pp. 88–9.

rebound on him, and when, in the 'Cyclops' section, we are told of 'the citizen and Bloom having an argument about . . . the Brothers Sheares and Wolfe Tone beyond on Arbour Hill',[25] it is clear from Joyce's own views recorded elsewhere that his sympathies are more likely to have been with what he referred to as 'the heroes of the modern movement – Lord Edward Fitzgerald, Robert Emmet, Theobald Wolfe Tone, Napper Tandy, leaders of the uprising of 1798' than with their detractors.[26] For Colin MacCabe, Emmet's 'refusal' of the heterogeneity of *writing* in his famous last words can only be explained by a regressive attachment to fixity and essentialism, 'the full unified identity offered by ultranationalism'.[27] But surely it means the direct opposite: the *deferral* (not the refusal) of writing. The inability to achieve the full inscription of the word within a subaltern or colonial culture points to a *lack* of definition, a transitory, indeterminate condition at odds with the homogeneity of the 'imagined communities' of print culture.[28] Emmet's aspirations may not have attained the stability of writing, but they are still words, albeit in an unresolved, transitional state, not unlike the desultory inner speech which many of the inhabitants of Joyce's Dublin carry around in their bodies. This faltering speech – awaiting a clearly defined speaking subject, unsure of its referent – attests not just to the uneven development of print culture, but to the loss of the 'mother tongue', the Irish language, in the wake of the forced modernisation of post-famine Ireland:

– The memory of the dead, says the citizen taking up his pintglass, and glaring at Bloom.
– Ay, ay, says Joe.
– You don't grasp my point, says Bloom. What I mean is . . .
– *Sinn Fein*! says the citizen. *Sinn fein amhain*! The friends we love are by our side and the foes we hate before us.[29]

[25] *Ulysses*, p. 305.

[26] Joyce, 'Ireland, island of saints and scholars', in *The Critical Writings of James Joyce*, ed. Ellsworth Mason and Richard Ellmann (London, 1959), p. 162.

[27] Colin MacCabe, *James Joyce and the Revolution of the Word* (London, 1979), p. 86.

[28] As Emer Nolan points out in her perceptive criticisms of MacCabe's argument, drawing on Benedict Anderson's influential work, writing and print culture were central to state formation in modern nationalism: Emer Nolan, *James Joyce and Nationalism* (London, 1995), pp. 67–8, 191. Elsewhere I have argued that this project of state formation was threatened by the instability of oral culture and its related 'hybrid' expressions, whether in script or printed forms such as political allegory, street ballads, melodrama and other disreputable strands of popular culture: Luke Gibbons, *Transformations in Irish Culture* (Cork, 1996), pp. 134–63. Instead of remaining 'pre-modern' and standing 'outside' writing, moreover, these pose a greater challenge to official hegemony when they are encrypted within manuscript and print culture.

[29] *Ulysses*, p. 306.

The citizen's toast to 'Sinn Féin' is not to Arthur Griffith's political movement, which had not yet been established in mid-1904, but is more likely to refer to the mute condition evoked in T. D. Sullivan's 'The West's Awake', which laments the loss of the Irish language – 'the stranger made that speech a crime' – and looks forward, with perhaps undue optimism, to the lifting of that great silence ('We found that dear tongue weak and low'), and to the restoration of Irish as a living tongue.[30]

The mutations of speech, then, can be seen as a profound cultural disability, but at another level it may testify to an interior history, a process whereby memory becomes part of the inner life of a community that gestures towards, even if it does not always achieve, articulation in public space. As Stephen goes home on holidays from Clongowes through country roads, 'the drivers pointed with their whips to Bodenstown'[31] – the burial place of Wolfe Tone, 'the holiest spot in Ireland' according to Patrick Pearse. This gestural association with Tone is not divulged in the text, but, as Christopher Woods observes, had passed into the local lore of Clongowes and its surrounding district as early as the 1820s.[32] The merging of landscape and history suffuses through Stephen again in the *Portrait* when he gazes out to sea from the Bull Wall, thinking of the Danes and other invaders at Clontarf: 'He heard a confused music within him as of memories and names which he was almost conscious of but could not capture even for an instant; then the music seemed to recede, to recede, to recede.'[33] Stephen's inchoate responses prefigure the stream of consciousness technique deployed in *Ulysses* to capture the sensory overload of the city, but as the example from the *Portrait* indicates, it is not just modernity but the debris of a shattered past which leads to this intensification of emotional life under colonialism.

In her study of the flâneur in modern literature, Anke Gleber relates the multiple array of images and impressions that characterise 'stream of consciousness' narration to the rapidly shifting perspectives experienced in walking through the modern city. For Joyce, however, it would seem that this involves a journey through time as well as space: as Stephen Dedalus gazes at the sea from Dublin Bay, 'So timeless seemed the grey warm air, so fluid and impersonal his own mood, that all ages were as one to him. A moment before the kingdom of the ancient city of

[30] Don Giffard with Robert J. Seidman, *Ulysses Annotated* (2nd edn, Berkeley, CA, 1988), p. 333.
[31] *Portrait*, p. 17.
[32] C. J. Woods, 'Tone's grave at Bodenstown: memorials and commemorations 1798–1913', in Dorothea Siegmund-Schultze (ed.), *Irland: Gesellschaft and Kultur* VI (Halle, 1989), p. 141.
[33] *Portrait*, p. 181.

the Danes had looked forth through the vesture of the hazewrapped city.'[34] In his essay 'On the Difficult Art of Taking a Walk', Franz Hessel, friend and collaborator of Walter Benjamin, describes how the aimless movement of the flâneur through the city subverts the routinised and functional pleasures of the tourist or sightseer: '*Sight seeing.* What a forcible pleonasm!' The tourist guide, he explains, 'now forces our gaze' towards national monuments, 'or is directed towards the Prussian State Bank, meanwhile I glance over at the famous cellar which E. T. A. Hoffman used to frequent'. While the tourist is spirited through the city on a bus, which leaves little time to linger on the sights, the flâneur prefers *site* to *sight*-seeing, unearthing the hidden histories and unexplained details of what is presented to him.[35] This calls to mind one of the rare appearances of the tourist in *Ulysses,* when Stephen finds himself once more outside Trinity College, this time in front of Goldsmith's rather than Moore's statue:

> Two carfuls of tourists passed slowly, their women sitting fore, gripping frankly the handrests. Pale faces. Men's arms frankly round their stunted forms. They looked from Trinity to the blind columned porch of the bank of Ireland where pigeons roocoocooed.[36]

While Hessel's flâneur is diverted by the memory of a great writer, the narrative in *Ulysses* takes a different train of thought, alluding to submerged political rather than literary associations. The Bank of Ireland was, of course, formerly the Irish House of Parliament, and this helps to explain other arrivals at College Green: 'By the stern hand of Grattan, bidding halt, an Inchicore tram unloaded straggling Highland soldiers of a band.' Foley's statue of Grattan bids a halt to the tram, but unlike his illustrious real-life precursor, is in no position to prevent the imperial progress of the army itself, which is last seen, a 'rout of bare-kneed gillies smuggling implements of music through Trinity's gates'. The subdued Celts of another century, like the abject harp in 'Two Gallants' outside the Unionist bastion of the Kildare Street Club, are now reduced to entertaining their colonial masters. According to Gleber, Hessel's version of the flâneur is intent on formulating 'a critique of the collective spirit of edifices that seek to serve a unified representation of German

[34] Ibid., p. 184. For Enda Duffy, the cinematic techniques of the 'Sirens' section produce effects of consciousness not unlike those of a highly mobile flâneur, darting between different spaces of the city: *Subaltern Ulysses*, pp. 89–90. My argument is that such effects traverse time as well as space.

[35] Cited in Anke Gleber, *The Art of Taking a Walk: Flânerie, Literature and Film in Weimar Culture* (Princeton, NJ, 1999), pp. 71–2.

[36] *Ulysses*, p. 228.

nationalism' by retreating into personal or literary reveries, but, as she observes, this also means turning a blind eye towards the more disturbing, political memories associated with certain locations.[37] The grim scene of Rosa Luxemburg's infamous murder, for example, is passed over with insouciant disregard, other than remarking how it 'desecrates' the 'stillness of this bridge'. Nothing could be further removed from the unsettling echoes of the past in Joyce's Dublin, where the jarring perceptual strategies of the colonial flâneur were all too aware of the 'nightmare of history', and could not but register the re-awakening of the nation as it attempted to throw off the dead weight of imperial torpor.

As with the immobile protagonists of Beckett's and Flann O'Brien's fiction, for whom movement of any kind is a heroic endeavour, walking for Stephen Daedalus, often in endless circles around the city, seems to provide a passage of sorts between an enervated body and a troubled soul. As he prepares the paper he is to deliver to the College debating society, Stephen's days, we are told,

> were consumed in aimless solitary walks during which he forged out his sentences. In this manner he had his whole essay in his mind from the first word to the last before he had put any morsel of it on paper. In thinking or constructing the form of the essay he found himself much hampered by the sitting posture. His body disturbed him and he adapted the expedient of appeasing it by gentle promenading. Sometimes during his walks he lost the train of his thought and whenever the void of his mind seemed irreclaimable he forced order upon it by ejaculatory fervours. His morning walks were critical, his evening walks imaginative and whatever had seemed plausible in the evening was always rigorously examined in the light of day.[38]

It was nothing for Stephen and his brother to walk in from Clontarf to the National Library, a distance of several miles, only to 'decide that it was too late to go in to read and so they would set their faces for Clontarf and return in the same manner'.[39] Walking is not pursued as a form of invigorating, outdoor exercise, akin to the Eugene Sandow-type physical jerks recalled by Bloom in *Ulysses*, but rather becomes for Stephen a mode of articulation, a lexicon for the disorienting sensations of the city:

> As he walked through the ways of the city he had his ears and eyes ever prompt to receive impressions. It was not only in Skeat that he found words for his treasure-house, he found them also at haphazard in the shops, on advertisements, in the

[37] Gleber, *Art of Taking a Walk*, p. 79.
[38] James Joyce, *Stephen Hero*, ed. Theodore Spencer (London, 1961), p. 74.
[39] Ibid., p. 41.

mouths of the plodding public. He kept repeating them to himself till they lost all instantaneous meaning for him and became wonderful vocables.[40]

This kind of walking encyclopaedia, the literal embodiment of shifting signifiers, reaches its apotheosis in *Ulysses* in the scene noted above of the 'five tallwhitehatted sandwichmen between Monypeny's corner and the slab where Wolfe Tone's statue was not' who 'eeled themselves turning H.E.L.Y.'S and plodded back as they had come'.[41]

THE FLÂNEUR, MEMORY AND THE SUBALTERN CITY

It is hard to imagine how any careful reader of Joyce could possibly entertain the idea that what is gone is past and fixed. There is no such reassurance to be found in Joyce's writings. On the contrary . . . he illustrates how the present can alter the past and also how the past can burst into the present and shatter it.[42]

The sandwichmen's gesture of turning back at this particular site recalls that of a much greater crowd, the 100,000 or so who thronged the streets of Dublin six years earlier to participate in the ceremony of laying the foundation stone for Wolfe Tone's memorial. Stephen 'remembered with bitterness that scene of tawdry tribute', but the tawdriness is due in his mind not to the ideals of Tone and Parnell, but to their corruption by the alliance between the Catholic church and constitutional nationalism which brought down Parnell.[43] Entering the University building, with its echoes of the rakish Protestant Ascendancy, 'he knew that in a moment when he entered the sombre college he would be conscious of a corruption other than that of Buck Egan and Burnchapel Whaley . . . The Ireland of Tone and of Parnell seemed to have receded in space.'[44] Yet, while falling short of full political articulation, the physical act of 100,000 people moving through the streets of Dublin may have helped to re-awaken the ideals of Tone and Parnell, even among those who, like Mr Kernan in *Ulysses*, were most unsympathetic to them. It was, in fact, the physical traversal of space involved in a grand funeral procession which helped to infuse the parliamentary politics of Parnell with the revolutionary ideals of 1798 in popular memory for, during

40 Ibid., p. 36.
41 *Ulysses*, p. 229.
42 Joseph A. Buttigieg, *A Portrait of the Artist in Different Perspective* (Athens, OH, 1987).
43 Stephen was not alone in expressing his cynicism over conservative nationalist attempts to wrest control of the centenary celebrations: others such as James Connolly and Maud Gonne also drew attention to the gap between the visionary politics of the United Irishmen and what they considered the obsequious careerism of the leading lights in the Irish Parliamentary Party.
44 Joyce, *A Portrait of the Artist*, *Portrait*, p. 199.

his funeral in October 1891, the organisers took the roundabout route of directing the huge cortege past Thomas Street where Lord Edward Fitzgerald was captured and where Robert Emmet was executed.[45] This insurrectionary detour also provided the meandering route for the procession which carried the foundation stone for the Wolfe Tone memorial through the streets of Dublin in 1898, and it is along this route that Mr Kernan in the 'Wandering Rocks' section in *Ulysses* undertakes his business, having washed down a 'good drop of gin' to help him on his way.

Kernan's local knowledge of Irish history has less to do with race memory or a mystical spirit of the place than with the pedestrian fact that he is unconsciously following in the footsteps of the centenary procession six years earlier. As M. J. F. MacCarthy describes the beginning of the vast parade, which 'first defiled past Tone's house in Stafford-street':

> It then pursued its way, with bands and banners, to St Michan's Church, in the vaults of which lie the remains of the Brothers Sheares – unburied, but marvellously preserved; a gruesome sight! – also the remains of Oliver Bond, Jackson, and, it is said, Robert Emmet . . . Moira House, the town residence of Lord Moira in 1798, where many of the United Irishmen were sheltered and entertained by its owner, was next passed. It is now called the Mendicity Institution! Next in order came the site of Robert Emmet's execution in Thomas-street; and the house, No. 151, in the same street, where Lord Edward Fitzgerald was arrested on May 19th, 1798.[46]

Thus, as the lord lieutenant's cavalcade winds its way through nearby streets in the 'Wandering Rocks' section of *Ulysses*, 'Tomgin' Kernan has another reason for thinking of the lord lieutenant's wife as he comes in sight of Thomas Street:

> Down there Emmet was hanged, drawn and quartered. Greasy black rope. Dogs licking the blood off the street when the lord lieutenant's wife drove by

[45] As Pauric Travers points out, this was following the precedent of the Fenian organisation of Terence McManus's funeral in 1861: see Travers, 'Our Fenian dead: Glasnevin Cemetery and the genesis of the republican funeral', in James Kelly and U. MacGearailt (eds.), *Dublin and Dubliners* (Dublin, 1990), pp. 52–72. It is striking that, notwithstanding the timorous outlook of the Irish Parliamentary Party, the Parnellite wing led by John Redmond also drew on the legacy of 1798 for some rhetorical sabre-rattling: 'Its [the '98 centenary's] intensity will be increased by the temporary breakdown of Parliamentary and Constitutional methods which have followed the abandonment and destruction of Mr Parnell, and it will be evidence that, if only the means were at hand, Irishmen would not be loathe again to take up the weapons of revolution to forward their ends. This much the demonstration will certainly mean, and if it succeeds in destroying the idea that because Ireland to-day is peaceful and crimeless therefore she has abandoned the national struggle it will have served a useful end': cited in Senia Pašeta, '1798 in 1898: the politics of commemoration', *Irish Review*, 22 (1998), 49.

[46] Michael J. F. MacCarthy, *Five Years in Ireland: 1895–1900* (London, 1901), p. 396.

in her noddy. Let me see. Is he buried in St Michan's? Or no, there was a midnight burial in Glasnevin. Corpse brought in through a secret door in the wall. Dignam is there now. Went out in a puff.[47]

Kernan's musings have merged here with those of Bloom who had earlier pondered the fate of Emmet as he chanced upon the name of one Robert Emery on a grave in Glasnevin: 'Who lives here? Are laid the remains of Robert Emery. Robert Emmet was buried here by torchlight, wasn't he? Making his rounds.'[48] As Kernan makes his rounds near Island Street, his mind drifts again towards 'Times of the troubles', lamenting the fate of Lord Edward Fitzgerald 'when you look back on it all now in a kind of retrospective arrangement':

Somewhere here Lord Edward Fitzgerald escaped from major Sirr. Stables behind Moira House. Damn good gin that was. Fine dashing young nobleman. Good stock, of course. That ruffian, that sham squire, with his violet gloves, gave him away. Course they were on the wrong side. They rose in dark and evil days. Fine poem that is: Ingram. They were gentlemen. Ben Dollard does sing that ballad touchingly. Masterly rendition. *At the Siege of Ross did my father fall.*[49]

'The good stock' and patriotic credentials of the Fitzgeralds are prefigured in an earlier scene, set in the vaults of nearby St Mary's Abbey, when Ned Lambert shows the Rev. Hugh C. Love around 'the most historic spot in Dublin' where Lord Edward's ancestor, Silken Thomas 'proclaimed himself a rebel in 1534': 'Hot members they were all of them, the Geraldines.' The Rev. Love, according to Lambert, is 'writing a book about the Fitzgeralds . . . He's well up in history, faith.'[50] But Lambert and Tom Kernan are also imbued with history, even if their sense of the past has not found its way into writing. In Kernan's case, the wayward sentiments precipitated by the physical act of walking are at odds with his official deference towards colonial rule, as if his body doesn't know what his mind is doing. His patriotic reveries distract him from the passing cavalcade, causing him to miss a close-up view of the lord lieutenant: 'His Excellency! Too bad! Just missed that by a hair. Damn it! What a pity!'[51]

In this montage of distractions, it seems that history is indeed to blame. Instead of giving rise to the fixity of monumental time, history in a

[47] *Ulysses*, p. 240.
[48] Ibid., p. 114.
[49] Ibid., p. 241.
[50] Ibid., p. 231.
[51] Ibid., p. 241.

subaltern culture may undo the ossification of the past, countering the stasis and authority of official memory. 'In Ireland we are not a statue-building people', declared *The Nation* in 1888, 'few of our immortals live either in stone or in bronze.'[52] It is true that commemorative ceremonies, like public monuments, have the capacity to freeze and immobilise the past, and there is little doubt that it was with this in mind that the more conservative elements in the Irish Parliamentary Party, led by John Dillon, sought to place their stamp on the centenary celebrations. This helps to explain Stephen's aversion to the wooden responses of the delegates at the commemoration ceremony – the hapless French delegate carrying '*Vive l'Irlande!*' wedged on a stick – but his recoil from the stilted ceremony may also be seen as part of a more general indictment in Joyce's work of the deadening force of habit on people's lives. In their most authoritative, stately forms, commemoration ceremonies, like monuments, institutionalise habit at the heart of the public sphere, attempting not just to represent the past but to freeze it through pomp and ritual. Much of the routinised behaviour of Joyce's Dublin – the paralysis of Mr Duffy and Maria, the desiccation of Eveline and others casualties of domestic life, the clichés and second-hand sentiment that pass for political conviction – reveal its denizens to be creatures of habit, with all its unreflective, leaden imprint on everyday life.[53] Yet as Joseph Buttigieg and others have pointed out, this unthinking acquiescence in the face of the past is countered by a more radical somatic or 'involuntary' memory in which 'epiphanies' of sorts – chance encounters, random events or incidental details 'not exceeding the span of casual vision and congruous with the velocity of modern life'[54] – break up what Doris Lessing refers to as 'the paving stones of habit', thus allowing characters to escape, however momentarily, the tedium of their existence. As Buttigieg describes this form of counter-memory in Joyce:

> When the past escapes the deadness imposed upon it, when it manifests itself as something new and unknown, when it ceases to be the familiar object of a dull memory, then the past has the power to jolt the Dubliner into recognising for the first time what he previously thought he knew so well. This experience is

[52] Gary Owens, 'National monuments in Ireland, *c.* 1870–1914: symbolism and ritual', in Brian P. Kennedy and Raymond Gillespie (eds.), *Ireland: Art into History* (Dublin, 1994), p. 105.

[53] Habit, in this sense, may have less to do with the notion of an 'unthinking', premodern tradition, but may be precisely the product of the mechanised ennui and boredom of modern commodity culture. See Seamus Deane, *Strange Country: Modernity and Nationhood in Irish Writing since 1790* (Oxford, 1997), ch. 4, and Patrice Petro, 'After shock/between boredom and history', in Patrice Petro (ed.), *Fugitive Images: From Photograph to Video* (Bloomington, IN, 1995), pp. 265–84.

[54] *Ulysses*, p. 720.

disturbing and painful, like a birth, for it deprives one of mastery over a world rendered comfortable by habit.[55]

Though habit seeks to inure the individual against such transitory experiences, the distracted attention of the modernist flâneur is uniquely open to the vicissitudes of the rapidly changing city. What is striking in *Ulysses* is that popular memory under colonial rule is open to such incursions of chance and contingency, thus bringing the radical sensibility of the flâneur to bear on even the most carefully controlled spectacles of public demonstrations and commemorative rituals. We can assume, given his Unionist sympathies, that Tom Kernan does not consciously call up 'the memory of the dead', but that such thoughts, lodged in his body, are prompted by his participation in such rituals, his involuntary return, as it were, to the scenes of the crime. One turned a corner to encounter not just dislocations in space, but the shards and fragments of time. For Benedict Anderson, 'it is the magic of nationalism to turn chance into destiny',[56] but in the uneven temporality of Joyce's Dublin, this alchemy is reversed and destiny converted back into the dross of everyday life.[57]

The narrative equivalent of this traversing of historical space is the street ballad, the movement of words and music through the streets of the city. For Charles Gavan Duffy, ballads exert their 'involuntary influences' in a manner akin to the rhythms of walking: 'the snatches of old sayings that imply so much more than they express; the traditional forms into which the liquid thought runs as unconsciously as the body drops into its accustomed gait'.[58] It is not surprising, therefore, to find stray snatches of key ballads relating to '98 – 'The Memory of the Dead' and 'The Croppy

[55] Buttigieg, *A Portrait of the Artist in Different Perspective*, p. 31. As John S. Rickard describes it, drawing on Buttigieg's formulation, the past here operates not as a protective barrier against the present, but as a painful, involuntary stimulus opening up parts of people's lives they have been trying to escape from, and which for that reason exert all the more control over their lives. Involuntary memory, therefore, restores agency of a kind, if only by disrupting the force of habit: see *Joyce's Book of Memory: The Mnemotechnic of Ulysses* (Durham, NC, 1998), especially ch. 2.

[56] Benedict Anderson, *Imagined Communities: Reflections on the Origins and Spread of Nationalism* (London, 1991), p. 19.

[57] For a perceptive critique of this aspect of Anderson's analysis, drawing on Homi Bhabha's notion of uneven temporalities, see Selina Guinness's argument that 'there are reasons to suppose that the nation [in 1898] was a far less stable concept than this monumental emblem proposes': Selina Guinness, 'The year of the undead, 1898', in P. J. Mathews (ed.), *New Voices In Irish Criticism* (Dublin, 2000), p. 22. Guinness proceeds to argue, however, that the pervasiveness of the past results in an elision of the present. But the immersion of the flâneur in the quotidian details of the city can be seen as reinserting the present into narratives of the nation.

[58] Charles Gavan Duffy, 'Introduction' to *The Ballad Poetry of Ireland* [1845] (Dublin, n.d.), p. 25.

Boy' – punctuating Kernan's and others' movements through the colonial city. When Ben Dollard gives his 'trenchant rendition' of 'The Croppy Boy' in 'Sirens', the stanzas are dispersed through time and space in the wandering minds of those present: yet the ballad is as familiar to them as their own memory: 'They know it all by heart. The thrill they itch for', as they await the climax when the bogus priest hearing the boy's confession is exposed as a yeoman captain. Though Bloom sees this tragic past as over and done with – 'All gone. All fallen. At the Siege of New Ross his father, at Gorey all his brothers fell. To Wexford, we are the Boys of Wexford, he would. Last of his name and race'[59] – not the least of the ironies of his lament is that it is immediately preceded by the concept of 'metempsychosis' or eternal return which recurs throughout *Ulysses*. On this occasion, however, Molly's earlier mispronunciation – 'met him pike hoses' – takes on a new political resonance, the pike being the notorious standard weapon of the Wexford croppies in the rebellion.[60]

Commenting on the differences between two sets of patriotic and commemorative symbols in American political culture, Andrew Starks draws a distinction between symbols that are relayed through time, such as holidays, processions and official songs or music, and those that occupy space, such as flags and monuments:

> When it comes to official songs and holidays, the private individual – because it is he and not the State who must actively do the expressing or the observing – can far more easily detach himself from whatever it is they signify . . . This kind of capacity for personal disavowal – for a private individual to distance himself from whatever is represented by a particularly officially staged patriotic symbol – exists in the same way neither with flags nor monuments.[61]

Citizens can refuse to stand for the national anthem, or can remain silent, or can avoid official Fourth of July commemorations by 'spending the day playing games or frolicking in taverns'. By contrast, flags and monuments are unavoidable in that they 'constitute "Government speech". They identify all citizens, even though they profoundly dissent from them, with whatever ideas they represent.'[62] Stark's observation

[59] *Ulysses*, p. 285.

[60] At a more elliptical level, the eighteenth-century connotations of 'hoses' have been signalled earlier – 'Merrion square style. Balldresses, by God, and court dresses . . . any God's quality of cocked hats and boleros and trunkhose' (*Ulysses*, 267) – and 'met him' may refer to the famous evocation of Napper Tandy in 'The Wearing of the Green': 'I met with Napper Tandy, and he took me by the hand.' Stray fragments of the ballad (e.g. 'every country they say, our own distressful included' [*Ulysses*, 643]) recur throughout *Ulysses*.

[61] Andrew Starks, 'Flying the flag', *Times Literary Supplement*, 30 Apr. 1999, p. 6.

[62] Ibid.

is correct for the most part, even if it fails to allow for the distressed narratives of monuments such as the Vietnam memorial in Washington, and which call for movement through time as well as space. Significantly, these address (painful) private as well as public memory and are characterised by extensive verbal inscriptions – the names of the fallen – which cut across their arresting visual qualities. This decomposition of the sign is already captured in *Ulysses* in the vignette where one of the sandwichmen falls behind as the lord lieutenant's carriage passes by: 'At Ponsonby's corner a jaded white flagon H. halted and four tallhatted white flagons halted beside him, E.L.Y.'S while outriders pranced past and carriages.'[63]

The inability of language to transcend the limits of the body – if only due to physical exhaustion – points to a culture whose unresolved history remains impervious to the talking cure. No doubt the regimentation of the body in post-Famine Ireland – the 'stationary march' decried by Stephen – sought to compensate for this, dulling the body to the pain of cultural memory. Distinguishing between the bodily practices of habit, and the operation of memory, Paul Connerton writes that:

> in compulsive repetition the agents fail to remember the prototype of their present actions. On the contrary, they have the strong impression that the actions in which they are 'caught up' are fully determined by the circumstances of the moment. The compulsion to repeat has replaced the capacity to remember.[64]

It is in this sense that commemorative practices which impose the regularity of habit on history seek to bury rather than to praise the past – or at least to stifle the spirited and often explosive energy that attended the event that is being commemorated. In the subaltern city of *Ulysses*, by contrast, popular memory is lodged in the immediacy of the body, but, unlike habit, it incorporates the somatic intensity of the flâneur, the fractured, restless sensibility of a native adrift in his own surroundings. Instead of closing off the past, the effect is to re-activate contact with the vestigial traces of the fallen and defeated, barely discernible under the encrustations of habit and conformity. Events that have been consigned to oblivion through shame, humiliation or embarrassment – the neuroses of upward mobility and respectability under a colonial regime – come back to haunt the living, and to wake them, as Stephen says, from the nightmare of history.

[63] *Ulysses*, p. 253.
[64] Connerton, *How Societies Remember*, p. 25.

In a fine discussion of involuntary memory in Joyce, Carle Bonafous-Murat charts the different ways in which memory and environment merge in the physical act of walking the city, leading him to raise the question: 'is it the characters who use the town as a reservoir for their memories, or is it on the contrary the town which makes use of the characters to actualise its memories?'[65] The difficulty with the latter process, as he sees it, is that it induces habit and 'predispositions', depriving the characters of agency in their relationship to the past. For this reason, he concludes:

> it appears that most of the Dubliners are more willing to be kept in thraldom than to be liberated from the burden of the past. Indeed, between the community of Dubliners and their memories, there is always the intermediate structure of the Dublin grid, the network of streets and public buildings thanks to which connections are established, and though they may wish to be freed from their history they willingly accept to be imprisoned by the space they are in.[66]

As if in response to this, the commemoration of 1798 can be seen as activating a narrative grid in which by contrast passivity gives way to agency, the streets of the city empowering rather than imprisoning those who pass through them. Most accounts of the cultural revival at the end of the nineteenth century point to the literary movement, the founding of the Gaelic League, or sporting organisations such as the Gaelic Athletic Association, as the turning points in the resurgence of national sentiment that culminated in the Easter Rising of 1916. This is accurate, so far as it goes, but it may be that these formal, institutional initiatives themselves presuppose a deeper shift in the substratum of everyday life, unsettling the sedimented residues of colonial paralysis and opening up new possibilities of renewal and change. Contrary to the stereotype that nationalism itself was the sole repository of paralysis, these energies, like Robert Emmet's famous last words, were restless and unresolved and lent themselves more to shifting perspectives of walking and motion rather than the finality of monumental time. This results in a kind of popular memory which has less to do with plenitude and authenticity, the local colour of 'characters' at one with their surroundings, than with 'the lives of the submerged tenth',[67] what Foucault describes as 'subjugated knowledge': 'naive knowledges, located low down on the hierarchy, beneath the required level of cognition and scientificity'. So 'far

65 Carle Bonafous-Murat, 'Disposition and pre-disposition: the art of involuntary memory in *Dubliners*', in Francca Ruggieri (ed), *Classic Joyce* (Rome, 2000), p. 365.

66 Ibid., p. 368.

67 *Ulysses*, p. 646.

from being a general commonsense knowledge', this is 'on the contrary a particular, local, regional knowledge, a differential knowledge incapable of unanimity which owes its force only to the harshness with which it is opposed by everything surrounding it'.[68] One third of the population of Dublin took to the streets for the procession to lay the foundation stone for the Wolfe Tone memorial, but notwithstanding all the rhetoric, only an empty space greeted the casual glance of passers-by on the sixteenth of June, 1904. Fixity was for tenure and not for time in Irish culture. 'For God's sake, try to do something about the Wolfe Tone Memorial', wrote P. T. Daly, a leading IRB organiser, to John Devoy in 1905, 'Public promises are being thrown in our teeth every day by the talkers.'[69] In the colonial city, it would seem, it was not so much the talking cure as the walking tour which revitalised a culture on the verge of revolt.

[68] Michel Foucault, 'Two lectures' in *Power/Knowledge: Selected Interviews and other Writings*, ed. Colin Gordon (New York, 1980), p. 82. For an insightful application of this concept to Molly Bloom's soliloquy, see Carol Shloss, 'Molly's resistance to the Union: marriage and colonialism in Dublin, 1904', in Richard Pearce (ed.), *Molly Blooms: A Polylogue on 'Penelope' and Cultural Studies* (Madison, 1994), pp. 105–8.

[69] T. J. O'Keefe, 'The 1898 efforts to celebrate the United Irishmen: the '98 centennial', *Eire-Ireland*, 23 (1988), 72.

CHAPTER 7

'For God and for Ulster': the Ulsterman on the Somme

David Officer

In the early morning of 1 July 1916, men of the 36th (Ulster) Division advanced across No Man's Land from their positions on the edge of Thiepval wood. This was but one part of a larger strategic plan to find a way out of the war of attrition which had marked the conflict up to this point. One hundred thousand Allied soldiers were mobilised by General Haig with the express purpose of breaking through the enemy lines. The Ulster Division concentrated its attack on the 'notorious' Schwaban Redoubt, a defensive system of considerable strength. The initial stages of the fighting saw various brigades within the Division advance and, despite considerable losses, secure their immediate objective – the first three lines of German trenches. Whilst Allied forces faltered elsewhere the men of the Ulster Division appear to have held their ground, isolated from the rest of the Allied army in their vicinity. Denied adequate support – so the narrative histories of this engagement suggest – the German counter-attack later that day was able to drive the invaders back allowing them to reoccupy what had been momentarily surrendered. An empirical audit of the engagement reveals that no advantage had been immediately gained for the Allied cause. Indeed, it could be characterised as yet another moment of abject failure. At least 5,000 men of the Ulster Division did not answer to their name at a role call the following day. About half that total lay dead on the battlefield.[1]

This event did not differ remarkably from many of the other engagements during the course of the First World War. The limited consequences of the attack, seen within the context of the broad struggle to defeat the Axis powers, was a hallmark of the war, providing a key

[1] The best general accounts of the Ulster Division and its role in the Battle of the Somme are Cyril Falls, *The History of the 36th (Ulster) Division* (Belfast, 1922) and Philip Orr, *The Road to the Somme* (Belfast, 1987).

theme of the general histories of this period.[2] Yet, as much international literature testifies, the significance attached to the extraordinary moments that wars occasion cannot be accounted for through the ugly rationality of 'military accountancy'.[3] Whatever the focus of loyalty and identification – be it empire, nation, locality, race or ethnic group – war has a tendency to accentuate those social processes associated with the production and reproduction of 'imagined communities'. In Ireland, too, considerable effort has been expended in the attempt to disclose the complex interaction between past conflicts and contemporary efforts to recoup their significance in the present. The 'troubles' in Northern Ireland suggested that this problematic was of pressing political significance. Memories of previous conflicts – and conflicts over memories – formed a vital aspect of the struggle to legitimise particularistic visions of the world and the consequences, sometimes violent and bloody consequences, which have then ensued.

It is within this context that the fate of the Ulster Division on the Somme battlefield is frequently evoked, an estimation that would appear to be borne out by the prodigious efforts to re-remember the event within certain sections of the Ulster Unionist community. The heroic, if tragic story continues to be perpetuated in a wide variety of forms. The ritualistic practices of the Orange Institution or the British Legion, the display of artifacts and the dissemination of information by the Somme Association or installations such as the Somme Heritage Centre at Newtownards represent the more respectable means through which this is achieved. The evocation of the battle on gable walls, in loyalist songs or paramilitary displays constitute just a few of the more demotic and less respectable forms through which the event continues to be evoked and memories purposefully rekindled.[4]

[2] See, for example, Lyn Macdonald, *The Somme* (London, 1983). Many Loyalists tend to direct particular, and sometimes quite bitter, criticism towards this book since the role of the Ulster Division appears grossly underplayed in her broad description of the battle.

[3] An example of this literature would be that which dwells on the relationship between the Gallipoli debacle and the cultivation of national sentiment in Australia and New Zealand. See, for example, Alistair Thomson, *Anzac Memories: Living with the Legend* (Oxford, 1994) and Bruce Kapferer, *Legends of People – Myths of State: Violence, Intolerance, and Political Culture of Sri Lanka and Australia* (Washington, DC, 1988).

[4] Whilst the ubiquity of the Somme story and its transmission is frequently noted, this process remains generally unexplored within academic literature. The exceptions to this are Jane Leonard, 'The twinge of memory: Armistice Day in Ireland since 1919', in Richard English and Graham Walker (eds.), *Unionism in Modern Ireland* (London, 1996), pp. 99–114, and Edna Longley, 'The Rising, the Somme and Irish memory', in Máirín Ní Dhonnchadha and Theo Dorgan (eds.), *Revising the Rising* (Belfast, 1991), pp. 29–49.

Clearly, a complex variety of social processes have played their part in the continued reconstitution of the Somme as narrative, myth, memory and symbol. This chapter has the limited ambition of exploring how the immediate experience of the event was absorbed by important public representatives of the Protestant and Unionist community in the North of Ireland. It also suggests how attempts were made to articulate mass grief through a process of what Gillian McIntosh has described as 'abstraction', both simplifying and conventionalising the event's meaning.[5] In doing so, particular attention is paid to the ways in which the experience was incorporated into pre-existing ethno-religious myths and memories which had themselves been elevated in the struggle against Home Rule, valued as a means through which legitimation and sharp definition could be given to communal efforts to defend the Union and preserve the ontological security of the loyal Ulsterman.[6]

Consequently, the concern here is not with individual memory but the social framework of memory within which the Somme experience was absorbed, made intelligible and rendered significant.[7] Emphasis is placed on the variety of claims swiftly advanced by those who self-consciously identified with the fate that had overtaken the Ulster Division. The religious leaders, civic representatives and prominent figures within local institutions such as the Orange Order who contributed to this process are considered here as entrepreneurs who sought to interpret the event and establish the fixity and unity of their ethnic group. This was a community imbued with a sense of cultural uniqueness and historical continuity through which members were united despite internal differentiation along a range of other social dimensions. It is vitally important to recognise the realm of social subjectivity in the reproduction of such communities rather than what might be apprehended as

[5] Gillian McIntosh, *The Force of Culture: Unionist Identities in Twentieth-Century Ireland* (Cork, 1999), p. 14.

[6] This ethno-religious population category laid explicit claim to a territorially rooted mode of being, a bounded social subject which not only had a range of naturalised capacities and dispositions but possessed historical depth – 'heritage', and a promised future within which true being would at last be revealed to the world – 'destiny'. For an elaboration of the importance of these claims for Ulster Unionism during the late nineteenth and early twentieth centuries see Peter Gibbon, *The Origins of Ulster Unionism* (Manchester, 1975) and James Loughlin, *Ulster Unionism and British National Identity Since 1885* (London, 1995). For a more recent discussion of this theme see David Officer and Graham Walker, 'Scottish Unionism and the Ulster Question', in Catriona Macdonald, *Unionist Scotland, 1800–1997* (Edinburgh, 1998), pp. 13–26.

[7] The first significant sociological investigation of this process was conducted in France immediately after the end of the First World War: see Maurice Halbwachs, *Les cadres sociaux de la mémoire* (Paris, 1925). For a useful overview of the more recent elaboration of this mode of investigation see James Fentress and Chris Wickham, *Social Memory* (Oxford, 1992).

a shared, objective, ethnic reality. The relative solidity of constitutive myths, memories, symbols, values and common modes of expression within an ethnic culture are at once the hallmarks of distinction from others and a means through which to make sense of the world. At the same time they have been crystallised over time and transmitted from one generation to another; and whilst they may become gradually modified, they limit and condition the perceptions and interactions of the people who inherit them. Anthony Smith offers a useful synopsis of the significance of such cultural attributes:

> the features of any *ethnie*, whatever its distant origins, take on a binding exterior quality for any member or generation, independent of their perceptions and will; they possess a quality of historicity that itself becomes an integral part of subsequent ethnic interpretations and expressions.[8]

This exploration of a particular constellation of memories which began to circulate around the Somme suggests their continued resonance and utility for contemporary entrepreneurs within the *ethnos* who would offer them as evidence of the objective boundedness which continues to distinguish the Protestant and Unionist community from others. Whatever the veracity of the accounts which have emanated from within an *ethnos*, the emphasis placed on its cultural uniqueness plays a vital part in distinguishing between particular population groups and confers a sense of collective identity claimed by members and usually recognised by others. An investigation of this sort proceeds by attempting to disclose the ways in which shared experiences are collectively interpreted and experienced, how meaning is then conferred and disseminated not only between contemporary members of the *ethnos* but across time, from one generation to the next. Expression, interpretation and transmission are processes which are shaped by the changing conditions within which they are effected; thus modification occurs despite the fact that the members of an *ethnos* may impute a timeless or 'traditional' quality to what is inherited.

The formation of the 36th (Ulster) Division within weeks of the declaration of war in 1914 was followed by an intensive period of recruitment and training, but it was not until May 1915 that the Division left Belfast for France, and not until over a year later that it was given orders to engage the enemy. If the fate of this generally inexperienced fighting unit was sealed within hours of 'going over the top', the news of what had transpired did not filter back to Ireland until a number of days later.

[8] A. D. Smith, *The Ethnic Origins of Nations* (Oxford, 1986), p. 22.

Consequently, in the absence of detailed evidence of either the general success or otherwise of the offensive, and the particular fate of the locally raised Division, attention was at first directed towards the broader significance of the engagement.

During the first four days of July a number of common themes surfaced which played their part in preparing the ground on which the event could be signified. The population were cautioned not to assume that the engagement was a 'thunderbolt stroke' which would result in a swift victory but a 'slow, continuous and methodical thrust' which might signal a gradual turning of the tide of war.[9] It was clearly impossible to ascribe a decisiveness to a major campaign which was only just beginning to unfold. This difficulty, combined with only scant details from the Front, meant that the Belfast press was engaged in an attempt to piece together the potential significance of what was happening elsewhere by deciphering the phraseology used by correspondents present in the vicinity of battle.[10]

Coincidentally, the first day of the Battle of the Somme coincided with the anniversary of the Battle of the Boyne (1 July 1690, O.S.), a synchronicity instantaneously imbued with considerable significance. Yet, at least a month before the traditional parading was due to take place on the Twelfth, the annual celebration had been postponed. Citing the expectation that July would witness a significant demand for war materials it was felt best to suspend an occasion which would disrupt war production.[11] However, the wider threat to public peace which the Twelfth might have posed was not far from the minds of those in Dublin Castle. Following the Easter Rising all public parades were banned; if the Orange Institution had not conformed with the request to suspend its celebration the authorities could have invoked the Defence of the Realm Act. As it was, those in authority within the Ulster Unionist movement, with the exception of the Independent Orange Order, acquiesced to this demand.[12]

[9] *Belfast Newsletter*, 3 July 1916.

[10] Both Belfast- and London-based journalists were reading and filtering official dispatches and reported observations from the Front. Belfast newspapers were piecing together their war narrative by using a mixture of news from a variety of agencies. The London Letter in the *Belfast Newsletter* commented on this process – 'it is perhaps more prudent to strike an average and so arrive at a happy medium', *Belfast Newsletter*, 5 July 1916.

[11] See the news reports and official notice in the Belfast papers published on 22 June 1916. Postponement extended beyond Ireland to Scotland. It is significant that these plans were primarily aimed at the shipyards in Belfast and on the Clyde with the expectation that others would follow the lead of shipyard workers in remaining at work: an indication of the strength and significance of Orangeism in those workplaces.

[12] The Independent Orange Order was adamant in exerting their right to march to the very last. It was only a matter of days before the Twelfth that the Independent Institution bowed to pressure and announced a substitute meeting in an Orange hall on Great Victoria St, Belfast: *Belfast Newsletter*, 13 July 1916.

However, the traditional anniversary church services did proceed, providing the first public event within the Protestant and Unionist community to mark the significance of events in France. It is worth dwelling on both the form and content of the religious services held that day, since in many respects they prefigure some of the dominant means through which the Somme would be remembered in years to come – this before any news of the fate of the Ulster Division had reached Ireland. What characterised these religious ceremonies was an expression of a complex ethnic consciousness which took as its self-referential subject the Ulsterman, and his part in the war raging in Europe and also the conflict in Ireland.[13]

Orangemen proceeded from their local Orange Halls to a central place of worship, donning their regalia only when they had entered the church so that travelling the route could not be construed as a parade. Two of the largest events that Sunday were given prominent coverage in the Unionist newspapers which reproduced the sermons delivered from the platform or pulpit, thus heightening the significance of the event by transmitting what had occurred to a mass readership.[14] Brethren from Sandy Row made their way to the Ulster Hall where a local clergyman introduced the proceedings by announcing what he believed to be the victories already secured in the current offensive in France. Standing, the audience sang the doxology and the opening stanza of the National Anthem, which was followed by a sermon delivered by the Rev. Louis Crooks. The narrative conjured effortlessly a scriptural message conjoined with a sense of crisis, an estimation of values and qualities which animated the Northern Protestants at home and overseas with an overall justification of the war effort as an attempt to secure the continued existence of the empire. The Rev. Crooks began by asserting that scripture taught that 'the path to peace was often by the deadly and implacable and bloody and ruthless path of war'; the allied forces were engaged in achieving that objective.[15] The Boyne commemoration was an act of remembrance of the same ambition: 'their main purpose was to strengthen and encourage the great national and Imperial resolve which was animating the British race the world over'. The momentous nature of the crisis through which they were living rendered the mundane world of petty politics obsolete:

[13] The exclusively male participation in the Somme event effortlessly reinforced the unselfconsciously masculine form in which the subject was invariably named. The Ulsterman stood as representative of the whole community. This unerring masculinity can, in part, be understood as an oppositional dualism in contrast to the essentialised femininity of the Celt. See M. Chapman *The Celts: The Construction of a Myth* (London, 1993), pp. 216–17.

[14] See, for example, *Belfast Newsletter*, 3 July 1916.

[15] Ibid.

'Even the most urgent local questions sank into insignificance in comparison with this vast war of the forces of good against the powers of evil.' Turning to matters closer at home, the Ulster Division was elevated as the paradigm of the sacrificing, patriotic self:

> the Empire might well be proud of the Ulster Orangeman and the Ulster Volunteers – proud of their patriotism, proud of their self sacrifice and proud of their most gallant sons who nobly responded to the call of King and country. England needed them, the Empire needed them and without waiting to fix their price, and without counting the cost or the sacrifice they gave themselves loyally and royally. . .

In conclusion, Crooks heightened those proven qualities by contrasting them with others, evoking the 'disgraceful Rising of Easter week in Dublin and the South and West'. The service formally ended with the playing of the National Anthem.

A familiar pattern is discernible in this narrative, a pattern which was to serve as a means through which the Somme was given signification. The necessity of sacrifice was stressed, as was a biblically sanctioned opposition between the forces of good and evil which not only incorporated the Axis powers but also local Irish nationalism. This was a binary opposition which defined those qualities demonstrated by the Ulster Division on the battlefield, qualities which also extended to the whole of the northern Unionist community.

Over the following days the general phraseology of war was supplemented and partly displaced by detailed accounts of the battle and its consequences. Not only did the news become increasingly ominous as time went on, but the personal human tragedy for friends and relatives waiting in Ireland began painfully to unfold. It was becoming clear that the Ulster Division had been overtaken by a catastrophe. The warning signs were there: 'let it be admitted [that] the resisting power of the enemy in the front of the British is hardening'.[16] Vivid attempts to describe the experience were also beginning to surface, one of the most striking being an Irish soldier, who, like many of his compatriots 'spoke with glowing eyes and weird phrases of the battle scene' as being 'like a Belfast riot on Vesuvius'.[17] Elsewhere, an anonymous commanding officer gave away little detailed information but commented that sixteen out of twenty-three of his officers had been killed or wounded in a recent assault: 'Our

[16] *Belfast Newsletter*, 5 July 1916.

[17] Quoted in the *Northern Whig*, 5 July 1916, from a report the previous day in the London *Daily News*.

Irish National Foresters' banner depicting Patrick Pearse, by courtesy of Neil Jarman

men are not bullet proof. When they enter a zone of living fire they get hit; but till they get hit they balk at nothing. . . Our men walked through that raging fire exactly as though they were on parade.'[18] The conflicting

[18] *Belfast Newsletter*, 5 July 1916.

images of a 'Belfast riot on Vesuvius' and a walk through the battlefield as if it were a parade reflected the difficulties with which combatants absorbed a shocking experience. This sense of order and disorder violently conflicting constituted the first recorded attempts to convey to others what had occurred, no doubt generating great anxiety back in Ireland.

Other details of the Ulster Division's conduct in the battle were emerging. It was at this point that a story began to circulate in both the public media and private conversation that sealed the significance of the event as a display of Ulster Unionist intent rather than simply an expression of greater British patriotism. The original source was a letter sent from the battlefield by an English staff officer to Colonel Crawford, Grand Master of the Orange Order in Belfast: 'Our gallant fellows marched into a narrow alley of death, shouting 'No Surrender' and 'Remember the Boyne'. I am not an Ulsterman, but yesterday, the 1st of July, as I followed their massing attack I felt that I would rather be an Ulsterman than anything else in the world.'[19]

This outward appearance of a specifically Orange self-consciousness amongst some of the troops as they engaged in battle was widely reported in the British press. The contents of the letter to Crawford were circulated by the Press Association and surfaced in accounts of the battle published in the *Daily Mail* and the London *Times*. An important refinement of this image of massed ranks of Northern combatants collectively asserting their Orange identity in conditions of extreme stress surfaced the following day. Whilst published accounts of the battle from a number of correspondents noted the shout 'No Surrender' from some, however, a composite report suggested that this was not generalised: 'one or two remembering the ancient watchwords, sang out 'No Surrender' and 'Dolly's Brae' but for the most part they kept a stiff upper lip and the clenched teeth which meant death or victory . . .'[20]

Whatever the truth, the original letter to Colonel Crawford was nevertheless valued because it suggested the animating spirit which guided the actions of the Ulster Division. Further, there was an authority attached to those observations not only because they originated with a staff officer in the army hierarchy but also because he also happened to be an Englishman. To express the sentiment: 'I would rather be an Ulsterman than anything else in the world' was to confer high praise indeed, praise which heightened the imputed significance of the event. It also suggested an absolute identity of interests between the Ulsterman

[19] See both *Irish News* and *Belfast Newsletter*, 7 July 1916.
[20] *Belfast Newsletter*, 8 July 1916.

and his English counterpart which was reiterated at a very different level in a speech delivered by Balfour and reported in the Belfast press:

> we might say at this moment that one of the bonds of the British Empire was the British army because it was spontaneously composed of elements from each of the self-governing Dominions fulfilling their own part of the national destiny. Working with a single heart and will for a common purpose and united in the same magnificent and glorious deeds, it would be able to look back on a joint heritage of heroism.[21]

What the Belfast-based Unionist newspapers offered was a multilayered narrative which rooted the experience of the Ulster Division into a familiar pattern of signification.[22] A unit of the British Army, it was nevertheless unique in being composed of 'Covenanters', motivated to band together in order to resist 'attacks on their hard won liberties'.[23] This historical allusion was not the only one that came to hand: the Division was animated by the 'same feelings which inspired Cromwell's Ironsides'. Elsewhere it was asserted that this unifying spirit arose out of its 'family character' which guaranteed a 'oneness of mind and purpose . . . closer and more intimate' than anything else to be found on the battlefield. This unity was also manifest in qualities and dispositions demonstrated by their conduct, an 'unconquerable spirit', 'dauntless courage', 'discipline', 'determination' and 'devotion'. On the one hand, the Division was described as exemplifying 'the finest traditions of the British Army', merely the modern manifestation of a long martial lineage. Their sacrifice,

> has raised them to an equality with any of the men who stormed the bloodstained heights of Alburea or dashed themselves against the defenses of the Redan, or stood, prepared to die but not to surrender, in the stem of British squares on the fields of Waterloo.[24]

The location where this tradition was re-joined only compounded this truth. The River Somme had played 'a great part in our history': it was from here that Edward III marched to Crecy, while Henry V's army negotiated it on the way to Agincourt. Yet, the 36th Division also stood

[21] *Belfast Newsletter*, 5 July 1916.

[22] This observation extends beyond those newspapers published in Belfast. For a brief overview of the narratives disseminated elsewhere, see Loughlin, *Ulster Unionism and British National Identity*, p. 83.

[23] The following quotes from *Belfast Newsletter*, *Northern Whig* and *Belfast Evening Telegraph* appear in editorials published on 7 July 1916 and 8 July 1916. As there appears to be little significant variation between these narratives they are presented here in composite form. Where substantial extracts are quoted the source is referenced.

[24] *Northern Whig*, 7 July 1916.

in the lineage of the Covenanters and the Ironsides, 'a unique unit in the British Army' who had been 'true to the splendid traditions which they have inherited as their birthright'. These were 'UVFers', described elsewhere as 'Ulstermen' or of 'Ulster Loyalist stock'.[25]

Other estimations of the composition of the Ulster Division also vied for attention. Its actions prompted a pride in both 'province' and 'race' in the proven attachment to king, country and empire. In a striking continuity with the ethno-histories that had been produced over the previous thirty years, the *Northern Whig* commented on how the Division's actions exemplified the intrinsic character of the community: 'We have combined the fiery energy of the Irish in attacking what we dislike with the dogged endurance of the Scottish in defending what we love.' Other renditions offered a variation on this basic estimation by sometimes incorporating distinctly English characteristics. The achievements of the Division arose out of the 'combination of Irish impetuosity, Scottish valour and English coolness', which made 'the fighting of the Covenanter incomparable'.[26]

What permeated these narratives is a strong sense that a historical tradition, a cultural or ethnic continuity, had been practically demonstrated. In short, a grand process of reacquaintance with some fundamental disposition in the world had taken place. Consequently, modern accretions had been stripped away to expose once again what was always said to have been there. Importantly, this revelation had occurred within the interested gaze of others, magnifying its importance at it addressed those who had only a passing, and frequently problematic, familiarity with the Ulsterman.

It was the representative nature of the Ulster Division as an exemplification of the Protestant and Unionist population of the North which helped to secure the Somme's abiding importance. This recognition of the representativeness of the Division, both back in Ireland and as it was finally revealed to others, was succinctly captured in the following editorialising remark:

> for the Loyalists of Ulster [the Ulster Division stands] as no other Division can stand for any other section of the people of the United Kingdom. It typifies us in all that we cherish and stand for, and all that we are in the eyes of the rest of the nation whatever view they take of us. By its record in the field of battle we knew before the 1st of July we would be judged and in some quarters the judgement

25 Ibid.

26 Editorial, *Northern Whig*, 14 Aug. 1916. For the Ulster Scot, see Ian McBride, 'Ulster and the British question', in English and Walker, *Unionism in Modern Ireland*, pp. 1–18.

would be strict, even to harshness, if there was the possibility of making it so. We never had any fear on that score, however, for we knew our own, we Ulster Loyalists, as we knew ourselves.[27]

If the Somme was rendered as a dramatic act of revelation it was simultaneously seen as an act of transformation: 'The old battle-cry of the Ulster loyalist has been derided and ridiculed by those who are opposed to the Ulster sentiment. But it has won a new glory which no one will dispute.' What had occurred was understood not only as a continuation of, but also a significant advance upon, what had gone before. The prominent Orangeman Colonel Robert Wallace commented in the *Belfast Newsletter* that the Twelfth now took on a 'new and even greater importance', and the past achievements of the Ulsterman would now be 'seen as small in comparison'; a 'fresh lustre' had now been added to his story.[28] This was, in the words of Bishop Charles F. D'Arcy, an event,

> the most glorious in the annals of Ulster . . . they have, indeed, surpassed all ancient records of chivalry. Wherever Ulstermen go they will carry with them something of the glory of the great achievements of the 1st of July. The spirit of willing sacrifice for the sake of those great ideals of liberty and progressive humanity which belonged to all that was best in the British race, and which has inspired Ulster throughout her recent struggles was never more magnificently exhibited.[29]

What these sentiments also capture is how a memorialisation process was set in motion as part of the complex attempts to make sense of this traumatic experience on the Home Front. There was perceived to be a pressing necessity to record what had happened. To place the event, which had unfolded a matter of days before, alongside other written records, 'ancient records of chivalry' and the 'glorious . . . annals of Ulster'. This impulse to inscribe, in what was hoped would be an indelible form, can be understood as an effort to compose the first day of the Somme in such a way that it was fitfully commensurate with an imputed history accruing to the Ulsterman. 'The name of Ulster has been written in glorious chapters on almost every page of British history for three centuries', and a new chapter had been opened.[30]

The Ulster Division was presented not only as unambiguously displaying a transcendental essence which united past generations but also as a model for future generations – an ideal representation, in a modern

[27] *Belfast Newsletter*, 8 July 1916.
[28] Ibid.
[29] Ibid.
[30] Ibid.

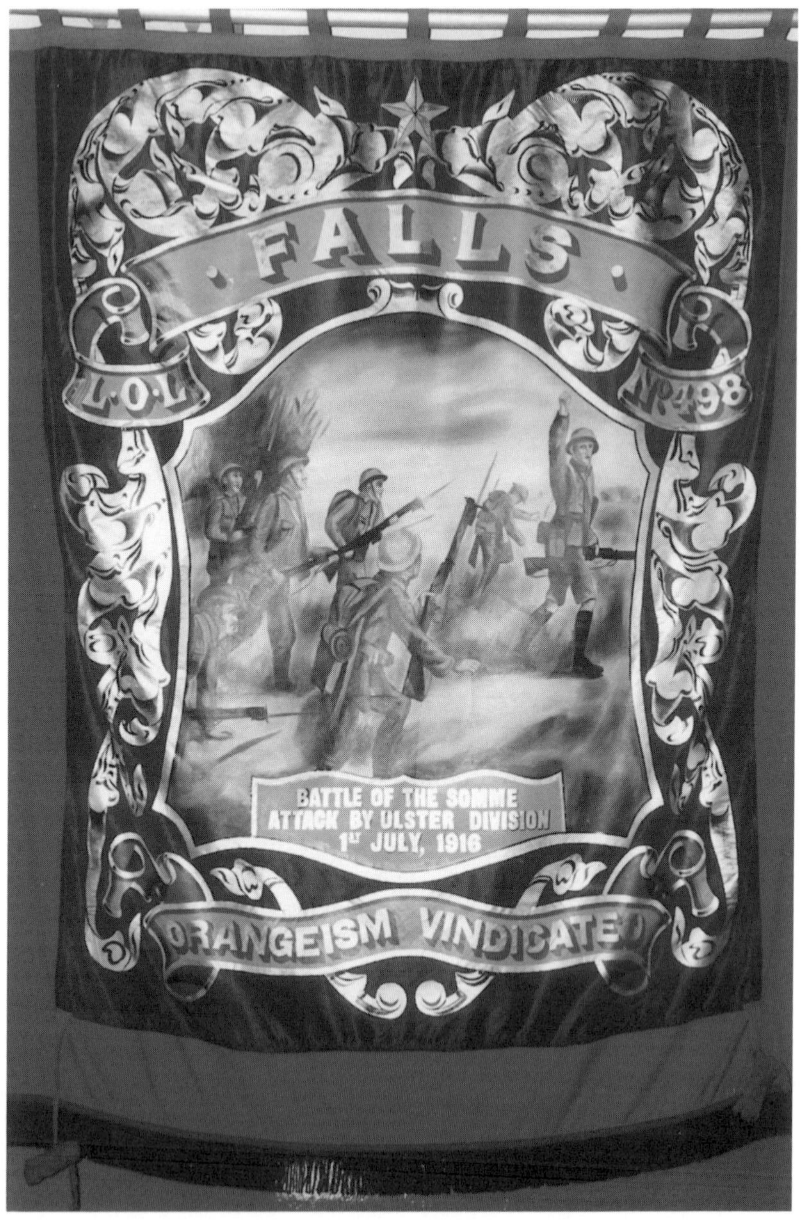

Orange banner depicting the Ulster Division at the battle of the Somme, 1916, by courtesy of Neil Jarman

setting, of a trans-historical being in the world which would demand an obligation from those who came after. '[F]uture generations will find in their dauntless courage a great and noble inspiration.'[31] Elsewhere it was observed that 'a new chapter has been written which will thrill and inspire generations of Ulstermen as yet unborn'.[32] These narratives naturalised a set of capacities and characteristics which served to highlight that 'Ulstermen may be destroyed but they will never yield when they know that their cause is just.'[33] This 'heroic band of brothers' were not only inspired by a desire to defend the secular demands for liberty, conscience and freedom but also animated by an otherworldly spirit – a fight 'For God and Ulster'.[34] To have seen 'self-sacrifice' without 'craven fear or selfish materialism' and 'willingly . . . engaged in a sacred cause' not only placed the fallen closer to God but also provided a sanctified model for future conduct in the world:

> We are undergoing the most severe test to which our people have been subject and seeing that our soldiers in the field have acquitted themselves so gloriously we, if we are to be worthy of them, must also display a similar spirit of heroism, self-sacrifice and endurance.[35]

Clearly there was a real degree of unanimity evidenced within the pages of Belfast's Unionist press about the appropriate form and content through which to make sense of the Ulster Division's fate. This was not shared by the nationalist *Irish News*. In important respects an estimation of the event's significance was given a quite different inflection. The communal character of recruitment to the Ulster Division was evidenced by the lack of detailed news coverage that the *Irish News* judged to be worth publishing. It was not until 6 July that any extensive coverage was given to what had occurred to the Northern Division in the Battle of the Somme. Ironically, the first fatality recorded by the Belfast papers in that battle was a Private Patrick Hanna of the Royal Inniskilling Fusiliers: a Catholic, and formerly an active member of the Wolfe Tone Branch of the United Irish League, he died on 1 July.[36]

Less than two weeks after the opening of the Battle of the Somme a rich and complex web had been woven around the event and its significance for Ireland in general and the North in particular. Politicians, journalists

[31] Ibid.
[32] *Northern Whig*, 7 July 1916.
[33] *Belfast Newsletter*, 7 July 1916.
[34] Ibid.
[35] *Northern Whig*, 7 July 1916.
[36] *Irish News*, 4 July 1916.

and clergymen had all participated in a struggle to give meaning to what had befallen the Ulster Division. Although the Orange Institution had acceded to the cancellation of the Twelfth it was nevertheless felt that this date, already heavy with symbolic importance, might provide an important occasion on which to express a public remembrance of the dead. The Independent Orange Order had intended to process as usual on the day itself but had failed to gain permission from the appropriate authorities who had invoked the Defence of the Realm Act to proscribe public parades because of the tense political situation in Ireland.

The Twelfth of July became an officially sanctioned occasion of mourning, the lord mayor in Belfast issuing a request that for five minutes, from the stroke of midday, traffic and work, both public and domestic, should cease as a mark of respect. How universally this request was observed is difficult to judge; the conflation of Orange day with a specific remembrance of the Ulster Division's fate suggested a particularistic significance of the commemorative process. However, the centre of Belfast was marked by a near-total observance of the instructions. On the stroke of twelve, Belfast became 'a veritable city of immobility'.[37] One journalist, standing at Castle Junction, recorded the scene as the clock struck noon:

> the cessation of vehicular and pedestrian traffic, the stoppage of all business commerce was almost instantaneous. The blinds of all the banks, shops, offices and warehouses were drawn, the people stood in long ranks without attempting to pursue their ordinary avocations. Looking down the vistas of High St, Donegall Place and Royal Avenue, one saw the trams standing motionless; horse drawn vehicles of all descriptions were also stopped, and the policemen on point duty stood stiffly to attention, and the minutes passed leaden footed. It seemed an immensity of time before the hands of the clock passed the five minutes stage, and meanwhile one had cause and opportunity for reflection.[38]

Standing in the rain, standing 'out of time', attention was said to be collectively directed towards the revealed meaning of the Somme battle. Despite journalistic attempts to record an imputed unity to the thoughts and emotions which passed through people's minds, it was impossible to grasp what was being invested in silent reflection as 'Abide with me' was played by the bells of Church House in Fisherwick Place. Private narratives of grief, political obligations sealed in blood, distress, pride or cold calculation all had their place. The sense of being 'out of time', of making a fleeting break from the normal routines of life and

[37] *Belfast Newsletter*, 12 July 1916.
[38] Ibid.

holding in abeyance the normal calenderical importance of 12 July, was an important symbolic act for many citizens in the city centre, and it was also repeated elsewhere in the North. A correspondent in the *Belfast Evening Telegraph* recorded the scene in the Belfast Rope Works where 3,000 women stood with bowed heads and clasped hands in silence for 5 minutes, commenting that, 'never in all the past have we had such a memorable five minutes as that which Noon gave us today, when the many heart beats of the city were as one'.[39]

Thousands attended a service of Intercession in St Anne's Cathedral whilst others were conducted on a similar basis elsewhere. Rather than observe the Twelfth by parading, various Orange Lodges participated in religious services within their districts. Yet another opportunity was presented for the Somme to be given a particular significance: the obligation to those who fell at Theipval meant that 'those who remain at home [were] doing their utmost to safeguard their interests';[40] that the Ulster Division's conduct had proved that 'Loyalty was ingrained in them';[41] that the threat posed by the possibility of Home Rule was a betrayal of the fallen which would be met by 'the binding of the Ulster Covenanters more closely together'.[42] For the first time since the suspension of the Party Processions Act there had been no Orange celebrations on the Twelfth, apart from a small Orange arch erected by children in Ballymena, an Orange flag flown from Walker's monument in Derry and a single flute band which toured the streets of Coleraine. When a Union flag was flown in public places it was done so at half-mast. Yet, in the absence of the Twelfth, the most significant date in the Orange calendar had been reinforced if not given even greater depth: 'An added measure of sacredness is given to the day', commented the editorial in the *Northern Whig*, 'and when we celebrate it in the future it will be fuller and richer because of the imperishable deeds of the Ulster Division.'[43]

An important indication of this specifically Orange meaning given to the commemoration of the Somme engagement was the response to these efforts by the Nationalist community in the North. The *Irish News* had been, at the very least, sparing in its coverage of the Ulster Division's fate, and this extended to the events which marked what had occurred. The public silence on 12 July was reported in a small three-line observation that, 'In compliance with the suggestion of the Lord Mayor,

39 *Belfast Evening Telegraph*, 12 July 1916.
40 Sir James Stronge, Grand Master of the Orange Order, *Belfast Newsletter*, 13 July 1916.
41 Rev. Louis Crooks, addressing Orangemen in Sandy Row Orange Hall, ibid.
42 Brother Edward Leathem's address at the Clifton St Orange Hall, *Belfast Newsletter*, 17 July 1916.
43 *Northern Whig*, 13 July 1916.

business and traffic was suspended for five minutes at Noon.'[44] In contrast to the Unionist press, the Nationalist paper also repeated criticisms of the conduct of the war which appeared elsewhere, particularly where it affected Irish soldiers in the field.

Reports of those who were dead, missing or wounded did not begin to arrive in the North until five days after the engagement began. It was not until 8 July that the local press began to reflect the full extent of the death and destruction which had been visited. For the next week or so whole pages in the press carried notifications of those who had been affected. Whilst the *Newsletter* changed the title of its column from 'Ulster and the War' to a 'Roll of Honour', the *Belfast Evening Telegraph* carried individual photographs of the dead. By 25 July the back page of the paper had displayed no less than 111 individual portraits. It was perhaps in this way that the full human tragedy of war was grasped in a concrete form for the first time. This evidence, both in the individualised image of a particular soldier but also in the conglomerate portrait which it presented to the public, realised the Unionist and Protestant community in the North in a way which had never been achieved before. In a sense this was no longer an 'imagined community'; its ideal representation was personified on the printed page for all to see.

On 4 August, just over a month after the first day of the Somme, the second anniversary of the beginning of the war was marked by an open-air service in the Belfast shipyards. Workers gathered on Queen's Island to hear a delegated representative from the workforce move a motion that recognised the inspiration that the soldiers on the battlefront had instilled back home. The simple retelling of what had happened was now well known from circulated accounts. As the delegate told it: 'They had read of the advance made by the gallant Ulstermen of the First of July when their battle-cry was "No Surrender".'[45]

Elsewhere that same day the ethnic variant of the same story was reiterated. Preaching at a United Presbyterian service in Londonderry, the Rev. Dr McGanahan noted how the battle had proven that, 'The Ulster Scot had not lost the characteristics of his race, tenacity of purpose, strength of devotion, adherence to principle.'[46] Finally, the annual Apprentice Boys parade round the city walls of Derry later that month offered another opportunity not only to highlight the display of Orange virility in battle but also to claim that spirit as alive and well back home.

[44] *Irish News*, 13 July 1916.
[45] *Belfast Newsletter*, 5 Aug. 1916.
[46] Ibid.

Sermonising to assembled Apprentice Boys the Bishop of Derry observed that, 'The casualty lists – the Roll of Honour – were a witness that the spirit which held the Walls of Derry long ago still lived in their midst.'[47] The *Newsletter* reproduced a standardised letter from General Ricardo dispatched to the parents of the fallen which echoed the theme of continuity and reinforced the impression of a general Orange spirit abroad on that fateful day: 'I doubt if they were taken prisoners for "No Surrender" was the feeling that day in the Ulster Division, and I should be wrong if I encouraged you to hope that they had survived.'[48] The significance for the Protestants and Unionists who had remained was also subject to an editorialising disclosure of the reconvened relationship between the past and present which carried a future promise:

> It has been suggested from time to time that the men who commemorate the Siege of Derry might be found, if the day of trial came, to be wanting in the qualities of heroism and fortitude which they praise in the Apprentice Boys. But the war has shown that they are not. The thousands of Ulstermen who have voluntarily offered themselves for the defence of the Empire are worthy successors of those who closed the gates and held the city in spite of every privation and suffering until relief came.[49]

The narratives spun, the memories evoked and the rituals practised in the months following the event suggest the ease with which the fate of the Ulster Division was assimilated as a recognisable stage in the teleological progress of the ethno-religious subject. Almost immediately a framework of remembrance had become established, much of which has continued into the present. The first anniversary of the Battle of the Somme was a time for personal mourning but it also marked the beginning of the conventionalisation of forms through which civic remembrance was accomplished. The First of July 1917 fell on a Sunday, guaranteeing the distinctively religious means through which the events of the previous year were raised in the public consciousness. Specifically, throughout the North, church services were held in almost every Protestant place of worship, the press articles the following day reporting many of these in considerable detail.

The forms of worship were valued for their directness and simplicity combined with the frequent observation that in many places extra seating had to be secured for the considerable numbers who attended. In some cases a Union flag, bordered by black drape, was placed around

[47] *Belfast Newsletter*, 14 Aug. 1916.
[48] Ibid.
[49] Ibid.

the pulpit; the presence of military bands in many of the larger venues who not only recited the 'Death March' but concluded services with the National Anthem, sealed the greater British nationalist content of these events. The sermons preached evoked a variety of patriotic images, imputed a series of qualities to those who had died on the battlefield and lifted the event out of mundane history onto a higher, spiritual plane. There was a recognition that what had occurred was beyond the experience of those gathered to remember, 'that brilliant advance which could only be pictured by their imaginations';[50] however, in the imaginative recreation of the event an increasingly orthodox form was imposed on the event and its meaning. This was a supreme symbolic act of sacrifice that had been motivated by the temporal defence of the empire, Britain and Ulster, but also a spiritual act of selflessness in pursuit of the higher good. It was also an occasion on which the specific contribution made by Ulster to the war effort could be reiterated, and highlighted in contrast with the conduct of others in Ireland. The release by the authorities of leading members of Sinn Féin who had participated in the Easter Rising during the same week provided a vivid point of reference in asserting this claim.[51]

Other notable features of these first anniversary events were the development of public occasions organised outside the confines of a church by a variety of civic bodies in accessible, central locations. In Coleraine the Urban Council orchestrated an event in the Diamond at the heart of the town. Wreaths were laid for the fallen in front of an old Russian gun which had been captured during the Crimean War. Described as an 'informal' occasion, friends, relatives, members of the Orange Order, local civic leaders and townsfolk gathered, laid their floral tributes and stood in silence for a number of minutes before quietly dispersing.[52]

What also surfaced was a ceremonial emphasis on a single soldier as representative of both the Division for whom he fought and the community from which he came.[53] William McFaddan died on the first

[50] Sermon delivered at St Anne's Cathedral, *Belfast Newsletter*, 2 July 1916.

[51] The Belfast newspapers reported the release of Eamon de Valera and Kevin Boland from custody in Dublin. A large crowd greeted them and bonfires were lit across the capital, including, as an overtly symbolic gesture, a fire in the ruins of the GPO. The presence of 'rebels' within Ulster was demonstrated by the arrival of another liberated prisoner, John McEntee, who arrived by train in Belfast to be greeted by a pipe band and 150 cheering supporters before the crowd made its way up the Falls Road.

[52] For this and other reports of the services and events held on the Saturday and Sunday see *Northern Whig* and *Belfast Newsletter*, 3 July 1917.

[53] This individuation of remembrance made the fallen recognisable but also underscored the intimate nature of the sacrifice made. This also found a correlate in the intimate and 'family like'

day of the battle in circumstances that won him the Victoria Cross, emblematic of the human cost of war but also confirmed as an individual exemplification of the moral virtue of the Ulsterman: he died in an attempt to save the lives of others. On 1 July a memorial tablet was unveiled which incorporated the regimental badge, the UVF badge and a Red Hand of Ulster, bordered by Irish scroll work intertwined with roses, thistles and shamrocks. The service in Newtownbreda Presbyterian Church combined testimony to his military prowess with an estimation of his character as a Christian and brother to his comrades, although the sermonising minister was careful not to suggest that 'the young hero [was] a spiritual phenomenon'.[54]

The humanising of the Ulster Division through the elevation of a representative individual provided a recognisable point of reference for those who wished to remember all those who had fallen on the battlefield. Whilst personal and private mourning was an essential function of the ceremonies and commemorations that took place across the North they also served as a important political resource in a situation where the battle over the future of Ireland was still to be decided. The conduct of the Division was presented as a sacrifice for England in England's time of need. The unique character of that exemplified loyalty was an established fact that offered a clear demarcation between the Ulsterman and others, a boundary that the imperial centre might be tempted to forget.

The Twelfth, 1917, provided the other major anniversary date upon which to reanimate and present on centre stage the proven military prowess of the Ulsterman. Unlike the previous year, the day was accorded the status of a holiday and the major parading routes were walked for the first time in two years. The depleted ranks of Orangemen served as a demonstrable counterpoint to the platform speech at the field which not only advertised the heroic qualities of the Ulsterman but the specific role played by the Loyal Institutions in the various armed services. The particular contribution of Orangemen to the war effort was demonstrated by the place taken in the marching ranks by de-mobbed soldiers who were identified by the display of a white disc. These disabled soldiers were a highly visible reminder of the human cost of war which militated against

relations which the Division was said to exemplify. At a fete for wounded soldiers, Carson cast himself as the soldier's father – 'they were his "own boys"'. Having led the first batch of recruits to the Old Town Hall in September 1914, he went on to say that 'hardly one of them he did not know personally, and many an honest hand that now lived no more had shaken his on many an occasion in Ulster'. *Belfast Newsletter*, 3 July 1917.

54 Ibid. See also *Belfast Newsletter*, 29 June 1917.

a simple and unambiguous presentation of war as innocent adventure. However, the patriotic impulse that animated Ulstermen both at home and abroad was emphasised by the display of Union flags at the head of each participating district replacing the banners customarily carried on the Twelfth.

The field speeches invariably asserted the reconvention of Orange tradition that linked the Boyne and the Somme as definitive expressions of the same trans-historical subject, a continuity clearly demonstrable by the common characteristics which united the struggle for liberty of one generation with the other of an eminently modern vintage. In Downpatrick, James Craig addressed the assembled Orangemen. He was there to

> take part in the celebration of what to Ulster was the outstanding landmark in Irish history, particularly as it was now embellished, and for all time would be, by the heroic deeds of the Ulster Division. Would it be practicable in future to emblazon 'Theipval' on their orange colours, for surely that supreme sacrifice of Ulster's manhood symbolised just as profoundly their struggle for civil and religious liberty as 'Derry, Aughrim and the Boyne'.[55]

Elsewhere in Ulster 'Theipval' had already become conspicuously displayed alongside its illustrious counterparts of the Williamite campaign. In Loyalist districts, traditional Orange arches had incorporated the recent battle: at Connswater 'Remember our Fallen Heroes' joined the injunction 'No Surrender' and 'Remember 1690' on an arch across the main road through the village. Similar manifestations appeared in working-class Belfast; in the east of the city and on the Shankill, the traditional Orange iconography of the Twelfth celebration had effortlessly incorporated the Somme event.

Other platform speeches that day evoked the Ulster Division but within the context of contemporary political difficulties. A convention had been proposed to consider the future of Ireland, the prospect of limited Home Role and the place of the north-eastern counties in any future arrangement. Within this context there was a noticeable shift in the rhetorical references to Ulster and the Ulster Division. The relationship of the six north-eastern counties within Ireland was expressed as one of increasing alienation, to the extent that General Sir William Adair, speaking in Ballyclare, made explicit the necessity for a reimagining of national points of reference: 'They must not think of themselves as Irishmen today but as British citizens.'[56] The retreat from the wider

[55] *Belfast Newsletter*, 13 July 1917.
[56] Ibid.

invocation of Ireland and Irishness as it accrued to the Ulsterman was a developed tendency in the speeches delivered by prominent members of the Orange Order.[57]

Whilst the commemorations that took place the following year were similar, in many respects, to those forms established in 1917, the process of conventionalisation continued apace. The role of civic leaders in organising public events, distinguishable from the formal religious services offered by the churches, conformed to similar practices in Britain. In 1918 the first major memorial event was held in the grounds of Belfast City Hall. By 1 July a 'memorial screen' with a panel inscribed 'For God and King and Country' was erected in front of the statute of Queen Victoria; intended to occupy a prominent location where floral tributes could be laid. In situ for the coming week, it provided a temporary focus for silent remembering: 'many affecting scenes were witnessed as the parents and other relatives of men who had made the supreme sacrifice in the war inspected wreathes and read the simple inscriptions attached to them'.[58] The screen memorial, which had been the initiative of the Lady Mayoress, also provided a symbolic space to which a variety of organisations paraded in homage to the fallen; Boy Scout troops, Orange lodges and parties of (Protestant) schoolchildren all made the journey to the City Hall. Other, more permanent forms of memorialisation were also brought into being elsewhere in the North. Again, reflecting an increasingly orthodox method of achieving this, a memorial park was re-dedicated in Ballymena, commemorative meetings were held to remember particular individuals and wreaths were laid in towns and villages where Unionists predominated.

A process of an increasingly conventionalised form of memorialisation had been set in motion which continued to gather pace over the coming years and in doing so the remembrance of the Somme battle conformed in many ways to a more general European 'myth of the war experience' explored by George Mosse amongst others.[59] However, the part played by the Ulster Division and their organic relationship with the UVF on the one hand and the Orange Order on the other served to root the remembrance of the war in local soil. This act of a specifically local

[57] Denis Kennedy, *The Widening Gulf: Northern Attitudes to the Independent Irish State* (Belfast, 1988), p. 27, observes that by late 1918, Carson 'feared the term "Ireland" had become one almost of reproach among the people of Great Britain and the Empire'.

[58] See reports in *Belfast Newsletter*, 3 July 1918 and 8 July 1918.

[59] See George Mosse, *Fallen Soldiers: Reshaping the Memory of the World Wars* (Oxford, 1990); and, more recently, Jay Winter, *Sites of Memory, Sites of Mourning: The Great War in European Culture History* (Cambridge, 1995).

remembrance, resonant with a general message about the particularity of the Ulsterman's contribution to the war effort, coalesced around the ceremonial practices which were annually reconvened on 1 July. Armistice Day, which eventually evolved into Remembrance Sunday, was a related event; however it carried a different inflection. The religious services and parades of 11 November were valued as a national act of remembrance, a day in which the wider British nation, the empire or, later still, the Commonwealth, momentarily cohered as an imaginatively solidified whole. By implication, those who did not define themselves as part of those local, national or international collectives did not feel themselves part of what was being celebrated. Neither, it must be said, were they generally made to feel as if they were welcome.

The formation and subsequent history of the Ulster Division during the war clearly had a vital symbolic importance that it performed to good effect. As a locally raised Division within the British Army it exemplified in a clear and unambiguous form the contribution of the North to the defence of Britain and of an empire of which it was strenuously asserted that Ulster formed an integral part. The blood sacrifice on the Somme was a final seal on the contractual obligations that the state owed to the Ulsterman. Importantly, this was a compact that was now lifted on to a higher, religious plane, guaranteed by the dead on the battlefield.

The heroic exploits of the Ulster Division were also clearly demonstrable as the paradigmatic model of the ideal Ulsterman, displaying qualities in the thick of battle – in the realm of action – proving who he was, indeed who it was that he always had been. The avid cultivation of his part in the Battle of the Somme is in clear and marked contrast to the contemporary remembrance of Northern Ireland's contribution to the Second World War. In the later war the Ulsterman was dispersed across many different regiments, divisions and services, and his progress was difficult to discern.[60] In the Great War, the locally raised Division was identifiable and clearly demarcated as the Northern answer to the patriotic call to defend the motherland. What was much easier to achieve here was a rendition of the war in which the Ulsterman played a vital part in the total war effort but could nevertheless be extricated

60 The remembrance of the Second World War by Ulster Unionists does not tend to focus on organised bodies of armed men but on single individuals. The paradigmatic Ulsterman in this conflict is located in the example of Blair Mayne, founder member of the SAS.

and localised, a distinctive contribution specific to the North and its people.[61]

Whilst there was a wide range of different messages which the northern participation in the Great War and, more specifically, the fate of the Ulster Division at the Somme could be employed to convey, one message thus tended to predominate over others. The Ulsterman had proved himself on the battlefield – proved to himself that he was as he imagined and proved to others that the Ulsterman had not been merely constructed in words – a work of mere fiction.

[61] It should not be assumed that these conditions were peculiar to the raising of the Ulster Division in the North of Ireland. W. Reader comments in his *At Duty's Call: A Study in Obsolete Patriotism* (Manchester, 1988), p. 108, that in the same period immediately after the declaration of war, 'Nothing was more characteristic of the voluntary effort . . . than the raising of "pals' battalions".' In retrospect, as one contemporary observer noted, 'The idea of men of the same town all serving together caught hold of the people's imagination and aroused all that was best in local patriotism and emulation': Basil Williams, *Raising and Training the New Armies* (London, 1918). Bob Bushaway in his 'Name Upon Name: The Great War and Remembrance', in Roy Porter, *The Myths of the English* (London, 1992), p. 142, has commented that 'at least at the outset of war, the pattern of recruitment had emphasised the sense that Britain's total military effort was the sum of contributions from local communities'; he concludes that, given this, there was a 'powerful link between British military fortune and the local community'.

CHAPTER 8

Commemoration in the Irish Free State: a chronicle of embarrassment

David Fitzpatrick

I

Life in Ireland has long been troubled by the recurrent, insistent, ceremonious invocation of the dead. The functions of commemoration vary according to the relationship between the dead and their celebrants. The commemoration of dead heroes or saints, and the events by which they left their mark, is an essential element of Irish political, religious and social organisation. By invoking past triumphs or struggles, current organisers seek not only to authorise and justify their aims and actions, but also to mobilise supporters in public affirmations of solidarity. Public commemorations such as funerals, memorial meetings, processions and subscriptions for monuments, assert a depth of commitment transcending everyday preoccupations. In the private domain, the memory of the dead may be partially recovered through mourning at a funeral, tending a grave, taking out a photograph or letter, fingering a souvenir or conjuring the lost physical presence in a dream or a séance. Even personal remembrance is seldom strictly private, since our strategies for coping with death often involve an appeal for supportive grief from others and for public participation in the ceremonies of mourning.[1] The funeral, the headstone and the notice *in memoriam* invite a wider public to offer respect to the dead, so providing additional reassurance to the bereaved that somebody of consequence has been lost. Yet such extensions of the domain of mourning always threaten to desecrate or trivialise personal recollection, particularly if the motive for public involvement is political advantage rather than personal regret. Partisan manipulation of private funerals and anniversaries tends to arouse resentment despite the compensating advantage of an impressive turnout. The contest for possession of the Irish dead is unremitting, dividing the bereaved, pitting strangers

[1] For the overlap between private and public commemoration of those lost in the Great War, see Jay Winter, *Sites of Memory, Sites of Mourning* (Oxford, 1995), ch. 1.

against intimates, and providing a sharp focus for factional and political conflict.

The ceremonies of commemoration range in frequency from the singular monument or funeral to the centennial or jubilee extravaganza. Such occasions typically entail heavy expense for little lasting benefit, since the impact of the ceremony soon fades from public consciousness. More cost-effective is the anniversary procession or demonstration, in which running costs are relatively small since reiterated use is made of an existing stock of regalia, musical instruments, weapons, banners, flags, trinkets, choreographic expertise, set speeches, pseudo-historical narratives and other forms of commemorative capital. Throughout the nineteenth and twentieth centuries, many Irish political parties, fraternities and other societies have demonstrated an astonishing mastery of commemorative technique. This is evident in the intricate and well-oiled machinery by which tens of thousands of Orangemen, Blackmen and Apprentice Boys are mobilised in elaborate annual processions and loyalist commemorations, according to an almost invariable calendar and protocol. Similar processional skills are displayed by the Ancient Order of Hibernians in their annual processions on St Patrick's Day and Lady Day (15 August), by the Irish National Foresters on the first Sunday in August, and by republican organisations in their commemorations of Wolfe Tone or Bloody Sunday as well as in paramilitary funerals.[2] The main models for these secular commemorations are military and religious ritual, often reapplied in bizarre and perhaps sacrilegious juxtaposition.

Irish commemorative expertise is apparent not only in processions and funerals, but in the mass production of souvenirs and medals (as after the Rising and the first Battle of the Somme in 1916) and the proliferation of polemical histories and hagiographies. There are close parallels and multiple connections between ceremonial and literary commemoration. Popular histories, biographies and almanacs, along with school textbooks, familiarised readers with a judicious selection of names, events and precise dates, supplying essential preparation for associated ceremonies.[3] The commemorative ceremony was itself a teaching tool, reinforcing

[2] See Belinda Loftus, *Mirrors: Orange and Green* (Dundrum, Co. Down, 1994), Anthony D. Buckley and Mary Catherine Kenney, *Negotiating Identity: Rhetoric, Metaphor, and Social Drama in Northern Ireland* (Washington, 1995), and Neil Jarman, *Material Conflicts: Parades and Visual Displays in Northern Ireland* (Oxford, 1997), for analysis of the imagery and anthropology of both loyalist and nationalist processions.

[3] Detailed historical calendars were included in Arthur Griffith's *Leabhar na hÉireann: The Irish Year Book* (Dublin, 1908–12) and the *Irish National Almanac* published by the National Association of the Old IRA (Dublin, 1944).

the lessons from books or conversation with powerful visual and aural imagery. Commemoration taught participants about their place in a venerable political, religious or social tradition, an affiliation less transient and more difficult to escape than mere adherence to a contemporary movement. For better or worse, Irish public life continues to dwell in imagined pasts as well as an equally fictionalised present, the link being most powerfully expressed through commemoration.

Since commemoration was already an integral part of Irish political life before 1922, it is not surprising that subsequent governments have attempted to exploit and control its political implications. In the Irish Free State, both Cosgrave and de Valera used commemoration for partisan purposes after taking power in 1922 and 1932 respectively. Their initial attempts to mobilise support by appropriating past rebellions and dead heroes were energetic and bitterly contested. Yet in Ireland, as elsewhere, official commemoration soon developed the more ambitious intention of reconciling hostile factions through identification of some episode of common inspiration or shared suffering in the past. This ambition continues to justify public expenditure on projects commemorating disasters such as the Great Famine and the rebellion of 1798, just as it justifies the search, so far futile, for a non-contentious 'peace memorial' in Northern Ireland.[4] This chapter examines the often painful and embarrassing experience of official commemoration in southern Ireland between 1922 and 1939. The survey is illustrative rather than comprehensive, being based largely on papers deemed sufficiently important or controversial to merit the government's attention.

II

The Irish Free State emerged from four bitter conflicts, between Irish and English, Catholics and Protestants, 'constitutional nationalists' and 'separatists', and finally 'Treatyites' and republicans. The rulers of the new state represented a sub-group within Catholic and nationalist Ireland, their triumph being bitterly resented by many Irish Protestants as well as by Catholic republicans and unreformed constitutionalists. In their attempts to secure the compliance and integration of disaffected opponents, Cosgrave's governments responded warily and wearily to the innumerable problems raised by partisan commemoration. Few sustained

[4] The best surveys of Irish commemorative practices are Jane Leonard's *The Culture of War Commemoration* ([Dublin], 1996) and *Memorials to the Casualties of Conflict: Northern Ireland, 1969 to 1997* (Belfast, 1997).

attempts were made to use official commemoration as a tool for reconciliation, since no event or hero seemed capable of incorporating all factions in common veneration.

Even the history of Christianity, although somewhat less contentious than past wars or rebellions, had pitfalls for secular commemorators. The constitution of 1922 precluded establishment of the Catholic Church, which even in 1937 was accorded nothing more secure than a 'special position'. It was therefore appropriate that state sponsorship of specifically Catholic commemorations should be muted and infrequent. Catholic Emancipation, the Eucharistic Congress and Father Mathew's temperance movement were deemed sufficiently uncontentious to be marked by postage stamps in 1929, 1932 and 1938.[5] When ministers and officers of state participated in religious commemorations and pilgrimages, they generally did so as pious parishioners or official suppliants, leaving the direction and organisation of such events to the clergy. The subordination of secular to spiritual authority was most conspicuous in the Eucharistic Congress of 1932, at which leaders of both major parties celebrated the supposed sesquimillennium of the birth of St Patrick by public obeisance to the hierarchy and the papal nuncio.[6] Since the saint's appropriation by the Roman Catholic Church had long been disputed by Protestants, this commemorative alignment of southern politicians with the Catholic hierarchy had unwelcome sectarian overtones.

In practice, governments seldom took a prominent part in the annual celebration of St Patrick's Day on 17 March, which remained largely under clerical and sometimes Hibernian control with some assistance from local authorities in organising parades. There were, however, two early attempts to harness the saint to the state. In 1925, the national holiday was celebrated in Dublin by a military parade, the minister for defence taking 'the salute from the troops at College Green'.[7] Next year, at the suggestion of J. J. Walsh (minister for posts and telegraphs), it was belatedly agreed to arrange a St Patrick's Day dance for over 1300 guests at Ballsbridge. Walsh cannily suggested that 'in view of the likelihood of invitations to Ministers from other quarters on this subject, it would be advisable to have an excuse for their remaining here in Dublin'. Cosgrave instructed the wives of his ministers that 'costumes and dress of Irish

[5] Ewan Morris, 'Our own devices: symbolising state and nation in Ireland, 1922–1939', Ph.D. thesis, University of Sydney (1997), p. 120.

[6] Ronan Fanning, *Independent Ireland* (Dublin, 1983), pp. 129–30. The minister for education (J. M. O'Sullivan) spoke on 'St Patrick's Apostleship' at the Mansion House, Dublin, on 19 June 1929: *Catholic Emancipation Centenary Celebrations: Advance Programme* (Dublin, 1929), p. 21.

[7] Executive Council [EC] Minutes, C 2/174, National Archives, Dublin [NA].

material and workmanship [were] to be worn . . . For the information of the ladies I might say that tailors may not recommend dress suits for men in Irish material. But that such material is available I am in a position to answer any one concerned.' In the event, the dance was cancelled as no hall with adequate cloakroom facilities could be secured.[8] Thereafter, state involvement in 'the national feast of Ireland'[9] was mainly restricted to the display of flags on prisons and buildings controlled by the Board of Works, military ceremonies, presidential wireless broadcasts and the mailing of shamrocks to selected 'exiles'. In 1931, Cosgrave sent no less than 1,356 shamrocks to 42 addresses in the United States, including batches of 100 or more to the Emerald Society in Brooklyn, the Friendly Sons of St Patrick, the 165th Infantry, the Irish Fellowship Club of Chicago and the United Irish Societies in Columbus, Ohio.[10] Such sentimental outpourings could not quite obscure the divisive implications of the state's collusion, however modest, in the hierarchy's hijacking of a Christian and national festival. As a Newtownards Unionist remarked in 1931: 'To St. Patrick we owe our National emblem, the Shamrock, and the symbol of the Trinity is honoured and respected by practically all denominations . . . The North was far more hospitable than the South to the Saint and his headquarters were in Armagh.'[11]

One of the few political anniversaries which initially seemed capable of ameliorating rather than sharpening intranationalist animosity was the birth of Theobald Wolfe Tone on 20 June 1763. Tone's professed desire to unite Catholic, Protestant and Dissenter in a common cause invited his commemoration as an apostle of reconciliation among Irishmen, if not between Ireland and Britain. In fact, the annual pilgrimage to his grave at Bodenstown, Co. Kildare, was invariably contested by several factions, each claiming Tone's mantle. The outcome was sardonically described by a Dublin accountancy student writing in 1925 to a republican in Australia:

> At 12 oc noon, Mr Hughes, Minister of Defence, with 2,000 Free State troops carrying English guns, entered Bodenstown churchyard. From a specially erected platform Mr Hughes harangued his troops for half-an-hour. He told them that were Wolfe Tone alive to-day that he (Tone) would be proud to carry a rifle in the Free State Army. He informed them that they had got the freedom for which Tone died and several other things besides. At 1.30 p.m. the Staters,

[8] Walsh to Cosgrave, 15 Jan. 1926; Cosgrave to wives, 1 Feb. 1926: EC Memoranda, S 599.

[9] This description was conveyed by the Department of External Affairs to the Spanish Consulate on 17 Aug. 1928: EC Memoranda, S 5724.

[10] EC Memoranda, S 4917B.

[11] *County Down Spectator*, 21 Mar. 1931.

having played the Last Post and fired volleys over the grave, vacated the position. At 2 oc. Eamonn de Valera and some thousands of Republicans took up the position and a fresh harangue took place, E. de V. assuring his audience that they had not got the freedom which Tone fought for etc. etc. What poor old Tone would have thought of it all had he been there in the flesh, I'm sure I don't know.[12]

Tone's reputation as a symbol of reconcilation was further fractured on 31 October 1969, when his tomb at Bodenstown was blown apart by a bomb.[13] Few other national leaders or events antedating 1914 received any official recognition. Perhaps because it was so closely associated with the discredited Home Rule movement, even the memory of the Manchester Martyrs on 23 November 1867 was left unretouched by all Free State administrations. Likewise, no government cared to claim the inheritance of the Repeal or Home Rule movements.[14] The history of pre-revolutionary nationalism remained divisive, since it could not be detached from the unresolved conflict over the measure of independence secured in 1922.

In the case of 'loyalist' anniversaries, the practical alternative to official indifference was not participation but suppression. It is noteworthy that the Free State's dwindling legion of Orangemen was never ostensibly prohibited from walking in regalia on 12 July, despite the risk of disorder and attacks by republicans. Instead, the police and occasionally the army offered some protection to the marchers while attempting to minimise disturbance. In 1923 Ernest Blythe, an Ulster Protestant intimately familiar with Orangeism, advised Kevin O'Higgins about the government's reponse to the forthcoming celebration of the Twelfth near Clones, Co. Monaghan. Local people had 'suggested that it would be a good thing if the Civic Guard and the Military took special, but *unostentatious*, precautions, to ensure that no unpleasantness occurred'. The police were instructed to act accordingly, and Assistant-Commissioner Éamonn Ó Cugáin reported that 'everything passed off very quietly', despite four prosecutions following the seizure of 'a large quantity of intoxicating liquor'.[15] Processions in Monaghan and Cavan continued until 1931, when unchecked disturbances erupted at Cootehill, Co. Cavan. The County Grand Lodge of Monaghan would never again

[12] Liam [Billy Judge] to Liam Corrigan, 24 June 1925: Corrigan MSS 1887/4/7, National Library of Australia.

[13] National Graves Association, *The Last Post* (2nd edn, Dublin, 1976), pp. 24–5.

[14] De Valera's government seems to have ignored the centenary of O'Connell's Repeal movement (launched in 1832) and the jubilee of the first Home Rule Bill in 1936.

[15] Department of Home Affairs files, H 75/15, NA. Blythe and O'Higgins were then ministers for Local Government and Home Affairs respectively.

authorise any public procession in regalia.[16] Indeed, it seems that no further traditional 'Twelfths' were held in the Free State outside Donegal (where an annual demonstration is held at Rossnowlagh on the first Saturday of July). The effect was to diminish both enthusiasm and recruitment in an institution deeply engrossed in public as well as private rituals of commemoration. Though some southern Lodges attended processions in Northern Ireland, this means of compensation was restricted by the expense and inconvenience of travel, and the enduring resentment of Orangemen in the 'three lost counties' towards their fickle northern brethren.

The Free State's reluctance to curtail loyalist commemoration exemplified a broader determination by both Cosgrave and de Valera to appear even-handed in their treatment of 'the minority', in mitigation of the religious and political bigotry of many of their supporters. This attitude was also evident in the official response to demands from local authorities and Fianna Fáil *cumainn* for the removal from Leinster Lawn of Queen Victoria's statue, and its replacement by a monument to Lord Edward Fitzgerald or Christ the King.[17] In March 1938, a party activist demanding the removal of 'imperialistic emblems and Monuments' was informed that 'it is not the policy of the Government to remove public monuments or sculpture on public buildings solely for the reason that they are associated with the former British regime'. This course might be justified only if 'it could be clearly shown that removal would be of definite national advantage'.[18] A decade passed before de Valera's opponents, during the spasm of symbolic renunciations culminating in their declaration of the republic, dismantled the 4 ton 'Famine Queen' and with some difficulty removed her from the sight of legislators.[19]

16 MSS minute books of the Grand Orange Lodge of Co. Monaghan (1932–42, 1943–60), kindly made available by the archivist, Grand Orange Lodge of Ireland.

17 EC Memoranda, S 6412A. Already in 1933, when two Cumann na nGaedheal deputies placed wreaths of leeks and broccoli on the monument in order to ridicule de Valera's tillage policy, it was rumoured that Queen Victoria would be replaced by Thomas Davis: *Irish Times*, 20 May 1933.

18 Draft letter from secretary, Department of the Taoiseach, to Liam Rapple, 16 Mar. 1938: EC Memoranda, S 10570. Similar phrases were used to rebut a similar proposal from the Fianna Fáil *ard fheis* in 1946.

19 Leonard, *War Commemoration*, p. 17. It was demonstrated by trial and error that a supine, but not a sitting queen could be squeezed through the ornamental gates: *Belfast Telegraph*, 22 July 1948, cutting in Evangelical Protestant Society Scrapbooks, i, p. 75, Linen Hall Library, Belfast. Four decades later, Queen Victoria was presented to the City of Sydney, which further abused her memory by reassembling the statue at the entrance to a shopping arcade.

III

In principle, commemoration of the Great War might have become a tool for reconciliation between Ireland's Catholic and Protestant communities, which had supplied roughly equal numbers to the wartime forces. As demonstrated throughout post-war Europe, it was perfectly possible to combine public mourning for the victims of war with repudiation of the 'war aims' of all protagonists. In the Free State, however, the rhetorical legacy of Sinn Féin made it impracticable to separate the issues of personal suffering and political conviction, all servicemen living and dead being damned by the flag under which they had served. Denunciation of enlistment was one of the defining features of wartime Sinn Féin, and nationalist disenchantment with the war had been crucial to Sinn Féin's campaign to supplant 'constitutionalism'. For the revolutionary generation, war service signified betrayal of the Irish nation, mitigated yet not excused (in the case of Home Rulers) by their deluded belief that the Allies were fighting for the freedom of small nationalities. These views survived the fragmentation of Sinn Féin after 1921, being eventually transmitted to Cumann na nGaedheal as well as Fianna Fáil and its diehard rivals. The lingering animosity of both major political parties towards ex-servicemen made all governments wary of publicly endorsing commemoration of Irish participation in the war.

Yet the scale of that participation, reflected in the survival of nearly 200,000 Irish veterans with personal connections touching every parish and most families, made it imprudent for any government to repudiate commemoration altogether. This factor was compounded by the Free State's obligations, reluctantly and incompletely fulfilled, as a dominion in the British Commonwealth. Alone among the dominions, the Free State declined to contribute its share to the expenses of the Imperial War Graves Commission, which was left to mark and maintain the graves of tens of thousands of Irishmen buried in foreign battlefields. In grudging compensation, the Executive Council agreed in June 1924 to 'take over the entire charge of British Military Graves in the State', eventually raising about 2,500 headstones for 'British' soldiers who had died in the twenty-six counties between August 1914 and August 1921. These included men killed in the Anglo-Irish conflict as well as Irish victims of the Great War who had died after returning home. Though entrusted with this task in December 1926, a decade later the Commissioners of Public Works had yet to complete it, progress having been impeded by objections from local authorities in Sligo and Clare to the inclusion of regimental badges on headstones in graveyards under their control.[20]

In Southern Ireland, as in Britain, the erection of collective war memorials, tablets and rolls of honour began even before the Armistice and peaked in its immediate aftermath. Though mainly funded by parishes, schools, firms and local authorities, these pre-Treaty initiatives included the inauguration under vice-regal patronage of an Irish National War Memorial, in July 1919.[21] Faced with the *fait accompli* of a subscription and trust to create a national memorial, Cosgrave's government restricted itself to postponing rather than countermanding the project. The trustees themselves took five years to settle upon an acceptable substitute for the soldiers' home originally proposed, and to recommend that Merrion Square should be acquired as a public park incorporating a memorial. After another three years, the government withdrew its initial acquiescence following objections in the Oireachtais to placing this reminder of a discredited conflict so uncomfortably close to Leinster House. The decision to develop a site at Islandbridge as a public park, reserved for the use of veterans 'on one or two days in the year in connection with the annual memorial ceremony', was taken only in late 1929. While regretting the government's procrastination, Cosgrave reminded an ex-Unionist senator that the fact could not be ignored 'that there is a certain hostility to the idea of any form of War Memorial'. Though agreeing in principle to augment the trust fund to facilitate the necessary capital investment and maintenance, Cosgrave allowed a further long delay before making the decision public.[22]

When asked to participate in other acts of remembrance, the government's response was usually equivocal. Even under de Valera, the Free State was regularly represented by its high commissioner at the Cenotaph ceremony in Whitehall; but neither the president nor the governor-general laid wreaths during Irish Armistice Day processions, which were frequently marred by republican violence and insults against ex-servicemen. Cosgrave attended a special Catholic mass in Cork on 11 November 1923; yet civil servants were refused leave to mourn the dead

[20] EC Minutes, C 2/112; EC Memoranda, S 9273. Less than a quarter of these graves were in cemeteries controlled by the Commissioners.

[21] Jane Leonard, 'Lest we forget', in Trinity History Workshop, *Ireland and the First World War* (Dublin, 1986), pp. 59–67.

[22] Cosgrave to Jameson, 2 Dec. 1929: EC Memoranda, S 4156B; cf. Keith Jeffery, 'The Great War in modern Irish memory', in T. G. Fraser and Keith Jeffery (eds.), *Men, Women and War* (Dublin, 1993), pp. 145–6.

at Dublin's College Green by an eleventh-hour ruling of 10 November 1925.[23] In the intervening year, the Executive Council had felt impelled to ask the Legion of Ex-Servicemen (shortly to amalgamate with other veterans' bodies as the British Legion, Free State Area) to withdraw its request for official representation at the erection of a temporary wooden cross in College Green. 'It was felt that the time was not ripe for the Government to publicly associate itself with functions of this nature.' Cosgrave's 'personal view' was 'that it would be hypocritical for him, having regard to the fact that he was imprisoned by the British Government during the world-war, to accept'. Yet the government decided three days later to allow Senator Maurice Moore to lay a wreath on its behalf, a gesture presumably designed to minimise offence to all parties.[24]

Two years later, this sequence was replicated when Stanley Baldwin invited Cosgrave with his colleagues to join other dominion premiers at the unveiling of a tablet in Westminster Abbey, commemorating the million lost by the empire in the Great War. Cosgrave reminded Baldwin that he and several members of the Executive Council had been 'actively engaged in the hostilities' of 1916, through which 'a considerable amount of feeling was naturally aroused and bitter words were spoken'. Fearing that his presence might 're-open old wounds that are not yet quite healed', and ruminating that 'it is so easy to hurt and so difficult to heal', Cosgrave nominated Kevin O'Higgins, whose brother Michael was among the lost million and 'to whom no similar objection exists'. Far from provoking contempt by this long-winded evasion, Cosgrave was complimented by Leopold Amery (the Dominions secretary) for his 'chivalrous thoughtfulness', and at Amery's suggestion the letter was made public.[25] Despite such timorous displays of tact, Cosgrave's government was reviled by republicans for its tolerance of war commemoration and the imperial patriotism which this supposedly implied. As Terence MacSwiney's sister Annie snarled in 1928: 'Poppy day is coming on now. How the poppies fly in Ireland since the Free State

[23] Deputies and senators with appropriate connections laid wreaths in Dublin, on behalf of the government, annually until Nov. 1933. See Jane Leonard, 'The twinge of memory: Armistice Day and Remembrance Sunday in Dublin since 1919', in Richard English and Graham Walker (eds.), *Unionism in Modern Ireland: New Perspectives on Politics and Culture* (Dublin, 1996), pp. 99–114; EC Memoranda, S 3370A.

[24] EC Memoranda, S 3370A. Maurice George Moore (1854–1939) had the multiple qualificiations of being Catholic, nationalist, a senior officer in both the Irish and National Volunteers, and a retired colonel in the Connaught Rangers.

[25] Baldwin to Cosgrave, 8 Oct. 1926; Cosgrave to Baldwin, 13 Oct. 1926; Amery to Cosgrave, 15 Oct. 1926; report by Michael McDunphy, 19 Oct. 1926: EC Memoranda, S 5276.

came into existence – Union Jackery of every description foisted on the country by Collins and Mulcahy and the rest.'[26]

De Valera's accession in 1932, though marked by a sequence of studied symbolic denials of the imperial connection, had strikingly little effect on official attitudes towards Irish commemoration of the Great War. Work on the memorial park at Islandbridge having begun only in December 1931, two months before Cosgrave's defeat in the general election, de Valera continued to subsidise construction despite allocation of half of the labour to 'British' ex-servicemen.[27] By March 1937, his minister for finance (Seán McEntee) displayed less uneasiness with the legacy of the Great War than Cosgrave had done when in power: 'a formal handing over of the War Memorial Park by the Trustees and acceptance by the Government would be a graceful gesture which . . . could be treated as symbolical of the unification of all elements in the community under an agreed democratic Constitution which guarantees respect for the rights of all citizens'. This message of reconciliation was premature, and an uncertain Cabinet left it to de Valera to determine whether an official opening should be held. In December 1938, de Valera 'intimated in favour of opening ceremony in summer with himself present', after his return from an American tour. Four months later, he advised a delegation from the British Legion to postpone or else restrict the scale of their proposed opening. 'The tenseness of the international situation . . . and the consequent ferment here had altered the situation'; and the threat of conscription in Northern Ireland exacerbated the risk that a formal ceremony 'might evoke hostility'. Prompted by an explanatory letter urging unqualified postponement, the British Legion was induced to retract leaked predictions of an opening ceremony on 30 July 1939, and to announce that the event had been 'indefinitely postponed' because of the international situation.[28]

The British Legion nevertheless applied as usual for permission to hold church services, poppy sales and a parade to the Phoenix Park (where a wooden cross was to be erected) in November 1939. The Gárda Siochána objected that both a parade and the erection of a cross would risk public disorder, and cited the cancellation of public processions in London and Belfast in response to wartime lighting restrictions and 'present conditions'. Yet the Cabinet approved all ceremonies except a procession, subsequently revoking the ban on parades after receiving

[26] Annie MacSwiney to Sheila Humphreys, 29 Oct. 1928: EC Memoranda, S 8049.
[27] Judith Hill, *Irish Public Sculpture: A History* (Dublin, 1998), p. 161.
[28] EC Memoranda, S 4156B.

an assurance from the British Legion. Official tolerance of Armistice Day ceremonies was again displayed in 1940, when the British Legion was permitted for the first time to hold a ceremony at Islandbridge, though without any public parade to or from the city. The wartime abandonment of Armistice Day processions was not peculiar to neutral Ireland, having already been applied throughout the United Kingdom. Shortly before the novel ceremony of 1940, de Valera concluded that 'in view of the war conditions, the question of State assistance for further works at Islandbridge Memorial cannot usefully be pursued at present'.[29] Nearly half a century of neglect followed until the official opening of the park in 1988, without participation by Haughey's government, and a further ceremony in 1994 at which Ahern pronounced the construction of the memorial to be complete.[30] Despite this unhappy record of subsequent official procrastination, it seems likely that de Valera would have made the long-contemplated gesture in 1939, but for rising domestic and international tension. If so, his government would have been the first to ascertain whether commemoration could indeed be deployed as a tool for reconciliation among Irishmen.

IV

Though repugnant to the dwindling bands of Unionists and constitutional nationalists, the rebellion of 1916 offered a credible focus for reconciliation between supporters and opponents of the Treaty. The Easter Proclamation and Pearse's writings remained seminal texts for both major parties, and the 'martyrs' were celebrated with competitive enthusiasm by all factions descended from revolutionary Sinn Féin. In practice, these competing claims to the Easter legacy made it impracticable to erect a memorial acceptable to all parties. This became evident after October 1923, when Clement Shorter offered to contribute £1,000 from his wife's estate, to enable her sculpture commemorating the executed rebels to be fashioned in Carrara marble, set on a pedestal of Irish limestone, and erected in Glasnevin cemetery. Its centrepiece was to be an image of Patrick Pearse.[31] Cosgrave remarked that Mrs Pearse's response would 'be largely affected by the contact which the Government has with

[29] EC Memoranda, S 4156B; S 3370B.

[30] Leonard, 'Twinge of memory', pp. 109–11.

[31] Shorter to James MacNeill, 12 Oct. 1923: EC Memoranda, S 3357A. Clement King Shorter (1857–1926) edited the *Illustrated London News* and from 1900 the *Sphere*. His wife Dora (d. 1918) was a sculptor, poet and daughter of Dr George Sigerson (1836–1925), who was nominated by Cosgrave to the first Seanad.

the proposal', demurred at the proposed exclusion of those killed by other means, and suggested that any memorial should be erected outside Leinster House rather than at Glasnevin. He feared that the unmodified proposal would make it 'look as if we wanted to have one last slap at the British'.[32] Nevertheless, in December 1923, the Executive Council approved both the memorial and its erection in Glasnevin.

As usual, acceptance in principle was followed by a tiresome sequence of setbacks and quandaries. In November 1925, the government rejected two sites at Glasnevin, fearing that in one location the memorial would have been dwarfed by existing tombs; whereas its erection in the other would 'hide President Griffith's grave from persons passing along the walk, and would undoubtedly be resented by his relatives, who it is understood are arranging to have a cross erected on the grave'. Although a third site was chosen, pitfalls remained. After yet another year, the Executive Council scrutinised the wording in minute detail, and directed that the names of all fallen rebels, including Roger Casement but specifically excluding Francis Sheehy-Skeffington, should be inscribed on parchment and cased in lead within the memorial.[33] In May 1927, this commitment was qualified by a characteristic decision to avoid any 'formal ceremony' of unveiling and hence reduce the risk of an unseemly public squabble over the Easter inheritance.[34]

Partisan rivalry had long since characterised the annual observance of the Republic's proclamation on Easter Monday, 1916. In 1924, the first official ceremony at Arbour Hill (burial-place of the executed rebels) was marred by 'a good deal of dissatisfaction' on the part of notabilities who 'should have been regarded as entitled to be present at any such celebrations'. Worse still, only Mrs Mallon among the twenty-five invited 'relatives of the deceased' condescended to attend.[35] The next ceremony incorporated a requiem mass at the garrison church, a slow march with bands, wreath-laying, a grave-side rosary, the firing of a volley and performance of 'The Last Post'. Attendance was by invitation

[32] Note in Cosgrave's hand, *c.* 20 Oct. 1923: EC Memoranda, S 3357A.

[33] EC Minutes, C 2/34, 2/224; EC Memoranda, S 3357A. Neither Sir Roger Casement (1864–1916) nor the pacifist Francis Sheehy-Skeffington (1878–1916) participated in the Rising, being nevertheless hanged at Pentonville prison and murdered in Portobello barracks, respectively.

[34] Shorter having expired during the four years of negotiation, contradictory samples of his correspondence were produced: some proposing that Cosgrave should unveil the monument, others 'protesting against any particular political party having charge of any ceremony of the kind': EC Minutes, C 2/338; EC Memoranda, S 3357A.

[35] Invitations were sent to close relatives irrespective of their views on the Treaty, with the exception of those deemed 'Irregular': EC Memoranda, S 9815A; EC Minutes, C 2/187. Mrs Mallin's husband Michael (1880–1916) had been chief of staff in James Connolly's Irish Citizen Army.

to about 400 ministers, deputies, senators, clergy, civil servants, soldiers, policemen and relatives of the deceased, along with a 'General list' of 200. In 1926, several awkward relatives were removed from the list, and the protocol was varied to substitute 'De Profundis' and 'A Soldier's Song' for the rosary.[36] The ceremony remained closed, and rival republican commemorations continued unabated, notably in 1929 when the IRA ordered its units to observe Easter Sunday as a 'Day of National Commemoration' for 'the memory of all who gave their lives for the Sovereign Independence of Ireland'.[37] After a procession from the city with six bands, Frank Ryan unveiled a modest memorial (since replaced) to sixteen obscure rebels who had been buried coffinless at Glasnevin.[38]

In commemorating 1916, de Valera proved less reticent than his predecessor in claiming the mantle of the martyrs. In March 1932, within a month of taking power, his first government had decided in principle to admit the public to the graveside after the 'usual celebration' at Arbour Hill Barracks. In the following year, the minister for defence (Frank Aiken) admitted that 241 names had been removed from the invitation list, ostensibly in order to accommodate 'the relatives of those who were killed or executed from 1916 to 1923'. This medley of mourners was littered with republicans increasingly hostile to Fianna Fáil. The protocol in 1937 was almost identical to that in 1926, except that all relatives were now excluded from the procession, only immediate connections of the dead leaders being accorded so much as a privileged vantage-point. The Mallon family, unique in their representation in 1925, proved an embarrassment to the organisers in 1941, when Michael Mallon's son demanded to be invited along with the hero's father and brother.[39]

The absence of an enduring and conspicuous monument to the Rising was eventually remedied on Easter Monday, 1935, when de Valera unveiled a memorial at the General Post Office, following a military parade and an inspection of the Old Dublin Brigade. The memorial was surmounted by Oliver Sheppard's magnificent bronze, *The Death of Cuchulainn*, modelled in plaster nearly a quarter of a century before. Fianna Fáil's appropriation of the Rising was predictably challenged by the subsequent arrival at the GPO of a rival republican procession, *en route*

[36] EC Memoranda, S 9815A.

[37] EC Memoranda, S 8049.

[38] National Graves Association, *The Last Post* (Dublin, 1932), p. 17; *ibid.* (2nd edn, Dublin, 1976), pp. 15–16. Frank Ryan (1902–44), commandant of the IRA's Dublin Brigade, led an Irish contingent in support of the Spanish Republic in 1936.

[39] EC Memoranda, S 9815A.

to its own commemorative ceremony at Glasnevin.[40] In the following year, undiscouraged, de Valera presented the National Museum with an ornamental Roll of Honour listing thousands of supposed participants in the Rising, both living and dead. Speechless and protected by dark glasses after ophthalmic surgery, he presided over a ceremony enlivened by mounted troopers and a military band performing 'The Last Post' and the 'Dead March' from Handel's *Saul*.[41] Despite these spectacular displays, neither Fianna Fáil nor any other party had yet managed to secure sole custody of the Easter legacy when, recently and quite suddenly, it became worthless.

V

The conflict accompanying the creation of the state provided ample opportunity for divisive commemoration by both protagonists, so testing the degree to which each party when in government would subordinate partisan to national interest. The Civil War had scarcely begun when Michael Collins revealed to Desmond FitzGerald his plan for a multitude of propagandist films to counteract the 'verbal thunder' of their opponents. These were to include a 'war film' depicting 'Leading National Generals' as ordinary people (such as 'McKeon – Blacksmith'), and also showing pictures and funerals of dead national soldiers. Collins had 'thousands of other possible Films' in mind, which died with their creator at Beal na mBláth a few weeks later.[42] As the Civil War receded, the government's focus changed from topical propaganda to partisan celebration of the birth of the Free State. Two years after its formal inauguration on 6 December 1922, the government celebrated 'Independence Day' for the first and last time. The anniversary was marked by flying flags from all public buildings and barracks, but not by a procession or military march. Kevin O'Higgins, Cosgrave's vice-president, delivered the rather drab message that 'given energy and honest endeavour there is no

[40] Hill, *Irish Public Sculpture*, pp. 156–7; Theo Snoddy, *Dictionary of Irish Artists: 20th Century* (Dublin, 1996), p. 457. Oliver Sheppard, RHA, RBS (1865–1941) had exhibited a plaster cast of the sculpture in the Royal Hibernian Academy in 1914, two years before the event that it was to commemorate.

[41] EC Memoranda, S 8874. The government also decided in 1938 to build a garden of remembrance as a national memorial to Irish freedom fighters, but the garden in Parnell Square was not opened until 1966: Hill, *Irish Public Sculpture*, pp. 157–8.

[42] Collins to FitzGerald, 12 July 1922: EC Memoranda, S 595. Seán MacEoin (1893–1973), a Longford guerrilla hero who played a major part in suppressing Irregular resistance in the midlands and Connacht, acquired the epithet 'Blacksmith of Ballinalee' after a bloody ambush at Clonfin in Feb. 1921.

reason why we should not speedily succeed in re-establishing ourselves', expressing 'feelings of renewed confidence' following 'the removal of the reign of terror'. Next year a senior civil servant presumed that a similar message was to be delivered, only to be informed by the secretary to the Executive Council that 'pressure of other business rendered any action in this matter impossible'.[43] On this irritable note, discussion of how best to commemorate the foundation of the state appears to have ceased.

A more sustained attempt was made to sanctify the memory of its architects, Michael Collins and Arthur Griffith, dual heads of government after approval of the Treaty, who both died at the peak of the Civil War in August 1922. In May 1923, the Irish-American Eugene Kinkead, who had collaborated in a botched attempt two years earlier to smuggle nearly 500 Thompson sub-machine guns for use by Collins and the IRA, undertook to pay the cost of building a burial mound for Griffith and an army plot at Glasnevin with Collins's grave at its centre.[44] As the first anniversary of their deaths approached, the director of publicity (Seán Lester) busied himself with securing suitable historical films, lantern slides and hagiographical features in the press.[45] Picture houses were supplied with 156 sets of five lantern slides displaying portraits of both leaders, Griffith entering the Mansion House, Collins at an open-air meeting in Cork, and a message from General Mulcahy observing that 'Griffith was the greatest sower and Collins the greatest reaper that Ireland ever knew'.[46] The commemorative highlight was Cosgrave's unveiling of a cenotaph on Leinster Lawn before 2,000 invited guests, accompanied by the laying of a wreath, a presidential oration, a salvo of guns at the Phoenix Park, a military parade with artillery and armoured cars along Merrion Street, salutes and a solemn requiem mass. The cenotaph used in 1923 was a miserable hodge-podge of timber and expanded metal covered by concrete plaster, with bust portraits in plaque of the two leaders in its base.[47] The occasion was somewhat spoiled by a demand from Mrs Griffith that 'her husband's name [be] erased from such a senseless show. It is

[43] EC Memoranda, S 4178, indexed under 'Independence Day'.

[44] On 2 May 1923, the Executive Council accepted this lavish proposal for expenditure of some £13,000 from Eugene F. Kinkead (1876–1960), an ex-major in American military intelligence who had become active in Irish republican organisations in the United States: EC Minutes, C 1/97; Kinkead to John W. Goff, 2 Dec. 1918: Cohalan Papers, 7/23, American Irish Historical Society, New York; interview with Liam Pedlar, O'Malley Notebooks, University College Dublin Archives [hereafter UCDA], P 17b/94.

[45] Piaras Béaslaí and Kevin O'Higgins wrote articles on Collins, while Griffith's memory was celebrated by Éamonn Duggan and John Chartres.

[46] Lester to FitzGerald, 11 and 23 July 1923: FitzGerald Papers, UCDA, P 80/303/2, 6.

[47] Memorandum by Michael McDunphy, 6 July 1932: EC Memoranda, S 8362.

more important to finish his grave, his remains are there in consecrated ground. This stunt is not at all in concord with his life of sacrifice and honesty.'[48] The private distress caused by public appropriation of the dead has seldom been so clearly exposed.

Undeterred, the Executive Council prepared the way for an even more ambitious personality cult in the following year, appointing a heavy-weight 'Griffith–Collins Anniversary Committee' which first met on 25 June 1924.[49] The ceremony was based on that for 1923, with Cosgrave laying a single wreath at the cenotaph 'representing the Nation' and delivering an oration before a military march-past, followed by the laying of further wreaths at Glasnevin and also a ceremony at Béal na mBlath, Co. Cork, on 22 August. Chairs or cloth-covered benches were to replace the 'unsightly' wooden seating of 1923; the plaques on the still temporary cenotaph were to be regilded; and the ceremony was put forward from 3.00 to 12.30 to avoid coincidence with the inter-provincial hurling and football finals. The committee rejected a proposal for 'a stall in the vicinity where tourists could obtain literature such as the Collins–Griffith Album, Speeches of the Leaders, etc. etc.', but agreed to ask 200 booksellers to 'make a special display of the literature in question during August'. The guest list was remodelled along ecumenical lines, Dublin's legion of parish priests being excluded whereas invitations were sent to the three major Protestant churches and the rabbinate. Other recipients of invitations included Provost Bernard and the seven senior fellows of Trinity College; the editors of all provincial weeklies except the *Waterford News*; friends of the 'late General Collins' such as Miss Kiernan and the disgraced army mutineers Tobin and Dalton; the novelist Brinsley MacNamara; and the former Home Rule leaders Dillon and Devlin.[50] Preparations were again disturbed by Mrs Griffith, who was asked to postpone removal of her husband's remains to a family grave until after the 'anniversary celebration'.[51] On 10 August she grudgingly agreed to

[48] Mrs [Mary] Griffith to organising committee, 30 July 1923, demanding publication of her views in the daily press: copy or précis in FitzGerald Papers, UCDA, P 80/303/8.

[49] The chosen date was 17 Aug. 1924, intermediate between the anniversaries of Griffith (12 Aug.) and Collins (22 Aug.). The committee was chaired by FitzGerald with Seán Lester as secretary, and two or three generals usually in attendance: EC Minutes, C 2/108; Mulcahy Papers, UCDA, P 7/B/330.

[50] Minutes of committee meetings in Mulcahy Papers, UCDA, P 7/B/330. Those named were John Henry Bernard (1860–1927), previously archbishop of Dublin; Catherine Bridget [Kitty] Kiernan (1892–1945); Major-Gen. Liam Tobin and Col. Charles Dalton, authors of the ultimatum issued by the Old IRA Organisation on 6 Mar. 1924; John Weldon, *pseud.* Brinsley MacNamara (1890–1963), author of *The Valley of the Squinting Windows* (Dublin, 1918); John Dillon (1851–1927); and Joseph Devlin (1871–1934).

[51] EC Minutes, 28 June 1924, C 2/112.

distribute tickets for 'the Cenotaph show', but protested that 'shows and stunts are all that is the thing now. When something is done to honour my husband's memory alone, I'll help and take part.'[52] Undaunted, Cosgrave renewed his bond with the dead with uncharacteristic euphoria: 'Founders of the State! the State lives and grows: Leaders of the people! the people are faithful: Revivifiers of the Gael! the pulse of the Gael throbs with life: Great pair ! . . . Rest in peace.'[53]

The anniversary celebration long remained the occasion for adherents of the Treaty to renew their faith and venerate their founders. After the murder of Kevin O'Higgins in July 1927, his portrait was added to the still temporary cenotaph and his name added to the already cumbersome designation of the anniversary. In 1928, the ceremony was 'simplified by omission of the oration', and the Board of Public Works offered the fairly reassuring prediction that the cenotaph would 'retain its appearance' for another five years. Twenty-two years were to pass before Raymond McGrath's granite obelisk with its three bronze medallions was erected, never to be unveiled.[54] De Valera made no attempt to prohibit the ceremony at the cenotaph, but discontinued the customary military parade and the attendance of ministers, leaving its organisation to Cumann na nGaedheal, the Association of the Old Dublin Brigade and the Army Comrades' Association.[55] This indulgence was abruptly terminated in 1933, when the commemoration was banned on the pretext that O'Duffy's National Guard intended to precipitate a *coup d'état.* No comparable anniversary derived from events or deaths in the Civil War was observed by de Valera's government, although in later years he and his ministers regularly unveiled monuments to individual republicans and to the activities of IRA units throughout the period 1916–23. By contrast with Cosgrave, de Valera based his primary claim to legitimacy on the link with 1916 rather than the less exalting tumult of 1922.

Cumann na nGaedheal's ineptitude in the manipulation of symbols was painfully evident in its protracted attempt to immortalise the founders in busts based on their death-masks. Already in October 1922, General Mulcahy had insisted that 'immediate steps should be taken to secure' the death masks of Griffith and Collins, and prevent their removal from the country.[56] Oliver St John Gogarty acted as go-between

[52] Mrs Griffith to Seán Lester, 10 Aug. 1924: copy in Mulcahy Papers, UCDA, P 7/B/330.

[53] Duplicated script in Devoy Papers, National Library of Ireland, MS 18124.

[54] EC Memoranda, S 8362; Hill, *Irish Public Sculpture*, pp. 154–5.

[55] Memorandum by Michael McDunphy: EC Memoranda, S 8362.

[56] EC Memoranda, S 1827A. Richard Mulcahy (1886–1971) commanded the army after the death of Collins.

with the sculptors Albert Power and Francis Doyle-Jones, both of whom had taken casts from Collins shortly after the arrival of his corpse in Dublin.[57] Power was commissioned to fashion busts from the death-masks in November 1922, but proved far from energetic in completing the assignment and answering correspondence. By June 1923, Cosgrave had ascertained from Gogarty that busts based on both masks were in Power's studio, and urged their inspection to ensure that justice had been done to Collins. Power's enthusiasm was negligible by February 1925, possibly, as Gogarty surmised, because 'the National Gallery has now a quite satisfactory bust by the Sculptor Doyle-Jones'. Three months later, Gogarty had managed to view Power's two plaster casts, which he thought might be improved by 'cutting off the edge of the shoulder' to render Griffith less 'stocky', and by draping Collins in a great-coat with 'one lapel thrown open' and remodelling him 'in the "heroic size" as the Kettle bust was'.[58] By 1928, the plaster was 'crumbling back into dust', and Bishop Fogarty of Killaloe urged the government to secure the busts and if possible have them cast in bronze or marble – advice which, as Cosgrave wearily informed his 'dear Lord Bishop', had been the intention of the government since the order was first placed in 1922.[59] The government's appetite for masks and busts remained undimmed, for in April 1930 the Executive Council authorised Oliver Sheppard to make a bronze bust from the death-mask of Kevin O'Higgins.[60] Two months later, another intermediary (Frank Duff) expressed 'little hope of early completion of the work' commissioned from Power, 'a man who appears to live in a chronic state of stagnation'.[61] In March 1931, Gogarty reported after an interview with Power that 'the Collins bust has been irreparably broken, having been lurched down by children'.[62] Cosgrave left office without the satisfaction of seeing his mentors immortalised in bronze.

[57] Oliver St John Gogarty (1878–1957), surgeon, senator, and polymath; Albert George Power, RHA (1881–1945); Francis William Doyle-Jones (1873–1938).

[58] Memorandum by Cosgrave, *c.* 2 June 1923; Gogarty to O'Hegarty, 18 Feb. and 7 May 1925: EC Memoranda, S 1827A. Power's bust of Thomas Michael Kettle (1880–1916), former Home Ruler and Lieut., 9th Royal Dublin Fusiliers, was exhibited in 1922 but not erected in St Stephen's Green until 1937: J. B. Lyons, *The Enigma of Tom Kettle* (Dublin, 1983), pp. 305–6.

[59] Fogarty to Cosgrave, 22 Apr. 1928; Cosgrave to Fogarty, 26 Apr. 1928: EC Memoranda, S 1827A. Dr Michael Fogarty (1859–1955) had bitterly denounced de Valera's rejection of the Treaty, and became Cosgrave's closest friend and mentor in the hierarchy.

[60] Sheppard's bust of O'Higgins, in marble not bronze, was completed in 1932 and placed in the National Gallery of Ireland: Snoddy, *Dictionary of Irish Artists*, p. 457.

[61] McDunphy's minute of conversation with Duff, 26 June 1930: EC Memoranda, S 1827A. Francis Michael Duff (1889–1980) and the Legion of Mary, founded in 1921, pursued a relentless campaign for the redemption of prostitutes.

[62] Notes on Gogarty's visit to Power, 3 Mar. 1931: EC Memoranda, S 1827A.

His successor, far from abandoning the quest, saw an opportunity to convert a partisan commemoration into an act of reconciliation. In January 1935, having secured an audience with the elusive Power, de Valera proposed that the state should buy both busts from Power for casting in bronze by Sheppard, and also commission fresh busts of the republican heroes Brugha and Stack. £1,500 was allocated to this purpose in the estimates for 1935–6, and by November 1936 the state had secured possession of Collins and Griffith in both plaster and bronze, for consignment to oblivion in the National Museum.[63] Stack had been modelled in clay by 1940, but Brugha's likeness had to be taken from a photograph rather than his death-mask, following objections from his widow. The rumour that Sheppard's bronze was shortly to adorn 'the so-called Dáil building' drew a scathing response from Mrs Brugha: 'I must emphatically protest on behalf of my late husband's family and myself against this threatened insult to his memory. I consider it a piece of gross impertinence, to say the least of it, for men who have abandoned the ideals for which Cathal Brugha died to attempt to shelter themselves in the reflected glory of one who died for the Republic.'[64] De Valera was languishing in opposition when the bronzes were finally delivered in 1951.

This chronicle of embarrassment demonstrates the obstacles confronting successive governments of the Irish Free State in their portrayal of the lessons of history through monuments and public rituals. Partisan appropriations of the past were invariably resented and contested, so that year by year Bodenstown and Glasnevin became battlegrounds rather than sites of veneration. When in power, both parties made some attempt to reconcile disaffected groups by involving the state in non-partisan commemoration of the 1916 Rising and the Great War. These somewhat ecumenical enterprises proved no less contentious, not least because of resentment from those whose mourning was personal and specific. Since all political factions drew their legitimacy from competing interpretations of the Irish past, all commemoration was tainted by politics and potentially counter-productive. Justifiably fearful of history and its power to rekindle unresolved conflicts, both governments were hesitant in exploiting the emotional capital accumulated through the fabled seven centuries of national struggle.

[63] Memorandum by Seán Ó Muimhneachain, 22 Jan. 1935: EC Memoranda, S 1827A. Cathal Brugha (1874–1922) and Austin Stack (1879–1929) were likewise to be fashioned in plaster by Power and cast in bronze by Sheppard. The estimates also provided for Sheppard's bronze of Pearse, completed in 1936: Snoddy, *Dictionary of Irish Artists*, p. 457.

[64] Mrs [Cathleen] Brugha to *Irish Times*, 26 Jan. 1939: EC Memoranda, S 1827A.

CHAPTER 9

Monument and trauma: varieties of remembrance

Joep Leerssen

I

With the exception of the Vatican, Great Britain is probably the European state where the official trappings of church and state are most closely intertwined.[1] The close link between church and state in the Orthodox countries and in Poland has vanished since the mid twentieth century (although it is now re-emerging in parts of eastern Europe); the privileged position of Catholicism in Portugal, Spain and Ireland has evaporated as a result of secularisation and modernisation during the 1960s and 1970s; and in most west European countries the legacy of the French Revolution has resulted in a rigid and uneasy division between the civil and ecclesiastical authorities.

Not so in high-church England. To visit Westminster Abbey or the cathedrals of Canterbury, Lincoln and York is to enter into shrines which celebrate a transcendent moral union between state and spirituality stretching from the Middle Ages into the twentieth century. The graves of princes, prelates and nobility; the commemorative plaques; the regimental flags; Poets' Corner: all these add up to an impression of 'establishment' in the firmest sense of the word. The continuity, the solidity and the ongoing affirmation of a shared sense of decorum and greatness are manifested in all these trappings, and turn such places into prime examples of *lieux de mémoire*. The cathedrals of high-church England are statements of enduring presence, continuity of usage and

[1] This is largely because England has an established 'state church', a situation unique in western Christendom. The role of religion, more especially of Anglican church ritual, in the development and maintenance of an Engish sense of nationality has been studied by scholars like Linda Colley: see her *Britons: Forging the Nation, 1707–1837* (New Haven, CT, 1992); or her article 'Britishness and otherness: an argument', in Michael O'Dea and Kevin Whelan (eds.), *Nations and Nationalisms: France, Britain, Ireland and the Eighteenth-Century Context* (Oxford, 1995), pp. 61–78. More abrasive is David Cannadine's 'The context, performance and meaning of ritual: the British monarchy and the "invention of tradition", *c.* 1820–1977', in Eric Hobsbawm and Terence Ranger (eds.), *The Invention of Tradition* (Cambridge, 1983), pp. 101–64.

reappropriation by each succeeding generation, in a moral sphere where religious and 'national' community overlap seamlessly. As in the case of state rituals, institutionalised traditions and ceremonies, such monuments proclaim a Burkean sense of national community – 'community' both in a synchronic sense (encompassing all those who share the location and its symbolic charisma) and in a diachronic one (linking present-day users to the past ones).

Would it not be churlish to speak of 'invention of tradition', or to spoil the noble dream by pointing out the partial, exclusive and triumphalist nature of such idealised communal symbolism? For a more sympathetic discussion of such celebrations of stability one might turn to the great sociologist of the reactionary American right, Edward Shils, in his perceptive study on *Tradition* (1981). 'Invented' or not, this tradition of a blithely consensual Anglican decorum, like so many other anglocentric cultural artefacts and attitudes,[2] becomes much more contentious as it is disseminated further afield to other, more peripheral parts of the empire or the United Kingdom – let alone to Ireland.

St Patrick's Cathedral in Dublin is a muted, muddled echo of the triumphant cathedrals of high-church England – much as the Church of Ireland is a foothill in the mountain range of anglocentric episcopalianism. It is a shrine to the elite's values of greatness and decorum: here, too, are the regimental flags, the graves of young officers killed in distant parts of the empire, of revered churchmen and politicians; the plaques listing the names of dignitaries succeeding each other in office over centuries (the longer the list, the heavier the weight of historical continuity and greater the prestige and charisma); and the names inscribed everywhere, names of gentry, nobility and patricians, reading like a Court Circular, a Peerage or a Who's Who.[3] There is a difference with the English counterparts, of course: this elite celebrated its values in a social context of unrootedness and isolation; its cathedrals were considered, by the

[2] The falsity and partiality of such ideals, and their hegemonistic intent, have been the subject of much critique in the last few decades. Much of that critique was necessary and justified; however, it would hamper us in our proper understanding of the historical and social function of traditions and rituals if we were to view them, exclusively and by definition as it were, from the peeved point of view of those who were left out. In order to balance and complement *that* perspective, it would be useful to consult the work of Edward Shils. For all his deep-dyed conservatism, his conceptualisation of societal centre–periphery relations has enduring methodological value, and his book on *Tradition* (London, 1981), analysing those aspects of public life embodying permanence through changing temporal circumstances (buildings, heirlooms, monuments, institutions, customs and ceremonies) anticipates the work of David Lowenthal and Pierre Nora.

[3] On the various mementoes and monuments in St Patrick's Cathedral, Dublin, see the highly informative guide by Victor Jackson, *The Monuments in St Patrick's Cathedral, Dublin* (Dublin, 1987).

mass of the population, as hijacked and desecrated places of Protestant heresy. The triumphalism of Anglican conservatism was reared on thin demographic ice, underpinned as it was, not by 'community' or local populace, but by reliance on the British 'mainland'. What in Britain can count as shared, official decorum[4] (almost effortlessly drowning out non-conformist traditions), is a much more partial and contentious presence on Irish soil. Nowhere in Irish public space does the colonial nature of the Protestant Ascendancy show itself more clearly than in the hollow spaces under its politico-religious monumentalism. How such Anglican monumentalism sits awry in the Irish context is also indicated by the case of Burke himself: for the premier spokesman for the patina of tradition and of decorum as a stabilising force in political relations was also the one who pointed out the limited extent to which Ireland, under its system of colonial-religious apartheid, participated in the harmony of English liberties.

With certain exceptions, to which I shall return later on, the monuments in St Patrick's Cathedral show, on the whole, a dogged determination to ignore the hollow space under their feet. Witness the amusingly bombastic eulogy carved on the base of the statue to George Ogle, Wexford MP, colonel in the Volunteers and opponent of Catholic Emancipation, whose main claim to Irish national rootedness was perhaps his authorship of the evergreen 'Molly Astore'. For reason of its prolixity and rhetoric the inscription is worth quoting in full:

> This statue of the Right Honble George Ogle is erected by his countrymen and friends as a tribute of affectionate veneration for the man who by a combination of transcendent qualities shone conspicuous among the highest, the brightest and the purest of the age in which he lived. For twenty-eight years he represented the County of Wexford in Parliament during which period the incorruptible integrity, the brilliant talents and the ardent patriotism with which he discharged the duties of that sacred trust secured to him the unalterable attachment of his constituents followed by whose unfeigned regret he withdrew from public life in the year 1796.
>
> In 1798 a memorable era he was called from retirement by the spontaneous and unanimous choice of the citizens of Dublin to the representation of that loyal city. A distinguished and unsolicited mark of confidence founded on the undaunted and unvarying firmness he uniformly displayed in supporting with almost chivalrous enthusiasm the constitution in church and state.
>
> In private life he shed a lustre on every Society in which he moved. To the attractions of an accomplished scholar he added suavity of manners, a

[4] Sharply analysed, of course, by scholars such as Raphael Samuel, e.g. his collection *Patriotism: The Making and Unmaking of British National Identity* (3 vols., London, 1989).

scrupulous sense of honour and a steadiness of friendship peculiarly his own. He lived as he died, enthroned in the hearts of all who had the happiness of his intimacy or acquaintance. Of such a man it may be truly and usefully recorded that he exhibited a perfect model of that exalted refinement which in the best days of our country characterised the Irish gentleman. Nat. 19th October 1742. Ob. 10th August 1814.

Such verbosity almost cancels the distinction between monument and discourse. While it would be interesting, or at least amusing, to undertake a 'close reading' of this cliché-ridden and overblown panegyric, dedicated as it is to a portly ex-Volunteer who helped to suppress the '98 rebellion in Wexford, the quotation is adduced here mainly to exemplify the extent to which monuments can become rhetorical and discursive. An even more extreme example of the same tendency to fuse marble monumentality with textual expatiation can be found elsewhere in Ascendancy Ireland: St Barrahane's church in Castletownshend, Co. Cork, has hung upon its inner walls, engraved on three enormous marble slabs, a lengthy and prolix extract from Debrett's Peerage on the descent and manifold branchings and alliances of the illustrious Townshend family.

Such engraved testimonials are prime examples of a type of historical consciousness (and of a type of history writing) which, in Friedrich Nietzsche's famous distinction, must be characterised as 'monumental' – as opposed to 'antiquarian' or 'critical'. Monumental history, in Nietzsche's view, is a selection of the great achievements from the past, as a palliative against the individual's sense of transitoriness and insignificance. These great pinnacles of human achievement, selected from the past, give an edifying sense that greatness was once possible, and is possible still. Monumental history is useful because it provides present generations with inspiration. This inspirational value is absent in antiquarian history (which, in Nietzsche's view, bespeaks a nostalgic yearning for things as they used to be – a type of exoticist escapism into the past) or critical history (which is the province of those who are burdened by, and rebel against, the misery of their times).[5]

The fetishistic historical awareness analysed by Nietzsche dominated most of the nineteenth century and can be traced back to the Romantic period. Precisely while Ogle's monument was being erected, in 1814–15, the German legal philosopher Savigny was trying to come to terms with what he felt was a new attitude to the relationship between past and

[5] Friedrich Nietzsche, 'Vom Nutzen und Nachteil der Historie für das Leben', second of his *Unzeitgemäße Betrachtungen* (1874).

present. He diagnosed a 'historicist' condition[6] when he wrote that 'historical sense is woken up everywhere' and that history was 'the only way to a true knowledge of our condition'. Among historians, the Romantic generation, influenced by philosophers like Schelling and Hegel, and by a belated discovery of Giambattista Vico, turned this into a veritable historiographical agenda. When Jules Michelet wrote his resounding history of France (centred around his celebration of the French Revolution) he saw history as a battlefield between transcendent principles usually manifested in a struggle between the nation and tyranny; for Carlyle, the battle was between chaos and order, with heroic willpower for an intervening third party. The Hegelian idealism as pioneered by these romantic historians was to reach its national-triumphalist peak in historians like Treitschke at the time when Nietzsche wrote his 'Observations against the times'. Ernest Renan, critical as he himself was of national essentialism, located an overriding sense of national identity, precisely, in a shared historical awareness: *the knowledge of having achieved great things together and the will to achieve more.*[7]

In other words, monumental history, as it is evinced by the symbolical language of *lieux de mémoire* like St Patrick's Cathedral, Dublin, gravitates to the register of national triumphalism. It celebrates the greatness of the nation's past, the achievement of the illustrious dead, and holds this up for emulation. The sense of decorum and edification derived in this way is a powerful bonding agent for the community in question. That is not a surprising conclusion in itself; but it becomes more meaningful, perhaps, if we realise that this modality of monumentalisation is by no means the only form of historical continuity and remembrancing.

[6] 'Historicism' means many things. Not only is there the specific Popperian meaning of the term (the fallacy that knowledge of the past can be extrapolated into 'historical laws' and thus underpin predictions about the future), there is also the sense which is usually associated with a Romantic/positivist school in the tradition of Ranke, which held that the past should be studied in its own moral frame of reference and things ought always to be seen in their own historical context, without the judgement of hindsight. Thirdly, however, and not least importantly, the German *Historismus* (analogously to 'fetishism') denotes a pathological monomania, a cramped obsession which sees History behind everything.

[7] On Savigny and his context, see Anna Morpurgo Davies, *Nineteenth-Century Linguistics* (London, 1998). On Michelet and Romantic history-writing, see Ann Rigney, *The Rhetoric of Historical Representation: Three Narrative Histories of the French Revolution* (Cambridge, 1989); the same author has dealt more closely with Carlyle in her article 'The untenanted places of the past: Thomas Carlyle and the varieties of historical ignorance', *History and Theory*, 35 (1996), 338–57. On Renan, see Ernest Renan, *Qu'est-ce qu'une nation?* (1882), new edition with an introduction by Joep Leerssen (Leiden, 1994); on nineteenth-century historical awareness, especially in Ireland, see generally my *Remembrance and Imagination: Patterns in the Historical and Literary Representation of Ireland in the Nineteenth Century* (Cork, 1996).

II

Even the most triumphant celebrations of the illustrious dead cannot bring them back to life. At the core of monuments and commemorations, there is death, absence, transience, a sense of loss resisted, denied, shouted down. The most elaborate ceremonials of national affirmation often concern defeats and losses: the Armistice Day celebrations in Britain, processions and wreath-laying at the Cenotaph, the Two Minutes' Silence on the eve of Liberation Day in The Netherlands; and in the heart of Paris, the very space in the middle of the Arc de Triomphe occupied by the grave of the Unknown Soldier.[8]

The triumphalist, inspirational value of monuments, foregrounded though it may be to contemporary critics, is not their primary signification or motivation; such monuments are erected as an act of resistance against the transience of an important person or event, an anchor to resist creeping obsolescence or oblivion. The admonition to commemorate and to remember is, primarily, inspired by the apprehension that one might forget. Our sense of mortality, or sense of loss at the death of esteemed and honoured compatriots, is transcended in the celebration of their enduring inspirational value. Pearse was by no means aberrant when he saw the efficacy of death and defeat; it is not an Irish monopoly to draw the most powerful inspiration for collective solidarity from, of all things, funerals. The burials of Princess Diana and of King Hussein of Jordan are highly similar in their symbolical value for the communities concerned to republican funerals in the North of Ireland.

Those who control obituaries, control history. The monumental value of cathedrals like St Patrick's lies precisely in this control over a central public point of congregation where the record of the past and the reputation of the dead is officially laid down, carved in marble and cast in bronze. It is here that grief, loss and death are transmuted into the recognition of achievement, as much as in patriotic texts like Tennyson's poem on the charge of the Light Brigade, or Laurence Binyon's still-moving recessional on the British casualties in the First World War.[9]

[8] The most outstanding work on war commemoration is Jay Winter's *Sites of Memory, Sites of Mourning: The Great War in European Cultural History* (Cambridge, 1995).

[9] 'They shall grow not old, as we that are left grow old. Age shall not weary them, nor the years condemn. At the going down of the sun and in the morning, We will remember them.' The text first appeared in *The Times* in 1914, and spontaneously achieved a prayer-like currency. In the face of the loss of the fallen and the waning of the survivors, the text offers a strong, almost religiously edifying effect, by combining two factors: the affirmation of a shared volition to remember, and the regularity of remembrance at sunrise and sunset. It thus reflects a very deep-seated human urge to redeem order from nature's cruel chaos.

This is not completely a British or Ascendancy monopoly. In Irish history, similar texts abound, such as Ferguson's elegy on Thomas Davis or that ballad giving 'Glory, O, to the bold Fenian men'. But on closer consideration the differences will be obvious. For the best part of history, the native tradition in Ireland had no control over the dedication and monumentalisation of public space; indeed, precisely in that condition do we find the very definition of its subaltern and oppressed situation. Catholic Ireland had no castle or cathedral to display its regimental flags or the monuments to its heroes; the emergence of a nationally oriented Catholic middle class in Ireland can be faithfully registered in its slow but steadily increasing grasp on monumental space. The process begins with the O'Connell monument in central Dublin, and the renaming of metropolitan spaces such as Sackville Street and Carlisle Bridge; it obtains an important focus with Glasnevin cemetery (itself made possible only as a result of Catholic Emancipation), which quickly developed into an open-air shrine for the Catholic, nationalist portion of Ireland. Towards the later part of the nineteenth century, there is a noteworthy intensification of nationalist markers in public space: monuments to Young Irelanders and 1798 pikemen can now be found in almost every market town.[10]

But all these are novelties, markers of a fresh development. In contrast to the long accumulation of memorials in St Patrick's, there are almost no pre-1850 monuments or *lieux de mémoire* embodying a 'national' Irish, anti-Ascendancy historical consciousness. Some heirlooms persist, semi-obscure, in private hands (e.g., Carolan's harp, kept by the O'Conor Don family); others are slowly collected into the more public, accessible property of bodies like Dublin University or the Royal Irish Academy and its incipient museum. But there is nothing in the way of public spaces. Even the resonating name of Tara does not refer to a place of social congregation. At best, there are the 'round towers' and high crosses, only surviving remains of a pre-English native culture. These scarce monuments of ancient civility accordingly obtain, in nineteenth-century iconography, a high symbolical 'national' prestige.[11]

The emergence of a nationalist groundswell, carried by an emerging Catholic middle class in Ireland, can be illustrated in no better terms than in this gradual appropriation of public space for the remembrancing of their particular history. The struggle for dominance in the public

[10] Judith Hill, *Irish Public Sculptures: A History* (Dublin, 1998).

[11] Cf. Jeanne Sheehy, *The Rediscovery of Ireland's Past: The Celtic Revival, 1800–1830* (London, 1980), and my *Remembrance and Imagination*.

sphere between unionist and nationalist, between Protestant Ascendancy and Catholic middle classes, is a struggle for the public manifestation and controlling of monumentalised commemoration. Indeed St Patrick's Cathedral itself, ironically, bears witness to this strenuous shift, which was to culminate in the present century with the Gaelic-inscribed tomb of Douglas Hyde. St Patrick's monumental value nowadays resides, not in the regimental flags and the statues to the likes of George Ogle, but rather in the grave of the one maverick dean who himself became an icon in the gallery of nationalist Ireland. Most tourists who visit St Patrick's Cathedral see its Irishness legitimised in the grave of Jonathan Swift. And there are some markers that even in the nineteenth century there were attempts to participate in the growing monumentalisation of a 'national' Irish past – witness the remarkable plaque, placed by none other than Lady Morgan, to the memory of Carolan. It shows the profile of the harper in marble relief, and carries the following inscription:

> Erected by the desire of Sydney Lady Morgan to the memory of Carolan, the last of the Irish bards. Obiit AD MDCCXXXVIII aetatis suae an. LXVIII.[12]

I will not here dwell on the portentous phraseology 'the last of the Irish bards' or on the obvious competition between the two nineteenth-century champions of the Irish harp-icon, Thomas Moore and 'Glorvina' Morgan;[13] the more important point is that even in this inner sanctum of Ascendancy Ireland, moves were made to participate in the heritage of the 'national' (non-English) past.

What I have said about public edifices and monuments also goes for public discourse: the obituaries of the past, the praise and blame allotted to public men, the 'official stories' which explain and interpret events are a matter for competition. It is by now a trite cliché that history is always the history of the victorious party, and that the vanquished are silent and lost in the past without a representative voice; but the cliché is worth looking into a little more deeply, because if there is any merit in the current historiographical concern for collective memory and collective remembrancing, it must lie in the fact that this forms an interface between history-as-past and history-as-story-about-the-past, between *res gestae* and *historia rerum gestarum*. By that I mean that the praxis of collective memory and collective remembrancing is, precisely, 'history in the making', the

12 The plaque was actually placed in 1874; Morgan had left a provision in her will for this purpose: Jackson, *St Patrick's Cathedral, Dublin*, p. 4.

13 Regarding which, see Fiona Stafford, *The Last of the Race: The Growth of a Myth from Milton to Darwin* (Oxford, 1994).

Memorial to Carolan, 'the last of the Irish bards', in St Patrick's Cathedral, Dublin. Photo: Lensman

very filter by which past events, almost immediately upon their passing, are transmuted into a memory for succeeding generations. I must explain myself more closely.

Historical theory in the wake of Hayden White has placed great stress on the 'constructed' nature of historical discourse and the radical division between historical discourse and that ideal-typical Rankean past 'as it actually was'. As a result, historical theorists over the last twenty years or so have emphasised, most of all, the idea that history is fabricated *ex post facto* by its discursive verbalisation on the part of latter-day historians. By now, there are some reasons to nuance this extreme constructivism slightly. These can be linked to the names of Paul Ricoeur and Maurice Halbwachs, respectively. To begin with, as Ricoeur has argued in *Temps et récit*, interpretation is not the monopoly of hindsight-ridden historians, but is shared by the historical actors themselves. Historical acts and decisions are not random natural occurrences to be freely interpreted by historians, but are intentional, which means that the past, inasmuch as it consists of human actions, carries a pre-programmed interpretation of intentionality.[14] Historians need not be bound by this but would be foolish to ignore it. More importantly for my present argument, there is no chronological vacuum between then and now, between the past which happened 'once upon a time', *in illo tempore*, on the one hand, and our contemporary latter-day observation of that past on the other hand. A continuum of human interpretation, of human sense-making, described by Maurice Halbwachs in his old but still-influential *Les cadres sociaux de la mémoire*, joins us to the past.[15] The *res gestae*, past events and occurrences, took on meaning even as they occurred, and from that moment onwards have been transmitted in an ongoing process of reckoning and remembering. What makes the notion of 'collective memory' interesting is that as a social praxis it mediates between the events as social reality, as they occurred, and events as past phenomena, as subject-matter for historical understanding. The notion of collective memory can therefore transcend the division between historical reality and historical discourse.

But to return, after this theoretical digression, to the case in point: nineteenth- and early-twentieth-century Ireland. Much as the social and ideological tensions of that country in those decades can be registered in the competition for monumental public space, so too can we register it in a competition for control over public discursive remembrancing: rivalling versions of history present the past in the meaning that it had for different, opposing sections of society, and as the Catholic, nationalistically minded middle classes emerge, one primary concern is the establishment of a print culture which can disseminate their view of society and of Irish history. Publishing houses like James Duffy (linked as it was to the Young Irelanders, the Fenians and the Catholic Church) are of cardinal importance in this development.

It is a historical novelty to see a nationalist historical awareness 'going public', and staking its claim in the public sphere of printing and

[14] Paul Ricoeur, *Temps et récit* (3 vols., Paris, 1983–5).
[15] Maurice Halbwachs, *Les cadres sociaux de la mémoire* (Paris, 1925).

reading. The 'Hidden Ireland' had been 'hidden' precisely because it had no access to that sphere. Catholic Ireland in penal days was hermetically sealed off from a public forum. Gaelic culture was restricted to the ambit of an incomprehensible language, a proscribed religion, a seditious interpretation of the nation's past, with only a very restricted access to public large-scale media or communication. As a result, the social make-up of Catholic Ireland was largely pre-modern, had no 'official' organs, and little proprietary access to large-scale media or to the public sphere to rely on. Communication was almost exclusively face-to-face, and social organisation was tied to the pre-modern structure of the small-scale community. The nineteenth century sees Catholic Ireland bursting into print culture and appropriating the media and the public voice to cement what Benedict Anderson sees as the prime effect of print media: nation-making. Catholic, nationalist Ireland emerges as a large-scale common concern, joined together by shared access to a print culture and a voice broadcast far and wide into the public sphere.[16]

And this, in turn, crucially affects the patterns of historical reckoning and public remembrancing. Remembrancing for Catholic, anti-British Ireland had for a long time been an informal communitarian concern, often in oral face-to-face transmission by way of balladry and folktale with only limited mediatisation in written or printed form, let alone by way of public monumentalisation. No Laurence Binyon could use the columns of a newspaper of the stature of *The Times* to give 'official' form to shared grief or trauma. The hallmark of a subaltern culture is that it has no newspaper like *The Times*; its historical memory remains inchoate, uncanonised, informal; a matter of folklore and local communities rather than of state-sanctioned political life or academic scholarship. We can see that this 'folklore' element remains the defining trait as Catholic, nationalist Ireland begins to penetrate into the public media: what is published is Minstrelsy, popular poetry, as in the collections of Hardiman and O'Daly, in a quasi-oral idiom which is perpetuated by the Young Irelanders and the poets around *The Nation*.

Thus we broadly distinguish between two modes of collective remembrancing. It follows to some extent the sociological distinction between

[16] A lively debate on the 'hiddenness' of Gaelic Ireland during the penal period has grown up since Louis Cullen reassessed Corkery's concept in *Studia Hibernica*, 9 (1969), 7–48. I do not wish to intervene in the finesses of that debate, as to the extent of illegitimate subterfuge and 'undergroundness' of native culture at the time. Regardless of the extent, it is obvious that the communication and dissemination media of print culture in mid-eighteenth-century Ireland excluded the Catholic population and its political opinions almost completely, and that this exclusion had been wholly removed by the mid-nineteenth century.

'society' and 'community'. Like any schematisation it is overly facile and black-and-white, and I offer it merely as a heuristic device, a suggestion of how to look at things, not as a serious and watertight analysis. So here goes: on the one hand, there is state-sanctioned public commemoration, which is highly mediatised, invokes a conservative ideal of social harmony where elite culture rests on the broad assent of a collective nationwide constituency, and which canonises the acts and personalities of individuals into an 'official' version of history. I would suggest that this mode is broadly speaking proper to autonomous states, elites and institutions and that its default mode is what Nietzsche calls monumental. Let us call this, for short, 'society remembrancing'.

On the other hand, there is what I shall call 'community remembrancing': it is sub-elite and demotic, carried largely by local or small-scale communities rather than by the elites of nations-at-large, perpetuated by oral or folkloristic face-to-face means rather than mediatised in print or monuments. The collective will 'not to forget' is not shored up by officially instituted public landmarks but persists by traditionary renewal, self-repetition and re-enactment. It is the mode of rebel songs, paramilitary murals in Belfast housing estates, and Orange Lodge parades. And although the 'monumental', triumphalist mode can be encountered here as much as in St Patrick's Cathedral, it is not as dominant. Even in Orange marches, the brash assertiveness is an act of defensive defiance rather than the mere proclamation of supremacy which we encounter in the monuments of Louis XIV or Queen Victoria, or in the crowds singing 'Land of Hope and Glory' at the last night of the Proms. Rather, the demotic and in many cases subaltern nature of 'community remembrancing' in very many cases evinces a different sense of history, one which sees history from the point of view of the losers, the bereaved, the victims. This view of history is now becoming known as the 'traumatic' paradigm.[17]

III

Ernest Renan wrote his famous *Qu'est-ce qu'une nation?* roughly at the time when Nietzsche wrote his 'Observations against the times'. There is no need here to dwell too extensively on a text which will be so well

[17] For a discussion of the links between 'collective memory' (as an approach in the historical sciences in the tradition of Maurice Halbwachs) and the 'traumatic paradigm', see Jean-Pierre Rioux, 'La mémoire collective', in J.-P. Rioux and J.-F. Sirinelli (eds.), *Pour une histoire culturelle* (Paris, 1997), pp. 325–53, and especially the excellent article by Lucette Valensi, 'Traumatic events and historical consciousness: who is in charge?', in Joep Leerssen and Ann Rigney (eds.), *Historians and Social Values* (Amsterdam, 2000), pp. 185–95.

Battle of the Bogside mural showing a boy with gas mask and a petrol bomb, Rossville Street, Derry, 1994. Photo: ©Bill Rolston

known to most readers; I only wish to highlight two aspects (both of them, again, famous) in this rich, seminal work. The first is the fact that Renan, for all that he is aware of the importance of a unified historical consciousness as bonding agent for a nation, realises that this mode of triumphalist national historiography is a hegemonic master story, imposed by brutal force by the victors on the vanquished. French national unity was obtained by smothering the Albigensians and the Vendée in blood, and a shared sense of Frenchness must therefore necessarily relegate the grievances of Albigensians and Vendéens to oblivion. Hence Renan's famous dictum that forgetfulness and even historical error are indispensable for the achievement of national unity.[18] We can read this statement

[18] Renan, 'L'oubli, et je dirais même l'erreur historique, sont un facteur essentiel de la création d'une nation', 'Qu'est-ce qu'une nation?', p. 8.

at various levels. It means that national unity is obtained by dint of acquiescence on the part of the non-privileged, and that, as a result, political conservatism and reactionary politics (say, again, one-nation Toryism in the wake of Burke and Disraeli) must necessarily invoke an ideal of the underprivileged cheerfully submitting to their station in life. An idyllic, harmonious ideal of national 'community' can persist only by dint of imagining faithful servants and rustic village yokels happily tugging the forelock and playing their allotted part. And as in societal relations, so too in historical memory. Harbouring grievances, wishing to 'pay back' the oppressor for past misdeeds, threatens the ideal of harmonious solidarity. Thus the conservative stance is often remarkably anti-historicist and tends to stress the need to let bygones be bygones. One of the things that Burke hated most of all in the French Revolution was precisely this tendency to settle old scores, which, Burke felt, threatened national cohesion in a historical sense much as its class struggle threatened national cohesion in a societal sense. Since Burke's time, the refusal 'to forgive and forget' has been deplored by the paternalist elite as cramped intransigence and a mark of political immaturity. Examples abound: the showdown between Samuel Ferguson and James Hardiman; the conservative review which countered Thomas Moore's motto 'Let Erin Remember' with the exasperated headline 'Let Erin Forget'; the similar exasperation of Lloyd George that his Irish counterparts interrupted all practical negotiations by dwelling on Cromwell; and, we may add, contemporary attitudes which blame the problems in Northern Ireland on a hypertrophy of historical awareness.

But it was not just smug conservatism that led Renan to emphasise the expedience of oblivion. Rather, he pointed out that behind each national-triumphalist historical consciousness there was a cupboard full of skeletons; and such an observation, coming as it did in 1881, was remarkably perceptive. Renan followed it with a prediction which was nothing short of prophetic. He pointed out that, as the historical sciences were progressing, the unsavoury facts which until then had been sanitised out of the historical record would come to light and might rekindle and fuel the flames of resentment within each nation. Marginalised minorities, Renan warned, would become aware of their roots, their defeats and the injustice and brutality they had suffered, in a process which would threaten the solidarity and cohesion of the nation-states.[19]

[19] Ibid., 'C'est ainsi que le progrès des études historiques est souvent pour la nationalité un danger. L'investigation historique, en effet, remet en lumière les faits de violence qui se sont passés à l'origine de toutes les formations politiques', p. 8.

The twentieth century has amply borne out Renan's prediction. Historical investigation has turned from victors and triumphant elites to the downtrodden, the persecuted, the victimised. Entire groups have become the locus of historical investigation, and have accordingly emerged as politically meaningful categories, in the sense predicted by Renan: women, homosexuals, non-European races, workers, and various regional or ethnic minorities have discovered their identity and have done so partly by a search for historical roots – roots which had to be painstakingly reconstructed from dispersed archival fragments and community remembrance because they had not been taken into account of 'official' history and 'official' commemoration. In all these cases the shared experience which constitutes a joint identity is not of the type that has given rise to the triumphalism and edifying dignity of Anglican cathedrals; it is an experience of oppression, of defeat, of injustice and grievance. And these, let me stress, are very powerful bonding agents. Renan had already pointed this out.

> Oui, la souffrance en commun unit plus que la joie. En fait de souvenirs nationaux, les deuils valent mieux que les triomphes; car ils imposent des devoirs; ils commandent l'effort en commun.[20]

If we look at 'identity politics' in the late twentieth century the overriding sense is that each fragmented identity which has staked out its position on the map has done so on the basis of past trauma. History writing nowadays is concerned almost exclusively with underdogs; indeed underdoghood is indispensable to obtain political or historical sympathy, and anyone daring to take an interest in upperdogs will be confronted by questions about whether this is not elitist and perpetuates the injustice of old hegemonies. In our historical narratives, all must be represented: women, colonial races, workers, homosexuals and other marginal or 'overlooked' groups.

The commemoration of shared trauma has thus become intensified. No longer in the Binyon/Tennyson mode of transmuting loss and grief into edification and catharsis, but rather in a 'never again' mode. Demands for apology are addressed to popes and Swiss bankers, and the lesson to be drawn from past injustice is one of vigilance and assertiveness at best. Even monumental history is beginning to incorporate the subaltern view of history from below, from the fringes. In other words,

[20] Ibid., 'Yes, shared suffering unites more firmly than shared joy. When it comes to national memories, mourning matters more than triumphs, for mourning instills a sense of duty and exacts a joint effort', p. 28.

the distinction between community and society remembrance is blurring even as I am making it.[21]

Even so, a number of features in community remembrancing and in the traumatic paradigm can be named which may help to account for some interesting and salient practices in 'subaltern' history. To begin with, a remembrance which is based so deeply in folk memory, in the complicity of oral transmission, will set up pieties which are not easily falsified. I use the word 'piety' without irony and indeed with a sense of respect. The very praxis of community remembrance is an act of piety, salvaging respect for the acts and experiences of earlier generations from the entropy of the passage of time. But the fact remains that the sense of the past as transmitted through such channels is not easily disproved. Indeed historians who set out to disprove the historical awareness transmitted in community remembrance place themselves in a quixotic and impossible position; for it cannot be the task of academic scholarship to *direct* the patterns of culture at large. If the hallmark of scientific procedure, following Popper, lies in its openness to the test of falsification, then community remembrance, given its unfalsifiability, is outside scholars' reach. This places historians, structurally, in a most awkward position *vis-à-vis* popular culture and its interest in the past as evidenced by films like *Braveheart* and *Michael Collins*.

Second, community remembrance is iterative, predicated on repetition. There are a number of reasons why this should be so. To begin with, the praxis of community remembrancing is a performative one. It does not solidify into objects occupying public space, such as monuments, but it persists by dint of being always performed afresh. The songs are sung and sung again, the stories told over and over again. It is a feature which I have also noticed in nineteenth-century nationalist history writing. Whereas academic, professionalised history writing progresses (in the sense that new generations step into the obsolescence of earlier insights and improve upon these), popular nationalist history writing solidifies into a canon which maintains an indefinite shelf-life. The histories of Abbé MacGeoghegan, of John Mitchell, of Thomas Davis, become

[21] The Veterans' Memorial in Washington, DC, is a telling case in point. The 'official', state-commissioned monument to the Vietnam War is a black marble chevron half-sunk into a trench listing the names of the dead and missing, and thus opts for a funereal register of grievance and mourning; the public's use of that monument is, accordingly, a communitarian one, as it can be encountered in local cemeteries (flowers, meditative touching, reading out of names). Ironically, while the official monumentalisation addresses the traumatic dimension of the Vietnam war, the veterans themselves felt the need for a more monumental celebration of their valour, and accordingly the official inscribed wall is flanked by a realistic statue of heroic GIs in combat dress.

literary classics, are reprinted again and again and lay down the truth of the story of Ireland much as Melville has laid down the story of the Pequod. Much as community remembrancing resists revision and has a pious sense of the enduring validity of its established truths, so too its standard texts are recycled continuously.

Elsewhere I have discussed at greater length this recycled maintenance of older historical interpretations, which, as I see it, bespeaks an indeterminacy of the generic border between history-writing and story-writing, in a manner not covered by Roy Foster's analysis of that issue.[22] The net effect of such reiterative reworkings of older histories is one of a nightmarish sameness. The insistent return of a historical consciousness to a past that is familiar and yet uncomfortable, haunting and drearily returning in predictable patterns, matches the notion of Irish history as a recurrent nightmare of oppression, resistance, defeat and renewed oppression, so prominent in Irish nationalist history-writing of the nineteenth century. In one of his more astute essays, Freud has described such nightmarish recurrences, characterised by their combination of repetitive familiarity and their disconcerting repulsion, as 'uncanny' [*unheimlich*]. In Freud's view, the repetitiveness of the uncanny manifests the fears and preoccupations of childhood, and is linked to childhood-based obsessions and neuroses; like our childhood nightmares and phobias, the uncanny harks back to a state of threatened helplessness and powerlessness.

There is no reason whatsoever to deride or to denounce the needle-in-groove nature of the Irish historical consciousness. To begin with, I find it significant that this condition is shared by both parties in the Northern conflict, and that it is precisely in this quality that Protestant and Catholic betray their joint Irishness. For both, history is uncanny, broken by rivers and battles like the Boyne or the Somme, by a sense of betrayal or threat. I think it has something to do with the subaltern nature of the memories which are at issue. These are of a 'traumatic' nature; and as various historians have pointed out, it lies in the very nature of trauma that the sense of hurt and wounding recurs, makes itself felt time and time again, in self-renewing fresh manifestations of the original experience. Trauma is more than the experience of pain or injury: it is a wound-licking impulse which returns to, and revives, the painful memory in an ongoing recurrence. In Freudian terms, trauma is an obsessive preoccupation with past injury, a pain which refuses to alleviate or go

[22] *Remembrance and Imagination*, pp. 152–4, commenting on Roy Foster's *The Story of Ireland* (Oxford, 1995), more recently reiterated in his article 'Storylines: narratives and nationality in nineteenth-century Ireland', in Geoffrey Cubitt (ed.), *Imagining Nations* (Manchester, 1998), pp. 38–57.

away. Hence an impulse to return, again and again, to the scenes, to describe the event or the story over and over again and yet feel that it is never adequately described or formulated in a final, definitive form.

Most moving in this respect, and formative for historians' understanding of the predicament, are the experiences of holocaust survivors: the fact that, even in the most gruesome death camps, one of the strongest impulses to survival lay in the wish to bear witness to these atrocities; the fact that often survivors initially encountered a devastating lack of interest in, or sympathy with, the story of their experiences; and the phenomenon that the full trauma of the holocaust hit Western culture after an incubation period of some twenty to thirty years, in the late 1960s. On the one hand, a sense of tongue-tied speechlessness in the face of such overwhelming horror; on the other, an insistent, urgent and recurring retelling of the cautionary horror-tale; Adorno's statement as to the impossibility of poetry after Auschwitz was accompanied by the poetry of Celan, by the testimonies of Elie Wiesel and Primo Levi. A similar sense of the insufficiency of representation combined with an insistently repetitive attempt to tell the tale can be found in other cases sharing this traumatic quality.[23]

To some extent, then, traumatic remembrancing results from the fact that injury or loss was initially unacknowledged, lacked proper 'official' recognition and catharsis. Accordingly, Freudian psychoanalysis places great value on the idea of verbalising the trauma, speaking about it, putting it into discourse. It has been pointed out that this is essentially a form of self-historicisation, of constructing a personal historical narrative.[24] To that extent, the official monumentalisation of history does provide a form of catharsis, and official celebrations or poems like that of Laurence Binyon are, in the deepest sense of the term, therapeutic – as much as the sympathetic listening ear of the psychoanalyst is therapeutic. Luke Gibbons, insightful as usual, has called Derry's Bloody Sunday massacre (exacerbated into trauma by the Widgery inquiry's refusal to give official recognition and acknowledgement to the catastrophic

[23] Cf. my '1798: the recurrence of violence and two conceptualizations of history', *Irish Review*, 22 (1998), 37–45.

[24] Cf. Michael S. Roth, *Psychoanalysis as History: Negation and Freedom in Freud* (Ithaca, NY, 1987). See also the same author's 'Trauma, Representation und historisches Bewusstsein', in Jörn Rüsen and Jürgen Straub (ed.), *Die dunkle Spur der Vergangenheit. Psychoanalytische Zugänge zum Geschichtsbewusstsein* (Frankfurt/Main, 1998), pp. 153–73. A number of contributions in the same collection are highly illuminating as to the 'traumatic paradigm' in historical theory, especially that of Werner Bohleber, 'Transgenerationelles Trauma, Identifizierung und Geschichtsbewusstsein' (pp. 256–74) and Brigitte Rauschenbach, 'Politik der Erinnerung' (pp. 354–74).

experience) 'history without the talking cure':

> In the therapeutic encounter, stories are detached from their emotional setting and told to an impartial spectator with whom one has a professional rather than a personal relationship. In a city such as Derry, however, still suffused by oral culture and memories of the dead, such impartiality is at a premium.[25]

Wide gulfs separate St Patrick's Cathedral from Bloody Sunday. Both are concerned with commemorating the past; one, in the idealised serenity of decorous catharsis, the other in self-renewing bitterness. One is smug, the other strident. The historian is caught between the two – indeed, as recent revisionism and post-colonialism debates have shown, the historical profession as a whole is somehow torn between the two.

A possible way out of what looks like a debilitating division may be that loss and bereavement is nobody's monopoly; and that at least a recognition of each other's past sufferings will make some understanding between inimical parties possible. The Protestant tradition in Ulster, which in the Republic is despised for its red-necked triumphalism and insistence on monopolising the King's Highway for partisan purposes, is sympathetically appreciated when its losses at the Battle of the Somme are brought forward – witness the remarkable success of Frank McGuinness's play on that topic in Dublin. As the Republic and the North are inching closer, the most meaningful gestures may well be those which involve a recognition of each other's past traumas – like the Republic's new-found respect for the casualties of the First World War. These Irishmen, who fell before a border was drawn around the Six Counties, were given a commemorative monument in Flanders in 1998. Shaped as a Round Tower, it was inaugurated jointly by President McAleese and Queen Elizabeth II. The attempt to find a non-sectarian Irish symbol in the shape of a Round Tower, of all things, may call forth historical comment from those who are familiar with the vicissitudes of that particular icon of Irishness. Be that as it may, its presence on a Belgian field, denoting, as it does, shared mourning rather than monopolist triumphalism, is much less incongruous that Carolan's plaque in St Patrick's.

[25] Luke Gibbons, 'History without the talking cure: Bloody Sunday as "modern event"', in Trisha Ziff (ed.), *Hidden Truths: Bloody Sunday 1972* (Santa Monica, CA, 1998), pp. 101–9.

CHAPTER 10

Northern Ireland: commemoration, elegy, forgetting

Edna Longley

I

Northern Ireland seems made for students of what John R. Gillis terms 'memory and identity in time and space'.[1] It exemplifies, for instance, the religious basis of secular remembrance; the transition from older encodings to 'modern memory'; how endemic division maintains sites of memory as sites of conflict. Also on the syllabus are: tension between metropolitan and local constructions of national memory; the reflexes that read history into current events, and *vice versa*; remembering the world wars; the problem of remembering civil war; the problem of forgetting it; the mnemonic role of literature and art; newer (sometimes contradictory) themes like identity politics, post-nationalist memory, commemoration as healing or 'mourning work'; conflict between custodians of popular memory and those who would modify its practices or relativise its premises; the identical way in which competing 'ethnic' groups vaunt 'precedence, antiquity, continuity, coherence, heroism, sacrifice';[2] the fact that *lieux de mémoire* can denote not only particular monuments or numinous places, but territories marked inwardly by communal mediations of history, outwardly by insignia and ritual.

That is to say, first, the culture and politics of Northern Irish memory correspond to European and transatlantic patterns; second, they manifest these patterns in a peculiarly intense way. So I question a view expressed by Joep Leerssen elsewhere in this book. While Leerssen rightly notes that 'the refusal to "forgive and forget" has been deplored by the paternalistic elite as cramped intransigence and a mark of political immaturity', less elite groups now ponder that difficult precept, and can sympathise with 'attitudes which blame the problems in Northern Ireland on a hypertrophy of historical awareness'. History 'itself' is indeed structurally

[1] John R. Gillis (ed.), *Commemorations: The Politics of National Identity* (Princeton, NJ, 1994), p. 3.
[2] Ibid., p. 44.

to blame, as are specific contests over power and sovereignty. Yet a toxic point has been reached when cultural insecurities, maximised by political actors, turn a whole (i.e., fragmented) society into a *lieu de mémoire*, a locus where monuments are inseparable from tombs. It is not as if the people have no room for choice along the spectrum between those cultures that aim at amnesia, and those that aim at total recall. Thus, as many argue, solving Northern Ireland's problems may be equally inseparable from remembering the past in new ways: a remembering that enables forgetting. Later I will suggest that, by reinventing genres of commemoration, 'Troubles elegy' inscribes parameters for 'new remembering'.

Discussing 'Building Pasts in Germany', Rudy J. Koshar finds that commemoration, as it tries to assuage the insecurity that begets it, 'assumes historically specific forms that [depend] on numerous layers of political action, numerous permutations of the political culture'.[3] This is borne out by Northern Ireland. For instance, the language at a 'commemorative rally' in Derry on the twenty-eighth anniversary of Bloody Sunday (30 January 2000) combined old and new elements in a way that reflected both Sinn Féin participation in a devolved Executive, and Sinn Féin opposition to the Executive's being suspended because paramilitaries have been slow to decommission arms:

> [Bairbre] de Brún was enthusiastically applauded by the crowd when she was introduced as the first Minister of Health to address a Bloody Sunday commemoration. She said everyone would require healing from the 'intensity of what we have all been through' over the past 30 years in Northern Ireland. She said 28 years on there was still no recognition of the role the 'British government played in what was a premeditated attack on unarmed demonstrators by members of the parachute regiment.'[4]

Dominic Bryan's studies of Twelfth parades have shown them to be

> diverse events involving many people with different motivations . . . The Twelfth is supposed to reflect tradition but so much of it symbolises change . . . A whole new array of symbols have appeared over the last thirty years, displayed on drums, on flags and on uniforms . . . And replacing the Stormont ministers that used to stand and congratulate their own Government on what a wonderful job they were doing, there are speakers reflecting the splits in unionist politics and the disillusionment with successive British Governments.[5]

[3] Koshar, 'Building Pasts: Historic Preservation and Identity in Twentieth-Century Germany', in Gillis (ed.), *Commemorations*, p. 230.

[4] *Irish Times*, 31 Jan. 2000, 7.

[5] Gordon Lucy and Elaine McClure (eds.), *The Twelfth: What it Means to Me* (Belfast, 1997), pp. 21–2.

In *Remembrance and Imagination* (1996) Leerssen argues that nineteenth-century nationalist remembrance involved the substitution of

> the historical *Nacheinander* by a spectacular *Nebeneinander*. The mutability of history, with its shifting and multifarious warring parties, is reduced to a conspectus of scenes on an invariant formula of English misrule and Irish resistance (always the same England, the same Ireland . . .). Remembrance from Moore to Davis becomes a cardinal element in the unification of history; towards the end of the century it becomes institutionalised in the penchant for centenary commemorations . . . and in the cult of funerals.[6]

'A conspectus of scenes on an invariant formula' also describes Orange rituals that try to deny insecurity and mutability. The current 'peace process' might be described as an effort to bridge the cognitive gulf from *Nebeneinander* to *Nacheinander*.

For Koshar, greater alertness to the contingency of memorial constructions could 'defuse conflict in a situation in which states or ethnic groups defended what seemed to be absolutely irreconcilable collective positions'.[7] 'Cultural Traditions' work of this kind has been underway for over a decade in Northern Ireland. For example, the 'Remembering 1690' tercentenary exhibition at the Ulster Folk and Transport Museum

> adopted the rhetorical conceit that the specific popular histories of the Williamite-Jacobite wars were not incorrect but incomplete . . . The exhibition therefore sought to affirm the validity of the popular histories of both sides. By doing so, it hoped to uphold the worth not only of the popular curators who looked after these histories, but also of the more general public, who gave the histories more distant support.[8]

Less soothingly, the Tower Museum in Derry uses a corridor to dramatise the 'concept of parallel stories arising out of a contested space'.[9] An ambitious memorial project, *An Crann/ The Tree*, fuses approaches to painful short-term memory with approaches to long-term historical memory:

> As with Holocaust museums . . . *An Crann* aims to counsel as well as educate . . . Two key elements are planned for this museum. A massive mural will

[6] Joep Leerssen, *Remembrance and Imagination: Patterns in the Historical and Literary Representation of Ireland in The Nineteenth Century* (Cork, 1996), p. 226.

[7] Gillis, *Commemorations*, p. 231.

[8] Anthony D. Buckley and Mary Catherine Kenney, *Negotiating Identity: Rhetoric, Metaphor and Social Drama in Northern Ireland* (Washington, DC, and London, 1995), pp. 228–9.

[9] Faith and Politics Group, *Remembrance and Forgetting: Building a Future in Northern Ireland* (Belfast, 1998), p. 9.

depict the historical, cultural and religious experiences that engendered contemporary Northern Ireland. A central offertory room, like the function of a cairn in earlier societies, can be visited by those seeking a private place of contemplation. Here tributes to the dead, in the form of letters, photographs and artefacts can be placed, as is done at the Vietnam Veterans' Memorial in Washington.[10]

Ideologically liberal, such enterprises promote respect for both communal narratives (and other narratives). This relativising itself constitutes or initiates critique – although too much 'parity of esteem' might defeat the educational purpose. Yet some interested parties are also becoming more historically self-conscious, as with the 'revisionism' in unionist quarters too. The Island pamphlets, whose cultural thinking informs the politics of the (Shankill Road based) Progressive Unionist Party, have challenged Sinn Féin's ideology of history and culture by asserting a 'common inheritance' that mingles Irish and British elements.[11] In 1997 the Ulster Society published two symposia: *The Twelfth: What it Means to Me* and *Remembrance*, which focuses on Remembrance Day. These special days were presumably picked because they complement one another as identity-affirming occasions that bind Ulster Protestants to a territorially defined community and to the British state. The one 'maintains' local presence by invoking the foundational Williamite moment forgotten by London (where once 'the story of English Protestant deliverances provided one of the distinctive ligaments of national political culture');[12] the other invokes deeper and wider British kinship 'reinforced in the modern age through two world wars'.[13] More may ride on Remembrance Sunday in the context of increased Protestant insecurity, as well as in the related absence of the old Stormont which used to organise displays of British patriotism now unthinkable in Northern Ireland. The special days intersect where Orange banners memorialise the Ulster Division at the Somme, and in Remembrance Sunday services. Religion, however, provides more than liturgy or the motive/motif of defending the Protestant faith. It influences primitive underlying structures (not entirely forgotten by London) that sanctify the UK polity and 'sacrifices' made on its behalf: the idolatry whereby a commemorating nation

[10] Jane Leonard, *Memorials to the Casualties of Conflict: Northern Ireland 1969 to 1997* (Belfast, 1997), p. 29.

[11] Shankill Think Tank, *A New Beginning*, Island Pamphlets 13 (Belfast, 1995). Among other Island Pamphlets are: *Ulster's Scottish Connection*, *Ulster's Shared Heritage*, *Ulster's European Heritage*, *Beyond the Fife and Drum*.

[12] Gillis, *Commemorations*, p. 71.

[13] Gillian McIntosh, *The Force of Culture: Unionist Identities in Twentieth-Century Ireland* (Cork, 1999), p. 3.

(or community) 'worships itself'.[14] This also applies to Irish nationalist re-workings of Christ's 'Do this in remembrance of me' – as at Wolfe Tone's grave. For Frank Wright, 'Nationalisms are not merely "like" religions – they are religions.'[15] Stephen Howe discloses that the murdered loyalist Billy Wright 'has his own memorial website, complete with full-screen colour photos and commemorative verse, both maudlin and menacing'.[16]

The Twelfth and *Remembrance* admit heretics into the Ulster Society's more respectable memorial sanctum. Besides Protestants who ascribe orthodox meanings to the Twelfth and the world wars, contributors include Catholics, other 'outsiders' and – an important category – critical Protestants whose attitude has been changed by the Troubles. Johnston McMaster, a Methodist minister, criticises the Orange Order's behaviour over the disputed 'traditional' walk at Drumcree and thus distinguishes Christian from self-idolatrous motives: 'Where God becomes identified with any political structure or ideology, prophetic faith must raise critical and subversive questions.' Not so for Evelyn Hanna who writes: 'Perhaps the greatest and most celebrated cultural festival of the world, [the Twelfth] summarises the best of our Ulster Protestant heritage. A celebration of *our beliefs* (and of religious and civil liberty for all), it is also a social gathering, a folk festival . . .'[17] Orange custodianship of Protestant memory – in part, because politically counter-productive – is being increasingly challenged by the wider community, as in the proposal for the Ulster Unionist Party to sever its links with the Order. Similar clashes can be found in *Remembrance*. Bill Barbour feels that Remembrance Day 'is becoming more militaristic . . . losing its original purpose of commemorating the dead and the horrors of war . . . [and] should be allowed to fade away'; whereas Alice Quinton, whose mother was killed by the IRA at the Enniskillen war memorial, sees the day's traditional meaning as renewed by the Troubles and, again, forgotten or muddled by the metropolis: 'My mother played her part in the campaign against fascists in World War Two, when, as a country, we had eventually realised that appeasement encourages tyranny. Modern-day fascists murdered her, but we seem to be back in the grip of appeasement.'[18]

[14] Jay Winter, *Sites of Memory, Sites of Mourning: The Great War in European Cultural History* (Cambridge, 1995), p. 93.

[15] Frank Wright, 'Reconciling the histories of Protestant and Catholic in Northern Ireland', in Alan D. Falconer (ed.), *Reconciling Memories* (Dublin, 1988), p. 75.

[16] Review of *Lost Lives* (see note 22 below), *New Statesman*, 14 Feb. 2000, 53.

[17] Lucy and McClure, *The Twelfth*, pp. 113, 59.

[18] Gordon Lucy and Elaine McClure (eds.), *Remembrance* (Belfast, 1997), pp. 12, 163.

The peace process has brought remembering and forgetting – perhaps prematurely – into the political foreground. In the late 1990s several publications presented overviews of Northern Ireland as *lieu de mémoire.* In *Memorials to the Casualties of Conflict* (1997), a report commissioned by the Community Relations Council and the Arts Council of Northern Ireland, Jane Leonard discusses 'Case-studies from other conflicts', 'Partisan memorials to the Northern Ireland conflict', and 'Existing and proposed general memorials'. Leonard warns against optimism regarding the latter category since partisan memorials in locations identified with one community – churches, cemeteries, buildings, streets – greatly outnumber general memorials such as *An Crann / The Tree* with its ambition to 'gather stories about the "Troubles", in the hope that their humanness will resonate across divisions'.[19] A more specifically Christian concern with historical ecumenism has been pioneered by Alan D. Falconer of the Irish School of Ecumenics, who edited *Reconciling Memories* (1988). From the same constituency comes *Remembrance and Forgetting: Building a Future in Northern Ireland* (1998). Its authors (the Faith and Politics Group) re-emphasise how Northern Irish memory works symbiotically to repress and exclude; how it excuses/erases casualties inflicted by 'our' side; how it also 'forgets' positive shared experience. Yet, while they insist that 'proper' forgetting enjoins active 'repentance' and redress, they match Leonard's caution about a shared peace memorial with their ambivalence about a truth and reconciliation commission: the latter 'appear[s] to work best when there is a powerful political consensus that "truth" must be established . . . a fragile peace, where there have been no decisive endings, may be unpropitious'.[20] The latent contradictions between truth and reconciliation are exposed in Martin McDonagh's play *The Lonesome West* which satirises the tenacity of Irish grievance together with the international vogue for historical apology. The Cain and Abel brothers, Valene and Coleman, follow a priest's advice and 'step back' to apologise not only for what each knows the other did in the past, but also for hidden crimes:

VALENE I did pour a cup of piss in a pint of lager you drank one time, Coleman. Aye, and d'you know what now? You couldn't even tell the differ . . .

COLEMAN I do take your poteen out its box each week, drink the half of it and fill the rest back up with water. Ten years this has been going on. You haven't tasted full strength poteen since nineteen-eighty-fecking-three.

VALENE (*drinks, pause*) But you're sorry for it?

[19] Ibid., p. 85.

[20] Faith and Politics Group, *Remembrance and Forgetting*, p. 18.

COLEMAN I suppose I'm sorry for it, aye. (*Mumbling.*) Making me go drinking piss, and not just anybody's piss but *your* fecking piss . . .[21]

Eventually reconciliation breaks down under the pressure of too much truth or the absence of a genuine paradigm-shift. Roy Foster has criticised apology 'as a rather questionable therapy for historical traumas of long standing'.[22] It also corresponds to a Catholic confessional model (as when the Pope recently apologised for the sins of Christianity). The ecumenical authors of *Remembrance and Forgetting* inject a touch of sterner conscience when they recommend truth-telling on a wider front. The imperative of 'some encounter with truth so that we can have freedom from the past . . . may point to the need for various groups and institutions (e.g., churches) to engage in a process of structured self-examination of their role in the conflict'.[23] This is 'new remembering' as self-criticism, as parity of disesteem.

A truth and reconciliation commission is also thought problematic by Sir Kenneth Bloomfield in *We Will Remember Them: The Report of the Northern Ireland Victims Commissioner*. The Commission was established in October 1997 'to look at possible ways to recognise the pain and suffering felt by victims of violence arising from the Troubles of the last 30 years, including those who have died or been injured in the service of the community'. Help for survivors is recognised as the crucial strand, then non-physical memorial schemes that promote education and reflection. Bloomfield's recommendation for a physical 'Northern Ireland Memorial' is a building 'set in a peaceful location amidst beautifully landscaped gardens', incorporating artworks, an archive and the kind of therapeutic environment pioneered by *An Crann / The Tree*. At the same time, his vision is haunted by continuing divisiveness: the desire to attribute blame; the perceived impossibility of remembering, say, RUC dead and republican dead in the same gesture; the 'uncoordinated' voices of victim-survivors.

Some of the latter are coordinated by political groups or victims' groups; others resist coordination; some are unheard by any group or media; some seek vengeance; most want no retaliation: the late Gordon Wilson, whose daughter Marie was killed at Enniskillen, forgave her killers in a way that came to personify the possibility of new remembering. Meanwhile, on the Lower Ormeau Road, where Catholics were murdered in Sean Graham's betting-shop, and there has been strong

[21] Martin McDonagh, *The Lonesome West* (London, 1997), pp. 58–9.
[22] *Independent on Sunday*, 18 July 1999, 25.
[23] Faith and Politics Group, *Remembrance and Forgetting*, p. 18

resistance to Orange parades (understandably, since some outriders mocked the dead), a wall carries a legend which represents much feeling on both sides: 'In memory of their victims they shall not pass.' Remembering Catholic victims is not a priority in most unionist manifestos. And Sinn Féin's demand for public inquiries into deaths caused by the security forces contrasts with the lack of information the IRA have given to families of the Disappeared. One family came up with a subversive – if theoretical – form of commemoration when they dreamed of 'put[ting] up a headstone in Milltown Cemetery with the words: "Reserved for the body of Jean McConville who has disappeared and was murdered by the Provisional IRA"'.[24]

Nonetheless, in the commemorative continuum that binds the Northern Irish Troubles, *via* other twentieth-century Irish and European wars, to battles long ago, victims are now entering the memorial record on a more individual basis (the Vietnam Wall precedent being much invoked). The apotheosis of earlier ventures that documented or represented all the casualties together is *Lost Lives* (1999). This massive dossier presents chronologically 'The stories of the men, women and children who died as a result of the Troubles.' *Lost Lives* puts flesh on the bald statistics offered by Bloomfield: as of December 1997, 3,585 people had been killed: 91 per cent male, 74 per cent under 39, 53 per cent civilians, 28.8 per cent from the security forces, 12.5 per cent republican paramilitaries, 3 per cent Loyalist paramilitaries. Later I will relate several elegies to entries in *Lost Lives*.

Historical ecumenism, inclusive commemoration, individual attention to victims – dead or alive – have a long way to go before they can really compete with older habits. Indeed, it might be argued that the peace process (shaky, as I write in February 2000) has pressed the Northern Irish antagonism back into its ritual cultural forms rather than begun its cultural resolution. Thus opposition to Orange parades from 'Concerned Residents' has itself become a powerful mode of 'ritual protest'. Commemoration now functions as a contradictory site of conflict and conflict-resolution. So does it provide homeopathic doses against violence, or keep the pot simmering until needed? Here are some anecdotal impressions of a debate in Derry during the twenty-sixth Bloody Sunday anniversary at which I suggested that we should build a monument to

[24] David McKittrick, Seamus Kelters, Brian Feeney and Chris Thornton, *Lost Lives: The Stories of the Men, Women and Children who Died as a Result of the Northern Ireland Troubles* (Edinburgh and London, 1999), p. 302; Sir Kenneth Bloomfield, *We Will Remember Them: Report of the Northern Ireland Victims Commissioner, Sir Kenneth Bloomfield* (Belfast, The Stationery Office, 1998).

Amnesia and forget where we put it. This was unpopular, even though I said that the Bloody Sunday commemoration obviously constituted healthy (rather than morbid) remembrance as defined by Milan Kundera: 'The struggle of man against power is the struggle of memory against forgetting.'[25] The very fact of the debate, speculation as to whether the Bloody Sunday 'March for Justice' would be the same in a hundred years (in 1998 Bairbre de Brún's ministerial attendance was not anticipated) and other signs showed that the Bloody Sunday Trust desired more 'progressive' means of commemoration. Nor is the Trust or every victim's family necessarily aligned with Sinn Féin. Yet the large numbers who attended the debate (or felt welcome there) were almost all Catholic, and going to Derry was a salutary encounter with the implacability of Irish memory. Another unpopular speaker was Robert Cooper, head of the Fair Employment Commission. Cooper had ruled that the Bloody Sunday black ribbon was political, and hence could not be worn in Derry workplaces. I was told, however, that people had worn the ribbon chiefly in *mixed* workplaces. The Northern Irish practice of 'coat-trailing' adds a preposition to the verb 'remember' – remembering *at*. This has been termed 'rhetorical history'. Extreme readiness to be annoyed in this way might be called 'rhetorical umbrage'. There is also a darker readiness: readiness to desecrate inscriptions, monuments, statues, headstones, wreaths and other memorials. Such actions counter-symbolically erase the Other's historical narrative, culture, territorial presence.

In the Republic, historical ecumenism proceeds more freely, though with sudden replays of looptapes between past and present. In 1995 Proinsias O Drisceoil warned that 'commemoration is likely to become a primary site of cultural politics'. Many interpretive communities, including more powerful groups than the academy, take a proprietary interest in the Irish past. O Drisceoil's main example of cultural politics converging on commemoration was the Famine, whose popular reinvention he was among the first to construe as driven by Irish America, and as serving the interests of 'nationalist ideologues and tourist promoters' handed 'an unsurpassable opportunity to combine in "re-living" (and in selling) a Catholic Irish trauma which transferred to North America and which can capably match the *weltschmerz* of any ethnic competitor'.[26] Introducing *Irish Hunger: Personal Reflections on the Legacy of the Famine*, the Irish-American senator Tom Hayden writes in self-worshipping style: 'The popular Irish musical *Riverdance*... re-enacts the native imagination of the

[25] Milan Kundera, *The Book of Laughter and Forgetting* (London, 1996), p. 4.
[26] 'Sites of Commemoration', *Times Change*, 5 (Summer / Autumn 1995), 23.

original Irish people, followed by the trauma of Famine, death and emigration, and goes on to celebrate the energising of the Irish as they flowed and mingled with other cultures of the world . . .'[27] The incidence of 'trauma' and 'repression' in *Irish Hunger* confirms the responsibility of Irish-American *weltschmerz* for introducing psycho-babble, as well as *Riverdance*, into the theatre of Irish memory. Many contributors – including some Irish writers – evince a kind of false memory syndrome by free-associating upon what they yet agree to be 'silence'. Here imported identity politics combines with soft-focus indigenous nationalism in what David Lowenthal, analysing contemporary 'heritage', calls 'a self-congratulatory swamp of collective memory'.[28]

Some also claim that there has been 'silence' in Ireland about the Famine through most of this century, although it was forgotten neither by the Free State/Republic's school history syllabus nor by nationalist rhetoric. However, there was no Famine walk, no performance artist weeping in public, no concept of 'survivor guilt' borrowed from the Holocaust. (The most powerful commemorative symbol created in the mid 1990s was John Behan's unrhetorical sculpture of a coffin-ship, skeletons entangled in the rigging, sited near Westport.) Perhaps, as Roy Foster suggests, a change in heritage styles has also combined with contemporary politics. Even a serious project, such as the Famine Museum in Strokestown, Co. Roscommon is more emotively conceived than Famine commemoration in the 1940s as summarised by Foster: 'the actual centenary . . . was marked by a government-funded programme of folk-lore retrieval and a heavyweight volume of essays'.[29] It is also a nationalist trope to accuse the present-day Irish of forgetting their heroic or tragic past. Hence, as cultural politics, all this implicated contemporary Northern Ireland (Tony Blair's 'apology' was propagandised as being 'for the Famine' rather than for its maladministration). It also aggravated the critique of historians who do not 'break up their lines to weep'.

The jury is still out on the 1798 bicentenary: one day to be investigated, just as the heavyweight historiography that abounded in 1998 included studies of the 1898 commemoration. Yet perhaps some enthusiasts offered this anniversary as post-traumatic stress therapy after those Famine tears: a chance for Irish people to feel good about themselves as opposed to bad about the Brits. On 16 November 1995, at a mass for Famine

[27] Tom Hayden (ed.), *Irish Hunger: Personal Reflections on the Legacy of the Famine* (Boulder, CO, and Dublin, 1997), p. 9.

[28] Gillis, *Commemorations*, p. 41.

[29] *Independent on Sunday*, 18 July 1999, 25.

victims, Minister of State Avril Doyle TD stressed the Famine's 'emotional scars', saying: 'We need the therapy of grief.' On 24 November she launched 1798 commemoration plans:

> the United Irishmen . . . imaginatively created a vision of a non-sectarian, democratic and inclusive politics, which would attract and sustain all Irish people in all their inherited complexities . . . Firstly, we must discard the now discredited sectarian version of '98, which was merely a polemical post-rebellious falsification. Secondly, we must stress the modernity of the United Irish project, its forward looking democratic dimension, and abandon the outdated agrarian or peasant interpretation.

The 1798 bicentenary intersected with the peace process in a manner that produced different emphases North and South. In the North (exclusive of republican events) the main focus was a carefully mounted exhibition in the Ulster Museum which won a prize for effective outreach to groups in both communities. In the Republic, the United Irishmen's radical theory was stressed more than the 'vicious, chaotic civil war' that ensued in practice (and whose sectarian aspect has not, in fact, been 'discredited'). Thus Comóradh '98, which organised the bicentenary events in Wexford, came up with 'a Wexford "Republic" that never existed, and . . . a "Senate" that never met'. Tom Dunne, from whom I have been quoting, found Comóradh to be 'intent on presenting a sanitised and politically correct version of the rebellion that is in tune with the common nationalist perception of the current "peace process", a lost dream of "United Irishmen", which we can still make a reality'. He also noted slippages 'from commemoration to celebration' which fit the self-worshipping model of such occasions.[30] Mic Moroney interviewed Bill Murray, a Wexford farmer who gathered 300 pikemen (the largest single contingent) for a re-enactment (21 June 1998) of the Battle of Vinegar Hill, and who attacked government attempts to tone down any militancy. Murray said: 'Of course, it's republican, 90%, I'd say of the pikemen are republican in sympathy, not that they'd be into violence. It's a very solemn occasion, it's about commemorating the dead, about walking in the shoes of those dead men . . .' In February, Sinn Féin had organised a national commemoration at Vinegar Hill, 'with thousands bussed in from the north', at which Murray presented a replica pike to Gerry Adams.

Here tension between official and local commemorative styles appears in its nationalist mode. Another Comóradh organiser said: 'I think

[30] Tom Dunne, unpublished essay, 'Memory, History, Commemoration'.

around here, people don't like to be told how they should or shouldn't commemorate their history and culture.'[31] Yet Irish popular memory does not bubble up from below as instinctively as Luke Gibbons assumes when he writes: 'What we are dealing with here are different registers of memory, one that is contained and legitimised within the confines of the monument and the museum, and the other having to do with the endangered traces of collective memory, as transmitted by popular culture, folklore, ballads and so on.' Gibbons then inconsistently commends an art exhibit which 'features an accordion mounted on a wall whose intake and expelling of air allows it to double up as an artificial lung attached to the barely decipherable image of the republican hunger-striker, Bobby Sands'.[32] Orangeism does not usually qualify as Irish 'collective memory'. But it hardly supplies the only evidence of (legitimising) organisation in this area, where the transition to modern memorial practices is clearly marked. Comóradh (copying battle enactments in Britain, marketing '98 heritage) and Sinn Féin's interest in Vinegar Hill, rather than the Ulster Museum or Presbyterian United Irishmen, are proof of that. Also, in the Republic, a relatively short thread connects political parties, government, academics, museum curators, local festival organisers and blokes dressed up as pikemen. In 1998, for example, Kevin Whelan figured as heavyweight historian, Comóradh scriptwriter and translator of 1798 into peace-process language for the Irish government.

At Vinegar Hill, Mic Moroney noticed 'that thrumming funereal chord in Irish culture and . . . republican commemoration'.[33] Updating Leerssen on the circularity of funeral cults, Malachi O'Doherty writes in *The Trouble with Guns* (1998):

> Catholicism and republicanism offer a form of immortality in the memory of those who honour the martyrs. Many republicans in Belfast wear medallions engraved with the image of Mairead Farrell or other republican martyrs, as other Catholics wear similar medallions bearing the image of the Virgin Mary or one of the saints. Republicanism sustains itself, in part, for the work of respecting the dead. It knows the need to do that. If the cause collapses, there may be no-one left to tend their graves or honour their memory. Conversely, if people forget to honour the dead, the cause will collapse . . .[34]

[31] *Irish Times*, 23 June 1998, 14.
[32] Luke Gibbons, *Transformations in Irish Culture* (Cork, 1996), p. 172.
[33] *Irish Times*, 23 June 1998, 14.
[34] Malachi O'Doherty, *The Trouble with Guns: Republican Strategy and the Provisional IRA* (Belfast, 1998), p. 22.

Probably owing to divergent paths taken at the Reformation, Ulster Protestant commemorative culture is less funereal in form, but also depends on compacts with the dead. Protestant ancestor-worship invokes 'fathers', rather than spirit emanations, of the present community.

The world wars' changing role in Irish memory potentially links new ways of remembering the longer-term past with shared ways of remembering the years and deaths since 1969. Irish Catholic/nationalist participation in the wars was, of course, officially and culturally repressed for years: Jane Leonard has tellingly mapped the conflicts over Armistice Day in Dublin.[35] Today, tangible realisations of historical ecumenism are the Irish National Memorial at Islandbridge, opened in 1995, and the Messines Peace Park, jointly inaugurated by President McAleese and Queen Elizabeth in November 1998. (Two sponsors of Messines, Tony Crowe, a Derry local historian with ties to the Apprentice Boys, and Lieutenant-General Gerry McMahon, formerly chief of staff of the Irish army, have mentioned the significance of 'revisionist' history in securing this outcome.)[36] Still more remarkably, Tom Hartley of Sinn Féin promotes remembrance of the Great War dead from both the Catholic and Protestant communities. Yet, especially in the North, most nationalists persist in seeing the poppy as only a provocative British and Protestant symbol – remembering *at.* They are partly right: Tom Collins regrets that some 'unionists (you can tell them by the size of their poppies) have made the emblem a badge of identity rather than a symbol of humanitarianism'.[37] Conversely, some relatives have objected to the peace doves added to the Enniskillen war memorial, seeing them as a generic contradiction rather than vital hybrid or additional testimony to 'a sacrifice which must never be allowed to happen again', as Jay Winter terms the civic function of 'war memorial art'.[38] More than once, the doves have been removed. Again, an obelisk recently built at Thiepval, to commemorate Orangemen who

[35] See Jane Leonard, 'The Twinge of Memory: Armistice Day and Remembrance Sunday in Dublin since 1919', in Richard English and Graham Walker (eds.), *Unionism in Modern Ireland: New Perspectives on Politics and Culture* (Dublin, 1996), pp. 99–114.

[36] At a symposium in the Ulster Museum (11 Nov. 1999) McMahon ascribed his interest in Messines to his attendance at evening classes in History at University College, Dublin when 'revisionist history' was in its heyday. Crowe (who also spoke at the symposium) links the 'superbly refurbished, unmolested Islandbridge' with 'the revisionist approach to such commemoration by the chattering classes of Eire', Lucy and McClure, *Remembrance*, p. 49.

[37] *Remembrance*, p. 4.

[38] Winter, *Sites of Memory, Sites of Mourning*, p. 95.

died at the Somme, has been criticised as a partisan memorial in aesthetic as well as moral bad taste – the former being a function of the latter. Further, by thus appropriating the Somme, it fosters ideas about Orangeism and the Ulster Division which have little evidential basis.[39]

Perhaps a case could be made that certain kinds of attention to the Great War or the Famine or 1798 evade more pertinent engagement with more recent events. It is, of course, not only in Irish contexts that commemoration may infinitely defer taking responsibility for history. Yet, for different reasons, neither unionists nor nationalists in Ireland have fully undergone western European processes of twentieth-century post-war grieving. In *Sites of Memory, Sites of Mourning* (1995) Jay Winter argues that, whatever the ideological factors and varying cultural tropes, we should not lose sight of commonalities: the sense of 'the post-war world as composed of survivors perched on a mountain of corpses'; the 'need to bring the dead home, to lay the dead to rest, symbolically or physically'; the localised and familial rather than national compulsion to memorialise; 'the absence of hatred, or triumph, or worship of the military *per se*'. Lutyens's ecumenical and abstract monuments, including his monument to the missing at Thiepval, are 'an extraordinary statement about mass death and the impossibility of triumphalism'.[40] Hence the extreme dissonance of that Orange obelisk, which also runs counter to John Keegan's description of the war graves gardens as 'a site of universally venerable sanctuary'.[41] With respect to the experiential gulf between middle-class and working-class unionism, Progressive Unionist Party politician Billy Hutchinson quotes as his favourite poem, Siegfried Sassoon's 'Suicide in the Trenches': 'Sneak home, and pray you never know / The hell where youth and laughter go.' Troubles elegy, then, emerges in a context to which Sassoon, Owen and other 'war poets' are directly relevant. It is also relevant that the Omagh bombing, which killed twenty-nine people, induced a universal recognition of common tragedy. Its first commemoration, on Sunday, 15 August 1999, was 'an extraordinary statement about mass death'.[42] Lament had become elegy.

[39] For the argument, see Ruth Dudley Edwards, *The Faithful Tribe: An Intimate Portrait of the Loyal Institutions* (London, 1999), pp. 250–3; George Fleming, review of *The Faithful Tribe*, *Irish Review*, 25 (Winter/Spring 1999/2000), 173–5.

[40] Winter, *Sites of Memory, Sites of Mourning*, pp. 17, 28, 98, 107.

[41] *Prospect*, Nov. 1997, 25.

[42] See *Irish Times*, 16 Aug. 1999, 6.

II

Proposals for inclusive commemoration often cite or quote poetry. Witness the title of the Bloomfield Report (Laurence Binyon), its quotations from Northern Irish poets, its proposal that the War Memorial building (whose imagined gardens recall the war graves) should incorporate 'inscriptions drawing upon appropriate words written by poets of this painful time'.[43] Here there may be an expectation that poets' words will always transcend difference. Frank Ormsby's anthology, *A Rage for Order: Poetry of the Northern Ireland Troubles* (1992), shows this not to be the case. Yet elegy, as a memorial structure, may have special ways of interceding between the mess of history and the perspectives that mourning brings. Only a minority of the poems in *A Rage for Order* are strictly elegies. Only a small number of poems by any individual poet are strictly elegies. Only a small number of victims get elegised. Yet elegy, I would suggest, is the genre that poets have made most distinctively expressive with reference to the Troubles, a genre on which other kinds of poem converge or from which they depart. Hence Troubles elegy has also contributed to the reinvention of elegy itself.

At the beginning of *Poetry of Mourning: The Modern Elegy from Hardy to Heaney* (1994) Jahan Ramazani denies that 'modern elegy' is a contradiction in terms:

> Sometimes regarded as opposites, modern poetry and the elegy should be seen instead as inextricable. Despite the common misconception that twentieth-century poets forsake mourning and genre, many of them perpetuate and intensify the ancient literary dialogue with the dead.

He qualifies this by stating that 'modern poets reanimate the elegy not by slavishly adopting its conventions; instead they violate its norms and transgress its limits'. Hence they attack 'the psychological structures and literary devices specific to the elegy [especially] the psychological propensity of the genre to translate grief into consolation'.[44] With elegies for the dead of the Northern Irish Troubles, further factors come into play. First, the local adherence to nineteenth-century Irish and British commemorative modes makes tensions between pre-modern and modern memory a live issue. This influences what elegists take from earlier war poets. Second, civil-war deaths bring public and personal mourning into mutual relation and question. Third, Troubles elegy revives modern

[43] Bloomfield, *We will Remember them*, p. 47.

[44] Jahan Ramazani, *Poetry of Mourning: The Modern Elegy from Hardy to Heaney* (Chicago, IL, and London, 1994), pp. 1, 3.

elegy as 'protest elegy' by implying an attitude to causes of death. Finally, I would argue that Troubles elegy supports Jay Winter's case, in *Sites of Memory, Sites of Mourning*, that there is a less clear divide between traditional and modern mourning than Ramazani maintains. Winter sees the 'enduring appeal of many traditional motifs – defined as an eclectic set of classical, romantic, or religious images and ideas' as 'directly related to the universality of bereavement in the Europe of the Great War and its aftermath'. His findings lead him to question 'the cultural history of the Great War as a phase in the onward ascent of modernism'. For Winter, the strength of war memorials often derives from 'the power of traditional languages, rituals, and forms to mediate bereavement'.[45] Yet the marked persistence of religious motifs in Troubles elegy does more than mediate grief. On the one hand, 'consolation' is not only metaphysically but (as for Owen) politically problematic. On the other, recast religious structures may assume a less passive role than that described by Winter.

It might seem paradoxical to combine 'elegy' with 'forgetting'. But to dwell on forgetting is to take a strategic step away from memory and its addicts – from Irish mnemophilia – even though remembering and forgetting are inseparable processes, whether for individuals or groups. My real concern, of course, is with poetry's critique and redirection of memorial schemata. This introduces some precursor poets who have influenced Troubles elegy. Perhaps (in any memorial context) the nouns memory-remembrance-commemoration mark sequence as well as variation: a sequence in which recollection becomes progressively less fluid, contingent and interior; more institutional, ceremonial and communal – as is generally the trajectory in Northern Ireland and other militarised societies. (At the same time, differences in religious culture and language mean that Protestants are more into 'remembrance', Catholics into 'commemoration'.) Thus when Leerssen describes James Joyce as ending 'the poetics of anachronism',[46] he may not allow for the extent to which the nineteenth century has been alive and morbid in Northern Ireland. And, where genre is part of the picture – poetry, as well as elegy and elegy's generic subdivisions – so is the complementary role of Yeats in disrupting and reinventing Irish commemorative systems.

I will focus on three points: Yeats's revision of the Moore-Davis ballad; his redirection of memorial emphases; a deeper dialectic between memory and forgetting which more radically questions memorial forms. Here, Yeats the autobiographer intersects with Yeats the national poet. Writing

[45] Winter, *Sites of Memory, Sites of Mourning*, pp. 5, 115.
[46] Leerssen, *Remembrance and Imagination*, p. 231.

on autobiography, and criticising theorists who neglect 'cultural influence' on the structures as well as content of memory, Eamonn Hughes argues that 'memory has two orientations, towards the past and towards the future rendered as a purposeful modification of memory', as translating cognition into 'conation'. Hughes also emphasises how Yeats's memory is 'strategically deployed against other memories, other schemata, then abroad'.[47] Leerssen says of Moore: 'the true political importance of the Melodies lies in their cultivation of remembrance. "To remember" is continually held out as an ethical and political imperative ("Remember the glories of Brian the brave" . . . "Let Erin remember . . .")'.[48] I have written elsewhere on Yeats's 'Easter 1916' as a critique of Davisite tropes.[49] Here the poem may have both anticipated revisionist history and initiated a dialectic between commemorative tropes. This is exposed by how the republican National Graves Association misreads 'Easter 1916'. In recommending the inscription, 'We know their dream . . . they dreamed and are dead', it elides Yeats's cognitive complication ('Enough / To *know* they dreamed') which divorces knowledge of the dream from any implied necessity to act on that knowledge. In fact, Yeats's own formulation may be a way of avoiding the verb 'remember', especially its imperative mood, as he does throughout the poem. By 'number[ing] in the song' or 'writ[ing] it out in a verse', he transfers power from the memorial tropes that prepared, and are prepared, for the event, to the poet, who himself devolves some power to his readers as they construe the ambiguities of his representation. Here, poetic commemoration becomes creatively 'purposeful' in modifying the schemata (and stigmata) to which the Rising appealed.

There is an exception to the rule that Yeats never uses 'remember' in the hortatory, political, imperative style of the Young Ireland ballad. This occurs in the 'Three Marching Songs' which have a complex history. Seeking to adapt 'O'Donnell Abu' for General O'Duffy's Blueshirts, and finding that he could not rival the Young Ireland legacy in this respect, Yeats eventually rewrote the songs in 1938: 'Remember all those renowned generations, / Remember all that have sunk in their blood, / Remember all that have died on the scaffold . . .'. The first version of 'remember' was 'justify'. This textual shift spells out what the 'poetics of anachronism' encode: directed memory as spur to political action. 'Justify' and 'remember' are linked to the 'unremembering hearts

[47] Eamonn Hughes, unpublished article.

[48] Leerssen, *Remembrance and Imagination*, p. 81.

[49] See Edna Longley, 'The Rising, the Somme and Irish memory', in Longley, *The Living Stream: Literature and Revisionism in Ireland* (Newcastle upon Tyne, 1994), pp. 69–85.

and heads' attacked in 'Under Ben Bulben' – the people's amnesia criticised once again, but from an unorthodox angle as earlier in 'September 1913'.

In the *Concordance* to Yeats's poetry, variants on memory and forgetting suggest a significant complex of concepts and forms. That imperative 'remember' reflects his final hectic effort to 'engross the present and dominate memory' ('The Circus Animals' Desertion') in his own mnemonic terms. He had already created a powerful symbolic memory-bank to rival Young Ireland's 'rhymed lesson-book': not only a different stylisation of historical events but a placing of different events and names – cultural and artistic – in the foreground. 'September 1913', with its startling appropriation of Moore-Davis tropes for a cultural nationalism that criticises Irish Catholics, began the process that led to 'Coole Park, 1929' and 'The Municipal Gallery Revisited'. The climax of both poems lays down new memorial ritual. 'Coole', proleptically ruined, becomes a shrine where we are asked to 'take [our] stand'

> And dedicate – eyes bent upon the ground,
> Back turned upon the brightness of the sun
> And all the sensuality of the shade –
> A moment's memory to that laurelled head.

At the end of 'The Municipal Gallery', a more explicit redirection of political-nationalist idiom commands, with regard to Synge, Lady Gregory and the poet who elegises himself by elegising his 'friends': 'Ireland's history in their lineaments trace'. That is, rather than in the political 'images' that other paintings present. Yet Yeats ultimately asks us to remember not artists, but art which implicates a life (sun, shade, friendship) beyond commemoration.

'Forgetting' occurs in the last stanza of 'The Municipal Gallery': 'And here's John Synge himself, that rooted man / "Forgetting human words..."' 'Forgetting human words' quotes a poem by Synge about becoming so absorbed in or into the Wicklow countryside that he loses his human bearings. In a simpler sense, this is where Yeats's poetry comes in – the Ossianic Island of Forgetfulness, the 'forgotten beauty', 'forgotten truth' of the *fin-de-siècle*; where the point is not 'remembering' forgotten beauty since its being forgotten constitutes its paradoxical charm. This a feminine world, remote from the macho world of patriotic action, which Ossian/Yeats is finally compelled to remember and resume. Now and then the half-forgotten, long-forgotten, world-forgotten renew their imaginative sway in more complex terms. At the end of 'Paudeen', forgetting in the sense of self-extrication from history becomes the condition of vision: 'on that lonely height, where all are in God's eye / There cannot be, confusion of our sound forgot, / A single soul that lacks a sweet crystalline cry.'

Yet forgetting the world is also allied to being forgotten by it, just as remembering (as in 'The Municipal Gallery') is allied to being remembered. 'Forgetting and forgot' appears in 'Meditations in Time of Civil War', a sequence which reflects on the fate of memory together with that of tradition and the literary movement. As it does so, it initiates further generic complications digested by the poetry of a later civil war. Here Yeats identifies with the man at arms whose 'dwindling score and he seemed castaways, / Forgetting and forgot'. This, however, presents an opportunity to reprogramme memorial schemata as 'Befitting emblems of adversity'; to restock 'the empty house of the stare' with new symbols – of which the stare's nest itself is one. For Yeats, civil war has widened the breach between public and private commemorative language. The arrival of two civil-warriors at the poet's door dramatises his necessary retreat into interiority, the 'cold snows of a dream'. That dream reflexively pioneers civil-war poetics as a tension between pointless mutual cannibalism ('Trooper belabouring trooper, biting at arm or at face') and domestic nurture, the natural world, artistic creation. Yeats characterises the warriors themselves as entirely present-minded: 'an indifferent multitude . . . Nor hate of what's to come, nor pity for what's gone.' Section VI incorporates a significant cross-over from Great War protest elegy: the unusually stark, factual utterance, 'Last night they trundled down the road / That dead young soldier in his blood.' For all Yeats's dismissals of Wilfred Owen, this echoes 'Dulce et Decorum Est' with its 'wagon that we flung him in'. At the same time, 'Meditations' unites elegy with a quest for reconstruction: 'Come build in the empty house of the stare.'

The Anglo-Irish War and Civil War confirmed Yeats as also a poet of the European war, and hence as an exponent of generic hybridisation. This turns on differences both between memorial systems and between their dismantlings. On the Moore-Davis system, remembrance of the (often remote) glorious past should inspire present action to enable a future. Although Yeats, in 'Easter 1916', revises both premise and outcome – the event exists textually between an ambiguous past and ambiguous future – he does not thereby give up on conation, on heroic role-models and significant action. Thus, 'In Memory of Major Robert Gregory' celebrates a culture-hero rather than a war-hero, or rather than lamenting a victim of 'futility'. The companion elegy, 'An Irish Airman Foresees his Death', is equally anomalous in celebrating a self-sacrifice allegedly divested of patriotic motive: 'Those that I fight I do not hate, / Those that I guard I do not love.' This politically careful focus on a 'lonely impulse of delight' also produces a transcendental sense of the artist-hero (Gregory) and hero-artist (Yeats) that contrasts with the humiliations suffered by art in 'Meditations', Great War elegy and Troubles elegy. 'An Irish Airman' discloses the tension between Irish and British (both patriotic and anti-war) commemorative tropes, as Yeats's elegy for the Anglo-Irish Gregory tries to outflank them all.

To return to forgetting: at its most radical, Great War protest elegy (absorbed by the poets discussed later) not only destroys the poetics of imperial patriotism, but strikes to the heart of remembrance itself, as in Lutyens's anti-transcendental monuments. The cenotaph is another 'empty house'. Charles Sorley's sonnet 'When you see millions of the mouthless dead' never loses its power as a pre-emption of memorial edifices, even of Adorno: 'Say only this, they are dead.' Edward Thomas's 'The Word' may seem a less obviously subversive poem. Yet, written shortly before he joined up in July 1915, it belongs to a group of poems that reflect on memory and identity in the context of this decision. Its literary context is his distinction between patriotic verse and poetry: 'but a small number of poems destined to endure are directly concerned with the public triumphs, calamities, or trepidations, that helped to beget them. The public, crammed with mighty facts and ideas it will never digest, must look coldly on poetry where already these mighty things have sunk away . . .'[50]

> There are so many things I have forgot,
> That once were much to me, or that were not,
> All lost, as is a childless woman's child
> And its child's children, in the undefiled
> Abyss of what can never be again.
> I have forgot, too, names of the mighty men
> That fought and lost or won in the old wars,
> Of kings and fiends and gods, and most of the stars.
> Some things I have forgot that I forget . . .

The speaker's vast forgetfulness is a way of rearranging memorial (and male) hierarchies. What he finally retains as significant is 'an empty

[50] *Poetry and Drama*, 2/8 (Dec. 1914). See Edna Longley (ed.), *A Language Not to be Betrayed: Selected Prose of Edward Thomas* (Manchester, 1981), p. 135.

thingless name' that problematises human consciousness:

> While perhaps I am thinking of the elder scent
> That is like food, or while I am content
> With the wild rose scent that is like memory,
> This name suddenly is cried out to me
> From somewhere in the bushes by a bird
> Over and over again, a pure thrush word.

Language and memory, abused by humanity, are displaced to the natural world as a form of critique. The fruitful paradox for Sorley and Thomas, as for all poems that work through processes of forgetting or not remembering, is that memory and poetry are as inseparable as memory and forgetting. These poems also strategically challenge St Augustine's view that we cannot 'remember forgetting'. A memorably ambiguous line is 'Some things I have forgot that I forget.' In *Elegy and Paradox* (1994) W. David Shaw says: 'When we try to remove one of the contradictory elements [from elegy] – the consolation from the inconsolability; the remembering from the forgetting; the certainty from the uncertainty – we are in danger of making death noncontradictory or devoid of strangeness.'[51] (One might add, the anger from the *requiescat*: hence 'protest elegy'.)[52] What these paradoxical poems do, then, is invite us to remember in difficult new ways. Sorley's tactic is to set up, then interrupt, memorial tropes with statements like 'It is easy to be dead.' Thomas gives what is forgotten or unimportant a ghostly presence before his poem becomes possessed by the clarity of present-tense consciousness: 'a pure thrush word'. That mantra resembles the 'pure crystalline cry' at the end of 'Paudeen': the cry of poetry against the noise of history. However, Yeats's anxiety about Irish memory, which conditions his belief in 'the Great Memory', keeps commemoration on the agenda. This contrasts with Sorley's questioning of remembrance and Thomas's ambivalence about historical memory.

I now want to relate three Troubles elegies to the terms which I have tried to establish. The elegies are Seamus Heaney's 'Casualty', Paul Durcan's 'Poem Not Beginning with a Line by Pindar' and Michael Longley's brief elegiac sequence 'Wreaths'. Ramazani refers to 'difficult, melancholic mourning' that produces 'not transcendence or redemption of loss but immersion in it'.[53] Civil War compounds all the elegiac

[51] W. David Shaw, *Elegy and Paradox: Themes and Conventions* (Baltimore, MD, and London, 1994), p. 6.
[52] Ibid., p. 155.
[53] Ramazani, *Poetry of Mourning*, pp. 14, 4.

difficulties. Intrinsic to politics rather than unique to modernity, these difficulties have not yet been resolved in the United States, Spain or the Republic of Ireland: countries which can show few shared civil-war monuments in public space. Moreover, the Northern Irish struggle has been war between communities who often claim separate ethnic identities (and who would also war about the category 'civil war'). Nevertheless, Troubles elegy may qualify as well as confirm Ramazani's stress on the anti-consolatory, anti-therapeutic properties of modern elegy – in part, because 'new remembering' implies 'conation' as a quest for sociopolitical healing. Indeed, Ramazani sometimes contradicts himself, as when he finds in modern elegies 'aesthetic gains' for elegy itself which keep it in touch with traditional literary and cultural structures; or when he argues that modern poets defy the institutional anonymity of death by 'moving from the categorical and universal to the intimate and particular'.[54]

Lost Lives rescues Louis O'Neill from statistical anonymity:

259. February 3, 1972
Louis O'Neill, Tyrone
Civilian, Catholic, 49, married, 6 children
From Killmascally, Ardboe, Co. Tyrone, he was killed when a bomb exploded without warning at the Catholic-owned Imperial Bar in Stewartstown. A 15 lb device blew out the front of the building, burying the owner and five customers under rubble. Louis O'Neill died instantly and five others were seriously injured . . . The pub was officially closed, like other bars, in mourning for those who died on Bloody Sunday, but some customers had gone in the back door for a drink . . . It is believed loyalists were behind the attack. There was initial newspaper speculation that the IRA had bombed the bar because it had not closed completely after Bloody Sunday, but the incident fits the pattern of loyalist attacks in and around Co. Tyrone.[55]

Seamus Heaney's elegy for Louis O'Neill, 'Casualty', begins:

He would drink by himself
And raise a weathered thumb
Towards the high shelf,
Calling another rum
And blackcurrant, without

[54] Ibid., pp. 8, 18.
[55] McKittrick *et al.*, *Lost Lives*, p. 150.

Having to raise his voice,
Or order a quick stout
By a lifting of the eyes
And a discreet dumb-show
Of pulling off the top . . .
A dole-kept breadwinner
But a natural for work.
I loved his whole manner,
Sure-footed but too sly,
His deadpan sidling tact,
His fisherman's quick eye
And turned observant back . . .

Specificity is crucial to both these texts. Families of victims documented in *Lost Lives* can be upset by any error (for instance, the mother of Edmund Treanor, a Catholic killed by loyalists on New Year's Eve 1997, objects to his being called 'Eddie' in the book). Yet the detail of poetry differs from that of documentary prose: although factual accuracy still counts, 'getting things wrong' would more crucially be failures of tone, sensitivity, empathy. The implied reader of civil war elegy is not necessarily located in international academe. Like its author and object, he / she belongs to a web of local relations and perceptions – but also potentially to the broader human recognitions opened up by elegy's threeway transactions between the poet, the dead person, the audience. 'Casualty' magnifies certain details of O'Neill's life, ignores others. Heaney evokes him, for instance, not as a family man but in his roles as drinker (his tipples being specified) and fisherman, in his body language, in the particularity of his conversations with the poet as pub companion. When elegy brings dead people 'to life', the poet underlines what has been lost by assigning to it values that oppose the fact and manner of death. Heaney does this formally by means of swiftly stroked lines, each lilting with a new impression. This opening stanza mimics O'Neill's demeanour in its own 'tact' and tactics, and also seems a heightened version of how people talk about the dead at Irish wakes.

Besides establishing a distinctive mourning ritual, 'Casualty' weighs up other memorial and funeral rites. The poem's title, by suggesting a casualty of war, alludes to the impact on Heaney of Wilfred Owen's empathic ('tender-minded') methods.[56] The second stanza gives the facts of O'Neill's death in the context of the Bloody Sunday deaths for which the poem is also an oblique elegy; then Heaney portrays the atmosphere

[56] Seamus Heaney, *The Government of the Tongue: Selected Prose, 1978–1987* (London, 1988), p. 64.

of the 'common funeral' in Derry:

He was blown to bits
Out drinking in a curfew
Others obeyed, three nights
After they shot dead
The thirteen men in Derry.
PARAS THIRTEEN, the walls said,
BOGSIDE NIL . . .

It was a day of cold
Raw silence, wind-blown
Surplice and soutane:
Rained-on, flower-laden
Coffin after coffin
Seemed to float from the door
Of the packed cathedral
Like blossoms on slow water.
The common funeral
Unrolled its swaddling band,
Lapping, tightening
Till we were braced and bound
Like brothers in a ring.

The terrible graffito (a vengeful Protestant 'memorial' to the killings) contrasts with the communal kinship mourning which represents Irish Catholic funeral culture at its most powerful and justified. Later, Heaney imagines O'Neill's conventional private funeral, which he 'missed': 'Those quiet walkers / And sideways talkers . . . the respectable / Purring of the hearse.' The poem imitates as well as ponders the rhythms of both these rituals, but takes its final aesthetic cue, like its first, from the individual life of the victim whose individuality has contributed to his death. Heaney associates O'Neill out fishing with a 'freedom' which merges into his own distinctive utterance and revised view of the poet's commemorative role: 'As you find a rhythm / Working you, slow mile by mile, / Into your proper haunt / Somewhere, well out, beyond . . .' In 'Casualty' the sense of the individual soldier against impersonal powers, in war poetry, becomes still more 'intimate and particular'. It is a bold move of Heaney's (in both versions of O'Neill's death, he reneged on Bloody Sunday mourning) to step away from memorial commonalities, even represent their constricting as well as bracing force. By getting at Bloody Sunday through a mild renegade personally known to him, who 'would not be held / At home by his own crowd', he creates a hybrid elegy which calls into question – the poem takes shape as a mutual interrogation – the absolute loyalties that link all Troubles deaths with commemorative orthodoxy.

'Casualty' indicates how civil-war elegy can subvert 'the categorical and universal'. This need not mean that it divests individual victims of their social being. Rather, elegy frames the *relation* between self and society in a way that challenges a politics that *identifies* self and society. O'Neill is not, in fact, detached from his community: he shares, as does the poet's voice up to a point, its style of 'sideways talking'. But this represents the community in its cultural particulars rather than its political generality. Michael Longley's triptych 'Wreaths' includes two elegies given the title of the victims' occupations: 'The Greengrocer' and 'The Civil Servant'. By stressing social and civic functions, these titles implicitly question the political belief-systems that caused the deaths. 'The Greengrocer' begins with a clash between the values manifested by the dead man in his job and those of his (loyalist) killers – the life-enhancing as opposed to the 'death-dealing':

> He ran a good shop, and he died
> Serving even the death-dealers
> Who found him busy as usual
> Behind the counter, organised
> With holly wreaths for Christmas,
> Fir trees on the pavement outside.

An earlier elegy by Longley, 'Wounds', had invoked images from the Great War in relation to Catholic, Protestant and British Army victims of the Troubles. This affirmed the generic relevance of protest elegy; one point being – in its translation from the battlefield – that rupture of the cross-cultural human values which inform everyday intercourse (nurture, domesticity, hospitality) adds further 'futility': 'the Sacred Heart of Jesus / Paralysed as heavy guns put out / The night-light in a nursery for ever'. (On 14 August 1969 an RUC tracer bullet killed a Catholic child, Patrick Rooney, in his bedroom.) The verb 'serve', which links 'The Greengrocer' with 'The Civil Servant', makes a similar point. However, the latter title (to spare survivors at the time) disguises the fact that this elegy mourns a magistrate, Martin McBirney. I quote from his entry in *Lost Lives*:

1185. September 16, 1974
Martin McBirney, East Belfast
Magistrate, Protestant, 52, married, one child

A magistrate and formerly a well-known QC and literary figure, he was shot dead by the IRA as he sat down to breakfast at his home on the Belmont Road. Judge Rory Conaghan [a Catholic] was shot at almost exactly the same time on the same morning . . . As a lawyer, he had previously been Crown counsel in Belfast, but he was also known as a barrister willing to appear in . . . cases involving civil rights issues . . . he was closely identified with the Northern Ireland Labour Party . . . A Protestant married to a Catholic . . . He wrote a number of plays and documentaries for the BBC and was a friend of poet Louis MacNeice and of shipyard playwright Sam Thompson . . . A subsequent court case heard that when news of his death was broken to his sister-in-law, Frances Cooke, she died of a heart attack.[57]

> He was preparing an Ulster fry for breakfast
> When someone walked into the kitchen and shot him:
> A bullet entered his mouth and pierced his skull,
> The books he had read, the music he could play.
>
> He lay in his dressing gown and pyjamas
> While they dusted the dresser for fingerprints
> And then shuffled backwards across the garden
> With notebooks, cameras and measuring tapes.
>
> They rolled him up like a red carpet and left
> Only a bullet hole in the cutlery drawer:
> Later his widow took a hammer and chisel
> And removed the black keys from his piano.

Here poetic specificity emphasises the manner of death and, as with the 'nursery' in 'Wounds', precisely how a domestic interior has been violated. Although the poem does not directly allude to McBirney's profession or politics, 'Civil Servant' seems not only a disguise but a metaphor both for the liberalism of his public service and for a civilised life. One elegiac model here is the Second World War poet Keith Douglas, whose proximity to the enemy in the Desert War produces intense collisions between death and life (in 'How to Kill' the poet-killer elegises his victim by observing him through his gun's 'dial of glass'). In 'The Civil Servant', 'skull' presses on the disjunction between the bullet and the rich consciousness it has terminated. Besides suggesting how the shockwaves of any killing go on affecting victim-survivors, the last two lines underscore the poem's own discordant protest music, which yet confines itself to (apparently) factual reporting like the police 'notebooks, cameras and measuring tapes'.

[57] *Lost Lives*, pp. 474–5.

Why should every victim not have an elegy? a poem so fitted to their death (and life) that the massive memorial diversity would unignorably challenge Northern Irish memory? *Lost Lives* is not alone in taking such an approach. BBC Northern Ireland Radio currently broadcasts 'Legacy' in brief slots before the 9 o'clock morning news: memories of dreadful events spoken by victim-survivors. Apart from poets' incapacity, in every sense, to keep up, civil war elegists may need personal imaginative contact: the subject is often a friend, a neighbour, a local figure. Two other notable elegies by Heaney are for his friend Sean Armstrong and his cousin Colum McCartney. At the same time, compelling images in the public domain can provide an empathetic point of entry: thus in 'Wounds' Longley's impression of 'Three teenage soldiers, bellies full of / Bullets and Irish beer' is enabled by the poem's mediation of Great War images through the memories of his father who himself fought as a teenage soldier. The elegies discussed above observe various protocols that validate their authority to speak, the manner in which they speak. Exploitative poetry can effect a critique neither of violence nor of orthodox commemoration. Second, all Troubles elegies illuminate more than a single death. In that sense they are 'representative' or synecdochic, and quantity would blur rather than clarify. In addition to their immediate occasion, the existing elegies stake out a field of response which also implicates other kinds of poem. Yet, in another sense, they are metonymic: their 'individuality' deconstructs unified symbolic narratives together with their expression and continuance through commemorative ritual. Elegy has followed this war in transgressing the bounds between private and public domains. But it deploys a critical reversal whereby the personal is thereby licensed to interrogate the public.

The Kingsmills killings were a mass murder on a par with Bloody Sunday. To quote again from *Lost Lives*:

1566. January 5, 1976
Robert Walker, Armagh
Civilian, Protestant, 46, factory worker

The man from Half Acre, Listrunchon, Glennane, was one of ten Protestant workmen machine-gunned by a group calling itself the Republican Action Force. The shooting, which some referred to as the Kingsmills or Whitecross massacre, is thought to have been the work of the IRA in reprisal for the killing of members of two Catholic families, the Reaveys and the O'Dowds, in the area in preceding days.[58]

58 Ibid., p. 611.

Lost Lives goes on to record the other individual deaths, and reprint a moving account given ten years later by the one man who survived:

> Even now when I hear of an innocent person being killed the horror of the massacre all comes back and I can feel every bullet hitting me. Bessbrook lost its heart through that massacre. It was once a vibrant happy community full of life and enjoyment. What was done that night was a sheer waste, a futile exercise that advanced no cause . . .[59]

As with Bloody Sunday and its thirteen victims, 'massacre' seems an apt word for multiple deaths in this small-scale civil war. Also aptly, it evokes the historical 'massacres' perpetrated by Christian sectarianism. Paul Durcan uses the word 'massacre' in the title of several Troubles elegies: for instance, 'In Memory the Miami Showband – Massacred 31 July 1975', and his first response to the Kingsmill murders: 'The Minibus Massacre – The Eve of the Epiphany'. His second response takes a different tack. Its title, 'Poem Not Beginning with a Line by Pindar', indicates how Troubles elegy, like Great War protest-elegy before it, may criticise classical/pastoral elegy as a basis for new remembering. Durcan also takes off from 'Poem Beginning with a Line by Pindar' by Robert Duncan, which alludes to Goya:

> Having photocopied Goya by moonlight, the IRA
> Hijacked a minibus on a circular road
> In Armagh of the Nightingales,
> Tromboned ten Protestant workmen into lining up
> Along the footlights of the Armagh hills,
> To kick high their legs, look left, look right,
> And fed them such real midnight jazz
> That not even Goya on a high
> Could have improvised a tableau
> Of such vaudeville terror, such prismatic carnage,
> Bodies yearning over bodies,
> Sandwich boxes, Thermos flasks, decks of playing cards.

Here, through his own black grotesquerie, Durcan engages in Ramazani's untherapeutic 'difficult melancholic mourning'. His conceit of vaudeville chorus line and jazz syncopation highlights the appalling death-count. The poem also reflexively becomes a commemorative 'tableau' whose allusion to other art forms is a way of dramatising the point that unprecedented horror requires new aesthetic alignments. At the same time, protest comes politically upfront not only as satirical tone

[59] Ibid., p. 612.

or image, but as explicit indictment of the concealed sectarian dimension in Irish nationalism:

> Next morning at breakfast in the kitchen
> I enquire of Daddy his judgement.
> The President of the Circuit Court
> Of the Republic of Ireland,
> Appointed by the party of the Fine Gael,
> Scooping porridge into his mouth,
> Does not dissemble as he curls his lip,
> Does not prevaricate as he gazes through me:
> 'Teach the Protestants a lesson',
> And, when I fail to reciprocate,
> 'The law is the law and the law must take its course' . . .
> The party of the Fine Gael is the party
> Of respectability, conformity, legitimacy, pedigree,
> Faith, chivalry, property, virility,
> The party of Collins, O'Higgins, O'Duffy, Cosgrave,
> Great Men lining up at the bride's door
> Walk tall to the altar rail in pinstripe suit and silk tie . . .

Durcan writes perhaps the first anti-war protest poetry from a culturally nationalist quarter in the Republic. His revision of nationalist memorial tropes, in the context of Northern Ireland, is more radical than Yeats's. Here (although other poems manifest Durcan's own brand of cultural heroics) the speaker does not project a glorious past into the future, even the alternative future represented by Lady Gregory and others, but an inglorious present into the past: hence the disjunction between 'Armagh of the Nightingales' and 'real midnight jazz', a disjunction that also comments on the poem's aesthetic. Further, as contrasted with Yeats's litany in 'Easter 1916' ('MacDonagh and MacBride / And Connolly and Pearse'), however contextually qualified, Durcan lists Fine Gael worthies in unheroic style. The party's supposed ideals clash with its bourgeois, sectarian reality. Simultaneously, as in Great War poetry, patriarchal old men are seen as the enemy. By speaking in the voice of a younger, critical generation from (post)nationalist Ireland, Durcan's hybrid elegy licenses itself to strike the didactic note of Young Ireland even while urging a revisionist 'lesson'.

There is both rupture and continuity in the poem's relation to religious traditions too. When Durcan reproaches respectable Catholicism with 'the altar rail', as when he stresses the Epiphany in the title of his earlier elegy, he plays Christ against institutionalised Christianity. Michael Longley's 'The Linen Workers' (the opening poem of 'Wreaths'), which takes a more oblique elegiac approach to the same event, places Christ in the foreground:

> Christ's teeth ascended with him into heaven:
> Through a cavity in one of his molars
> The wind whistles: he is fastened for ever
> By his exposed canines to a wintry sky.
>
> I am blinded by the blaze of that smile
> And by the memory of my father's false teeth
> Brimming in their tumbler: they wore bubbles
> And, outside of his body, a deadly grin.
>
> When they massacred the ten linen workers
> There fell on the road beside them spectacles,
> Wallets, small change, and a set of dentures:
> Blood, food particles, the bread, the wine.
>
> Before I can bury my father once again
> I must polish the spectacles, balance them
> Upon his nose, fill his pockets with money
> And into his dead mouth slip the set of teeth.

Here the personal belongings that survive their owners, a poignant detail also noticed by Durcan, come to imply the impossibility of Communion: just as one item on the list, dentures, projects an incompletely resurrected Christ. Ramazani glosses melancholic mourning as 'unresolved, violent, and ambivalent'.[60] Longley's unresolved images in 'Wreaths', his Christ stuck between earth and heaven, further removes redemptive possibility from the crucified Christ of Great War elegy: the image recalls Walter Benjamin's paralysed angels. Yet, in this civil-war context, denial of elegiac consolation also functions as critique. The poem's 'immersion in loss' sets out tough conditions for sociopolitical redemption – such as acknowledging all guilt for 'massacre'. In Great War elegy an Old Testament *episteme*, which conditions the 'primitive' religio-nationalist base mentioned earlier, is subjected to New Testament perceptions. Troubles elegy replays the same conflict: not as anachronism but as contemporary politics. Thus 'The Greengrocer' may appear consolatory in that it imagines the Three Wise Men, *en route* to 'a small house up / The Shankill or the Falls', stopping at 'Jim Gibson's shop' to buy 'Dates and chestnuts and tangerines'. This suggests, however, that Christianity has not so much failed as never been tried. In 'The Strand at Lough Beg', his elegy for Colum McCartney, Heaney does effect some metaphorical consolation

[60] Ramazani, *Poetry of Mourning*, p. 4.

by 'burying' a Troubles victim who haunts his consciousness 'With blood and roadside muck in your hair and eyes'. But the poem's ritual, again adapted to the victim's domicile and manner of death, is less consolatory, more protesting, than it first appears (or than it appeared to Heaney when he revisited the murder in *Station Island*). Its imagery sufficiently accuses McCartney's loyalist killers; and, by introducing pagan nature into Christian consolation, implies the necessity to renew its spirit: 'With rushes that shoot green again, I plait / Green scapulars to wear over your shroud.'

Amos Oz asks of Israel, a country whose dominant ideology recycles a sanctified national-epic story: 'can any civilisation survive as a museum civilisation or does it only live when it wears the garb of dramatic improvisation?'[61] The dramatic improvisations of Troubles elegy seem in tune with emergent cultural forms discussed earlier. Its generic subversions and hybridisations incubate ways of 'new remembering': positive engagement with the European legacies that condition the Northern Irish conflict; critique of the morbid cultures of commemoration that inhibit its resolution; insistence on the humanity of each victim; recognition that 'healing' is difficult and demanding. Some effects are: deflections of focus, redistributions of significance, critical interpenetration of personal and public contexts, desacralisation or resacralisation; a switch from lament to mourning, from Old Testament to New, from the institutional to the internal, from blame to conscience, from destructive remembrance to constructive amnesia – and from cynical, selective forgetting to responsible, alarming memory.

[61] Amos Oz, *In the Land of Israel* (London, 1983), p. 137.

CHAPTER 11

'No lack of ghosts': memory, commemoration, and the state in Ireland

D. George Boyce

I

Modern scholarship invites the historian to temper his or her concern with the traditional (i.e. written, unpublished) sources, and attend to the kind of material that throws light on the mentalities and preoccupations of an age: architecture, sculpture, paintings, film, sport, popular novels and the like, to which might be added, mobile telephones. The author, on his way to Durham on 3 April 1998 to attend the Conference of Irish Historians in Britain, overheard one young businessman tell his office staff that he would be back the following Tuesday, when he would set to work 'packaging Scotland'. The characterising and marketing of a country is part of the modern preoccupation with promoting tourism, and is also a place where politics and commerce meet: a country's image cannot be wholly divorced, even for commercial gain, from its notion of what it stands for, and what its fundamental values are. The image of an England, essentially rural, is what Stanley Baldwin, amongst others, wanted to promote in 1930s Britain, to rally his divided nation around some common theme, some heartland of existence.

Baldwin sought to evoke a memory of a nation at ease with itself in a rural setting; even the urban dweller, recalling his country roots, kept his little plot of land, his little garden, in order to keep memory alive.[1] This raises the question of where individual memory and public memory intersect. Individual memories are often buried in the obscurity of the past; forgetting is part of remembering, in the sense that the private person will enjoy only selective recall; and most of what he or she recalls will be of an essentially private nature. But there are many private events that involve public affairs. War is the most significant of these, and the encapsulation of private memory in public war memorials helped shape Britain's attitude to the two world wars of the twentieth century. Local or

[1] Stanley Baldwin, *On England* (London, 1938), pp. 16–17.

regional sentiments were promoted; soldiers and civilians mingled at war memorials on Armistice Day; a sense of national unity was promoted and sustained.[2]

Memory, as Raphael Samuel remarks, so far from being merely a passive receptacle or storage system, an image bank of the past, is rather an active, shaping force, in that 'it is dynamic – what it contrives systematically to forget is as important as what it remembers – and . . . it is dialectically related to historical thought, rather than being some kind of negative other to it'. Memory, then is

> historically conditioned, changing colour and shape according to the emergencies of the moment; that so far from being handed down in the timeless form of 'tradition' it is progressively altered from generation to generation. It leaves the impress of experience, in however mediated a way. It is stamped with the ruling passions of the time.

This memory, 'like history, is inherently revisionist and never more chameleon than when it appears to stay the same'.[3]

The role of politics in controlling memory is a reflection of the 'ruling passions of the time'. Thus in France, the 'memory' of the counter-revolutionary movement in La Vendée was suppressed by Republicans, and revived by Monarchists bent on reminding France that it enjoyed another political tradition, and one inimical to Republicanism. It was only after this political battle that historians began to study the history of La Vendée, which hitherto they had ignored. History, memory and politics were then a potent and dynamic force.[4] The Southern Irish state at first permitted, then, after 1932, began increasingly to discourage, commemoration of the Great War, as part of the process of republicanising Ireland, and denying legitimacy to any other political tradition, and especially one associated with John Redmond and his imperialist Home Rulers.[5] The resonances of war were not only felt in Ireland, but surfaced as late as 1959 to bedevil Anglo-Irish and Anglo-American relations: on 3 November the British ambassador in Dublin drew the Commonwealth Relations Office's attention to the fact that the United States military attaché had laid a wreath on the James Joseph Daly memorial at the annual Connaught Rangers Mutiny Commemoration at Glasnevin

[2] Jay Winter, *Sites of Memory, Sites of Mourning: The First World War in European Culture* (Cambridge, 1995).

[3] Raphael Samuel, *Theatres of Memory*, vol. i, *Past and Present in Contemporary Culture* (London, 1994), p. x.

[4] For La Vendée see Sharif Gemie, *French Revolutions, 1815–1914* (Edinburgh, 1994), ch. 4.

[5] D. George Boyce, *The Sure Confusing Drum: Ireland and the First World War* (Swansea, 1993), pp. 1–5.

Cemetery. The ambassador remarked that the attaché's 'callisthenics' (in bending over backwards to 'please the Irish') 'could not have been more unfortunately timed, coming, as it does, at the beginning of the week ending with Remembrance Sunday'. As a soldier, the ambassador went on, the American military attaché 'should realise the extreme impropriety of honouring mutiny in the armed forces of a country that has been an ally in two wars . . .'[6]

The modern state is even more active in commemoration than its early modern predecessors, or even early twentieth-century predecessors. As William M. Johnston points out in his *Celebrations*, the European cult of anniversaries presupposed state financing of cultural budgets.

> Schools, universities, theatres, museums, literary organizations and cultural institutes abroad thrive on state funding. In return for investing in culture, state agencies expect these activities to enhance national identity. Intellectuals who get paid to organize and attend anniversary commemorations acquiesce in becoming retainers of the state. The device that more than any other eases such dependency is the cult of anniversaries. It mediates between the state's interest in promoting national identity and intellectuals' interest in playing a public role.[7]

The important point here is that the intellectual who thus participates 'need not have been an ideologue in order to personify national identity'. The mere fact of citizenship suffices to link a celebrant with the nation or locality that honours him. Thus 'a kind of commonwealth of Anniversaries has emerged in present-day Europe, whereby intellectuals accept subsidies for articulating national values, even when they disagree with much of what is done in the name of those values'.[8]

In the United States of America, the private sector funds such commemorations; the United States separated church and state, and also church and culture. But, in Europe, national agencies are the promoters of cultural values. British national identity, precarious in any case, is today more oriented towards capturing tourism than asserting a correct version of the national past; Jack the Ripper evokes more celebrations in the British press than the Spanish Armada, he is a true hero of popular culture.[9] Irish national identity, in what Fintan O'Toole calls a post-modern age – one that Ireland has entered without experiencing the

[6] G. Kimber to G. W. St. John Chadwick, Commonwealth Relations Office, 3 November 1959, Public Record Office, CRO, DO35/8035.

[7] William M. Johnston, *Celebrations: The Cult of Anniversaries in Europe and the United States* (New Brunswick, NJ, and London, 1991), p. 45.

[8] Ibid., p. 46.

[9] Ibid., pp. 39–40.

bit in between pre- and postmodernism – has shifted from a highly politically orientated commemoration world, to one that is, however, not wholly commercial, but is a rather uneasy combination of the two. What was peculiar about Ireland, O'Toole noted, was that it had become a post-modern society without ever fully becoming a modern one.

> We have gone from the few hungry acres to the Financial Services Centre with only a half-finished project of modernity in between. We have a society in which a husband and wife will go to jail over a few acres of bog (as happened in 1922), and at the same time a society in which landscape is a distant, emotion-free object to be 'interpreted'. The middle bit, the bit where landscape is a strange and sacred thing, is missing. Or at least it is present only in the half-developed form of a half modernised society.[10]

What Ireland ended up with was a landscape so strange that it had to be interpreted for its people, but one not strange enough to be accorded the 'wary reverence' that is given to the genuinely unknown. 'If we were still peasants, we wouldn't think twice about building a whole village on the top of Mullaghmore, if we had the money and the reason to do it. Yet, if we were fully Los Angelised, we wouldn't think twice about turning it completely into a product.' But, as it is, we are 'somewhere in the middle between these states of mind'; we offer 'a place like Mullaghmore the kind of interpretation that reduces it while pretending to honour it'. 'We give it a kind of pseudo meaning.'[11]

The intersection of commerce, culture and politics was, O'Toole noted, encapsulated in a Borde Failte document called 'Heritage attractions and development: a strategy to interpret Ireland's history and culture for tourism', which noted that

> While the folk culture of Ireland is relatively easily appreciated, Irish history, due to the influence of many peoples, cultures and conflicts, is not easily understood by visitors . . . Many visitors arrive with a limited awareness of a few elements of this heritage, but there is little common ground to start further exploration. Visitors' time is also limited, and in many cases is predetermined by tour operators, so it is important to help increase visitors' understanding by creating interpretative 'gateways' into our heritage. This will heighten their experience, increase satisfaction levels and help in awareness and appreciation of individual sites, the end result will be more repeat business, better 'word of mouth' publicity and the creation of a strong 'brand image' of Ireland as a quality heritage destination, with unique heritage attractions.[12]

[10] Fintan O'Toole, *Black Hole, Green Card: The Disappearance of Ireland* (Dublin, 1994), p. 35.
[11] Ibid., pp. 35–6.
[12] Ibid., pp. 39–40.

The gateways into this history were narratives. Everything was to be understood as part of a particular storyline, clustered around five key themes: live landscapes, making a living, saints and religion, building a nation and the spirit of Ireland. Instead of real history, there is a kind of history 'by way of our own pop images and simulacra of that history, which itself remains forever out of reach'.[13]

This 'kind of history' is represented in Brian Moore's novel *Fergus*, where the eponymous character contemplates the break-up of a long relationship. He lives in Los Angeles, 'a place where total artificiality, total efficiency and total depersonalisation seem to be the objectives of life'. Fergus, weeping for his lost relationship, is suddenly confronted by a series of manifestations from his past – his real past – which contrasts with the images represented in his apartment, which is exactly like the other apartments.

> "Take this carpet. It looks like real wool but it's made up of nylon thread. The pile is burnproof. These two reading chairs have polished wooden frames and maroon tweed cushions. But this wood is synthetic and so is the tweed. The chairs do not stain or burn . . . there is one picture in each apartment. The same picture. It appears to be an oil painting. But if you look at the back" – he turned the picture over and showed the girl and Dick Fowler, his friend, read the label:
>
> REALOIL
> Simulates the look and texture of the original oil painting:
> SUNFLOWER
> by Artist Vincent van Gogh.[14]

Synthetic objects are better than the real: they pose no problems, they do not stain, burn or warp lives in any way. They ease the people into a comfortable contemplation of their past. They help society cope with plurality and diversity, but in a way that orders and integrates society.

O'Toole offers a neat example of how this impacted on even the most dedicated searcher for a 'real Ireland', the romantic nationalist Patrick Pearse, who describes the Gael as the 'high priest of nature. He loves nature, not merely as something grand and beautiful and wonderful but as something possessing a mystic connection with and influence over man.' Pearse, in seeking to recreate that mystic communion with nature, peculiar to the Gael, brought a cinematograph operator to Connemara and gave an entertainment in an adjacent school.

[13] Ibid., pp. 40–1.
[14] Brian Moore, *Fergus* (London, 1983), pp. 112–13.

> But first of all he provided a plentiful supply of barn-bracks and sweets for the children. It was the first time that anything like it had ever been seen in the district and many funny remarks were passed thereon. One old woman tried hard to get behind the screen to see the real people! Her remark should be quoted in Irish in order to give the real full value. Padraig had beautiful rural scenes shown.

As O'Toole concludes, 'the process of making people observers of their own lives, audiences for their own culture, tourists of their own landscapes had been set in train'.[15]

Yet it is easy, as Raphael Samuel remarks, to make fun of the heritage industry.[16] The admixture of concern to recreate a nation's past with an equally deeply felt desire to provide toilet facilities and a car park, can hardly do other than provoke a certain, if superior, sense of mirth. The heritage industry is 'widely accused of wanting to commodify the past and turn it into tourist kitsch'.[17] But the Irish heritage industry bears closer examination, and raises more significant points about the cross-fertilisation of commerce, history and politics. And this in turn raises questions about what 'memory' is and how it is encapsulated, created, or rediscovered – all, or any, of these three.

II

There are various ways of approaching the question of how societies remember, and two may be singled out as illustrative of the methodology. But first, the role of the historian in explaining the past must be discussed. The historian seeks to distinguish history from memory, in that the historian tries to reconstruct a past which the individual, or the society, cannot have known. R. G. Collingwood offers the example of the historian who sketches the economic history of the Roman Empire, and in so doing depicts a state of things that no contemporary ever saw as a whole. The historical past 'is not a remembered past, nor a sum of individual remembered pasts; it is an ideal past, arrived at in the mind by a process of theorising and thinking', and to that extent resembles the world of the scientist.[18] 'The *mere* past is that which merely was; the historical past is that which not only was, but remains historically knowable.'[19] The

[15] O'Toole, *Black Hole, Green Card*, pp. 44–5.
[16] Samuel, *Theatres of Memory*, pp. 259–73.
[17] Ibid., p. 259.
[18] R. G. Collingwood, *The Principles of History and Other Writings in Philosophy and History*, edited with an introduction by W. H. Dray and W. J. Van der Dussen (Oxford, 1999), p. 136.
[19] Ibid., p. 222.

personal memory ('I remember this or that') is important in shaping our identity. But, Collingwood says, 'My identity with my own past does not depend on my memory, in memory I partially *discover* that identity.'[20]

A collective memory and a collective identity require some active agents who create and transmit that memory. Collingwood evolved this theory when he was analysing the reason why certain forms of art persisted after they had been overlaid by a new culture; specifically, he was interested in why Celtic design revived after the Roman conquest. He offered a modern, but parallel, example:

> If by (say) 1920 English peasants had stopped singing modal folk-songs, and had taken instead to hearing dance music on the wireless; and if no one had written their songs down and preserved them in libraries; would it not be very odd to find their descendants beginning to sing modal folk-songs again round about the year 2200?[21]

Collingwood's explanation of this was as follows: 'any process involving an historical change from P_1 to P_2 leaves an unconverted residue of P_1 encapsulated within an historical state of things which superficially is altogether P_2'. Encapsulation is not an 'occult entity', but the fact that a man who changes his habits, thoughts, etc., retains in the second place some residue of the first. 'He gives up smoking, but his desire to smoke does not thereupon disappear.' 'The desire survives in the form of an unsatisfied desire.' Thus, 'without any implications as to racial temperament or a "racial unconsciousness" the same thing may happen in a society'.[22]

> If the members of a certain society have been in the habit of acting or thinking in certain ways, and if at a certain time they try to stop acting and thinking in those ways, and do their best to act in different ways, the desire to go on acting and thinking in the old way will probably persist. It will certainly persist, and persist in a lively form, if they were accustomed to think and act in those ways very effectively and found great satisfaction in doing so. The tendency to revert to the old ways would in that case be strong.[23]

It might be thought that 'unless some occult entity like a racial temperament or an inheritance of acquired pyschical characteristics were at work, this tendency would not survive into the second generation . . . Well, you would be wrong.' If a 'warlike people, at a certain crisis in its history,

[20] Ibid., p. 132.
[21] R. G. Collingwood, *An Autobiography* (Oxford, 1987 edn), p. 138.
[22] Ibid., pp. 140–1.
[23] Ibid., p. 141.

turned entirely peaceful, then in the first generation warlike impulses would survive'. Children of that generation would be told on no account to indulge in the forbidden pleasures of war. The father's explanation would be that war was a wrong thing, but 'a grand thing while it lasted and that he would have to fight his neighbours again if only he did not know that he ought not'. These children would carefully pass all this on to their own children when the time came. 'Thus the transmission by educational means of any moral idea which involved the outlawry of an institution, or custom, and the repression of a desire for it, entails the simultaneous transmission of that desire itself. The children of each generation are taught to want what they are taught they must not have.'[24] Collingwood argued that, in time,

> the tradition which keeps alive the memory of the forbidden thing, and keeps alive at the same time the desire for it, may die out. Its disappearance will be greatly accelerated if the new way of thinking and acting proved to be one in which the converts find themselves successful and satisfied . . . In that case the 'folk-memory' (nothing occult; nothing inborn; simply the transmission by example and precept of certain ways of thinking and acting from generation to generation) of a success and satisfaction now no longer permitted will tend to fade away. [And] where you find the new ways of thinking and acting never displayed with more than a low degree of success, you may take it as certain that the discarded ways are remembered with regret, and that the tradition of their glories is being tenaciously kept alive.[25]

This theory, whilst it must not be accepted uncritically, is a useful tool for understanding the transmission of memory in nationalist Ireland between 1798 and 1916. In the immediate aftermath of the 1798 rebellion, controversy centred on the responsibility for the massacres that accompanied the rising, which both Catholic and Protestant historians deplored.[26] As constitutional nationalism, led by Daniel O'Connell and then revived by the Home Rule movement, seemed to promise success for the risen Catholic people, rebellion was not forgotten, but was praised, yet at the same time discouraged: a fine thing, but not to be repeated. But the memory was kept alive, and was all the more safe (it seemed) for not needing to be repeated: Home Rule would carry the day. Nuala Johnson makes this point in her study of the glorification of the 1798 rebellion in monuments and statues.[27] 'Monuments were not

[24] Ibid., pp. 142–3.
[25] Ibid., p. 143.
[26] D. George Boyce, *Nineteenth Century Ireland: The Search for Stability* (Dublin, 1990), pp. 263–5.
[27] Nuala Johnson, 'Sculpting heroic histories: celebrating the centenary of the 1798 rebellion in Ireland', *Transactions of the Institute of British Geographers*, n.s., 19 (1994), 74–93.

just decorative appendages erected to beautify cities and towns, and their location within public space was no historical accident. They represented a self-conscious attempt to solicit public participation in the politics of the day.'[28] The creation of icons of past heroes, the creation of memory, was not an exact repetition of the motives and ideals of the men of 1798, for different nationalist traditions competed for their place in the commemoration process. The Catholic Church sought to play an integral part in the event, and sought to push the commemoration towards 'faith and fatherland'.[29] The event itself was far enough away for the church to do this. It was also far enough away for constitutional nationalists to praise it, assure the younger generation that they wished to emulate it, but at the same time to stress that present conditions made it hard to emulate (they had no weapons) and that in any event the ongoing constitutional system would deliver freedom. Freedom's battle would be won without recourse to arms, though arms were a goodly thing, and their use was to be praised – in 1798.[30]

Likewise, in 1903, at the centenary celebrations of Robert Emmet's rebellion, it was the Fenian John O'Leary who claimed that the best way to honour Emmet's memory was 'to strive with might and main to bring about the time when his epitaph can be written. I have nothing more to say, but I and all of you have very much to do.' But it was the epitome of constitutional nationalism, the *Freeman's Journal*, which told its readers that Emmet 'represented with unmistakable clearness and boldness the lofty and uncompromising spirit of Irish nationality', and that it was fitting that 'the people of our time should show that his memory is still dear to them, and that on the centenary of his execution they should gather together to pay honour to that hallowed memory and resolve one and all to do everything possible to hasten the day when his epitaph can be written'. The *Freeman's Journal* noted on the day that the presence of the National Foresters, the Gaelic Athletic Association, the Gaelic League, and all the Boys' Brigades was a sign that they gave 'pledge of fidelity to the national cause when the young lads will have grown to man's estate'.[31] Emmet taught Ireland that it must persevere: the 'blood of the martyrs . . . is the soul of the Church; and the blood of Emmet, as it flowed in Thomas Street a

[28] Ibid., p. 78.
[29] Ibid., p. 85.
[30] Ibid., pp. 87–8. For another example of the significance of statues see Gary Owens, 'Nationalist monuments in Ireland, *c.* 1870–1914: symbolism and ritual', in R. Gillespie and Brian P. Kennedy (eds.), *Ireland: Art into History* (Dublin, 1994), pp. 103–17.
[31] D. George Boyce, *Nationalism in Ireland*, 3rd edn (London, 1995), p. 273.

hundred years ago, had fructified in many a young Irish mind since, at home and abroad, to the glory and credit and the practical benefit of Ireland'.[32]

This explanation of how memory is transmitted, and also altered to suit present political needs, contrasts with another version, the notion that there is some kind of hidden memory, some pre-existing memory, that only needs to be jogged into life by a stimulus. This might be called the *Wind in the Willows* depiction of memory. When the baby otter, 'Little Portly' went missing, Mole and Rat set out to find him. On their way down the river, they came to a scented, herby place. This set off reminiscences in the Rat. '"This is the place of my song-dreams", said Rat, "the place the music played to me." He whispered as if in a trance: "Here, in this holy place, here if anywhere, surely we shall find Him!"'[33] The 'Him' was not the missing otter, but some ancient, primordial memory. As they proceeded down the river, they heard the music again, and Rat quoted the words that were now, just, audible. '"But what do the words mean?" asked the wondering Mole. "That I do not know", said the Rat slowly. "I passed them on as they reached me. Ah! Now they return again, and this time full and clear! This time, at last, it is the real, the unmistakable thing, simple – passionate – perfect!"'[34]

This idea of a memory, not understood, but innate, only requiring a 'Him' to unlock the key to the mysteries, was what Patrick Pearse tried to tap in his writings and deeds. 'Our Gaelic League time', he wrote in *The Coming Revolution*, 'was to be our tutelage. We had first to learn to know Ireland, to read the lineaments of her face, to understand the accents of her voice; to re-possess ourselves, disinherited as we were, of her spirit and mind, re-enter into our mystical birthright.'[35] And again,

> the generation that is now growing old in Ireland had almost forgotten our heroes . . . But the soil of Ireland, yea, the very stones of our cities have cried out against an infidelity that will barter our old tradition of nationhood even for a thing so precious as peace. This is what the heroes have done for us; for their spirits indwell in the place where they lived . . .

'I live in a place', he continued, 'that is very full of heroic memories.' Thus a timeless tradition existed, waiting only to be tapped, to be revealed, and one who held the key could achieve this.[36]

32 Ibid., p. 274.
33 Kenneth Grahame, *The Wind in the Willows* (London, 1984), p. 134.
34 Ibid., pp. 141–2.
35 Patrick Pearse, *Political Writings and Speeches* (Dublin, 1918; reprinted 1966), pp. 22–3.
36 Ibid., pp. 66–7.

It is hard to see how a 'collective memory' can be formulated and asserted without some political necessity to express it, and the means of so doing. This is not to say that real, individual, family, or even group memories do not exist. Rather it is to say that they are mediated through political parties, institutions, media and the state, and might be suppressed because they do not accord with the memory that these activists wish to create and preserve. The playwright Sebastian Barry gives one such example in his introduction to the text of his play *The Steward of Christendom*. He made his play

> with two things really: a pair of shirt studs from the thirties that a friend found in an old house, and that I put on my desk for a year, to guide me; and an old childhood mental picture – childish vision I would almost say – of a man riding on a high white horse against a mass of black-coated strikers in Sackville Street. A man, it seems, who was my own great-grandfather, and who rose, as the singsong formulas of family stories go, as high as Catholic could in the Dublin Metropolitan Police.

But because of his place in life, and the fall of the Dublin Metropolitan Police with the demise of the British state in Ireland, Barry's grandfather and 'fellas like him don't figure in history books as names'. They 'become part of the general story of the demonic nature of the times, in his case the nameless demon who baton-charged Jim Larkin, arrested him, and in the course of a catastrophic few minutes, killed four good men and true on that day notorious in Trades Union history, notorious and emblematic, and its own fashion, true as daylight, or not untrue'. Barry went on to confess that

> When I first considered this, in the cold light of 1985, I was in fear of it being discovered that I had such a relative, hiding you might say in my very blood. I was eager to conceal him, indeed to keep him concealed, to seal him in, where he lay unnamed and unmentioned in official history. He was no cosy name around the fire of family. But a demon, a dark force, a figure to bring you literary ruin. What price my credentials as a real Irish writer...[37]

In another example of memory, Angela Bourke notes, in nineteenth-century Ireland 'folklore was fashionable, but only in so far as it could be accommodated within the dominant paradigm. Outside the pages of literary folklore, the storyteller's art became invisible or even came to be regarded as a disease: a symptom of lamentable backwardness.'[38]

37 Sebastian Barry, *The Steward of Christendom* (London, 1997), p. vii.

38 Angela Bourke, 'The baby and the bathwater: cultural icons in nineteenth century Ireland', in Tadhg Foley and Sian Ryan (eds.), *Ideology and Ireland in the Nineteenth Century* (Dublin, 1998), pp. 79–92, at p. 83.

Newspapers, not storytellers, became the tellers of 'what happened'.[39] And what happened was a vigorous sense of grievances not redressed, located within a culture that honoured the idea of providential deliverance.

III

Without some means of transmitting memory, every generation would forget the experiences of the one before. The state mediates these memories, encouraging some, discouraging or suppressing others. In Ireland, this created not only a nationalist, but a republican culture. At the same time the beginnings of historical revisionism began to make themselves felt, with challenges to the 'grand narrative' of Irish history, the narrative which saw that history as indeed the story of a people coming out of bondage. In more recent decades there came 'post-modern' history, which the Scottish historians R. J. Murray and Graeme Martin characterised thus:

> to some extent the history of nineteenth-century Scotland is part of what is happening to western historiography in general. The story of our nation has now become history, herstory, their story, our story – regions, industries, interest groups, ethnic groups, religious groups, technologies, professions and sexual orientations are all developing their own stories. For a post-modern society struggling to sustain tolerance between multiple identities the historiography of many stories is clearly essential . . .

These historians acknowledge that the writing of post-modern history is difficult, for 'the lack of a clear "modern" narrative of nineteenth-century story for Scotland contains subtle problems for these who would tell many stories'.[40] Perhaps the high water mark of postmodern history in the case of Ireland is the *Oxford Companion to Irish History* in which the patriot, T. F. Meagher, shares a page with an entry on meat-processing.[41]

But as many (though by no means all) historians watch with satisfaction the dissolution of the old, apparently solid ground of the grand narrative of Irish history (nationalist and Unionist), the state is obliged to stand between the two extremes: those of the fragmented past, which underlines its need for some agreed past that will help direct its future, and the necessity not to surrender to a narrative about the past that

[39] Ibid., p. 89.

[40] R. J. Murray and Graeme Martin, 'Where was Scotland?', *Scottish Historical Review*, 73 (1994), 89–99, at 97.

[41] S. J. Connolly (ed.), *The Oxford Companion to Irish History* (Oxford, 1995), p. 353.

will interrupt or jeopardise its efforts to modernise itself. It also needs to steer between these extremes in order to present a thematic past for commercial as well as political ends; but in Ireland these intertwine, for Irish politics were so used to drawing upon the past that when commerce reached out to touch history, it found itself more entangled in politics than, perhaps, it ever imagined. Moya Kneafsey observed that 'tourism plays a major part in the Irish economy', but also noted that heritage tourism 'may also serve a purpose for the community, acting as a focus for action and contributing towards a sense of awareness and pride in this heritage'.[42]

William Johnston notes the importance of the commercial factor, but he also emphasises the imperative need to buttress national identity.[43] In Ireland, this was well illustrated in the Irish state's commemoration of the 1916 Rising on its fiftieth anniversary. Germany, Italy and Austria stress culture, not politics, for obvious reasons. America emphasises the great continent-wide events, rather than great figures, for it is the constitution, and anything that reminds the varied peoples of the United States that they live under the constitution, that must be celebrated, and thus remind the population of where their loyalties are based. As Johnston says 'anniversaries help a nation to assimilate a tumultuous past'.[44] The Irish state, riven by civil war and partition, could take its stand upon the Easter Rising, on which all nationalists could find common ground.

For the Irish state, or any state, to survive, it is important to create a master narrative, to repeat the past consciously, to find significance to celebrated recurrence. But for the Irish state this raised problems in 1966, because the state was moving cautiously towards a rapprochement with Northern Ireland, and must be careful not to let the 'memory' of 1916 spill over into dangerous politics. To commemorate, as Johnston says, means 'submitting to conformity';[45] but conformity is not a characteristic of Irish politics. Hence the Irish government's plans for celebrating the Rising had various dimensions. The taoseach, Séan Lemass, fresh from his historic meeting with Terence O'Neill, the Northern Ireland prime minister, took control of the 1916 Commemoration Committee, determined to show that it was indeed the key legacy to modern Ireland,

[42] Moya Kneafsey, 'The cultural tourist: patron saint of Ireland?', in Ullrich Kockel (ed.), *Culture, Tourism and Development: The Case of Ireland* (Liverpool, 1994), pp. 103–16, at p. 111.

[43] Johnston, *Celebrations*, p. 174.

[44] Ibid., pp. 44–5, 82.

[45] Ibid., p. 65.

that it was part of the necessary struggle for freedom: 'Bequeathed from bleeding sire to son', as he put it in a speech.[46] Yet he wished to ensure that the commemoration would not interfere, or at least would interfere as little as possible, with positive cross-border relations. Lemass, however, remained determined to use the anniversary to re-educate the nation in appreciating the importance of the Rising for the Irish people, and the sacrifices made on their behalf by the men of 1916.[47]

Lemass's desire to reconcile these two goals was reflected in his speech on receiving back Pearse's flag, which had flown over the General Post Office in Dublin, from the British Imperial War Museum. He dwelt on the magnanimity of the British in restoring the flag to Ireland, rather than the circumstances in which it was taken in the first place. This was 'a gesture to the Irish people and . . . a further contribution by them for the building of goodwill and better relations between the two communities'.[48] When a spokesman for the '1916 Golden Jubilee Committee' organising an event in Northern Ireland requested that the CIE (Irish Railways) put on a special train to take a party of their members to Belfast for 17 April 1966, with the tickets overprinted with the words, 'Freedom Train 1966', Charles Haughey, the minister for justice, recommended that as the committee organising the trip was 'composed of members of the IRA, Sinn Fein and Cumann na mBan', the request should be refused. He believed that the attempt by this group to hire a special train in order to organise a parade in Belfast and an oration in Milltown Cemetery in the Falls Road, was 'for IRA organisational purposes'.[49]

Thirty years later, it seemed that heritage had replaced political considerations, commerce had triumphed in the sponsorship of collective political memory. But the heritage industry, though very conscious of the prime directive of making money, could not be unmindful of what it was doing in the Irish political context as well. In the 1980s and 1990s, Ireland still enjoyed a broad consensus on the national question: as Brian Girvin remarks, 'while the seam of neo-traditional nationalism was largely exhausted by 1989, this does not mean that nationalist aspirations have disappeared'. They had adopted a more gradualist

[46] Gillian Deeniham, 'Sean Lemass and Northern Ireland, 1959–66', M.Phil. Thesis, University College Cork (1999), p. 241.
[47] Ibid., p. 244.
[48] Ibid., p. 246.
[49] Ibid., pp. 255–6.

approach, and 'large proportions of Irish public opinion consider themselves to be nationalists and believed that Irish unity is something to hope for'.[50] Yet modern Ireland was driving forward to economic success on an unprecedented scale, and the heritage industry was an essential part of that drive, combining as it did commerce, history and – therefore – politics. Thus the heritage industry moved into the space left clear by those Irish historians who had helped destroy the grand narrative of the Irish past. Historians stressed contingency, difference, uncertainty, flux; the heritage industry stressed continuity, core, identity, a past firmly located in such a way as to enable the nation to reorient itself. A whole host of heritage-centred bodies – Bord Failte, the National Museum, regional tourist authorities, An Taisce – all cleared a space which the people could occupy. But this raised the problem of who was to be included, and who excluded. One heritage trainee was worried about the possibility that English visitors to Ireland might be offended by certain words or phrases engraved on Fenian memorials and sites: would they come to Ireland to spend their money for the sake of being insulted?[51] Bord Failte was anxious that nothing would be included in Cork City Jail's presentation that would offend British visitors, though one professional heritage manager concluded satisfyingly that Ireland's heritage 'belongs to us and its presentation is our responsibility'.[52] When the Kilmainham Jail exhibitions were being set up the curator refused to deal with this subject in a 'fashionable and revisionist manner' (*sic*), because 'this place is associated with Irish nationalism in an unapologetic way'. But the exhibits were explained (or 'interpreted') in terms that showed political awareness: 'An understanding of Irish Nationalism and Republicanism in its own terms remains essential to the process of developing fresh perspectives on this current in modern national history.'[53]

The keeping alive of memory, then, when placed in the hands of the state, or bodies responsible to the state, or even in purely commercial hands, reflected current political preoccupations.[54] Despite what the

[50] Brian Girvin, 'Nationalism and the continuation of political conflict in Ireland', *Proceedings of the British Academy*, 98 (1999), 369–99, at 382–3.

[51] Orlaith Mannion, 'Where the Fenians sleep: representations of Fenianism', MA Thesis, University College Cork (1997), p. 75.

[52] Ibid., p. 95.

[53] Ibid., p. 71. For the political significance of a theme park, in this case the Ulster–American Folk Park at Omagh, see David Brett, *The Construction of Heritage* (Cork, 1996), pp. 105–8, 154.

[54] For a perceptive discussion of this, see especially Brian Walker, *Dancing to History's Tune: History, Myth and Politics in Ireland* (Belfast, 1996), chs. 4 and 5.

heritage industry seemed to stand for, it was not handing down timeless history, timeless tradition, but was progressively altering these because of generational concerns. The political turmoil in Northern Ireland, and the divided politics of Catholic and Protestant, pushed the heritage industry in new directions. Anthony Buckley and Mary Kenney described these strategies:

(i) that schools and museums should be 'oases of calm';
(ii) that schools and museums should provide opportunities for intermingling between individuals of different ethnicities to encourage mutual understanding; and
(iii) that schools and museums should enable individuals of different ethnicities to explore their own and each others' cultural heritage.

Thus 'the practical goal of creating an oasis of calm quickly extended into the state schools and into the world of museums. Schools and museums were to be "neutral territory".'[55] Into them, the troubles should not intrude. As well as the mere physical exclusion of 'the men of violence', it was also hoped to keep out of the classroom and the museum gallery contentious forms of debate that could 'politicise' these places.[56] In the Ulster Folk Museum the purpose of the director, George Thompson, was 'to present to the people living in Northern Ireland a vision of what they had in common'.[57]

This decision to 'depoliticise' these places was, in its own way, a political decision. Like the Somme Heritage Centre outside Newtownards, it reflected contemporary concerns – legitimate and important concerns – about the present, presenting the past through the prism of the present. This need for the state, and other institutions, to mediate between memory and contemporary political exigencies was illustrated in the Irish Republic's approach to what it regarded as seminal events in its history. The search was on for a new narrative that would properly reflect the importance of these events, and yet would not be politically troublesome in the way that, for example, the 1966 commemoration of the Easter Rising proved to be. The search shaped the way in which the state commemorated its anniversaries in the 1990s. The celebration of the 75th anniversary of the Easter Rising was muted, so much so that it

[55] Anthony Buckley and Mary Kenny, '"Cultural heritage in an oasis of calm": Divided identities in a museum in Ulster', in Kockel, *Culture, Tourism and Development*, pp. 129–47, at p. 129.
[56] Ibid., p. 131.
[57] Ibid., p. 135.

provoked some more nationalist spirits to mount their own commemorations, and to stand where their forefathers stood: unashamed of their great tradition.[58] But far from handing on the torch from sire to son, they too were reacting in the context of the ruling passions of the time – in this case a reaction against the apparent *lack* of ruling passions. The celebration of the 1798 rebellion is even more instructive, compared to the commemoration in 1948. The *Round Table*'s Irish correspondent noted then, sourly, that 'ominous threats' were made, with Republicans, including Tom Barry, saying that the spirit of '98 'showed that all they needed was complete victory in order to march on the Six Counties and regain them'. He added that unfortunately the Irish prime minister, Mr Costello, had 'himself given every encouragement to illegal attacks on Northern Ireland by his declaration that he will never again take part in a Government which has to enforce order by extra-judicial measures'.[59]

In 1998 the atmosphere was different. Now the emphasis was on the capacity for unity demonstrated by the '98 rebellion; the word liberty was on the lips of Ulster Presbyterians. The idea was one of 'democracy and pluralism . . . triumphantly proclaimed'.[60] The commemoration of the event included contributions by historians who had accused revisionists of taking the pain out of Irish history, but who were now themselves engaged in the same enterprise. Memory was directed towards the significance of pluralist thinking in the Irish past, and academics mediated between the state and the citizen, playing a public role.

All this was done with the best of intentions; and the direction of public memory towards an agreed Ireland marked a major shift in the relationship between history, politics, and, in the case of the heritage industry, commerce. All were now on the same side, that of controlling the transmission of the past in ways that would help stabilise the present. But this enterprise, though in itself highly commendable, runs the risk of distorting the past in ways that make it harder to understand the present, especially the divided present; for if ghosts from the past are to be buried, then the search for the new consensus brings with it the

[58] Declan Kiberd, 'The elephant of revolutionary forgetfulness', in Maírín ni Dhonnchadha and Theo Dorgan (eds.), *Revising the Rising* (Derry, 1991), pp. 1–20, at pp. 1–5.

[59] *Round Table*, 154 (Mar. 1949), 152.

[60] Ian McBride, 'Reclaiming the Rebellion: 1798 in 1998', *Irish Historical Studies*, 123 (May 1999), 395–440, at 395.

paradox described by the Canadian poet Earle Birney:

> we French and English never lost
> our civil war
> endure it still
> a bloody civil bore
>
> the wounded sirened off
> no Whitman wanted
> it's only by our lack of ghosts
> we're haunted.[61]

[61] Earle Birney, 'Can. Lit.', in Margaret Atwood (ed.), *The New Oxford Book of Canadian Verse* (London, 1982), p. 116.

Index